Collected Poems

ALFRED NOYES

Collected Poems

IN ONE VOLUME

CLARK McCUTCHEON
1966

Library of Congress Catalog Number 66-16190

Second edition first published in the United States 1966

Printed in Great Britain by
Billing & Sons Ltd, Guildford and London
for Clark McCutcheon, 176 Main Street,
Port Washington, N.Y.

CONTENTS

4

AUTHOR'S PREFATORY NOTE

MY acknowledgments are due to Messrs. William Blackwood and Sons and to Messrs. Sheed and Ward for the use of poems published by them, and to *The Times, Punch, Blackwood's Magazine,* and *The Tablet* for those which originally appeared in their columns.

A. N.

Acknowledgment is made also to the Curtis Publishing Co. for use of the following poems which appeared in the *Saturday Evening Post:* THE ISLE OF MEMORIES, A SPRING HAT, A BALLAD OF BOYHOOD, THE CAVE, SEA DISTANCES Copyright 1920, 1931, 1933, 1951 The Curtis Publishing Co.

PREFACE TO THE SECOND EDITION

THE present edition of my father's poems is the most complete collection yet to have been published in one volume in England. In addition to the poems of the last collection, first published in 1950, I have selected a further nine which appeared in 1956 in a small volume *A Letter to Lucian*. These include one or two poems which I feel are among his finest work, particularly "Night Journey", written shortly after an unsuccessful eye operation when he knew that he would soon be blind.

Because of the gradual loss of his sight, these later poems were either dictated to a secretary or taken down on a wire recorder. I have also included, with the kind permission of the Editor of the *Contemporary Review*, his last poem, "Ballade of the Breaking Shell", written in May 1958, one month before his death. I am grateful also to Mr. G. D. Blackwood, who has given permission to include three poems, published originally by William Blackwood and Sons Ltd. in an early series of my father's works. These were not among the poems of the last collected edition which were chosen by my father as being those which he particularly wished to be remembered. Two of them, "Dobbin", and "The Man who Discovered the Use of a Chair", I have included because although not great poems, I remember them with affection from my childhood and also because I feel that their inclusion helps to illustrate the great range of my father's writing which could provide entertainment and interest for the smallest child as well as for the most learned scholar.

The third poem of this group, "The Old Fool in the Wood", is a particularly good example of his belief in the ultimate nature of things, and as he says in *The Unknown God*, in the universe, or "Nature", as an expression of the thought of God. It was this faith that enabled him to write a poem such as "Night Journey" at a time when he realized that he was soon to lose his sight which to him, whose whole life revolved around reading and writing, was so indescribably precious.

Throughout his life, his writings centred on the belief that the function of all great art was to establish a right relationship between things temporal and things eternal, so that, as he said in his reply of thanks to the friends who had organized a dinner to celebrate his

7

seventieth birthday, "what may appear chaotic and fragmentary in our daily life, seen in another aspect is part of a perfect whole". With Plato and Plotinus he saw beauty and truth as aspects of the divine perfection. Never, by eccentricity of expression, nor by the help of needless gimmicks, did he attempt to attract attention to his writings. What Walter Jerrold wrote about my father in 1930 was as true as on the day of his death: "He is not ashamed of having sat at the feet of Tennyson and his place is assured in the regard of those who rejoice in the simple culture of perennial beauty rather than any temporary cult of the ugly."

According to his wish he is today still close to Tennyson, for he is buried less than a mile from the poet's Isle of Wight home at Farringford.

H. N.

ALZUNA

The forest of Alzuna hides a pool.
  Beside that pool, a shadowy tree up-towers.
High on that tree, a bough most beautiful
  Bends with the fragrant burden of its flowers.
Among those flowers a nest is buried deep.
  Warm in that nest, there lies a freckled shell.
Packed in that shell, a bird is fast asleep.
  This is the incantation and the spell.

For, when the north wind blows, the bird will cry,
  "Warm in my freckled shell, I lie asleep.
The freckled shell is in the nest on high.
  The nest among the flowers is buried deep.
The flowers are on a bough most beautiful.
  The bough is on a tree no axe can fell.
The sky is at its feet in yonder pool.
  This is the incantation and the spell!"

A SONG OF SHERWOOD

SHERWOOD in the twilight, is Robin Hood awake?
Grey and ghostly shadows are gliding through the brake,
Shadows of the dappled deer, dreaming of the morn,
Dreaming of a shadowy man that winds a shadowy horn.

Robin Hood is here again: all his merry thieves
Hear a ghostly bugle-note shivering through the leaves,
Calling as he used to call, faint and far away,
In Sherwood, in Sherwood, about the break of day.

All the gnarled old thorn-trees are blossom-white for June.
All the elves that Marian knew were here beneath the moon—
Younger than the wild thyme, older than the trees,
Lob and Mab and Bramblescratch, on their unbridled bees.

Oaken-hearted England is waking as of old,
With eyes of blither hazel and hair of brighter gold:

9

For Robin Hood is here again beneath the bursting spray
In Sherwood, in Sherwood, about the break of day.

Love is in the greenwood building him a house
Of wild rose and hawthorn and honeysuckle boughs:
Love is in the greenwood, dawn is in the skies,
And Marian is waiting with her laughter-loving eyes.

Hark!   The dazzled laverock climbs the golden steep!
Marian is waiting: is Robin Hood asleep?
Where the last dark arrow fell, the white scuts flash away,
In Sherwood, in Sherwood, about the break of day.

Oberon, Oberon, the hazel copses ring,
Time to hush the night-jar and let the throstle sing,
Time to let the blackbird lift a bonny head,
And wake Will Scarlett from his leafy forest bed.

Friar Tuck and Little John are riding down together
With quarter-staff and drinking-can and grey goose feather.
The dead are coming back again, the years are rolled away
In Sherwood, in Sherwood, about the break of day.

Softly over Sherwood the south wind blows.
All the heart of England hid in every rose
Hears across the greenwood the sunny whisper leap,
Sherwood in the red dawn, is Robin Hood asleep?

Hark, the voice of England wakes him as of old
And, shattering the silence with a cry of brighter gold,
Bugles in the greenwood echo from the steep,
Sherwood in the red dawn, is Robin Hood asleep?

Where the deer are gliding, down the shadowy glen,
All across the glades of fern he calls his merry men—
Doublets of the Lincoln green glancing through the may
In Sherwood, in Sherwood, about the break of day—

Calls them and they answer: from aisles of oak and ash
Rings the *Follow!   Follow!*   and the boughs begin to crash,
The ferns begin to flutter and the flowers begin to fly,
And through the crimson dawning the robber band goes by.

Robin!   Robin!   Robin!   All his merry thieves
Answer as the bugle-note shivers through the leaves,

Calling as he used to call, faint and far away,
In Sherwood, in Sherwood, about the break of day.

THE HIGHWAYMAN

PART ONE

THE wind was a torrent of darkness among the gusty trees.
The moon was a ghostly galleon tossed upon cloudy seas.
The road was a ribbon of moonlight over the purple moor,
And the highwayman came riding—
        Riding—riding—
The highwayman came riding, up to the old inn-door.

He'd a French cocked-hat on his forehead, a bunch of lace at his chin,
A coat of the claret velvet, and breeches of brown doe-skin.
They fitted with never a wrinkle.   His boots were up to the thigh.
And he rode with a jewelled twinkle,
        His pistol butts a-twinkle,
His rapier hilt a-twinkle, under the jewelled sky.

Over the cobbles he clattered and clashed in the dark inn-yard.
He tapped with his whip on the shutters, but all was locked and barred.
He whistled a tune to the window, and who should be waiting there
But the landlord's black-eyed daughter,
        Bess, the landlord's daughter,
Plaiting a dark red love-knot into her long black hair.

And dark in the dark old inn-yard a stable-wicket creaked
Where Tim the ostler listened.   His face was white and peaked.
His eyes were hollows of madness, his hair like mouldy hay,
But he loved the landlord's daughter,
        The landlord's red-lipped daughter.
Dumb as a dog he listened, and he heard the robber say—

"One kiss, my bonny sweetheart, I'm after a prize to-night,
But I shall be back with the yellow gold before the morning light;
Yet, if they press me sharply, and harry me through the day,
Then look for me by moonlight,
        Watch for me by moonlight,
I'll come to thee by moonlight, though hell should bar the way."

He rose upright in the stirrups.   He scarce could reach her hand,
But she loosened her hair in the casement.   His face burnt like a brand

As the black cascade of perfume came tumbling over his breast;
And he kissed its waves in the moonlight,
(O, sweet black waves in the moonlight!)
Then he tugged at his rein in the moonlight, and galloped away to the
west.

PART TWO

He did not come in the dawning.   He did not come at noon;
And out of the tawny sunset, before the rise of the moon,
When the road was a gypsy's ribbon, looping the purple moor,
A red-coat troop came marching—
Marching—marching—
King George's men came marching, up to the old inn-door.

They said no word to the landlord.   They drank his ale instead.
But they gagged his daughter, and bound her, to the foot of her narrow
bed.
Two of them knelt at her casement, with muskets at their side!
There was death at every window;
And hell at one dark window;
For Bess could see, through her casement, the road that *he* would ride.

They had tied her up to attention, with many a sniggering jest.
They had bound a musket beside her, with the muzzle beneath her
breast!
"Now, keep good watch!" and they kissed her.   She heard the doomed
man say—
Look for me by moonlight;
Watch for me by moonlight;
I'll come to thee by moonlight, though hell should bar the way!

She twisted her hands behind her; but all the knots held good!
She writhed her hands till her fingers were wet with sweat or blood!
They stretched and strained in the darkness, and the hours crawled by
like years,
Till, now, on the stroke of midnight,
Cold, on the stroke of midnight,
The tip of one finger touched it!   The trigger at least was hers!

The tip of one finger touched it.   She strove no more for the rest.
Up, she stood up to attention, with the muzzle beneath her breast.
She would not risk their hearing; she would not strive again;
For the road lay bare in the moonlight;
Blank and bare in the moonlight;

12

And the blood of her veins, in the moonlight, throbbed to her love's
refrain.

Tlot-tlot; tlot-tlot!   Had they heard it?   The horsehoofs ringing clear;
Tlot-tlot, tlot-tlot, in the distance?   Were they deaf that they did not
hear?
Down the ribbon of moonlight, over the brow of the hill,
The highwayman came riding—
        Riding—riding—
The red-coats looked to their priming!   She stood up, straight and still.

Tlot-tlot, in the frosty silence!   *Tlot-tlot,* in the echoing night!
Nearer he came and nearer.   Her face was like a light.
Her eyes grew wide for a moment; she drew one last deep breath,
Then her finger moved in the moonlight,
        Her musket shattered the moonlight,
Shattered her breast in the moonlight and warned him—with her death.

He turned.   He spurred to the west; he did not know who stood
Bowed, with her head o'er the musket, drenched with her own blood!
Not till the dawn he heard it, and his face grew grey to hear
How Bess, the landlord's daughter,
        The landlord's black-eyed daughter,
Had watched for her love in the moonlight, and died in the darkness
there.

Back, he spurred like a madman, shouting a curse to the sky,
With the white road smoking behind him and his rapier brandished
high.
Blood-red were his spurs in the golden noon; wine-red was his velvet
coat;
When they shot him down on the highway,
        Down like a dog on the highway,
And he lay in his blood on the highway, with a bunch of lace at his
throat.

        .   .   .   .

And still of a winter's night, they say, when the wind is in the trees,
When the moon is a ghostly galleon tossed upon cloudy seas,
When the road is a ribbon of moonlight over the purple moor,
A highwayman comes riding—
        Riding—riding—
A highwayman comes riding, up to the old inn-door.

Over the cobbles he clatters and clangs in the dark inn-yard.
He taps with his whip on the shutters, but all is locked and barred.
He whistles a tune to the window, and who should be waiting there
But the landlord's black-eyed daughter,
　　Bess, the landlord's daughter,
Plaiting a dark red love-knot into her long black hair.

FORTY SINGING SEAMEN

"In our lands be Beeres and Lyons of dyvers colours as ye redd, grene, black, and white.　And in our land be also Unicornes and these Unicornes slee many Lyons. . . . Also there dare no man make a lye in our lande, for if he dyde he sholde incontynent be sleyn."—*Mediæval Epistle of Pope Prester John.*

ACROSS the seas of Wonderland to Mogadore we plodded,
　　Forty singing seamen in an old black barque,
And we landed in the twilight where a Polyphemus nodded
　　With his battered moon-eye winking red and yellow through the dark!
　　　　For his eye was growing mellow,
　　　　Rich and ripe and red and yellow,
　　As was time, since old Ulysses made him bellow in the dark!
Cho.—Since Ulysses bunged his eye up with a pine-torch in the dark!

Were they mountains in the gloaming or the giant's ugly shoulders
　　Just beneath the rolling eyeball, with its bleared and vinous glow,
Red and yellow o'er the purple of the pines among the boulders
　　And the shaggy horror brooding on the sullen slopes below,
　　　　Were they pines among the boulders
　　　　Or the hair upon his shoulders?
　　We were only simple seamen, so of course we didn't know.
Cho.—We were simple singing seamen, so of course we couldn't know.

But we crossed a plain of poppies, and we came upon a fountain
　　Not of water, but of jewels, like a spray of leaping fire;
And behind it, in an emerald glade, beneath a golden mountain,
　　There stood a crystal palace, for a sailor to admire;
　　　　For a troop of ghosts came round us,
　　　　Which with leaves of bay they crowned us,
　　Then with grog they wellnigh drowned us, to the depth of our desire!
Cho.—And 'twas very friendly of them, as a sailor can admire!

There was music all about us, we were growing quite forgetful
　　We were only singing seamen from the dirt of Londontown,
Though the nectar that we swallowed seemed to vanish half regretful
　　As if we wasn't good enough to take such vittles down,
　　　　When we saw a sudden figure,

14

Tall and black as any nigger,
  Like the devil—only bigger—drawing near us with a frown!
Cho.—Like the devil—but much bigger—and he wore a golden crown!

And "what's all this?" he growls at us! With dignity we chaunted,
  "Forty singing seamen, sir, as won't be put upon!"
"What? Englishmen?" he cries. "Well, if ye don't mind being haunted,
  Faith, you're welcome to my palace. I'm the famous Prester John!
    Will ye walk into my palace?
    I don't bear 'ee any malice!
One and all ye shall be welcome in the halls of Prester John!"
Cho.—So we walked into the palace and the halls of Prester John!

Now the door was one great diamond and the hall a hollow ruby—
  Big as Beachy Head, my lads, nay bigger by a half!
And I sees the mate wi' mouth agape, a-staring like a booby,
  And the skipper close behind him, with his tongue out like a calf!
    Now the way to take it rightly
    Was to walk along politely
Just as if you didn't notice—so I couldn't help but laugh!
Cho.—For they both forgot their manners and the crew was bound to
      laugh!

But he took us through his palace and, my lads, as I'm a sinner,
  We walked into an opal like a sunset-coloured cloud.
"My dining-room," he says, and, quick as light we saw a dinner
  Spread before us by the fingers of a hidden fairy crowd;
    And the skipper, swaying gently
    After dinner, murmurs faintly,
"I looks to-wards you, Prester John, you've done us very proud!"
Cho.—And we drank his health with honours, for he *done* us *very* proud!

Then he walks us to his garden where we sees a feathered demon
  Very splendid and important on a sort of spicy tree!
"That's the Phœnix," whispers Prester, "which all eddicated seamen
  Knows the only one existent, and *he's* waiting for to flee!
    When his hundred years expire
    Then he'll set hisself a-fire
And another from his ashes rise most beautiful to see!"
Cho.—With wings of rose and emerald most beautiful to see!

Then he says, "In yonder forest there's a little silver river,
  And whosoever drinks of it, his youth shall never die!
The centuries go by, but Prester John endures for ever
  With his music in the mountains and his magic on the sky!
    While *your* hearts are growing colder,

While your world is growing older,
There's a magic in the distance, where the sea-line meets the sky."
Cho.—It shall call to singing seamen till the fount o' song is dry!

So we thought we'd up and seek it, but that forest fair defied us.
First a crimson leopard laughs at us most horrible to see.
Then a sea-green lion came and sniffed and licked his chops and eyed us,
While a red and yellow unicorn was dancing round a tree!
We was trying to look thinner,
Which was hard, because our dinner
Must ha' made us very tempting to a cat o' high degree!
Cho.—Must ha' made us very tempting to the whole menarjeree!

So we scuttled from that forest and across the poppy meadows
Where the awful shaggy horror brooded o'er us in the dark!
And we pushes out from shore again a-jumping at our shadows,
And pulls away most joyful to the old black barque!
And home again we plodded
While the Polyphemus nodded
With his battered moon-eye winking red and yellow through the dark.
Cho.—Oh, the moon above the mountains, red and yellow through the
dark!

Across the seas of Wonderland to London-town we blundered,
Forty singing seamen as was puzzled for to know
If the visions we had seen was caused by—here again we pondered—
A tipple in a vision forty thousand years ago.
Could the grog we *dreamt* we swallowed
Make us *dream* of all that followed?
We were only simple seamen, so of course we didn't know!
Cho.—We were simple singing seamen, so of course we could not know!

BUCCANEER DAYS

The rain's on the roof.   The dark boughs tap at the pane.
I have heaped up the fire; and it shows me your face there again,
As it shone in our cave, when we cooked our sea-perch at a blaze
Of dry gorse and drift-wood, in boyhood's great buccaneer days.

The old cave by the fir-wood that slopes down the hill to the sea,
—I remember, we smoked our first pipes there, and had to agree
That either the clay was not ripe, or the 'baccy was damp.
You were breaking yours in for a sailor, you said.   I gave mine to a
tramp.

In a clearing above it, one fir-tree still whispers apart
With a magpie's big mud-plastered nest in its old crooked heart.
I can still feel the smooth mottled eggs, the strange warmth, the new
    wonder;
The beauty, the pity, that spared our first exquisite plunder.

And our "eyrie,"—that nook overhung by the cliff's dizzy brow,
I wonder if other young pirates are haunting it now.
There were red pungent flowers on the brink.   If I smell them to-day
I am kneeling, out there, on a cliff-top, the wide world away.

Could Araby match them?   They called them "rest-harrow" at home.
They were fringes of elfin-land there, hanging over the foam,
With magic about them, or why should that brink be so bright
With those queer little friends of my boyhood, across the long night?

I can see the brass ring of your spy-glass.   How brightly it shone
As you climbed through the crisp purple thyme to our eyrie alone.
I can see the smooth sun-burn that darkened our faces and hands
As we gazed at the merchantmen sailing away to those palm-shadowed
    lands.

I can hear the long sigh of the sea as we raced in the sun
To dry ourselves after our swim; hear the shout as we run
Out, again, through the waves, and ride back on the surf to the land,
To bask and grow brown on the dry drifting dunes of the sand.

Then up, in our breeches and shirts, to that buccaneer glow
In the cave.   Is it true we grow old?   Is the fire sinking low?
Come!   You shall be chief.   We'll not quarrel.   The time flies so fast.
There are ships to be grappled.   There's blood to be shed, ere our sum-
    mer be past,—

It is winter, mid-winter!   The dark boughs thresh at the pane.
Dying embers—white ashes—the windows are beaten with rain.

OLD GREY SQUIRREL

A GREAT while ago there was a school-boy.
    He lived in a cottage by the sea,
And the very first thing he could remember
    Was the rigging of the schooners by the quay.

He could watch them, when he woke, from his window,
    With the tall cranes hoisting out the freight.
And he used to think of shipping as a sea-cook,
    And sailing to the Golden Gate.

For he used to buy the yellow penny dreadfuls,
    And read them where he fished for conger eels,
And listened to the lapping of the water,
    The green and oily water round the keels.

There were trawlers with their shark-mouthed flat-fish,
    And red nets hanging out to dry,
And the skate the skipper kept because he liked 'em,
    And landsmen never knew the fish to fry.

There were brigantines with timber out of Norroway,
    Oozing with the syrups of the pine.
There were rusty dusty schooners out of Sunderland,
    And ships of the Blue Funnel line.

And to tumble down a hatch into the cabin
    Was better than the best of broken rules;
For the smell of 'em was like a Christmas dinner,
    And the feel of 'em was like a box of tools.

And, before he went to sleep in the evening,
    The very last thing that he could see
Was the sailor-men a-dancing in the moonlight
    By the capstan that stood upon the quay.

He is perched upon a high stool in London.
    The Golden Gate is very far away.
They caught him, and they caged him, like a squirrel.
    He is totting up accounts, and going grey.

He will never, never, never sail to 'Frisco.
    But the very last thing that he will see
Will be sailor-men a-dancing in the sunrise
    By the capstan that stands upon the quay. . . .

To the tune of an old concertina,
    By the capstan that stands upon the quay.

THE ADMIRAL'S GHOST

I TELL you a tale to-night
   Which a seaman told to me,
With eyes that gleamed in the lanthorn light
   And a voice as low as the sea.

You could almost hear the stars
   Twinkling up in the sky,
And the old wind woke and moaned in the spars,
   And the same old waves went by,

Singing the same old song
   As ages and ages ago,
While he froze my blood in that deep-sea night
   With the things that he seemed to know.

A bare foot pattered on deck;
   Ropes creaked; then—all grew still,
And he pointed his finger straight in my face
   And growled, as a sea-dog will.

"Do 'ee know who Nelson was?
   That pore little shrivelled form
With the patch on his eye and the pinned-up sleeve
   And a soul like a North Sea storm?

"Ask of the Devonshire men!
   They know, and they'll tell you true;
He wasn't the pore little chawed-up chap
   That Hardy thought he knew.

"He wasn't the man you think!
   His patch was a dern disguise!
For he knew that they'd find him out, d'you see,
   If they looked him in both his eyes.

"He was twice as big as he seemed;
   But his clothes were cunningly made.
He'd both of his hairy arms all right.
   The sleeve was a trick of the trade.

"You've heard of sperrits, no doubt;
   Well, there's more in the matter than that!

19

But he wasn't the patch, and he wasn't the sleeve,
   And he *wasn't* the laced cocked-hat.

"Nelson was just—a Ghost!
   You may laugh!   But the Devonshire men
They knew that he'd come when England called,
   And they know that he'll come again.

"I'll tell you the way it was
   (For none of the landsmen know),
And to tell it you right, you must go a-starn
   Two hundred years or so.

    .   .   .   .

"The waves were lapping and slapping
   The same as they are to-day;
And Drake lay dying aboard his ship
   In Nombre Dios Bay.

"The scent of the foreign flowers
   Came floating all around;
'But I'd give my soul for the smell o' the pitch,'
   Says he, 'in Plymouth Sound.

" 'What shall I do,' he says,
   'When the guns begin to roar,
An' England wants me, and me not there
   To shatter her foes once more?'

"(You've heard what he said, maybe,
   But I'll mark you the p'ints again;
For I want you to box your compass right
   And get my story plain.)

" 'You must take my drum,' he says,
   'To the old sea-wall at home;
And if ever you strike that drum,' he says,
   "Why, strike me blind, I'll come!

" 'If England needs me, dead
   Or living, I'll rise that day!
I'll rise from the darkness under the sea
   Ten thousand miles away.'

"That's what he said; and he died;
   An' his pirates, listenin' roun',

With their crimson doublets and jewelled swords
    That flashed as the sun went down,

"They sewed him up in his shroud
    With a round-shot top and toe,
To sink him under the salt sharp sea
    Where all good seamen go.

"They lowered him down in the deep,
    And there in the sunset light
They boomed a broadside over his grave,
    As meanin' to say 'Good-night.'

"They sailed away in the dark
    To the dear little isle they knew;
And they hung his drum by the old sea-wall
    The same as he told them to.

    .   .   .   .

"Two hundred years went by,
    And the guns began to roar,
And England was fighting hard for her life,
    As ever she fought of yore.

" 'It's only my dead that count,'
    She said, as she says to-day;
'It isn't the ships and it isn't the guns
    'Ull sweep Trafalgar's Bay.'

"D'you guess who Nelson was?
    You may laugh, but it's true as true!
There was more in that pore little chawed-up chap
    Then ever his best friend knew.

"The foe was creepin' close,
    In the dark, to our white-cliffed isle;
They were ready to leap at England's throat
    When—oh, you may smile, you may smile;

"But—ask of the Devonshire men;
    For they heard in the dead of night
The roll of a drum, and they saw *him* pass
    On a ship all shining white.

"He stretched out his dead cold face
   And he sailed in the grand old way!
The fishes had taken an eye and an arm,
   But he *swept* Trafalgar's Bay."

THE BARREL-ORGAN

THERE's a barrel-organ carolling across a golden street
   In the City as the sun sinks low;
With a silvery cry of linnets in its dull mechanic beat,
   As it dies into the sunset-glow;
And it pulses through the pleasures of the City and the pain
   That surround the singing organ like a large eternal light;
And they've given it a glory and a part to play again
   In the Symphony that rules the day and night.

And now it's marching onward through the realms of old romance,
   And trolling out a fond familiar tune,
And now it's roaring cannon down to fight the King of France,
   And now it's prattling softly to the moon,
And all around the organ there's a sea without a shore
   Of human joys and wonders and regrets,
To remember and to recompense the music evermore
   For what the cold machinery forgets. . . .

         Yes; as the music changes,
            Like a prismatic glass,
         It takes the light and ranges
            Through all the moods that pass;
         Dissects the common carnival
            Of passions and regrets,
         And gives the world a glimpse of all
            The colours it forgets.

         And there *La Traviata* sighs
            Another sadder song;
         And there *Il Trovatore* cries
            A tale of deeper wrong;
         And bolder knights to battle go
            With sword and shield and lance,
         Than ever here on earth below
            Have whirled into—*a dance!*—

22

Go down to Kew in lilac-time, in lilac-time, in lilac-time.
  Go down to Kew in lilac-time (it isn't far from London!),
And you shall wander hand in hand with love in summer's wonderland.
  Go down to Kew in lilac-time (it isn't far from London!).

The cherry-trees are seas of bloom and soft perfume and sweet perfume,
  The cherry-trees are seas of bloom (and oh, so near to London!),
And there they say when dawn is high and all the world's a blaze of sky,
  The cuckoo, though he's very shy, will sing a song for London.

The Dorian nightingale is rare, and yet they say you'll hear him there
  At Kew, at Kew in lilac-time (and oh, so near to London!),
The linnet and the throstle, too, and after dark the long halloo
  And golden-eyed *tu-whit, tu-whoo*, of owls that ogle London.

For Noah hardly knew a bird of any kind that isn't heard
  At Kew, at Kew in lilac-time (and oh, so near to London!),
And when the rose begins to pout and all the chestnut spires are out
  You'll hear the rest without a doubt, all chorussing for London:

Come down to Kew in lilac-time, in lilac-time, in lilac-time;
  Come down to Kew in lilac-time (it isn't far from London!),
And you shall wander hand in hand with love in summer's wonderland;
  Come down to Kew in lilac-time (it isn't far from London!).

And then the troubadour begins to thrill the golden street,
  In the City as the sun sinks low;
And in all the gaudy busses there are scores of weary feet
Marking time, sweet time, with a dull mechanic beat,
And a thousand hearts are plunging to a love they'll never meet,
Through the meadows of the sunset, through the poppies and the wheat,
  In the land where the dead dreams go.

  So it's Jeremiah, Jeremiah,
    What have you to say
  When you meet the garland girls
    Tripping on their way?

  All around my gala hat
    I wear a wreath of roses.
  (A long and lonely year it is
    I've waited for the May!).
  If any one should ask you,
    The reason why I wear it is—
  My own love, my true love, is coming home to-day.

And it's buy a bunch of violets for the lady,
  (*It's lilac-time in London!   It's lilac-time in London!*)
Buy a bunch of violets for the lady
  While the sky burns blue above.
On the other side the street you'll find it shady,
  (*It's lilac-time in London!   It's lilac-time in London!*)
But buy a bunch of violets for the lady,
  And tell her she's your own true love.

There's a barrel-organ carolling across a golden street
  In the City as the sun sinks glittering and slow;
And the music's not immortal; but the world has made it sweet,
And enriched it with the harmonies that make a song complete,
In the deeper heavens of music where the night and morning meet,
  As it dies into the sunset-glow;
And it pulses through the pleasures of the City and the pain
That surround the singing organ like a large eternal light,
  And they've given it a glory and a part to play again
In the Symphony that rules the day and night.

          And there, as the music changes,
            The song runs round again.
          Once more it turns and ranges
            Through all its joy and pain,
          Dissects the common carnival
            Of passions and regrets;
          And the wheeling world remembers all
            The wheeling song forgets.

          Once more *La Traviata* sighs
            Another sadder song.
          Once more *Il Trovatore* cries
            A tale of deeper wrong.
          Once more the knights to battle go
            With sword and shield and lance,
          Till once, once more, the shattered foe
            Has whirled into—*a dance!*

Come down to Kew in lilac-time, in lilac-time, in lilac-time.
  Come down to Kew in lilac-time (it isn't far from London!)
And you shall wander hand in hand with love in summer's wonderland.
  Come down to Kew in lilac-time (it isn't far from London!).

AT DAWN

O HESPER-PHOSPHOR, far away
    Shining, the first, the last white star,
Hear'st thou the strange, the ghostly cry,
That moan of an ancient agony
From purple forest to golden sky
    Shivering over the breathless bay?
It is not the wind that wakes with the day;
    For see, the gulls that wheel and call,
    Beyond the tumbling white-topped bar,
Catching the sun-dawn on their wings,
    Like snow-flakes or like rose-leaves fall,
Flutter and fall in airy rings;
    And drift, like lilies ruffling into blossom
    Upon a golden lake's unwrinkled bosom.

Are not the forest's deep-lashed fringes wet
With tears?   Is not the voice of all regret
    Breaking out of the dark earth's heart?
She too, she too, has loved and lost; and we—
We that remember our lost Arcady,
Have we not known, we too,
The primal greenwood's arch of blue,
The radiant clouds at sunrise curled
Around the brows of the golden world;
The marble temples, washed with dew,
To which with rosy limbs aflame
The violet-eyed Thalassian came,
Came, pitiless, only to display
How soon the youthful splendour dies away;
    Came, only to depart
Laughing across the gray-grown bitter sea?
For each man's life is earth's epitome,
And though the years bring more than aught they take,
Yet might his heart and hers well break
Remembering how one prayer must still be vain,
    How one fair hope is dead,
    One passion quenched, one glory fled,
With those first loves that never come again.

How many years, how many generations,
    Have heard that sigh in the dawn,

25

When the dark earth yearns to the unforgotten nations
    And the old loves withdrawn,
Old loves, old lovers, wonderful and unnumbered
    As waves on the wine-dark sea,
'Neath the tall white towers of Troy and the temples that slumbered
    In Thessaly?

From the beautiful palaces, from the miraculous portals,
    The swift white feet are flown!
They were taintless of dust, the proud, the peerless Immortals
    As they sped to their loftier throne!
Perchance they are there, earth dreams, on the shores of Hesper,
    Her rosy-bosomed Hours,
Listening the wild fresh forest's enchanted whisper,
    Crowned with its new strange flowers;
Listening the great new ocean's triumphant thunder
    On the stainless unknown shore,
While that perilous queen of the world's delight and wonder
    Comes white from the foam once more.

When the mists divide with the dawn o'er those glittering waters,
    Do they gaze over unoared seas—
Naiad and nymph and the woodland's rose-crowned daughters
    And the Oceanides?
Do they sing together, perchance, in that diamond splendour,
    That world of dawn and dew,
With eyelids twitching to tears and with eyes grown tender,
    The sweet old songs they knew,
The songs of Greece?   Ah, with harp-strings mute do they falter
    As the earth like a small star pales?
When the heroes launch their ship by the smoking altar
    Does a memory lure their sails?
Far, far away, do their hearts resume the story
    That never on earth was told,
When all those urgent oars on the waste of glory
    Cast up its gold?

Are not the forest fringes wet
With tears?   Is not the voice of all regret
Breaking out of the dark earth's heart?
She too, she too, has loved and lost; and though
She turned last night in disdain
    Away from the sunset-embers,
From her soul she can never depart;

26

She can never depart from her pain.
Vainly she strives to forget;
Beautiful in her woe,
    She awakes in the dawn and remembers.

IN OTHER WORLDS

"Few, few only are there left, with whom that world of memory is duly present."

PHÆDRUS

WHOSE was the radiant face,
That bent above me, from that happy place?
Whose the strange voice that whispered through the flow
Of waves and mountain fir-woods, *It is I,*
Love that was never born, and cannot die.
Ask thine own answering soul if thou would'st know
Who speaks to thee, through earth and sea and sky.

In other worlds I loved you, long ago.
    Love that hath no beginning hath no end.
The sea-wind in my fir-wood whispers low,
In other worlds I loved you, long ago.
The sea-waves murmur, and the mountains know
    The message that the setting sun shall send:
In other worlds I loved you, long ago.
    Love that hath no beginning hath no end.

Only two children, wandering by that sea
    Listened and understood.   The breathless West
Burned like the Phœnix in its incense-tree

Beyond Cathay, in Araby the Blest.
    Above the hill-ferns, the deep heather-bloom
From crag to crag, along each broken crest,

Rolled a dim sea of colour and fragrant gloom
    Whose billows rocked the drowsy honey-bee
Round saffron isles of nut-sweet gorse and broom.
    .   .   .   .

The hawk dropped down into the pine-forest;
    And, far below, the skylark ruffled her wings
Blossom-wise, over her clover-inwoven nest.

27

They came.   They heard the song that memory sings,
  Two bare-foot children, by the salt sea spray,
Avatars of the sweetness of lost Springs

And, in their eyes, a memory—far away.

    .   .   .   .

Once, once upon a time; and, o'er and o'er
  As aye the *Happy Ever After* came
The enchanted waves lavished their faerie lore,

And tossed a rainbow, like a dying flame
  Over their foam-kissed feet on that lost shore.
O, waves that break, and return, and are ever the same,
  Where are they flown?   Will they return no more?
And God sighed in the sunset; and the sea
  Moved with His breath against the coasts of Time,
Breathing His law and heaven's tranquillity

Through waves that rose in rhythm and broke in rhyme
  (Deep music that man's heart has never learned!)
Until it seemed as though the Love sublime

Uttered itself.   The moon rose.   The waves burned
  With little flaming crests of rose and green.
Then, like an opal river, the tide returned,

Flowing out of the sunset's pure serene,
  With mirrored tints of Dawn in its dark breast
Like glimmering thoughts of lovelier worlds unseen.

Grief, like a sea-bird, drifted down to rest;

And all earth's discords, all this dark world's wrong,
  Like molten notes of music were resolved
Into the bliss of Love's transcendent song;

Through which the suns and moons and stars revolved
  According to the Spirit's deep decree,
Till Time was but a tide of intervolved

And interweaving worlds of harmony.
  In other worlds I loved you, long ago,
The ethereal citoles breathed across the sea,

And unseen citerns answered, throbbing low
   Where airs of sunset into the sunrise wend,
In other worlds I loved you, long ago.
   Love that hath no beginning hath no end.

Only two lovers, wandering by that sea
   Listened and understood. The mystery
Of silent earth and sky was like a word
   Uttered, but all unheard;
Uttered by every glistening cloud and leaf
With all the immortal glory of mortal grief;
While every wave that out of the sunset rolled
To break in music on that darkening shore
Seemed telling, strangely telling, evermore,
   A story that must still remain untold:

     Love, of whom Life had birth,
       See, now, is Death not sweet?
     Love, is this heaven or earth?
       Both are beneath thy feet.

     Nay, both within thy heart!
       O, Love, the glory nears.
     The veils of Time are riven apart.
       The Rose of Heaven appears.

     What rhythmic ebb and flow
       Still rules the blissful throng
     That through its radiant mazes go
       Like pangs of visible song?

     Do they still taste of death,
       As music breathes farewell,
     That its own soul, and what it saith,
       In its own form may dwell?

     So that when Love is fain
       To touch the silent strings,
     At once, from their dark sleep again
       Awake the ecstatic wings.

     Love, of whom Death had birth,
       See now, is Life not sweet?
     Love, is this heaven or earth?
       Both are beneath thy feet.

In other worlds I loved you, long ago.
    Love that hath no beginning hath no end.
The may-boughs murmur, in the moon's first glow,
    In other worlds I loved you, long ago.
The fir-woods whisper, and the sea-waves know
    The message that the deepening dawn shall send:
In other worlds I loved you, long ago.
    Love that hath no beginning hath no end.

NIOBE

How like the sky she bends above her child,
    One with the great horizon of her pain!
No sob from our low seas where woe runs wild,
    No weeping cloud, no momentary rain,
Can mar the heaven-high visage of her grief,
    That frozen anguish, proud, majestic, dumb.
        She stoops in pity above the labouring earth,
            Knowing how fond, how brief
    Is all its hope, past, present, and to come,
        She stoops in pity, and yearns to assuage its dearth.

Through that fair face the whole dark universe
    Speaks, as a thorn-tree speaks thro' one white flower;
And all those wrenched Promethean souls that curse
    The gods, but cannot die before their hour,
Find utterance in her beauty.   That fair head
    Bows over all earth's graves.   It was her cry
        Men heard in Rama when the twisted ways
            With children's blood ran red.
    Her silence towers to Silences on high;
        And, in her face, the whole earth's anguish prays.

It is the pity, the pity of human love
    That strains her face, upturned to meet the doom,
And her deep bosom, like a snow-white dove
    Frozen upon its nest, ne'er to resume
Its happy breathing o'er the golden brace
    That she must shield till death.   Death, death alone
        Can break the anguished horror of that spell.
            The sorrow on her face
    Is sealed: the living flesh is turned to stone;
        She knows all, all, that Life and Time can tell.

Ah, yet, her woman's love, so vast, so tender,
  Her woman's body, hurt by every dart,
Braving the thunder, still, still hide the slender
  Soft frightened child beneath her mighty heart.
She is all one mute immortal cry, one brief
    Infinite pang of such victorious pain
      That she transcends the heavens and bows them down!
        The majesty of grief
  Is hers, and her dominion must remain
      Eternal.   Grief alone can wear that crown.

DRAKE

EXORDIUM

Ships and the ocean-sea; the man who sailed it,
Rending the veils of the west from those new worlds;
England, ablaze with colour; her Devonshire lads,
In steel and velvet, raking the Spanish Main
For emeralds, pearls, piratical red doubloons,
Or swaggering through the sunset into the dawn;
Her legends of old Cathay; her musical inns;
The ring of the hammers at Rye on her new fleet;
The smell of the great clean sails; the tang of the pitch,
The hemp, the pine, on the salt wind, singing for ever
Freedom enthroned, and all that fury of Spain.
A proud adventure of song, a task for youth,
And only youth to endeavour; but since each soul
Repeats in its own growth, from youth to age,
All the wild struggling history of mankind,
So now, in a golden year of dawning life,
When blood runs hot and far horizons call,
While colour enchants, and Gloriana's throne
Burns like a star in the mind's unclouded sky,
I take the challenge, attempt the enduring tale.

Long since on Hispaniola's loneliest hill,
Lost in the tropical forest's tangled maze,
Drake halted with his crew.   Bravely they shone
With musketoon and dagger; their tawny brows
Bound with soiled scarves of orange and sweat-stained blue,
They shook the sweat off, shaking the silver rings
A-flash in their sun-bronzed ears.   The lion-maned palms

31

Drooped smooth crisp fans, fountains of sharp black shadow
Hiding the world beyond them. Bee-like birds,
Darts of green fire, rose-tufted, needle-beaked,
Flew by, to thrill in their curled moon-tinted target,
A trumpet-orchid's throat. Lianas wreathed
Their long tough cords to baffle the cutlass blades.
A deep strange silence dreadfully besieged
Even those mighty hearts.
                                        Only they heard
Cries of the painted birds, troubling the heat
And shivering through the woods.
                                        Behind them lay
The old world they knew. Beyond that forest-ridge
None guessed what worlds were hidden; till Francis Drake
Unbuckled his sword, took hold on a dark-boughed tree,
The tallest near them, and clomb upward, branch
By branch.
                        And there, as he swung clear above
The steep-down forest, before his wondering eyes
Mile after glorious mile of struggling gold
Blazed the unknown immeasurable sea.
He hailed it, and turned home to Plymouth Sound
With sunset-oceans plunging through his mind
And new horizons calling. No man knew
By what wild roads to north or south a ship
Might enter that sea Paradise. But Drake
Vowed that, God helping, he would one day plough
Those virgin waters with an English keel.

So here, above a wide invisible sea,
In a boy's heart, another dream was born.
Far off, he saw the sails of England's youth
Like sunset clouds go by—a vision lit
With mighty prophecies, fraught with nobler dooms
Than great Æneas knew, yet all unsung.
Blind master of these opened eyes, be near me
While I assay this voyage, not in pride,
But with heart raised to a Power above my power,
And filled with it, as hearts are filled in prayer.
For he, our Devon seaman, who first sailed
The globe around, and crowned our white-cliffed isle
Against the paramount empire of the world
With that sea-glory, fought in a wider war
Even than he knew. He fought for a world's re-birth,
Championing our manhood as it rose

And broke its feudal chains in the face of kings.
He fought for the soul's freedom; fought the fight
Which, though it still rings in our wondering ears
Was won then and for ever—that great war,
That last Crusade of Christ against false priests,
Wherein Spain fell, behind a thunderous roar
Of ocean-triumph, over burning ships
And shattered fleets, while England, England rose,
Her white cliffs laughing out across the waves,
Victorious over all her enemies.

And while he crowned her queen on every sea,
Her loins brought forth, her fostering bosom fed,
Souls that have swept the spiritual deep
From heaven to hell, and justified her crown,
For, round the throne of great Elizabeth,
The stainless moon of England's epic song,
The Faery Queen, in silver music moved;
Her Ocean-shepherd, and those golden lads
Who sung the dawn in at the Mermaid Tavern
Broke through the clouds like stars; Drayton, a gleam
Like Hesperus over westering voyagers;
Marlowe, a fiery planet, ruddy as Mars;
Jonson, like huge Orion; and, over all,
The soul of Shakespeare brooding far and wide.
Lord of a realm that many an age to come
Must still leave undiscovered, unexplored.

Prosper my song then, England.   If it spread
Too wide a sail, it sails for love of thee.
Three hundred years ago, three hundred years
And five long decades, on the red-rock coast
Of wooded Devon, thou didst light this flame.
There, with wild branches swaying above the cliff,
And that white witchery of the foam below,
The tree that bore the raven's matted nest
Surrendered—smooth, warm loot!—the sea-green eggs
Mottled with sea-weed brown, to the daring hand,
Lean, sunburnt, hard, of the young-eyed privateer
Who now, astride the rough dark fork of the tree,
Gazed westward, Francis Drake.   There didst thou fill
His heart with beauty, feed his eyes with light.
Like a young eagle, gazing on a glory
Deeper than even he knew, there did he spread
And shut and spread those eager untried wings

Whose kingly power should bear him soon through heaven,
Climb with the dawn, majestic pulse for pulse,
And waft him round the world.   So prosper thou
His voyage in my song; for more than his
My need is, even than when he first set sail
In secret, with three ships and three-score men,
Not knowing if he went to life or death,
Nor caring greatly, so that he were true
To his own soul, which could not choose but hear
Through that red turbulence of the Spanish Main,
One deeper whisper, one undying call,
From ever-fading, ever-new horizons,
And shores beyond the sunset and the sea.

BOOK I

In Gloriana's dark old council-hall
The weather-shrewd pilots of her storm-tossed realm
Were privily mustering; for the threat of war
Was growing like thunder on the south-west wind.
The late light, near the windows, flickered on steel,
Burned on a ruby hilt, or softly bloomed
On such a cloak as Titian loved to paint
In days when colour warmed the world like wine.
Here, in the dusk, like a feather of sunset-cloud
A plumed cap kindled.   There, in the mellower gloom,
A doublet, slashed with rich Italian hues
Darkened or gleamed; but lean brown faces of men
Eagled it over the splendour.   Storm-shrewd eyes
Looked at the shadow of doom upon their seas,
And challenged it.
                   They waited for their Queen.
And now, the long bright silver trumpets pealed.
The tapers flashed.   Tall waxen torches burned.
The hidden throng blazed out into the light;
And, statelily, between their bending ranks,
She passed to her throne.
                        Then, with a clash of swords
All took their seats.   The hush that gripped all hearts
Was charged with lightning.   The dark fire of war
Smouldered in every eye.
                       First, Walsingham
Arose and spoke his thought;
                            "England, her queen,
And you, my lords, are surely at one to-night.

34

What choice is ours when every sea-wind tells
Of English galleons, grappled and gutted and sunk;
Of English seamen lashed to the galley-bench,
Flung into dungeons, burned in a yellow fool's coat
By those red hands of Spain?   She has locked all lands
In her imperial chains; but not the sea.
There lies your freedom, in that untamed realm.
Set all your ships and seamen free to claim it."

But, over all the murmurs of assent,
Round-shouldered Burghley rose and, with a smile
Of half-ironic admiration, praised him.
Then, watching close the small white face of the queen,
Clear-cut as a cameo over her wide-winged ruff,
And knowing her woman's craft would still prefer
His own more subtle strength, he straight began
To chill their fever.
                    "Would that I might regain
That reckless forth-right heart of fire," he said.
"But, though my way be tortuous, it makes straight
The way of England.   If it serve that end
Her friends would call it wisdom.   You know well"—
Shrewdly he watched that small white clear-cut face
Hardening to steel—"How Mary of Scotland waits
To strike us in the side.   In England still
Are many who pine to warm their hands again
At Spanish faggots, heaped on Smithfield fires."
    "So be it," growled Effingham, "painted figure-heads
Of Fleets Invincible make good fire-wood, Burghley!"
    "France," echoed Burghley, with his cold grave smile,
"France, hunting down her Huguenots, would kill
In English woods, before your ships brought home
Those faggots, my lord admiral.   Half the world
Awaits its hour to strike at us.   What shield
Can England raise?   I say that open war
Would shatter us; and piracy, my lords,
Is black, whoever practise it.   Our hands
Are not untainted.   Hawkins in the west"—
"Had pitch upon his hands," cried Howard again.
"My lords, the Spaniard had destroyed all law
Beyond the line.   God's death, must Spain haul down
All flags, forbid all cargoes but her own?"

Then through the halberds at the black-winged doors
A voice demanded entrance; and the guards

Made way; and through that conclave surged the blood
Of Agincourt; as up to the foot of the throne
Strode Leicester.   Hard behind him, with wild eyes,
Grey lips and twisted body, a man in rags,
A seaman—for the tawny weather-stains
Were not yet faded from his face and throat—
Came stumbling.
                    "Look," said Leicester, in a voice
Level and low and deadly as a sword.
"Before you judge our privateers, Lord Burghley,
Look on Spain's work.   He fell into her hands
On one of our chief city merchant's ships,
The Pride of London, one of Osborne's ships.
He has lain beside his comrades on the rack.
Look in his eyes.   They'll show you, like a glass,
The glare of the torture chamber.   He escaped—
How, let him tell you."
                    "I cannot tell it, sirs,
I cannot tell it."   The seaman's voice that, once,
Bore down the gale, quavered and broke, as the cry
Of a sea-mew driven before it.
                    "I escaped,
Because,"—he smiled a wild-eyed dreadful smile—
"Because my heart failed and I answered all
As they would have me answer.   All the rest
Were brave, sirs, very brave.   I was their captain;
And so the Spaniard, being very subtle,
Made me a crueller rack of my own thought;
For, when they stretched my naked spirit there,
It bore worse pangs than flesh could ever feel.
O, sirs, I only see blind faces round me;
Blind faces, each a bruise of white that smiles
In idiot agony, dribbling water and blood,
The face of some strange thing that once was man
And now can only turn from side to side
Babbling like a child, with mouth agape,
Where there is none to help it, none to hear,
But those black vizards in the furnace-glow,
Moving like devils at their hellish trade.
Sirs, I escaped."
                    The sweat ran down his face.
He shook from head to foot.   A crazy laugh
Broke from his lips.
                    "Yet something I did bear
Even in my flesh for England.   You shall see it."

He paused.   His memory sickened.   His brain **swooned**
Back into that wild glare of obscene pain.
Once more to his ears and nostrils horribly crept
The hiss and smell of shrivelling human flesh.
His head sank down, struggling in agony
With what all hideous words must leave untold,
He clutched the filthy rags upon his breast,
Tore them wide open, and shewed above his heart,
Seared in white lettering by the white-hot iron,
A word for England, branded there by Spain.
One low deep mutter, like that darker warning
When the storm gathers its might, and the sea draws **back**
To leap upon its prey, broke from all lips
And died again.
                        The voice of Walsingham
Rang like a trumpet through the council-hall,
"England has but one answer now to Spain.
Let all her seas deliver it!"
                                  Then the Queen,
Elizabeth, rose; and, in her tense hard face,
The imprisoned passion glowed like white-hot steel:
"My lords, this is the last cry they shall wring
From English lips unheeded.   Have no fear,
My lord of Burghley.   We shall not destroy
This England with an ill-timed stroke.   And you,
Walsingham, trust us also; for we know
Our answer now.   Only a little while,"
She dropt her voice to a whisper—"it must be dark.
It must be wide and secret as our sea.
And you, Lord Howard of Effingham"—her face
Gleamed like the face of a prophetess who looks
Through far horizons—"tell your Catholic friends
We'll wage no war of creeds; for you and I
Think first of England.   I will be Head of the Name
In this cause only; and when your children's children
Ask for a tale around the sea-coal fire
They shall see Fleets Invincible burning in it,
And hear how one small island set her heel
On Spain's imperial throat."
                                  On that same night,
Drake, in a Greenwich tavern, lay concealed;
For Spain, if it were peace, would have him die
A pirate's death.   There, all alone, he pored
By a struggling rush-light over his well-thumbed charts,
Re-sailing his late voyage, by palmy keys,

37

Woods of green parrots and sweet-mouthed Indian isles.
Charts, painted like a picture, in fair colours,
His brown hands turned, charts of the Spanish Main;
Of Mexico, where Spain had lashed his crew
On horse-back, naked, through the hot white streets;
Of San Domingo, island city of fruits,
Blood-marked, for payment by his guns, one day;
Of Darien, and his hidden harbour there,
Port Pheasant, marked *Here fish and birds abound;*
Of Nombre Dios Bay, long since inscribed
*Here Cimaroons will guide you through the woods
To El Dorado;* and one great fabulous chart,
Wavering and vague in outline as a cloud,
But marked with an old red thumb-print, where a hand
Had clutched it as chief treasure, even in death,
On Drake's first prize,—the secret Spanish chart
Of coasts that met the unknown Pacific sea.
There, fired with sunset to their crooked hearts,
Old harbours, crowned with crumbling peach-stained walls,
Glowed upon coasts with names like Spanish bells,
Castille del Oro, pealing through its palms,
Beragua, Nicaragua and *Peru.*

Hope whispered; but he dared not listen yet.
He bent above his charts, as in a cave
Of pirate booty, a seaman long-marooned
Upon an eastern island, weighs in vain
His raw rubines, his hyacinths and pearls.
He tiptoes to the heap.   He glances round
Askance.   He dreads to hear what erst he hoped,
A voice to break the hush.   He kneels.   He bathes
His gnarled brown arms with laughter in that cold fire.
He lets it trickle through his fevered palms,
Counts it, recounts it, losing count each time
For wonder at it.   Meanwhile, if he knew,
Passing the cave mouth, easily in hail,
A sail that might have saved him comes and goes,
And never comes again.
                              So Francis Drake
Counted his hidden treasure; but that sail
Passed not unseen; for now, like fate, there came
A firm and heavy footstep to the door;
Then a loud knocking; and, at first, he thought
"Death brings his warrant.   There is peace with Spain!"
But, as he looked across one shoulder, pride

Checking the fuller watch for what he feared,
The door opened; and cold as from the sea
The night rushed in, and there against the gloom,
Clad, as it seemed, with wind and cloud and rain,
There loomed a stately form and high grim face
Loaded with deadly thoughts of iron war—
Walsingham. In one hand he held a map
Marked with red lines. The other hand held down
The hilt of his lean sword. As when two eagles,
After blind wheelings through the storm-wrack, meet
On the same crag in silence, while the world
Unfolds below them through a rifted cloud,
Eyes challenged eyes, ablaze with what they saw.

The seaman rose. The soldier, cautiously
Closing the door, drew near the flickering light
And spread his map out on the table saying
"Mark for me here the points where we must strike,
To break this power at sea; King Philip's heel;
The joints in his harness."
                          And Drake looked at him,
Thinking, "If he betrays me, I am dead."
But Walsingham met his eyes and, with a laugh,
Drake, quivering like an eagle on poised wings
That freeze to stillness over the prey far down
Below, and quiver again as it moves on,
Stooped, with his finger pointing thus and thus—
"Here would I guard, here would I lie in wait,
Here would I strike him through the breast and throat.
Here are the secret fountains of his power
Beyond the Spanish Main,—Potosi's mines,
Where all day long his naked Indians dig
A sunset from the rocks; for, in the cliffs
That face the sunset and reflect its fires,
Another sunset burns, engendered there
Some say, by those warm colours of the sky;
A sunset of raw emeralds, blood rubines,
And hyacinths clustering in great veins of gold.
It is no dream; for here, by Panama,
Along the Cordilleras' tawny spurs
His mule-trains drag that sunset overland
To load the ships in Nombre Dios Bay.
But there he is on his guard. He is strong enough
To meet a navy there. Sir, I would strike him
Here, in his unattainable western sea.

Here, at one swoop, we might tear out the heart
Of all his riches; ballast our ships with it;
And bring it home to England.   We could build
A fleet with it, a power to match his own
And sail in freedom, then, on every sea."

Then as he spoke, he kindled, and began
To set forth his great dreams; and, as the moon,
Rising behind a mighty mountain-chain,
Will shadow forth in outline grim and black
Its vast and ragged edges, so that light
Of dreams, reflecting the true sun unseen,
Dawned upon Walsingham, and he, too, saw
For a moment of muffled moonlight and wild cloud
The proud sea-kingdom of the years to be.
But, even there, Drake paused, as one who strays
Beyond the bounds of caution, paused and cursed
His tongue for prating like a moon-struck boy's.
"I am mad," he cried.   "I am mad to babble so."
Then Walsingham drew near him with strange eyes
And muttered slowly, "Write that madness down,
Sign it, and let me take it to the Queen."
But the weather-wiser seaman warily
Answered him, "If it please Almighty God
To take our Queen Elizabeth to heaven,
Seeing that she is mortal as ourselves,
England might then be leagued with Spain, and I
Should here have knotted a rope around my neck.
I will write nothing."
                              So, across the charts
With that dim light on each grim countenance
The seaman and the courtier subtly fenced
With words and thoughts, but neither would betray
His whole heart to the other.   At the last
Walsingham gripped the hand of Francis Drake
And left him wondering.
                              On the third night came
A messenger from Walsingham who bade
Drake to the palace.   There the statesman met him
And led him, with flushed cheek and beating heart,
Along an echoing gallery, to a room
With carven black-winged doors.   Under their feet
They found a quietness as of fallen bloom.
Heaped on the deep-set hearth great beech-logs burned.
The soft red firelight fluttered on tapestries

From Flanders looms, leapt on their hounds and stags;
Or flushed, like colours from an evening sky,
Through forest-work: great knights with hawk on hand,
Riding for ever on their glimmering steeds
To their Belphoebe, that star-glorious face
Beyond the fairy fringes of the world.

Near the broad hearth, arranged as for a game,
An ebony chess-board stood, inlaid with squares
Of ruby and emerald, garnished with cinque-foils
Of silver, bears and ragged staves; the gift
Of Leicester, and his ancient arms.   The men,
Bishops and knights and elephants and pawns,
Were made of precious stones.   Sixteen were set
In silver white, the other sixteen gilt.

And as, for seeing eyes, the lives, loves, fates
Of all are written, even against their will,
On their own faces and within their houses,
So, close behind the darkly shining board
On the innermost wall, another parable shone.
There, the most delicate tissued cloth of all
Portrayed in glistening robes of gold and blue,
Penelope, with cold hands weaving still
The unending web, while in an outer court
The broad-limbed wooers, basking in the sun
On soft brown ox-hides, took from white-armed girls
Their golden bowls of wine.   'Tis thus, Drake thought,
Our own Penelope of England weaves
Her darker web, and ever again at night
Unravels it, to gain time for England's sake.
There, as he gazed, either the pictured arras
Moved, or the shadows tricked him.   Well had it been
Had he drawn sword and stabbed it through and through.
He saw the firelight fluttering.   Little he thought
In that still room of the gilded palace-rats,
The spies of Spain, or courtier-spies.   His mind
Was quietly drawn elsewhither; for he heard
Music within, the strings of a low lute,
An air of Dowland, like a choir of birds
At daybreak, after rain, in an April wood;
And then a maiden singing; to Queen Bess,
Or so he thought, for that great lonely spirit
Seemed to be near, and listening, but to thoughts

Beyond the music's reach.

                              Thus, long ago,
In Ithaca, the careless minstrel sang
Before the wooers, and the Queen laid down
Her endless web to listen.   Like a shadow
She stole from the upper chamber.   All unseen,
She stood beside a pillar of the door,
Covered her face and wept to find her grief
Too lonely for the song.

SONG

   Now the purple night is past.
      Now the moon more faintly glows.
   Dawn has through thy casement cast
      Roses, on thy breast, a rose.
   Now the kisses are all done.
      Now the world awakes anew.
   Now the charméd hour is gone,
      Let not love go, too.

   When old winter creeping nigh
      Mists with grey the golden hair,
   Dims the brightly glancing eye,
      Steals the joy that gentled there,
   Lad and lass imperial,
      Doff your crowns of sun and dew!
   Leaf by leaf your glories fall.
      Let not love go, too.

   Palaces and towers of pride
      Crumble, year by year, away,
   Creeds like robes are laid aside.
      Even our very tombs decay.
   When the all-conquering moth and rust
      Gnaw the princely raiment through,
   When the dust returns to dust,
      Let not love go, too.

The song ceased.   On the quiet air a power
Was darkly brooding.   A curtain rustled aside,
And fell back, like a shadow.   Then, Drake saw
Standing before him in the firelit gloom,
Pale, slender, proud, Elizabeth, the Queen.

42

All England in one woman, she drew near.
Behind her aquiline head, the ruff's wide wings
Gleamed like a phantom butterfly.   Emerald sparks
Flashed in her red-gold hair.   Her glimmering robe
Of white and green, was broidered round the hems
With grey doves' wings and serpents' emerald eyes,
And leaf-like listening ears of fox and fawn.
The buckles on her small green shoes burned red
As faerie gold, in the firelight at her feet.
But, in her face, a moment and no more
He caught a glimpse of an immortal power,
More beautiful than all her Dian's grace,
Terrible, haunting, sadder than the grave.
For, as a flame leapt upward on the hearth
She turned her head a little.   Her profile there,
With all its delicate clear-cut agate, shone
Stern as the death-mask of the Roman Cæsar
Gazing, through life and the world's unending war,
On his eternal City; an eagle face
With something of the austerer Florentine
Whom Virgil led through fire.

        She turned.   It vanished.
All woman again, she smiled.   "I have long wished
To talk with Captain Drake, that wicked pirate."
He knelt before her.

      Walsingham, bowing low,
Withdrew; then England caught her seaman's hands
And raised him to his feet.

       His whole heart burned
Knowing he talked with England, face to face.
He stood there, like a youthful knight at arms
Before his Gloriana.

      "My friend," she said,
"I have looked for truth too long in courtier's eyes.
Thank God, in yours, I see those honest friends
The sky and sea, deep friends that I can trust.
We must gain time.   We are not ripe for war.
Time, time, is our chief need.   But never think
I lack our ancient fire.   I am still Tudor,
And neither wholly meek, nor yet a king.
There is a Hand upon this helm of state
Guiding our England—and it is not mine;
But I can feel its ordinance and obey.
I cannot see the goal to which it steers;
And, as the winds change, so must I change too.

43

Let me be counted in the years to come
A wavering fool, because I blindly obey
The Power that guides our country to its goal.
Kings might have driven our ship to instant doom.
Therefore God armed me, in the appointed hour,
For England's sake, a woman and a queen.
They mock me for my thrift.   I know it.   I found
My country feeble.   I will leave her mighty.
I will build up our England.   If I hoard
My revenues like a miser—let them say it.
I gather my strength up as a woman draws
Her life into the breast that feeds her babe.
But were I thriftier even than fools account me
I'd furnish forth thy ships.   Put out to sea.
Let Burghley call thee 'pirate' for a while;
And though I must disown thee, and even feign
A willingness to hang thee, Drake"—she smiled—
"I share thy peril daily.
                            They reproach me,
My counsellors, that I keep two nations dangling.
They'd have me wed my speckled frog of France
And crown him at my side to frighten Spain.
He is Queen Catherine's son.   He knows her tricks.
A drugged rose, little grains of powdered glass,
A poisoned glove might conquer England, then;
And set my murderer with the Queen of Scots,
Exultant on my throne.   'Decide!   Decide!'
My wise men clamour.   Could they only know
One half, one hundredth of my intricate task!
I take my woman's way.   On every side
Spain lies in wait for me.   The assassin crept
Behind me, in my garden, yesternight
Fingering his hilt.   I saw it by the moon
Cold as death's eye; but, though I turned to meet him
Alone, England was with me, for I found
Only his dagger, lying at my feet.
Remember, then, though I desert thee, Drake,
I also wage this war.   Put out to sea.
Ransack their golden harbours of the west;
And though, at first, thou needs must sail alone,
And undefended, ere that end be reached,
When I shall give the word, nay, but one word,
All England shall be up and after thee,
The sword of England shall shine over thee
And round about thee like a guardian fire.

Meanwhile, we must be cautious.   Let no word
Escape thee.   That strong prophet of the law,
Burghley, would wreck thy voyage, if he knew.
He is my king of statesmen; and I chose him;
But England now takes counsel with her sea.
Hostis humani generis is Spain.
Thine is no piracy.   Nay, but take this sword,"—
She drew a glimmering weapon from the wall
And thrust the hilt towards him like a cross.
"Take it," she said, "a sign twixt thee and me,
That I, the lawful and anointed queen
Of England send thee out, where law is none,
To execute my judgment, on all seas.
Nay, let me buckle it round thee with my hands!"
There, at the word, she stooped to him.   His Queen,
England, stooped down to him and all his heart
Filled with her beauty, as her slim hands drew
The sword-belt round him, and the firelight shook
His worship and her glory in one flame.
"Farewell," she said.

     He bent above her hand,
A slender fragrant hand.   "God speed thee, Drake."
Then, through the dusk, drawing a curtain back,
She vanished, like a spirit of incantation;
And Drake, one hand upon his proud new hilt,
Strode out, afire with thought.

     At once, behind him
The embroidered arras moved.   A lean dark face,
Grey with its long eaves-dropping upon death,
Peered after him sharply, like a listening rat.
Then, like a streak of shadow, out slipt the spy
To seek his master, Doughty—a friend of Drake
In former years, but Burghley's watch-dog now.

Few suns had risen and set ere Drake made ready
Five ships, with guns and men, old sea-companions
From Bideford and Clovelly, Tavy and Dart;
Lads that had fought the Spaniard at San Juan;
Tried weather-beaten sea-dogs, old Tom Moon,
Will Harvest, who could sing a fo'c'sle song
To cheer sea-weary hearts; and, after these,
Some two-score gentlemen adventurers,
Blithe college lads and lawyers, whose young blood,
Chilled by the dusty Temple, leapt anew
At tales of the rich Indies and tall ships

Laden with ingots and broad bars of gold.
Already some had bought at a great price
Green birds of Guatemala, which they wore
On their slouched hats, tasting the high romance
And new-found colours of the world like wine.
By night they gathered in a black-beamed inn
Beside the dark and secret-flowing Thames,
And joyously tossed about a phrase that glowed
With perilous opal fire—a battered phrase
Old as Aladdin's lantern, whence a touch
Awoke a magical power—*The Spanish Main.*
Night after night, round their deep hearth, they filled
With blood-red wine their mighty loving cup
Of hammered silver, captured long ago
By Hawkins, in the west, and carrying still
The dints of that rough tussle.   Up to the brims
They filled and passed the ponderous glory round
Drinking to England and to Francis Drake.
Among them came a courtier.   No man knew,
Or asked who brought him; for he made his way
Cautiously, being a man with a smooth tongue.
His name was Doughty.   Most of all with Drake
His friendship grew and deepened, till at last
There seemed one heart between them and one soul.

BOOK II

FROM Plymouth Sound, with a crisp December wind,
Five ships put out to a mackerel-coloured sea.
It was their second sailing.   A black storm
Had struck their first, and driven them headlong home
Dismasted, and wing-broken like wounded gulls,
Before they had climbed their first Atlantic wave.
Bold ships,—their flag-ship only a hundred tons,
Their least too small for a North Sea fishing fleet—
Re-masted with Dartmoor pines, and ready once more
To dare the unfathomed night of the world's-end oceans,
Undauntedly, out to the swinging deep, they sailed.
The Pelican led the way, an immortal glory,
Ere long to be named anew *The Golden Hind.*
With three new masts that smelt of a sun-warmed coombe
Beneath Hey Tor, she carried in her strong heart
The fate of England.   A gray spray-misted throng
That seemed to rise and fall with the heaving tide
Waved from the Hoe.   They saw her captain, Drake,

High on the scutcheoned poop.   His trim gold beard
And crimson velvet cap shone vivid and sharp
As jeweller's work against a sun-washed sail.
The herring-gulls mewed around him, as he watched
All drawing, aloft, alow.   Already she held
A white bone in her teeth.   Her cannon grinned
Through dripping jaws of grim heraldic beasts,
Carven and gilded and gleaming with gem-like hues;
But, under the fair wet colours, her hard oak hull
Was built like a wave, or a stag, for strength and speed.
Black as an ebony figure-head in her bows
Diego soared, athirst for his land of palms.
One foot on a red wet anchor, he crooned to the clouds
The savage old Cimaroon war-cry, *Yo Peho.*
The clean green water around him swashed and sang;
And, high overhead, with the crackle of musketry,
St George's banner burned on the north-east wind.

Full in her milk-white wake, a fair new ship
Commanded by John Winter, a queen's captain,
The Elizabeth walked, a glittering sea-god's bride,
With streamers flying from all her slender spars
And all her close-fights hung with painted shields.
The Christopher next, a pinnace of fifteen tons,
Leapt out like a greyhound, leashed by old Tom Moon.
The Marygold, with her sixteen polished guns,
Raced on his lee.   Last, loaded deep with stores,
The Swan sailed, wallowing in her own bright foam.

And now, as though they went to a bridal feast,
A mellowing breeze of music filled their sails,
Airs of delight, from silver tubes and strings;
For, on their decks, the skilled musicians played
Whom Drake had brought to speed the boundless leagues
Of ocean, with old memories and new joy;
Not idly, but because the hearts of men
Grow mighty in song, and music moves the world.

Their crews, all told, were eight score men and boys.
They braved not only death's familiar face
Under known skies; but witch-crafts of the abyss
Beyond them, and the naked edge of doom.
Yet their first danger menaced them from within,
Not from without.   Their foremost enemy stood
—Stands always, in this voyage of man's life—

47

Unchallenged, on their flag-ship, like a friend.
Doughty stood smiling there.   Drake turned to him,
And, as the great rough coast-line opened out
Beyond St Nicholas Island, pointed west
Across the bulwarks, naming the well-loved names.
"There lies Barn Pool, beyond our wooded Ida,
Mount Edgcumbe, the dark beauty, with her pines.
That wide curved welter of silver is Cawsand Bay.
And there—that sparkle of foam is Penlee Point.
I have swum there; fished for bass, there.   We shall find
No better country upon the sunset road.
But, if our wings go wild, 'tis good to know
This will not change.   Home-keeping herring-gulls
Will still be wheeling here.   They will not lose
One brown speck in that pattern on their wings."
And Doughty laughed,—"If we return and find
A Spaniard on the throne."

                        Drake looked up quickly.
"I should put down my helm again," he said,
"And raid him till he sunk me."

                       As he spoke,
The thin, cold hand of a prophetic fear
Touched Doughty; for he thought, "If he suspect me,
The strange fanatical furnace in this man
Will shrivel all shams to ashes."

                       But, at once,
He shook the thought off; for Drake smiled at him,
Saying, "Come down, and drink a cup of sack
To our return."

                The tall cliffs dwindled down,
And swiftly vanished; for a prosperous wind
Carried the five ships onward.   The broad sun
Sank, and the dim grey chaos of the skies
Deepened into the miracle of the stars.
Frostily glittering, all the Milky Way
Lay bare, like diamond dust upon the robe
Of a great king.   Orion and the Plough
Glimmered, through drifting gulfs of silver fleece;
Watched by the lonely helmsmen on the ships,
And many a lonelier soul in Europe now
That sailed with them in spirit, unknowing, unknown,
As, far away, in Italy, that night
Young Galileo, looking upward, heard
The world-wide whisper from the abyss of stars
Which lured these other voyagers from their home.

But when the low grey clouds behind them turned
To orchards of ripe glory, right in front
They met, on heaving opalescent seas,
A mightier cloud that slowly, as they neared it,
Sharpened into a hull, with masts and spars,—
A carrack, with her high black shining prow
Stained by the crimson East.   She seemed asleep,
Swinging at ease with great half-slackened sails,
Majestically careless of the dawn;
And, sullenly rumbling out its gorgeous folds,
Over her rumbled like a thunder-cloud
The heavy flag of Spain.
                              Unseen, unheard,
The five small ships, like dolphins drawing near
A slumbering whale, grappled her lustrous flanks.
There, in her native seas, her own blue coasts
In sight across the waves, up by her guns,
The lithe bare-footed Devonshire seamen swarmed
With knives between their teeth.   Down, on her decks,
They dropped, like panthers; and the softly fierce
Black-bearded watch of Spaniards, all amazed,
Rubbing their eyes as if at a wild dream
Upraised their panic shout, *El Draque!   El Draque!*
Too late, for ere they flashed their weapons out,
The watch lay bound, and over every hatch,
Gleamed cutlasses on guard; till those below
Yielded their treasure; hilts encrusted thick
With emeralds; blades of chased Toledo steel;
Long rosaries of gems from Aztec crowns,
And chains of gold from Montezuma's land.
Then onward, over the great grey gleaming sea
They swept with their rich booty, day and night.
Five other prizes, under those enemy coasts
They caught at a swoop, and laughed, as they sailed away,
"Now have we singed the royal beard of Spain.
Now have we roused the imperial hornet's nest.
Nothing can save us now from faggot and fire
But our own hands, five ships and three score guns."

Triumphantly through the bay of storms they plunged,
And past Gibraltar.   It gazed across the waves,
A ghostly rock of prophecy, touched with gleams
Of distant hope, and love's most wistful fear,
As that small fleet went by.   Southward they sailed
Till like a Titan sentinel, towering dark

49

Before the Atlantic glory, they beheld
Tremendous over ocean, Teneriffe,
Cloud-robed, but crowned with colours of the dawn.

Already the traitors worked upon the crews;
Who knew not yet the vastness of their quest,
For Drake had kept it secret, and the thoughts
Of most set sail for warm West Indian isles,
And some for midnight woods in Mogadore
And that strange palace, built of chrysoprase
Where Prester John had reigned five hundred years.
And Sydon, river of jewels, through the dark
Enchanted gorges, rolled its rays along.
Some thought of Rio Grande; and to divert
All hearts from care, the skilled musicians played.
But Doughty, and his brother, who sailed with him,
Soon cunningly contrived, by nod and shrug
And chance-dropt words to awake a grisly fear
Of things that lay beyond the world they knew,
Till even the hardiest seamen almost quailed;
And now, at a whisper, they might all refuse
To venture near that fabled burning Void,
Or brave that *primum mobile* which drew
O'er-daring ships into the jaws of hell
Beyond the Pole Antarticke, where the sea
Rushed down through fiery mountains, and no sail
Could ever return, against its roaring stream.

But down the coast of Barbary they cruised,
Till Christmas Eve embraced them in the heart
Of summer.   In a bay of mellow calm
They moored, and as the musky twilight brought
The stars, they eased their hearts again in song,
While, out of the forest, to the water's edge,
The naked wild-eyed denizens of the night
Stole down, unseen, to watch that festal glare,
Unheard, to hear that music of strange gods,
Where, over the wash of the lanthorn-crimsoned tide,
Broad Devonshire voices in full chorus rang:—

SONG

Fill high!   Drink deep!   Our home-brewed ale
On Christmas Eve shall drown your care;

And, if one stoup shall not avail,
　　Fear nought—we've two more casks to spare.
Drink deep!　Fill high!　Give thanks to heaven
　　That gave us all we need on earth,
A song, a ship, a girl in Devon,
　　And ale, to brim our hearts with mirth.

　　　And he that will not merry be
　　　　With a pretty girl by the fire,
　　　May roost with owls in the hollow of a tree,
　　　　And hoot to his heart's desire.

Then let the Atlantic hurricanes blow;
　　While hands can steer we rule our fate.
For hands rule helms, as all men know;
　　But hearts rule both, if hearts be great.
Fill high!　The unknown world's before us.
　　Life like a feather of foam goes by;
But, up, up, up, with a rousing chorus,
　　And make you merry before you die.

　　　For he that will not merry be
　　　　With a pretty girl by the fire,
　　　May roost with owls in the hollow of a tree,
　　　　And hoot to his heart's desire.

Stronger than death is our redoubt
　　Against the storm's unholy din.
Fill high!　The boundless night's without:
　　But we've a mightier light within.
To heave the shouldering surge aloof
　　And roll the world's black waves away,
We've stout oak walls and a sloping roof.
　　(Drink deep!　To-morrow is Christmas Day).

　　　And he that will not merry be
　　　　With a pretty girl by the fire,
　　　May take and sail my ship at sea,
　　　　Or roost with owls in the hollow of a tree,
　　　Roost in the damp dark hollow of a tree
　　　　And hoot to his heart's desire.

A breeze awoke at dawn.　Hoisting their sails,
They kept their Christmas feast with out-spread wings,
And steered to southward, till the sloping sun

Laid a long road of gold across the waves,
A sea-road that to many an old marauder
Seemed plated with doubloons.   Then, all their prows,
With one immortal cry of *Westward Ho!*
Swung into its wrinkled dazzle and sailed on,
Following the sun's own way, across the deep.

And soon to the Fortunate Islands of old time
They came, but found no Paradisal calm
Whispering about them.   Bleak and desolate rocks
Those isles were.   On the largest of the seven
Drake landed Doughty with his musketeers
To seek supplies among the matted huts
Which, as the ships drew round a ragged cliff
Crept, like remembered misery, into sight.
And Doughty, with his men, ashore, alone,
Among the sparse wind-bitten groves of palm
Kindled their fears of all they must endure
On that immense adventure, muttering hints
That Drake was bent on voyaging far beyond
Magellan, who could only hound his crew
Onward, by threats of death, until they turned
In horror from the Threat that lay before,
Preferring to be hanged as mutineers
Rather than venture farther.   He sailed on,
And, with all hell around him, in the clutch
Of devils died upon some savage isle
By poisonous black enchantment.
                                        Not in vain
Were Doughty's words on that volcanic shore
Among the stunted dark acacia trees
Whose heads, all bent one way by the trade-wind,
Pointed north-east by north, south-west by west,
Ambiguous sibyls that with wizened arms
Mysteriously would urge two opposite paths
Homeward, and onward.   But, aboard the ships,
Among the hardier seamen, old Tom Moon
Would overbear all doubts with blither tales
Of how he sailed to Darien, and heard
Nightingales in November all night long
As down the coast of Paradise they cruised
By creeks of molten silver and sharp black palms
Like ebony fountains; while, at noon, canoes
Of bark, with slim brown crews of Indian girls
Crowned with red petals and eyed like wild-wood fawns

Brought them rich fruits, whose taste was honey and wine.
And once, a troop came swimming through the waves,
Fair as the sea-maids that Æneas saw,
The sea-maids, or the souls of his lost ships
(For Master Fletcher, when he told that tale
Dwelt much on souls) who, swimming round his keel
Called to him, softly, from the moonlit sea.
But these, like rounded fruit, from arm and breast,
Rosily ripening through the clear green tide,
Tossed back a light quick rainbow of sun-lit spray
With every stroke; and ere their small brown hands
Laid hold upon a rope, Drake fired a bombard
Over their heads, and split his sides to see them
Scurrying like sea-devilkins through the foam
Back to their sheltering palm-trees.
                                        "We will send
No Devonshire bridegroom to the Isle of Pearls
This voyage," he said, remembering his own friend
Who, on a lonelier coast than Circe ruled
Lay drugged with poisonous honey and forgot
The glory of his lost sails.
                              Then Moon would tell
Of how they robbed the mule-train from Peru,
Seized the great ox-hide bales of gold and gems,
And, finding them too heavy for their haste,
Poured their cold bars of silver and blood-rubines,
A kingdom's treasure, on the hot white sand,
And buried them in the land-crab's crumbling holes.
Thus would he hold them spell-bound, waiting there
For Doughty, in the hollow-waisted ship,
Or idly couched about the sun-washed decks,
On sails, or coils of rope, while overhead
A ship-boy climbed the rigging and looked out,
Westward, for Spaniards.
                           But, when Doughty came,
He came with a strange face of feigned despair,
And scant supplies; and, when Drake looked at him,
And at his musketeers, their eyes were strained,
Their faces wore a cloud.
                           So Drake, that night,
With subtle weather-wisdom, spread his crews
Anew, throughout the ships.   And, on the morrow,
Sailing, they saw a throng of small dark clouds
Behind them, on the clear horizon-line;
And then what seemed a city of masts arising;

And, from the crow's nest of *The Pelican*,
A seaman cried, "By God, the hunt is up!"
And, once again, the red rejoicing blood
Raced through their veins.   They crowded on their decks
To watch the tall avenging ships of Spain,
Eight heavy-jowled bloodhounds, nosing out their trail.
And Drake growled, "All you Bideford lads, I know,
Ache in your bones to fight them.   But we sail
For something mightier.   Fights like that must wait
Till our return.   You'll have your bellyful, then.
Yet I will not put on one stitch of sail;
So, clear the decks; and, if they are not too slow,
God give you joy of it."
                                        So the ships advanced
With decks all cleared, and shotted guns and men
Bare-armed beside them, hungering to be caught;
Until their enemy dwindled into the grey
And dropped below the sea-line; and the doubts
And cares that Doughty had sown awoke anew
And many a sunlit brow grew black again.

Then happily, and in good time, there came
At sundown, as their golden western road
Was growing dark around the plunging ships,
A chance that loosed heart-gnawing doubt in deeds.
For, through a mighty zone of golden haze,
A galleon like a floating mountain moved
To meet them, clad with sunset and with dreams.
Her masts and spars immense with jewelled mist
Shimmered.   Her rigging, like an emerald web
Of golden spiders, tangled half the stars.
Embodied sunset, dragging the soft sky
O'er dazzled ocean, through the night she drew
Out of the unknown lands; and round a prow
That jutted like a moving promontory
Over a cloven wilderness of foam,
Upon a lofty blazoned scroll her name
San Salvador challenged obsequious isles
Where'er she rode; who, kneeling like dark slaves
Before some great Sultan, must lavish forth
From golden cornucopias, east and west,
Red streams of rubies, cataracts of pearl.
The five small ships lay rocking in the gloom,
Like cormorants, in the dark troughs of the waves,
Letting her pass to leeward.   On she came,

Blazing with lights, a castle of the sea,
Belted with crowding towers and clouds of sail,
And round her bows a long-drawn thunder rolled,
Splendid with foam.   But, ere she passed them by,
Drake gave the word, and with one crimson flash
A hundred yards of black and hidden brine
Leaped into sight between them.   The fierce roar
Of his full broad-side shattered the peaceful night.
Then after her they drove, like black sea-wolves
Behind a royal high-branched stag of ten,
Hanging upon her bleeding foam-flecked flanks,
Leaping, snarling, worrying as they went
In full flight down the wind; for those light ships,
Much speedier than their huge antagonist,
Keeping to windward, worked their will with her.
In vain she burnt wild lights and strove to scan
The darkening deep.   Her musketeers in vain
Provoked the crackling night with random fires.
In vain her broadside bellowings burst at large
As if the Gates of Erebus unrolled.
For ever and anon the deep-sea gloom,
From some new quarter, like a dragon's mouth
Opened and belched forth crimson flames and tore
Her sides as if with iron claws unseen;
Till, all at once, rough voices close at hand
Out of the darkness thundered, "Grapple her!"
The grim claws gripped their hulk.   The Spaniards knew
The Dragon of that red Apocalypse,
And, with one panic cry, *El Draque!   El Draque!*
They cast their weapons from them; for the moon
Rose, eastward, and, against her rising, black
Over the bloody bulwarks, Francis Drake,
Grasping the great hilt of his naked sword,
Towered for a moment to their startled eyes
Through all the zenith like the King of Hell.
Then he leaped down upon their shining decks,
And after him swarmed and towered and leapt in haste
A brawny band of threescore Devonshire lads,
Gigantic as they loomed against the sky
And risen, it seemed, by miracle from the sea,
So small were those five ships below the walls
Of that huge floating mountain.   Smiling grimly,
Drake, from the swart commander's trembling hands
Took the surrendered sword, and bade his men
Gather the fallen weapons on an heap,

And placed a guard about them, while the moon,
Silvering the rolling seas for many a mile,
Glanced on the huddled Spaniard's rich attire,
As like one picture of despair they grouped
Under the splintered main-mast's creaking shrouds;
And the great swinging shadows of the sails
Mysteriously swept the gleaming decks,
Where rows of cannon heaved their smooth blind butts
Along the accoutred bulwarks or upturned,
As the ship wallowed in the rolling troughs,
Dumb mouths of empty menace to the stars.

And Drake made Doughty captain of that prize
Out of his friendship.   But the Spanish crew
He sent aboard a small new-captured barque
And set them free to make their own way home.
And Doughty's heart leapt in him.   Doughty saw
His hope draw near.   His purpose was not base;
For, like his master, Burghley, he believed
He served his country best by foiling Drake.
Wherever he moved, he sowed a discontent,
Now hinting at the smallness of their gain
—Since Drake was guarding all the wealth they won,
As treasure of war, for England and her queen—
Now muttering of the ransoms they had lost
By freeing their prisoners.
                              He could not discern
The tragedy shaping from this clash of faiths.
Courtier-like, he mistook simplicity
For weakness, and could see nor peril nor strength
In Etna's crude round crater and sleeping fires.
But, even while Doughty plotted on the prize,
Drake, in his cabin, pored on his two guides,
The Bible and the map.   Then, on his knees,
Blindly he drew the All-might into his soul.
"Steer Thou my ships, Lord.   Bring us to that land,
That sacred country shining on the sea.
There shall we see this dust of battle dance
Everywhere in the sunbeam of Thy peace.
There, in that New Atlantis of mankind,
Freedom shall reign for ever in Thy law.
Let these our sails upon their westward way
Herald across that golden wilderness,
The Soul, whose path our task is to make straight,
Freedom, the last great Saviour of mankind."

So, with closed eyes he saw, beyond his world,
That Vision, without which, the wise king said,
A people perishes.   Uttering not a word,
His thought prayed on.   "Far off, I have heard the song
Of mighty peoples rising in the west;
Wonderful nations that shall set their foot
Firm on the throat of all old tyrannies.
The sunset voices call me.   Steer my ships."

And, while he knelt, the last grey island rock
Faded behind them, and the sun once more
Began to lay its golden evening road
Across the earth-shaking shoulders of the broad
Atlantic, and the great grey slumbrous waves,
Crested with gold, swelled up to meet the keels.

BOOK III

WHISPERS of that dark plotting on the prize
At last reached Drake.   He pondered them a day,
And sent for Doughty at dusk.
                            Between them shone,
Under his cabin-lamp, a captured chart
From far Cathay, in elephant's ivory, carved
By old Chineses.   All its rough peaked isles,
Dwarf promontories, tiny twisted creeks,
And sea-snakes wallowing under elfin hills,
Were stained as if the painter's delicate brush
Had dipped in liquid gems.
                            Drake pointed to it,
Brooding upon it with the glowing eyes
Of boyhood, over a well-thumbed ocean-tale
On blue Twelfth Night, beside the crimson fire.
"I also worship images," he smiled.
"There lie my dreams in little.   But worlds like this
Are easily broken, Doughty.   Ships at sea
Bring even friends too near at times for peace;
And I have heard thy sailing-master irks thee.
But now—let anger cool.   Although, 'fore God,
I would not brook from other men alive
What thou hast spoken against me, I know well
How anger strikes at friends.   Thou shalt be vexed
With this division of mastery no more;
But take my *Pelican,* for her crew is trusty,

And I myself will sail upon the prize."
So saying, he picked the chart up, gripped the hand
Of Doughty, and left him, staring; for the faith
Of Drake bewildered him.
                              Then he laughed it by,
And straight began to weave another web
To snare his new companions.   Night and day
Between the adventurous gentlemen-at-arms,
Gallant in fight, but idlers all at sea,
And those whose rough tarred hands in battle or storm
Were ready at need, he stirred a subtle fire
Of jealousy, that swiftly grew to hate.
So fierce indeed the strife became that, once,
When Chester, Doughty's catspaw, played with fire,
A grim old seaman growled between his teeth
"Remember, sir, remember, and in good time,
Magellan's mutinous vice-admiral's end."
And Doughty, hearing, boisterously laughed.
"The yard-arm is for dogs, old fool, not men!"
Meanwhile, his brother, sly John Doughty, sought
To fan the seamen's fear of the unknown world
With whispers and conjectures; and, at night,
He brought strange books of Greek and Hebrew down
Into the fo'c'sle, claiming by their aid
A knowledge of Black Art, and power to tell
The future, which he dreadfully displayed
There, in the flickering light of the oily lamp,
Bending above their big rope-hardened palms
And tracing them to many a grisly doom.

So many a night and day westward they plunged.
The moon's blade grew to a glowing silver shield
Bruised with old dints, and dwined to a sickle again.
And always round them shone the sky's grey ring
Rising and falling with the Atlantic seas.
The sun, their fellow-pilgrim, every day
Arose behind them, soared above their sails,
And from the noon descending laid his road
Of evening gold before their plunging prows;
While, rising, sinking, with the wet bright decks,
The skilled musicians, dark against his light,
Struck their brave strings and followed him with a song,
Trolled to a joyous burden poets used
In old love-ditties, but filled with sea-born love

For England now, and deep-sea harmonies
To cheer their hearts, and speed their leagues along.

Queen Venus wandered away with a cry,—
  N'oserez vous, mon bel ami?—
For the purple wound in Adon's thigh;
  Je vous en prie, pity me;
With a bitter farewell from sky to sky
  And a moan, a moan, from sea to sea;
N'oserez vous, mon bel, mon bel,
  N'oserez vous, mon bel ami?

The soft Ægean heard her sigh,—
  N'oserez vous, mon bel ami?—
Heard the Spartan hills reply,
  Je vous en prie, pity me;
Spain was aware of her drawing nigh
  Foot-gilt from the blossoms of Italy;
N'oserez vous, mon bel, mon bel,
  N'oserez vous, mon bel ami?

In France they heard her voice go by,—
  N'oserez vous, mon bel ami?—
And on the May-wind droop and die,
  Je vous en prie, pity me;
Your maidens choose their loves, but I—
  White as I came from the foam-white sea,
N'oserez vous, mon bel, mon bel,
  N'oserez vous, mon bel ami?

The warm red-meal-winged butterfly,—
  N'oserez vous, mon bel ami?—
Beat on her breast in the golden rye,—
  Je vous en prie, pity me,—
Stained her breast with a dusty dye,
  Red as the print of a kiss might be!
N'oserez vous, mon bel, mon bel,
  N'oserez vous, mon bel ami?

Is there no land, afar or nigh—
  N'oserez vous, mon bel ami?—

But dreads the kiss o' the sea?   Ah, why—
   Je vous en prie, pity me!—
Why will ye cling to the loves that die?
   Is earth all Adon to my plea?
N'oserez vous, mon bel, mon bel,
   N'oserez vous, mon bel ami?

Under the warm blue summer sky,—
   N'oserez vous, mon bel ami?
With outstretched arms and a low long sigh,—
   Je vous en prie, pity me—
Over the Channel they saw her fly
   To the white-cliffed island that crowns the sea,
N'oserez vous, mon bel, mon bel,
   N'oserez vous, mon bel ami?

England laughed as her queen drew nigh,—
   N'oserez vous, mon bel ami?
To the white-walled cottages gleaming high,
   Je vous en prie, pity me!
They drew her in with a joyful cry
   To the hearth where she sits with a babe on her knee,
She has turned her moan to a lullaby,
   She is nursing a son to the kings of the sea,
N'oserez vous, mon bel, mon bel,
   N'oserez vous, mon bel ami?

At last, upon a faint-flushed April morn,
They saw beside them, rolling through the waves,
Vanishing and emerging, shoal on shoal
Of glittering porpoises.   Like a moving crowd
Of black bright rocks washed smooth by foaming tides
They stirred the heart with living hints of land.
And soon Columbus' happy signals came,
The signs that saved him when his mutineers
Despaired at last and clamoured to return.
For now, with awe triumphant in their eyes
They saw, lazily tossing on the tide
A drift of sea-weed and a berried branch,
Which silenced them, as if they had seen a Hand
Writing with fiery letters on the deep.
Then, a black cormorant, with long neck outstretched,
Went hurtling past them to its unknown bourne;
Then, a white cloud of mewing and wheeling gulls;
And, all at once, echoing across the waves

From crew to crew, there rose the shout of *"Land!"*
Tense, dumb, upon the rigging as they hung
Staring at it, a menace chilled their blood.
For, coloured like a thunder-cloud, from North
To South, there slowly sharpened into sight
A country like a dragon fast asleep
Along the west, with wrinkled purple wings
Ending in ragged forests over its spine;
And with great craggy claws out-thrust, that turned
As the dim distances dissolved their veils
To promontories bounding a huge bay.
There, over the hushed and ever-shoaling tide
The staring ships drew nigh and thought "Is this
The Dragon of our Golden Apple Tree?"
Till now, from out the softly mingled clouds
Of blues and greys upon that coast's deep flank
There crept a forest of enchanted boughs,
A forest of Aladdin's trees that bore
All-coloured clustering gems instead of fruit.
Height over height it grew, till sea-dazed eyes
Saw the huge splendour of the tropic hills
Thronged like a vast arena, cirque on cirque
With jewels and flowers ablaze on women's breasts
Innumerably confounded and confused
While lovely faces, flushed with lust of blood
Rank above rank upon their tawny thrones
In soft barbaric splendour lapped, and lulled
By the low thunderings of a thousand lions
Luxuriously smiled as they bent down
Over the scarlet-splashed and steaming sands
To watch the white-limbed gladiators die.
Such fears and dreams in Drake's nigh-fevered brain
Rose and dissolved as they drew near that shore.
New rumours had been borne to him; and now
He knew not whether to impute the wrong
To his mistrustful mind, or to believe
Doughty a traitorous liar; yet there seemed
Proof and to spare.   A thousand shadows rose
To mock him with their veiled indicative hands;
And each alone he laid and exorcised,
But, for each doubt he banished, one returned
From darker depths to mock him over again.

And, when they had anchored, Drake bade lower a boat,
And went ashore with sixteen men to seek

61

Water; and, as they neared the branch-hung beach,
Over the green translucent tide there came,
A hundred yards from land, a muttering sound
As of innumerable elfin drums
Drowsily mustering in the tropic bloom.
This from without they heard, across the waves;
But, when they glided into a steaming creek,
Where armoured turtles crawled, and those huge lizards
Named alligartas, drowsed like sunken logs
With their blunt noses at the water's brim,
Breathing, and wicked eyes that watched in sleep,
Under the sharp black shadows of jaca and palm
And red liana wreaths, the strange sound ebbed
Into the murmuring of those mighty fronds,
Prodigious leaves that in their veinings bore,
Fresh from earth's prime, the fingerprints of God.
There humming birds, like flakes of emerald fire
Flung from a passing seraph's plumage, beat
And quivered in blinding blots of golden light
Between the embattled cactus and cardoon;
While one huge whisper of primeval awe
Awaited the cool evening and the Power
Unseen, that walked His Garden as of old.
And there, Drake bade his comrades tarry a while,
And went, alone, into the trackless woods.
Round him, tormented with his doubt he saw
Only the battling image of his mind,—
The vast unending struggle of Titan trees,
Large internecine twistings of the world,
The dumb locked anguish of Laocoons
Grappling with death for thrice three hundred years.
Once, like a subtle mockery overhead
A black-armed chattering ape swung swiftly by.
But he strode on, gripped by one throbbing thought
"Was Doughty false?   Could it be wholly false,—
That joyous pledge of friendship, and the grasp
That sealed it?   Friendship?   Was there nothing sure?

Up, by a fern-fringed precipice, he clomb
To an eagle-haunted ledge, whence, looking down,
Across the forest, he beheld the sea;
And, in the bay below, his elfin ships
All six at anchor on the white-flecked tide.
Up to the summit he clomb; then, through the woods
He plunged once more with burning heart and brow.

Once more, like madness, through his tortured brain
Swung the black shapes of doubt and chattered and laughed,
Till he up-stretched his arms and cursed the name
Of Doughty, cursed the unhappy day they met;
Cursed his false face and skin-deep courtier smiles.

And there, at once, his own wild warring thoughts
Tore him another way—"If Doughty wished
To turn back home, he had but to speak the word,
And he might take his choice of all my ships.
Why should he sail at all, if he desires
To thwart me?   Why, this proves his innocence—
This very courtly carelessness which I,
Black-hearted evil thinker that I am,
In my own clumsier spirit so misjudge."
And yet again the torment of his doubt,
The madness of distrustful friendship, gleamed
From his fierce eyes, "He is an Englishman
Italianate, and that—as all men know—
Is deeper than the devil.   He wears no fault
Upon the gloss and frippery of his breast.
It is not that!   Why did he seek me out
To sail with me?   It is these hidden things,
Unseizable, the things I do not know
That I mistrust."
                          And as he walked, the skies
Grew full of threats.   A strange ensanguined cloud
Blotted the daylight out.   He took no heed.
Though that weird darkness filled the branching aisles
With horror, he strode on until his way
Ended abruptly at a precipice edge
That overlooked the sea again.   He stood
Gazing.   His right hand rested on the rock
That towered above him, like a derelict ship
With bouldered bones, a dark remembering hulk,
A huge ribbed shell upon a lonely height
Left by forgotten seas.   A whispering crowd
Of tree-ferns waved around it.   At its base
Drake flung himself with one sharp shivering cry,
Show me Thy ways, O God, teach me Thy paths.

Then the skies darkened.   All the woods grew still
Waiting the flash.   It came, like Michael's sword.
Out of the darkness, forest, and cliff and sea,
With five small ships at anchor in the bay,

Five ebony ships upon a sheet of silver,
(Drake saw not that!   Saw not that one was flown!)
Flashed in one blinding picture: then the skies
Crackled and split with thunder, and drowned the world.
But, in the deeper darkness, Francis Drake
Stood upright now, and with blind outstretched hands
Groped at that bouldered hulk.   In one blind flash
Æons had passed; and now the Thing in front
Made his blood freeze with memories that lay
Behind his Memory.   In the gloom he groped,
And with dark hands that knew not what they knew
He touched the enormous rain-washed belted ribs
And bones like battlements of a mastodon,
A rock in rock embedded till the doom.
After long centuries, other pioneers
Might read the history there of mortal life.
Drake, in the dark, could only feel the touch
Of some huge mystery, from beyond the world
Where men and nations warred and lived their day;
Yet there he felt, like Atlas touching earth,
His fellowship with eternal thoughts and powers.
All round him through the heavy purple gloom
Sloped the soft rush of silver-arrowed rain
Loosening the skies' hard anguish as with tears.
But now he touched beyond the wandering storm,
The vast composure of the universe,
Which comprehends the tumult of our days,
And, with that peace, the power to act returned.
There, with his back against the mastodon
He stared through darkness towards the roaring sea.
The rain ceased for a moment.   Only the slow
Drip of the dimly drooping fans of palm
Deepened the hush.
                Then, out of the gloom, once more
The whole earth leapt to sight with all her woods,
Her boughs, her leaves, her tiniest twigs distinct
In one wild lightning; but Drake only saw
That land-locked bay with those five elfin ships,
Five elfin ships in a cruddle of molten silver.
Where he had left six ships an hour ago,
And, as the thunder pealed across the sky,
One thought pealed through his brain, *"Doughty has flown!"*

Over the grim precipitous edge he hung,
An eagle waiting for the lightning now

To swoop upon his prey.   One iron hand
Gripped a rough tree-root like a bunch of snakes;
And, as the rain rushed round him, far away
He saw to northward yet another flash,
A scribble of God's finger in the sky
Over a waste of white stampeding waves.
His eye flashed like a falchion as he saw it,
And from his lips there burst the sea-king's laugh;
For there, with a fierce joy he knew, he knew
Doughty, at last—an open mutineer!
An open foe to fight!   Ay, there she went,—
His *Pelican*—he knew her by her sails—
A wild deserter scudding to the north.
Almost before the lightning, Drake had gone
Down the steep face of the precipice, holding fast
By root and trunk and rock, with loose stones plunging
Under his feet and the black gulf below.
Down by a narrow water-gully he slid.
Then, through the trackless forest he tore his way
Back to the shore; while, three miles to the north,
Doughty, upon *The Pelican's* wave-swilled poop
Stood smiling, little knowing what Drake had seen
From that dark eagle's tower, amidst the thunders.
And long had Doughty worked upon his crew,
Until he won them over, saying that Drake
Would never return, and bidding them slip away
Northward to Darien's golden coasts and join
The roystering feasters round those island fires,
Buccaneer camps in scarlet log-wood groves,
By old Port Pheasant and the Gulf of Wine.

And when Drake reached his boat, he found his crew
Under great eaves of leafage, tossing dice;
And none of them had seen *The Pelican go*,
But all along the coast the big dark waves
Pounded and crashed and whitened and savagely ebbed
To gather their might and return; and the seamen thought
Their boat could not be launched.   At a word from Drake,
And a glance of his eyes, they poled her down the creek,
Waiting their chance, between the bursts of spray.
Then all together, with brandished oars they thrust;
And on the fierce white out-draught of a wave
They shot up, up, and over the crumbling crest
Of the next, and plunged, like a sea-bird into the trough
Behind it.   Then they settled at their thwarts.

65

And the black water boiled before their blades,
As, with Drake's own firm hand upon the helm
They soared and crashed across the struggling seas.

He steered for *The Marygold*—in the hands of Drake
Their swiftest ship; and, ere the seamen knew
What power, as of a wind, bore them along,
Anchor was up, their hands were on the sheets,
The sails were broken out, *The Marygold*
Was flying like a storm-cloud to the north;
And like implacable granite on her poop,
Stiller than death stood Drake.
                                    One hour they rushed
Northward, with green seas washing across the deck,
And buffeted with wild splendours.   Then they saw
The Pelican with her torn mismanaged plumes
Floundering in peril of shipwreck; saw her fly
Half-mast, a feeble signal of distress,
Despite all Doughty's curses; for her crew,
Distracted by disputes amongst themselves,
All willingly now surrendered in their hearts
As close alongside swept *The Marygold*,
All trim and taut, and drawing, aloft, alow;
Her gunners waiting at their loaded guns
Bare-armed and silent; and that iron captain,
Alone, and silent, on his wave-washed deck.
There they hauled up into the wind and lay,
Rocking, while Drake, alone, without a guard,
Boarding the runaway, straight dismissed his boat
Back to *The Marygold*.
                              Then his voice out-rang
Trumpet-like over the trembling mutineers,
With quick commands, as in the day's routine;
And, ere they knew what power, as of a wind,
Impelled them, that half-wreck was trim and taut,
Her sails all drawing and her bows afoam;
And, creeping past *The Marygold*, with new speed
She led their southward way.
                                   And not till then,
Drake turned to Doughty, who furtively slunk near
With some new lie lost in the crackling laugh
Of deprecation upon his fear-parched lips.
Drake looked at him, then called four seamen out.
His words went like a cold wind through their flesh
As with a passionless voice he slowly said,

"There is your prisoner.   Bind him to the mast
Till I decide his fate."
                              And Doughty gasped
As at the world's blank end.   "Francis," he cried,
"Thou canst not thus misuse me."
                                    They gripped his arms.
He struggled and threw them off; and, in his rage,
Let slip the whole dark secret of his cause.
" 'Fore God," he foamed and snarled, "when we return,
Ye shall all smart for this!   Unhand me, dogs!
I have Lord Burghley's warrant!"
                                  In one flash,
Drake saw the truth, and Doughty saw his eyes '
Lighten upon him; and in those eyes he read
A depth of judgment, deeper than all speech,
That silenced him; and, round his breast and arms
The seamen lashed the courtier to the mast.
And when they had reached their anchorage anew
Drake, having now resolved to bring his fleet
Beneath a more compact control, removed
The guns and stores from out the Spanish prize,
And sent Tom Moon to set her hulk afire.
But Doughty and his brother he sent aboard
The pinnace *Christopher,* thinking it best to keep
The poisonous leaven apart, until they had won
Well southward, and the crews new-reconciled
Went forward on this voyage with hope again.
Then might they arraign the traitor, and themselves
Acquit him, or condemn.
                          And those two brothers
Thinking he sent them to his smallest ship
Because he meant to sink them secretly
By night, refused to go; till Drake, abruptly
Ordered them to be slung aboard with ropes.
And far into the night they saw the blaze
That lapt with crimson the abandoned hulk
Behind them, like an ocean hecatomb,
Marking the path of some Titanic will.
Many a night and day they southward drove.
Sometimes, at midnight, round them all the sea
Swirled into witches' oils and water-snakes,
Green, blue and red, with lambent tongues of fire.
Mile upon mile about the blurred black hulls
A cauldron of tempestuous colour coiled.
On every mast mysterious meteors burned;

And, from the shores, a bellowing rose and fell
As of great bestial gods that walked all night
Through unknown hells, too vast and wild for thought.
But many a muttered word began to pass
From watch to watch, of Doughty's wizard arts;
And his own boasts began to seal his doom.
By day, they saw strange coasts, with birds like men
Drilled upon long rock-ledges; and out of the foam,
Sea-lions raised their smooth black heads and hauled
Their sleek black bodies lazily into the sun.
The visible world grew strange, almost as dreams,
And dreams grew stranger still; for once a storm
Scattered the fleet so fiercely that they thought
The winds were ridden by demons, and obeyed
The Black Art of their prisoner.   When the ships
Gathered again, amidst the smoothing waves,
One of the five, the ship of Thomas Drake,
Was missing.   Francis Drake held on his way,
Learning, from hour to hour, to merge himself
In those unfaltering purposes and powers
Which steer the world; and as the four ships plunged
Southward, his world mysteriously changed,
Till, like a prophet's vision, it was fraught
With sacred signs, a world of hieroglyphs,
Wherein he seemed to read the innermost truth
For which the Roman augurs groped of old
When they foretold the future from the flight
Of birds.   And now, the shores that fleeted by
Grew wilder and bleaker with his growing soul;
Until, along the Patagonian coast
They cruised, and in the solemn midnight saw
A savage wilderness of frozen marl,
Petrified seas of lava, league on league
All stricken stiff and still beneath vast cliffs
With ragged gorges winding through the clouds
To monstrous craters, cauldrons long ago
For Hecate.   Behind, in darkness throned,
Gigantic mountains and volcanic peaks,
Catching the wefts of cirrus fleece appeared
To smoke against the sky, though all was cold
And lifeless now as the silver-cratered moon;
Or some huge passion of a slaughtered soul,
Prostrate under the marching of the stars.

At last, and in a silver dawn, they found
A broad-ringed river-mouth.   In the midst of it,
An island lay, and on its landward side
The ships found shelter and anchored.   There Drake held
His grim court-martial.   Two long hours he heard
Defence and accusation, then dismissed
The conclave, seeing that one thing was most sure.
Doughty would wreck this voyage, for the sake
Of England, as his master—Burghley—thought,
On whom Drake's mightier vision of the sea
Had never dawned.   Doughty had made large use
Of Burghley's name of late—to daunt his guards,
And win the voice of Fletcher who, chaplain-like,
Hoped for preferment through those powerful hands.
A dangerous prisoner—Doughty; and if he hoped
To help his country with this wrecker's plot
And worked for more than pay, more dangerous yet.
And Drake, still seeking everywhere a sign
To guide him, went ashore upon that isle;
And, as he turned a rugged point of rock,
He saw—a sign, like Death's own hieroglyph,
Scrawled by an awful hand against the sky;
For stark upon that lonely shore there stood
With broken arm-stump pointing out his way,
The grim black gallows where Magellan hanged
His mutineers.   Wreathed with a rusty chain,
A skeleton lay below it, flaked and white,
Picked by the gulls, and crumbling over the sand,
A dread sea-salt, dry from the tides of time;
Though, twisted still around the stump above,
Some links of chain, in the low soft evening wind,
Swung gently, tinkled quietly.
                                   It stood there,
Death's finger-post, like a forgotten truth
Risen from the grave of memory, a ghost
Reproaching him.   *"Were this man not thy friend,*
Ere now he should have died the traitor's death.
What wilt thou say to others if they, too,
Prove false?   Or wilt thou slay the lesser and save
The greater sinner?   Nay, if thy right hand
Offend thee, cut it off."   And, in one flash,
Drake saw his path and chose it.
                                   With a voice
Low as the passionless utterance of a soul
That comprehends all pain, but girds it round

With iron, lest some random cry break out
For man's misguidance, he gathered all his crews
Around him, saying, "Ye all know how I loved
Doughty, who hath betrayed me twice and thrice.
For I still trusted him.   He was no felon
That I should turn my heart away from him.
But now there comes a time when greater right
On lesser right must wage a bleaker war
Than ever it waged on wrong.   He served his cause
Unswervingly, as I must now serve mine.
He serves the cause of Burghley, who believes
He serves his country.   But in these my hands,
England herself, Elizabeth, the Queen,
Laid her own sword, for judgment on her seas.
Here are no laws but those our souls can make,
Who sail and seek a world beyond the worlds,
A vision past our seeing.   I dare not judge.
But ye who know the mighty goal we seek,
Ye who have seen him stir continual strife,
Ye who have seen him strike this last sharp blow,
Sharper than any enemy could have struck,
Because I loved and trusted him, judge ye.
His life is yours, if truth will let him live;
But, if ye think the truth would have him die,
Hold up your hands in silence."

His voice dropped,

And eagerly he whispered one quick word
Beyond the scope of Fate.   "In spite of all,
I would not have him die!"

He bowed his head

And waited.   On that desolate shore they stood,
A silent throng, with tawny faces, bowed
As if in prayer.   Along that lonely coast
The rhythmic thunder of eternal seas
With its unchanging measure, seemed the voice
Of universal law.   At last, one man
Up-thrust his arm.   Then a grey rustling throng
Of shadows lengthened on the sunlit sand
Under Drake's eyes.   He raised his head and saw
A brawny forest of brown arms up-raised
In silence, and the great sea whispered *Death*.

And Doughty laughed and said, "Since I must die,
Let us have one more hour of comradeship,
One hour as old companions.   Though we go

By different roads, it may be we shall meet
One day in England's honour.   Let us make
A feast here, on this island, ere I go
Where none may feast again."
                              Then Francis Drake
Held out his right sun-blackened hand and gripped
The hand that Doughty proffered him; and they made
A great and solemn banquet as the day
Decreased; and Doughty bade his friends unlock
Their sea-chests and bring out their rich array.
There, by that wondering ocean of the west,
In crimson doublets, lined and slashed with gold,
In broidered lace and double golden chains,
Embossed with rubies and great cloudy pearls,
They feasted, gentlemen adventurers,
Drinking old malmsey, as the sun went down.

And Doughty, fronting the rich death of day
And flourishing a silver pouncet-box,
With many a courtly jest and rare conceit
Out-braved them all; for like a sunset cloud
His murrey-coloured doublet, double-piled
Of Genoa velvet, puffed with ciprus, shone;
But over against him, with his loyal crew
In salt-encrusted rough sea-faring garb
Drake watched, not feasting, for he raised the cup
And set it down untasted.   As the sun
Grew ripe for death they rose.   The Eternal spoke
In breaking waves; and, black against their gold,
The gallows of Magellan stretched its arm.
Over the skeleton clicked that rusty chain.
It swung and tinkled in the solemn breath
Of evening, like a pendulum, measuring out
The moments that remained.   There, side by side,
Among the rocks, the prisoner and the men
Who judged him, took the holy sacrament,
Of Jesus' Body and Blood.   Then Doughty and Drake
Kissed each other, as brothers, on the cheek;
And Doughty knelt.   And Drake, without one word,
Leaning upon the two-edged naked sword
Stood at his side, with iron lips, and eyes
Full of the sunset, while the doomed man bowed
His head upon a rock.   The red sun dropped
Behind a cloud.   The land and sea grew dark.
Then Drake swung up the great two-handed sword

Over his head.   It seemed to sweep the heavens
Down in its arc as he smote, once, and no more.

Silence, for one dread moment, froze their veins,
Till, with a strange hoarse cry, a seaman stooped
And, like an eagle clutching up its prey,
His arm swooped down and bore the head aloft,
Gorily streaming, by the long dark hair.
And hoarsely rose their shout—"So perish all
Traitors!"   But, with a face of cold grey stone,
Drake turned to them and bade them to their ships.
Wondering, they left him.   As they thrust from shore
They saw him, leaning still upon his sword.
Larger and darker from his loftier ground,
Against the slowly gathering night of stars
He stood like granite, by his quiet dead,
Stiller than death, and gazing out to sea.

BOOK IV

DAWN, everlasting and almighty Dawn,
Hailed by ten thousand names of death and birth,
Who, chiefly by thy name of Sorrow, seem'st
To half the world a sunset, . . .
Bring wider seas and skies within my ken,
But help me still to grow in spirit with thee.
Dawn on my song which trembles like a cloud
Pierced with thy beauty.
All that long night, mocked by the breathing peace
Of sleeping seas, the lonely spirit of Drake
Wandered through hells behind the apparent world,
A dreadful darkness, where he clutched at ghosts.
Found fair of old, but now most foul.   For earth
Leered at him through its old remembered mask
Of beauty.   Even the grass that clothed the fields
Of England (shallow, shallow fairy dream!)
Sprang out of death, enriched with all decay.
And bird and beast and man, how fat they fed
On one another's blood.   His mind reeled back
Through time to that dark voyage on the coast
Of Darien, where his crews were stricken down
And dying by scores of some unknown disease;
Till Joseph, his own brother, in his arms

Died; and Drake trampled down all tender thought,
All human grief, and for his seamen's sake
Sought for the cause.   There, in his own dark cabin,
Lit by the wild light of the swinging lanthorn,
He laid the naked body on that board
Where they had supped together.   He took the knife
From the ague-stricken surgeon's palsied hand;
And while the dark waves lapped the rolling hulk,
And dreadfully in the hush the great beams creaked,
He opened his own brother's cold grey corse,
That wan deserted mansion of a soul.
He bade the surgeon mark, with his own eyes,
While yet he had power to use them, every clue
To that fell scourge, and whispered, with dry lips,
"Seest thou?   Seest thou?   Knowest thou what it means?"

Then, like a dream up-surged the belfried night
Of Saint Bartholomew,—scented palaces
Whence harlots leered upon the twisted streets
Of Paris, choked with slaughter.   Europe flamed
With human torches, living altar-candles,
Lighted before the Cross where men had hanged
The Christ of little children.   Cirque by cirque
The world-wide hell reeled round him, east and west,
To where the tortured Indians worked the will
Of lordly Spain in golden-famed Peru.
But, as heaven greyed, he whispered, "Dawn, at least
Brings us new hope of battle.   Men may fight
And sweep away that evil, if no more,
At least from the small bright circle of their swords."

Then, like the meeting after desolate years,
Face to remembered face, Drake saw the Dawn
Arise in naked splendour from the sea;
The same, yet never the same.   Strangely she gleamed
Across the crumbling lilac-coloured foam,
Touching Magellan's gallows with her light
Softly as ever she touched a woodland bough.
Strangely she glanced on velvet dusk and gold
Where that dark body was huddled on the sand,
Close to the creeping tide.   Drake stared at it.
His world was made anew.   Strangely his voice
Rang through that solemn freshness of the day,
Calling his men, and, stranger than a dream,
Their boats black-blurred against the crimson east,

Or flashing misty sheen wherever the light
Smote on their smooth wet sides, like seraph ships
Moved in a dewy glory towards the land.
Their oars of glittering diamond broke the sea
As by enchantment into burning jewels
And scattered rainbows from their flaming blades.
The clear green water lapping round their prows,
The words of sharp command as now the keels
Crunched on his lonely shore, and the following wave
Leapt slapping over the sterns, in that new light
Were more than any miracle.   At last
Drake, as they grouped a little way below
The crumbling sandy cliff whereon he stood,
Seeming to overshadow them as he loomed
A cloud of black against the crimson sky,
Spoke, as a man may hardly speak but once:
"My seamen, O my friends, now must I set
My seal upon the red wax of this blood,
Ere it grow cold. . . .
Not all the waters of that mighty sea
Could wash my hands of sin if I should now
Falter upon my path.   But look to it, you,
Whose word was death last night to this dead man.
Look to it, I say, look to it!   Brave men might shrink
From this great voyage; but the heart of him
Who dares turn backward now must be so hardy
That God might make a thousand millstones of it.
Yet if ye will be found so more than bold,
Speak now, and I will hear you.   God will judge.
But ye shall take four ships of these my five,
Tear out the lions from their painted shields,
And speed you homeward.   Leave me but one ship,
The Pelican, and five good friends, nay one,
To watch when I must sleep, and I will prove
This judgment just against all winds that blow.
Now ye that will return, speak, let me know you,
Or mutter no more in secret, for I swear
Over this butchered body, if any swerve
Hereafter from the straight and perilous way,
He shall not die alone.   What?   Will none speak?
Then mark, my friends, I'll have no jealousies
Aboard my fleet.   I'll have the gentlemen
To pull and haul with the seamen.   I'll not have
That canker of the Spaniards in my fleet.
You that were captains, I cashier you all.

I'll have no captains. I'll have nought but seamen,
You whose white hands are found too delicate
For aught but dallying with your jewelled swords!
And thou, too, master Fletcher, I have heard
Overmuch talk of judgment from thy lips,
God's judgment here, God's judgment there, upon us!
Whenever the winds are contrary, thou takest
Their powers upon thee for thy moment's end.
Thou art God's minister, not God's oracle.
Chain up thy tongue a little, or, by His wounds,
If thou canst read this wide world like a book,
Thou hast so little to fear, I'll set thee adrift
On God's great sea to find thine own way home.
Why, 'tis these very tyrannies of the soul
We strike at when we strike at Spain for England;
And shall we here, in this great wilderness,
Ungrappled and unchallenged, out of sight,
Alone, without one struggle, sink that flag
Which eagled it, once, through all the storms of death.
Nay, master Winter and my gallant captains,
I see ye are tamed. Take up your ranks again
In humbleness, remembering that ye serve
One little island till your lives' last end.
Comrades, mistake not this, our little fleet
Is freighted with the golden heart of England,
And if we fail that golden heart will break.
The world's wide eyes are on us, and our souls
Are woven together into one great flag
Of England. Shall it be rent asunder now
In little quarrels of contemptible tongues
Or shall it be blazoned, blazoned evermore
On the most heaven-wide page of history?
This is that hour, I know it in my soul,
When we must choose for England. Devonshire lads.
O, ay, but with a kingdom on that sea
Whose tang is in your nostrils. Ye must choose
Whether to re-assume it now for England,
And let her freedom with its glory roll
Round the wide world for ever, sweeping back
All evil deeds and dreams, or whether to yield
For evermore that heritage. Ye must learn
Here in this golden dawn our great emprise
Is greater than we knew. Eye hath not seen,
Ear hath not heard, the splendour of the goal
For which we sail,—new freedom and new hope

For all the world in one small sea-washed isle.
Come now, to sea, to sea!"
                                    And ere they knew
What power impelled them, with one eager cry
They lifted up their hearts to the new dawn
And hastened down the beach and launched their boats,
Thrust with their urgent oars, and the boats leapt
Out, and they settled at the groaning thwarts.
The swirling water boiled before their blades.
Swiftly they reached their ships, broke out their sails,
And like a wedge of sea-birds down the coast
To southward flew before the prosperous wind.

And when to Magellanus straits they came,
Drake named his ship anew—*The Golden Hind.*
Then, striking all their top-sails on the bent,
With ringing shouts of joy they entered in.
A mighty strait, it wound in narrowing calm
Between great silent mountains, crowned with snow.
From cliff to echoing cliff, on either side,
Like small white puffs of smoke that grew to clouds,
The clanging sea-birds rose, and all around
Unutterable loneliness rebuked
The strange new sacrilege of the prows that ploughed
Those time-forgotten tides.   But soon, rude flaws,
Cross-currents, tortuous channels, where the wind
Shifted at every turn, set the sails flapping
And sent them drifting perilously.   Once they saw
An elfin isle where goblin armies drilled,
And drawing nearer saw that all those ranks
Along the beaches were white-headed birds,
Penguins, that walked like men, and could not fly.
Whereat they landed, and with bludgeons killed
And stored their fleet with food for many a day.
And, after sailing many a league, they saw
The westward portal, like a cup of gold,
Full of the sunset.   Over roughening waves,
The wash of the Pacific storms, they reached
Capo Desiderato, and there beheld,
—A miracle in that lonely wilderness,—
Gaunt, black, and sharp as death against the sky
The Cross, the great black Cross, on Cape Desire,
Which dead Magellan raised to guide his ships,
Not knowing they had left him to his doom,
Not knowing how in distant years, with awe,

Another should come voyaging and read
Through tears, immortal guidance in that sign;
While, with a shout of joy, his seamen hailed
Beyond it, that broad waste of burnished gold,
League upon league, the great new ocean-sea.

Now, in those days, men thought that, south of the strait,
The firm land stretched to the white Antarticke Pole;
But when Drake turned to take his northward way
Up the Pacific coast, a great head-wind
Suddenly struck them, and the heaving seas
Increased all round them into billowy hills,
Dark rolling ranges, whose majestic crests
Like wild white flames, far-blown, and savagely flickering
Licked at the clouds; and in their sullen troughs
The small bright ships, wallowing like porpoises,
Or floundering like sea-lions through the foam,
Were scattered asunder.   Drake, on *The Golden Hind,*
One moment saw his comrades soaring up
Above him, on the mounded floods; the next,
A mile of sea had severed them.
                              One last glimpse
He caught of *The Marygold,* when some mighty vortex
Wide as the circle of the dark sea-line
Swept them together again.   He saw her staggering
With mast snapt short and wreckage-tangled deck
Where men like insects clung.   He saw the waves
Leap over her mangled hulk, like wild white wolves
Volleying out of the clouds down dismal steeps
Of green-black water.   Like a wounded stag
Quivering upon its haunches, the ship heaved,
Struggling to shake them off.   Then, in one mass
Of fury rushed the great deep over her
Trampling her down, as with a madman's wrath.
She rose no more.   And in the hurricane laughter
That roared across her grave, *The Golden Hind,*
With sails rent into ribbons, her masts all splintered,
Went hurtling to the South; until they found
Where even Magellan thought firm land had been,
Only a wicked wilderness of seas
That shook the world with their tremendous war;
From east to west, one awful shoreless waste
Wherein the mightier western ocean roared
Its greetings to the Atlantic, and both swept
In broad white cataracts, league on struggling league

Pursuing and pursued, immeasurable,
With Titan hands, grasping the rent black sky,
East, west, north, south.
                           And on *The Golden Hind*
Her midget seamen vainly fought to clear
The tangled wreckage from her streaming decks
With ant-like weapons.   Not their captain's voice
Availed them now.   They huddled down below,
Knee-deep in swirling water.   Yet if they dared
To raise their heads, in a momentary lull,
Above the deck, they saw through blinding spume,
By a lightning flash, one set and stubborn face
Like the last glimmer of faith among mankind,
Like the last hope of a world among its graves,
Where Drake stood, lashed to his post, beside the helm.
The black waves washed around him, burying him
Once to his waist.   Half-stunned he dashed away
The sharp brine from his eyes.   Lifting his head
He watched one moving mountain-range draw near
As if to o'er-whelm them utterly, one huge wave
White-crested, and up-heaped so mightily
That, though it coursed more swiftly than a herd
Of Titan steeds upon some terrible plain
Nigh the huge City of Ombos, yet it seemed
Most strangely slow, with all those crumbling crests,
—Each like a cataract on a mountain-side—
And moved with the steady majesty of doom,
High over him.   One moment's flash of fear,
And yet not fear, but rather life's regret,
Felt Drake, then laughed the low deep laugh of joy
That comes to men in battle; one low deep laugh,
One mutter, as of a lion about to spring;
And gallantly, up, up, up, *The Golden Hind*
Soared, well-nigh to the summit, and fell back,
Buried in blinding surf.   Then, like a falling sky,
The wave rolled down, and blotted out the world.

Meanwhile, in Devon, dreaming of her sailor,
His heart's bride waited.   Careless birds of Spring
Nested and sang in all the winding lanes;
But Bess of Sydenham neither saw, nor heard.
She locked her secret love within her breast,
And laid her music by, knowing what deaths
Must yet be conquered, ere that ship came home.

Then, on a dreadful summer morn there came
Borne by a wintry flaw, home to the Thames,
A bruised and battered ship, the last poor wreck,
Her seaman said, of Drake's ill-fated fleet.
John Winter, her commander, told the tale
Of how *The Golden Hind* and *Marygold*
Had by the wind Euroclydon been driven
Sheer over the howling edges of the world;
Of how himself, by God's good providence,
Was driven into the Magellanus strait;
Of how, on the horrible frontiers of the Void
He waited, reddening with his beacon-fires
The coasts of the black abyss, from which no sail
Ever returned.   Week after week he watched
Beneath Magellan's Cross, and only saw
Demoniac tempests devastating heaven
And driving the whole ocean headlong down
After the lost ships, in one cataract
Of endless fury and splendour and rolling doom.

And yet, not long thereafter, to the quays
Of Devonshire, and dark inns beside the Thames,
Though none knew how, there flew upon the wings
Of startled winds, from over the Spanish Main,
Strange echoes as of sacked and clamouring ports,
And battered gates of fabulous golden cities,
Whispers from Valparaiso's fluttering palms,
A sea-bird's wail from Lima; and all men knew
A sail had risen, beneath the sunset star.

BOOK V

With the fruit of Aladdin's garden clustering thick in her hold,
With rubies awash in her scuppers and her bilge ablaze with gold,
A world in arms behind her to sever her heart from home,
The Golden Hind *drove onward over the glittering foam.*

If we go as we came, by the Southward, we meet wi' the fleets of Spain!
'Tis a thousand to one against us.   We'll turn to the West again!
We have captured a China pilot, his charts and his golden keys:
We'll sail to the golden Gateway, over the golden seas.

Over the immeasurable molten gold
Wrapped in a golden haze, onward they drew;

And now they saw the tiny purple quay
Grow larger and darker and brighten into brown
Across the swelling sparkle of the waves.
Brown on the quay, a train of tethered mules
Munched at the nose-bags, while a Spaniard drowsed
On guard beside what seemed at first a heap
Of fish, then slowly turned to silver bars
Up-piled and glistering in the enchanted sun.
Nor did that sentry wake as, like a dream,
The Golden Hind divided the soft sleep
Of warm green lapping water, sidled up,
Sank sail, and moored beside the quay.   But Drake,
Lightly leaping ashore and stealing nigh,
Picked up the Spaniard's long gay-ribboned gun
Close to his ear.   At once, without a sound,
The watchman opened his dark eyes and stared
As at strange men in a wild Arabian tale,
Borne on a magic carpet, from the stars.
Then, with a courtly bow, his right hand thrust
Within the lace embroideries of his breast,
Politely Drake, with pained apologies
For this disturbance of a cavaliero
Napping on guard, straightway resolved to make
Complete amends, by now relieving him
Of these—which doubtless troubled his repose—
These anxious bars of silver.   With that word
Two seamen leaped ashore and, gathering up
The bars in a stout old patch of tawny sail,
Slung them aboard.   Swift loot, no sooner lifted
Than out of the valley, like a foolish jest
Out of the mouth of some great John-a-dreams,
A woolly train of llamas proudly came
Stepping by two and two along the quay,
Laden with pack on pack of silver bars.
The seamen greeted with profuser thanks
Their driver's punctual courtesy.   None the less
It pained them much to see a cavaliero
Turned carrier; and, at once, they must insist
On easing him of that too sordid care.

.   .   .   .

Then out from Tarapaca once again
They sailed, their hold a glimmering mine of wealth,
And steered for fabulous Lima, where they thought
The prize of prizes waited unaware.

For every year a gorgeous galleon sailed
With all the harvest of Potosi's mines,
Pearls from the glimmering Temples of the Moon,
And hyacinths from the Temples of the Sun,
To glut King Philip's coffers.
                                    To the first
That spied her topsails Drake had sworn to give
A kingly prize—the chain of gold he wore;
And every seaman, every ship-boy, watched.

Northward they cruised along a warm wild coast
That like a most luxurious goddess drowsed,
Her rosy breasts up-heaving their soft snow
In distant Andes, and her naked side
Bathed by the foam for half a hundred leagues.

But as they came to Arica, from afar
They heard the clash of bells upon the breeze,
And knew that Rumour with her thousand wings
Had rushed before them.   Horsemen in the night
Had galloped through the white coast-villages
And spread the dreadful cry "El Draque!" abroad,
And when the gay adventurers drew nigh
They found the quays deserted, and the ships
All flown, except one little fishing-boat
Wherein an old man like a tortoise moved
A wrinkled head above the rusty net
His crawling hands repaired.   He seemed to dwell
Outside the world of war and peace, outside
Everything save his daily task; for all
The pilot asked of him without demur
He answered, scarcely looking from his work.
A galleon laden with eight hundred bars
Of silver, not three hours ago had flown
Northward, he muttered.   Ere the words were out,
The will of Drake thrilled through *The Golden Hind*
Sharp as a trumpet-call, and ere they knew
What power impelled them, crowding on all sail
Northward they surged, and roaring down the wind
At Chiuli, port of Arequipa, saw
The chase at anchor.   Wondering they came
With all the gunners waiting at their guns
Close to the enemy.   But no sight or sound
Of living creature stirred upon her decks.
Only a great grey cat lay in the sun

Upon a warm smooth cannon-butt.   Cautiously
Drake neared her in his pinnace: cautiously,
Cutlass in hand, up that mysterious hull
He clomb, and wondered, as he climbed, to breathe
The friendly smell of the pitch and hear the waves
Crackling and slapping against her windward flank.
A ship of dreams was that; for when they reached
The silent deck they saw no crouching forms,
They heard no sound of life.   Only the hot
Creak of the cordage whispered in the sun.
The cat stood up and yawned, and slunk away
Slowly, with furtive glances.   The great hold
Was empty, the rich cabin stripped and bare.
Suddenly one of the seamen with a cry
Pointed where, close inshore, a little boat
Stole towards the town; and, with a louder cry,
Drake bade his men aboard *The Golden Hind.*
Scarce had they pulled two hundred yards away
When, with a roar that seemed to buffet the sky
And rip the heart of the sea out, one red flame
Blackened with fragments, the great galleon burst
Asunder!   All the startled waves were strewn
With wreckage; and Drake laughed—"My lads, we have diced
With death to-day, and won!
                              We'll overhaul
Those devils yet, with their treasure-ship.   Now pull hard,
Hard for *The Golden Hind.*"

. . . .

                              And so they came
At dead of night on Callao de Lima!
They saw the harbour lights across the waves
Glittering, and the shadowy hulks of ships
Gathered together like a flock of sheep
Within the port.   With shouts and clink of chains
A shadowy ship was entering from the north,
And like the shadow of that shadow slipped
The Golden Hind beside her through the gloom;
And side by side they anchored in the port
Amidst the shipping!   Over the dark tide
A small boat from the custom-house drew near.
A sleepy, yawning, gold-laced officer
Boarded *The Golden Hind,* and with a cry,
Stumbling against a cannon-butt, he saw

The bare-armed British seamen in the gloom
All waiting by their guns. Wildly he plunged
Over the side and urged his boat away,
Crying, "El Draque! El Draque!" At that dread word
The darkness filled with clamour, and the ships,
Cutting their cables, drifted here and there
In mad attempts to seek the open sea.
Wild lights burnt hither and thither, and all the port,
One furnace of confusion, heaved and seethed
In terror; for each shadow of the night,
Nay, the great night itself, was all *El Draque.*
The Dragon's wings were spread from quay to quay,
The very lights that burnt from mast to mast
And flared across the tide kindled his breath
To fire; while here and there a British pinnace
Slipped softly through the roaring gloom and glare,
Ransacking ship by ship; for each one thought
A fleet had come upon them. Each yielded up
The struggle as each was boarded; while, elsewhere,
Cannon to cannon, friends bombarded friends.

Yet not one ounce of treasure in Callao
They found; for, fourteen days before they came,
That greatest treasure-ship of Spain, with all
The gorgeous harvest of that year, had sailed
For Panama: her ballast—silver bars;
Her cargo—rubies, emeralds, and gold.

Out through the clamour and the darkness, out,
Out to the harbour mouth, *The Golden Hind,*
Like a great questing bloodhound leapt to the trail:
And where the way was blocked, her cannon clove
A crimson highway to the midnight sea.
Then northward, northward, over the jewelled main,
Under the white moon like a storm they drove
In quest of *The Cacafuego,* fourteen days
Ahead of them. At dawn the fair wind sank.
The Golden Hind lay chafing and becalmed;
While, on the hills, the Viceroy of Peru
Marched down from Lima with two thousand men,
And sent out four huge ships of war to sink
Or capture the fierce Dragon, who grimly smiled
To see them creeping nigh, urged with great oars,
Then suddenly pause; for none would be the first

To close with him.   And, ere they had steeled their hearts
To battle, a fair breeze broke out anew,
And northward sped the little *Golden Hind*
In quest of the lordliest treasure-ship of Spain.

.   .   .   .

Behind her lay a world in arms; for now
Wrath and confusion clamoured for revenge
From sea to sea.   Spain claimed the pirate's head
From England, and awaited his return
With all her tortures.   And wherever he passed
He sowed the dragon's teeth, and everywhere
Cadmean broods of armèd men arose
And followed, followed on his fiery trail.
Men toiled at Lima to fit out a fleet
Grim enough to destroy him.   All night long
The flare went up from cities on the coast
Where men like naked devils toiled to cast
New cannonry, and still to the northward sped
That world-watched midget ship of eighteen guns,
Undaunted; and upon the second dawn
Sighted a towering galleon, not their prize,
Yet worth a pause; for out of her they took—
Embossed with emeralds large as pigeon's eggs—
A golden crucifix, with eighty pounds
In weight of gold.
                          On, to the north they flew—
A score of golden miles, a score of green,
An hundred miles, eight hundred miles of foam,
Rainbows and fire, ransacking as they went
Ship after ship for news of the chase and gold,
Learning from every capture that they drew
Nearer and nearer.   At Truxillo, white
And indolent city, a-drowse with purple flowers,
She had paused a day to take a freight of gold!
At Paita—she had passed two days in front,
Only two days, two days ahead; nay, one!
At Quito, close inshore, a youthful page,
Bright-eyed, ran up the rigging and cried, "A sail!
A sail! *The Cacafuego!* And the chain
Is mine!"   And by the strange cut of her sails,
Whereof they had been told in Callao,
They knew her!
                          Heavily laden with her gems,

84

Lazily drifting with her golden fruitage,
Over the magic seas they saw her hull
Loom as they onward drew; but Drake, for fear
The prey might take alarm and run ashore,
Trailed wine-skins, filled with water, over the side
To hold his ship back, till the darkness fell,
And with the night the off-shore wind arose.
At last the sun sank down, the rosy light
Faded from Andes' peaked and bosomed snow.
The night-wind rose.   The wine-skins were up-hauled;
And, like a hound unleashed, *The Golden Hind*
Leapt forward thro' the gloom.
                              A cable's length
Divided them.   *The Cacafuego* heard
A rough voice in the darkness bidding her
Heave to! She held her course.   Drake gave the word.
A broadside shattered the night, and over her side
Her main-yard clattered like a broken wing!
On to her decks the British sea-dogs swarmed,
Cold steel in hand: that fight was at an end.

The ship was cleared, a prize crew placed a-board,
Then both ships turned their heads to the open sea.
At dawn, being out of sight of land, they 'gan
Examine the great prize.   None ever knew
Save Drake and Gloriana what wild wealth
They had captured there.   Thus much at least was known:
An hundredweight of gold, and twenty tons
Of silver bullion; thirteen chests of coins;
Nuggets of gold unnumbered; hyacinths, pearls,
Diamonds, emeralds; but the worth of these
Was past all reckoning.   In the crimson dawn,
Ringed with the lonely pomp of sea and sky,
The naked-footed seamen bathed knee-deep
In gold and gathered up Aladdin's fruit—
All-coloured gems—and tossed them in the sun.
The hold like one great elfin orchard gleamed
With dusky globes and tawny glories piled,
Hesperian apples, heap on mellow heap,
Rich with the hues of sunset, rich and ripe
And ready for the enchanted cider-press;
An emperor's ransom in each burning orb;
A kingdom's purchase in each clustered bough;
The freedom of all slaves in every chain.

BOOK VI

Now like the soul of Ophir on the sea
Glittered *The Golden Hind*, and all her heart
Turned home to England.   Enemy fleet on fleet
Awaited her return.   Along the coast
The very churches melted down their chimes
And cast them into cannon.   To the South
A thousand cannon watched Magellan's straits,
And caravels quartered all the sea like hounds,
With orders that wherever they came on Drake,
Although he were the Dragon of their dreams,
They should out-blast his culverin and convey,
Dead or alive, his body back to Spain.

And Drake laughed out and said, "My trusty lads
Of Devon, you have made the wide world ring
With England's name; you have looted half the seas
Of their rich sunsets.   In our oaken hold
You have packed the gorgeous Indies.   We shall sail
But slowly with such wealth.   If we return,
We are one against ten thousand!   We will seek
The fabled northern passage, take our gold
Safe home; then out to sea again and try
Our guns against their guns."

.   .   .   .

                              And as they sailed
Northward, they swooped on indolent Guatulco
For food and water.   Nigh the drowsy port
The grand alcaldes in high conclave sat,
Blazing with gold and scarlet, as they tried
A batch of negroes charged with idleness
In Spanish mines; dumb slaves, with bare scarred backs
And those deep hopeless eyes of oxen spent
From heavy ploughing.   The pompous judge arose
Relishing his own sentence.   At his words,
"The knotted lash," Drake and his pirate crew
Entered the court.   The grim judicial glare
Grew wider with amazement, and the judge
Staggered against his gilded throne.
                              "I thank
Almighty God," cried Drake, "who hath given me this—
That I who once, in ignorance, procured
Slaves for the golden bawdy-house of Spain,

86

May now requite a little of that wrong.
Unyoke the prisoners: tell them they are men.
But take these gold and scarlet cockatoos
Aboard my *Golden Hind;* and let them write
An order that their town shall now provide
My boats with food and water."
                                    Swift as a sword-cut,
The slaves being placed in safety on the prize,
The Golden Hind revictualled and the casks
Replenished with fresh water, Drake set free
His cockatoos, and plunging Northward still,
Off the blue coast of Nicaragua, found
A sudden treasure better than all gold;
For on the track of the China trade they caught
A ship whereon two China pilots sailed,
And in their cabin lay the secret charts,
Of silken sea-roads through that ultimate west
Where all roads meet and east and west are one.
And, with that mystery stirring in their hearts
Like a strange cry from home, northward they steered
And northward, till the soft luxurious coasts
Hardened, the winds grew bleak, the great green waves
Heaved threateningly around them, and the spray
Froze on their spars and yards. Fresh from the warmth
Of tropic seas his shivering crew was pinched
With cold; and when the floating hills of ice
Like pale blue shadows crowned with ghostly snow
Went past them with strange cracklings in the gloom,
Or gleamed with splintering colours in the dawn,
Their hearts misgave them, and they found no way;
But all was iron shore and icy sea.
And one by one the crew fell sick to death
In that fierce winter, and the land still ran
Westward and showed no passage. On they plunged,
Through opalescent seas, whose ice-cold spray
Crusted their prow with rainbows, as they drove
Northward, till lost in helpless wonderment,
Dazed as a soul awakening from the dream
Of death to some wild dawn in Paradise
(Yet burnt with cold as they whose very tears
Freeze on their faces where Cocytus wails)
All world-worn, bruised, wing-broken, wracked, and wrenched,
Blackened with lightning, scarred as with evil deeds,
And yet embalmed in beauty by that sun
Which never sets, bosomed in peace at last

The Golden Hind rocked on a glittering calm.
Seas that no keel had ever ploughed, from sky
To glistening sky, enringed her. Glory and gleam,
Glamour and lucid rapture and diamond air
Embraced her broken spars, begrimed with gold
Her battered hull, rocking as on a sphere
New made, mysterious with the primal Light,
Cold, pure, with subtle colours of the sky.
The uncharted ocean belted her dark hulk
With brilliance, while she dipped her jacinth beak
In waves of mounded splendour, and sometimes
A great ice-mountain flashed and floated by
Throned on the waters, pinnacled and crowned
With all the smouldering jewels in the world;
Or in the darkness, glimmering berg on berg,
All emerald to the moon, went by like ghosts
Whispering to the South.
                              There, as they lay,
Waiting a wind to fill the stiffened sails,
Their hearts remembered that in England now
The Spring was nigh, and in that lonely sea
The skilled musicians filled their eyes with home.

SONG

It is the Spring-tide now.
Under the hawthorn bough
   The milkmaid goes.
Her eyes are violets blue
Washed with the morning dew,
   Her mouth a rose.
      It is the Spring-tide now.

The lanes are growing sweet.
The lambkins frisk and bleat
   In all the meadows.
The glossy dappled kine
Blink in the warm sunshine
   Cooling their shadows.
      It is the Spring-tide now.

Soon, hand in sunburnt hand,
Through that dear sea-washed land,
   England, our home,

>   Whispering as they stray
>   Adown the primrose way,
>   Lovers will roam.
>   It is the Spring-tide now.

And when a fair wind rose, and still he found
No sign of the fabled passage by the north,
Drake, with a great new purpose in his eyes
Turned south and sailed into that Golden Gate
Where now the lights of San Francisco shine,
A solitude then; but all the cliffs were white
Like those of England, and the soft soil teemed
With gold.   There they careened *The Golden Hind,*
Her keel being thick with barnacles and weeds—
And made her ready, hull and masts and sails,
For new adventures, greater than them all.
And as the sound of chisel and hammer broke
The stillness of that shore, shy figures came,
Keen-faced and grave-eyed Indians, from the woods
To bow before the strange white-faced new-comers
As gods, and though the chaplain all aghast
Persuaded them with signs and broken words
That Drake was but a man, yet they would crown him,
With woven flowers and barbarous ritual,
King of New Albion,—for so Drake named
That coast, remembering the white cliffs of home.
There, for a moment, on that lonely shore,
Ringed by the storm-beat crew and those dark throngs,
A vision of England—in her distant glory—
Dawned upon Drake, a kingdom far away,
A Power before the lightning of whose arms
Darkness should die, and all oppression cease;
A realm of Freedom, bound in starry law,
Wherein the weak were strengthened, and the strong
Made stronger, in the increasing good of all;
Till even the wasteful rage of war were turned
To accomplish large and fruitful tasks of peace,
As men have turned Niagara's smoking wrath
To light their cities.
                    Thus did he foresee
What none may see with living eyes; but thou,
When all our hearts are dust, shalt see it, England,
Who like that angel of the Apocalypse
Setting one foot upon thy sea-girt isle,
And one upon the waters, in thy day,

In thy great day, shalt raise above the nations,
The trumpet of deliverance to thy lips.

At last, with keel as clean as a sea-gull's breast,
The Golden Hind was launched; her well-patched sails
Hoisted; and, while she glided out to sea,
The red-skinned throng, knee-deep in the swirling foam
Keening a wild farewell, all stood at gaze
Like men that, once, in all their innocent lives
Have walked with gods and seen them fade away
Into the boundless distance whence they came.
But westward sped the singing *Golden Hind*
Across the wide Pacific, following still
The dazzling heave and dip of the sunset-road.
Far out of sight of land they steered, straight out,
With all that gorgeous booty in their hold,
A splendour dragging deep through seas of doom,
A prey to the first great hurricane that blew,
Except by miracle; their only guide
The captured ivory chart from old Cathay,
And that strange homing cry of all their hearts
Which seemed to lead them further from their home.

BOOK VII

THE wrath of Spain, a sea of flouted power
Clamoured round England for the head of Drake.
"Drake and his ships are on their homeward way!
Ye swore that he had foundered! What reply,
What recompense can England yield our King
Except the head of Drake?"

To which the Queen
(Who saw, like skeleton castles wrapped in mist,
The monstrous fleets and armaments of war
That Philip prepared, growing from day to day)
Elizabeth, fighting still to gain more time,
Replied, as might a sibyl of old Rome,
"If Drake have hurt our friends, the head of Drake!"

And—while the tense world waited him, as men wait
The sound of cannon, quietly one grey morn,
Grey as a ghost, with none to welcome her,
A tattered ship came gliding into the Sound.
There was no voice to hail her from the quay,

90

And not an eye to read the faded scroll
Around her battered prow—*The Golden Hind.*
Above the harbour, through the drizzling streets,
Rumbled the death-cart with its dreary bell
Monotonously plangent; for the plague
Had spread through Plymouth as a yellowing fog
Spreads through a rotting woodland.   A boy, alone,
From one high window saw an anchor splash,
And gave tongue, like a terrier, as he ran.
Then through the dumb grey misty listless port
A rumour like the colours of the dawn
Streamed o'er the shining quays, up the wet streets,
In at the tavern doors, flashed from the panes
And turned them into diamonds, fired the pools
In every muddy lane with Spanish gold,
Flushed in a thousand faces, *Drake is come!*
Down every crowding alley the urchins leaped
Tossing their caps, *The Golden Hind* is come!
Fisherman, citizen, 'prentice, dame and maid,
Fat justice, floury baker, bloated butcher,
Fishwife, minister and apothecary,
Yea, even the driver of the death-cart, leaving
His ghastly load, using his dreary bell
To merrier purpose, down the seething streets,
Panting, tumbling, jostling, helter-skelter
To the water-side, to the water-side they rushed,
And some knee-deep beyond it, all one wild
Welcome to Francis Drake!
Wild kerchiefs fluttering, thunderous hurrahs
Rolling from quay to quay, a thousand arms
Outstretched to that grey ghostly little ship
At whose masthead St George's flag still flew.
Then, over all, in one tumultuous tide
Of pealing joy, the Plymouth bells outclashed
A nation's welcome home to Francis Drake.

The very *Golden Hind,* no idle dream,
The ship of ships that sacked the Spanish Main,
The Golden Hind, the wonder of the world,
Carelessly lying there, in Plymouth Sound—
A glory wrapt her greyness, and no boat
Dared yet approach, save one with Drake's close friends,
Who came to warn him: "England stands alone.
The Queen perforce must temporise with Spain,
The Invincible!   She hath forfeited thy head

To Spain, against her will. Philip, the king,
Is mustering ships and armies. Cadiz holds
A huge Armada, none knows where to strike.
Set not thy foot on shore. The Queen, weighed down
By Burghley, may be driven to make thy life
Our ransom, and deliver thee to Spain."

To whom Drake answered—"Gloriana lives;
And, while she lives, England can say 'All's well!'
I have brought her a good cargo—a world's wealth,
The golden keys of all the power of Spain;
But, lest the Queen be driven to yield them up,
I will warp out behind St Nicholas' Island,
Until I know her will."
                            And in his heart
He secretly thought to himself "If it be death,
I'll out again to sea, strew its rough floor
With costlier largesses than kings can throw,
And, ere I die, I'll singe the Spaniard's beard
And set the fringe of his imperial robe
Blazing along his coasts. Let him come out
And roll his galleons round my *Golden Hind,*
Bring her to bay, if he can, on the high seas.
Thank God, who left to all men and all ships
On every deep one always open road,
No power can make us yield. We can still fasten
Our flag's last shred upon the last stump left us,
And sink with our last shot."
                            So Drake warped out
His *Golden Hind;* and, past her, in the night
Fisher-boats glided, hearing with awe-struck pride
Songs that had risen from many a lonely sea;
For all of Devonshire knew the legend now
Of that strange pirate whose immortal hold
Was packed with burning sunsets of rubines,
Not for himself, but England; one who sailed
In kingly state, to a sound of violins,
With skilled musicians round him, turning all
Battle and storm and death into a song.

SONG

Our highway none knoweth,
    Yet our blood hath discerned it.

Clear, clear is our path now
    Whose foreheads are free.
Where the hurricane bloweth
    Our spirits have learned it.
        'Tis the highway of wrath, now,
            The storm's way, the sea.

No land in the ring of it
    Now,—all around us,
        Only the splendid
            Re-surging unknown.
How should we sing of it,
    This that hath found us
        By the great stars attended
            At midnight, alone?

Ah, the broad miles of it
    White with the onset
        Of waves without number
            Warring for glee;
Ah, the soft smiles of it,
    Down to the sunset
        Holy for slumber,
            The peace of the sea.

When the breakers charged thundering
    In thousands all round us,
        With a lightning of lances
            Up-hurtled on high,
When the stout ships were sundering,
    A glory hath crowned us
        Like the wild light that dances
            On the crests that flash by.

Who now will follow us
    Where England's flag leadeth us,
        Where gold not inveigles,
            Nor statesmen betray?
Though the deep midnight swallow us,
    Let her cry when she needeth us,
        We return, her sea-eagles,
            The hurricane's way.

But like a splendid hurricane through the night
A flying horseman from the Queen returned

93

In answer to Drake's message, bidding him come,
And bring such curious trifles of his voyage
As might amuse her.   Like a woman's smile
The words were; but the face that smiled at him
Was England's own.   So Drake with all his crew
Landed amid the jostling wide-eyed throngs,
And loaded twelve big pack-horses with pearls
Beyond all price, diamonds, crosses of gold,
And emeralds torn from El Dorado's crown.
Also, he said, we'll take three ox-hide bales
Of gold doubloons, pieces of eight, moidores,
Out of our ballast, for those noble lords
At court, lilies that toil not, neither spin,
And have lean purses, and almighty tongues.

Six days thereafter, a fearful whisper reached
Mendoza, plenipotentiary of Spain,
That Drake, the master-thief of the golden world,
Drake, even he, that bloody buccaneer,
Had six hours' audience with her Majesty
Daily, nay more, walked with her in her garden
Alone, among the fiery Autumn leaves,
Talking of God knows what.   The woman's hand,
The hand of England, that Mendoza held
So lightly, changed to steel.   And when he came
Demanding instant audience of the queen,
Her officers of state with mouths awry
Told him that she was close in conference now
With some rough seaman, pirate, what you will,
A fellow made of bronze, a buccaneer,
Maned like a lion, bearded like a pard,
With hammered head, clamped jaws, and great deep eyes
That burned with fierce blue colours of the brine,
And liked not Spain—Drake!   'Twas the very name,
One Francis Drake! a Titan that had stood,
Thundering commands against the thundering heavens,
On lightning-shattered, storm-swept decks and quaffed
Great draughts of glory from the untameable seas.
"El Draque," he choked.   The queen could promise nought
To Spain's ambassador, nor see his face
Again, while yet one Spanish musketeer
Remained in Ireland.
                              Vainly the Spaniard raged
Of restitution, recompense; for Drake
Had brought his *Golden Hind* now, up the Thames.
There, like a star, her worn, grey, battered hulk

94

Kindled in all men's eyes. Her sunburnt crew
Were princes as they swaggered down the streets
In weather-beaten splendour. Out of their doors
To wonder and stare the jostling citizens ran
When they went by; and through the length and breadth
Of England, the new glory of Liberty
Shone like the dawn. O'er hill and dale it streamed
Making a golden pomp of every oak
Whose brethren had so braved the tyrant seas.
In each remotest hamlet, by the hearth,
The cart, the grey church-porch, the village pump,
By meadow and mill and old manorial hall,
By turnpike and by tavern, farm and forge,
Men staved the crimson vintage of romance
And held it up against the light and drank it,
And with it drank confusion to the wrath
That menaced England, but eternal honour,
While blood ran in their veins, to Francis Drake.

But Bess of Sydenham, prisoned in her home,
Fenced by her father's angry watch, lest Drake
The landless king of the untamed ocean-sea
Should speak with her—as in old fairy-tales
The changeling maiden in enchanted woods
Looks for the starry flash of her knight's shield;
Or, on the further side of the magic west,
Sees pushing through the ethereal golden gloom
A blurred black prow, with loaded colours coarse,
Clouded with sunsets of a mortal sea,
And rich with earthly crimson—waited still
With lips apart, the slumber-shattering thrill
When that keel grates the coasts of Elfin-land.

And yet there came no sound to break the spell
That bound her, and no message from her love,
Or none that reached her restless, helpless hands.
Only the general rumour of the world
Borne to her by the gossip of her maid
Kept the swift pictures flashing through her brain:
Of how *The Golden Hind* was hauled ashore
At Deptford through a sea of exultation;
Of how the Queen with subtle statecraft still
Kept Spain at arm's-length, dangling, while she played
At fast and loose with France, whose embassy,
Arriving with the marriage-treaty, found

(And trembled at her daring, since the wrath
Of Spain seemed, in their eyes, to flake with foam
The storm-scarred hulk) a royal banquet spread
To greet them on that very *Golden Hind*
Which sacked the Spanish Main, a gorgeous feast,
The like of which old England had not seen
Since the bluff days of boisterous King Hal,—
Great shields of brawn with mustard, roasted swans,
Haunches of venison, roasted chines of beef,
And chewets baked, big olive-pyes thereto,
And sallets mixed with sugar and cinnamon,
White wine, rose-water, and candied eringoes.
There, on the outlawed ship, whose very name
Rang like a blasphemy in the imperial ears
Of Spain (its every old worm-eaten plank
Being scored with scorn and courage that not storm
Nor death, nor all their Inquisition racks,
The white-hot irons and bloody branding whips
That scarred the backs of Spain's pale galley-slaves,
Her captured English seamen, ever could daunt),
There with huge Empires waiting for one word,
One breath of colour and excuse, to leap
Like wolves at the naked throat of her small isle,
There in the eyes of the staggered world she stood,
Great Gloriana, while the live decks reeled
With flash of jewels and flush of rustling silks,
She stood with Drake, the corsair, and her people
Surged like a sea around.   There did she give
Open defiance with her agate smile
To Spain.   "Behold this pirate, now," she cried,
"Whose head my Lord, the Invincible, Philip of Spain
Demands from England.   Kneel down, Master Drake,
Kneel down; for now have I this gilded sword
Wherewith to strike it off.   Nay, thou my lord
Ambassador of France, since I be woman,
And squeamish at the sight of blood, give thou
The accolade."   With that jest she gave the hilt
(Thus, even in boldness, playing a crafty part,
And dangling France before the adventurous deed)
To Marchaumont; and in the face of Europe,
Knighted the master-thief of the unknown world,
Sir Francis Drake.

              And then the rumour came
Of vaster privateerings planned by Drake
Against the coasts of Philip; but held in check

And fretting at the leash, as ever the Queen
Clung to her statecraft, while Drake's enemies
Worked in the dark against him.   Spain had set
An emperor's ransom on his life.   At home
John Doughty, treacherous brother of that traitor
Who met his doom by Drake's own hand, intrigued
With Spain abroad and Spain's dark emissaries
At home to avenge his brother; until by chance
Drake gat the proof of his intrigues with Spain,
And hurled him into the Tower.

                              But all these tales
Were vague as dreams to Bess, as under the stars,
With window wide to the dark pine-scented air
She listened to that distant ebb and flow
Marking the pulse of ages; till one night
Its music died away.   The great sea slept
Quietly as a child.   It grew so still
That Bess could almost hear the white owl's wing
As, like a phantom, over the pines he swept;
So still that she could almost hear the stars
Crackling, like fairy fires.   A dry twig snapped
Beneath her window.   A glimmering face looked up,
Draining her face of blood, of sight, of life,
And whispering, all the glory of life and death,
In one small word—"sweetheart!"
                              The jassamine shook;
And Drake was at her side, his arms around her,
His lips upon her lips.

                    A mastiff bayed,
A foot crunched on the gravel.
                              "E'en here," smiled Drake,
"They are watching for this pirate's head of mine"—
"Hist!" whispered Bess.   The footsteps died away.
Then Drake let down his ladder of strong ship's tackle.
"Quickly," he said, "before he rounds the house
We must be gone."   But ere the words were out,
Bess reached the path; and into the breathless woods
They sped, his arm around her.
                              Once, in the dark,
She drew back with a cry, as four grim faces,
With hand to forelock, glimmered in their way.
Then, with a laugh, she heard their deep-sea voices
Wishing their captain joy.   The mastiff bayed,

97

Far off, then nearer, as if he had found the trail;
And then a cry as if in hot pursuit.
"This way," cried Bess, and plunging through the firs
They followed her, till they reached an inch-deep brook
Hurrying down to the sea.   Drake lifted Bess
And down the brawling watery bed they splashed
To baffle the clamouring hunt.   Then out of the woods
They stole, on the sea-ward side; and Bess, with a shiver,
Saw starlight flash from four bright blades of steel
As the mastiff bayed still nearer.

                        Swiftly they reached
The starrier foam that churned the silver gravel
Around a small black lurching boat, a strange
Grim Charon's wherry for two lovers' flight,
Guarded by old Tom Moon.   Drake took her hand,
And with one arm around her waist, her breath
Warm on his cheek for a moment, in she leapt
Daintily over the gunwale, and took her seat,
His throned princess, beside him at the helm,
Backed by the glittering waves, his lady and queen
With eyes like stars and glorious hair that seemed
Breathing back scents and colours to a sea
Which lived but to reflect the world's one rose.

Then, all together, with their brandished oars
The seamen thrust as a heavy mounded wave
Lifted the boat; and up the whitening breast
Of the next they soared, then settled at the thwarts,
And swung and pulled across the starlit seas
To where a small black pinnace at anchor pitched,
Dipping her rakish prow in the dawning moon.
Small was she, but not fangless; for Bess saw,
And laughed to see, the black and threatening muzzles
Of four grim guns above the tossing boat;
But ere his seamen or his sweetheart knew
What power, as of a wind, bore them along,
Anchor was up, the sails were broken out,
And as they scudded down the dim grey coast
Of a new enchanted world (for now had Love
Made all things new and strange) the skilled musicians,
Plucking their golden strings on the moonlit prow,
Through the sea's music poured their lovelier song —

SONG

Sweet, what is love?   'Tis not the crown of kings,
Nay, nor the fire of white seraphic wings!
Is it a child's heart leaping while he sings?
     Even so say I;
     Even so say I.

Also the springing spray, the little topmost flower
Swung by the bird that sings a little hour,
Earth's climbing spray into the heaven's blue bower,
     Even so say I;
     Even so say I.

Dawn, like a wild-rose in the fields of heaven
Washed grey with dew, awoke, and found their bark
At anchor in a little land-locked bay.
A crisp breeze blew, and all the living sea
Beneath the lucid colours of the sky,
Now like a myriad-petalled rose and now
Innumerably scalloped into shells
Of delicate fire, with dwindling wrinkles edged
Fainter and fainter to the unruffled glow
And pure white sunlight of the distant deep,
Shone with mysterious beauty for those two
Who watched the gathering glory.   In an hour,
Drake and his Bess went up the rough rock-steps
Of the small white sparkling seaport, to the church.
No peal of bells had they, but as they linked
Their wedded hands, they heard, through the open door,
A missel-thrush warbling in a hawthorn-tree,—
Earth's climbing spray into the heaven's blue bower,
     Even so say I;
     Even so say I.

BOOK VIII

Now like a white-cliffed fortress England shone
Against the mirk of chaos.   Close at hand
Those first fierce cloudy fringes of the storm,
The Armada sails, gathered their might; and Spain
Crouched close behind them with her hideous fires
And steaming shambles.   Under Parma's feet
Writhed all the tortured Netherlands, dim coasts
Right over against us, whence his mustering hoards
Might suddenly whelm our isle.   But all night long,

On many a mountain, many a guardian height
From Beachy Head to Skiddaw, little throngs
Of seamen, torch and battle-lanthorn nigh,
Watched by the unlit beacons of rough logs
And sun-dried gorse.   Round them the sea-wind blew
Warm scents of clover and aromatic thyme
High over the sounding coast, along whose cliffs,
The coast-guards paced their winding white-chalk paths
And gazed to seaward through the loaded gloom.
And while all England held her breath in doubt,
Swift rumours flashed from north to south as runs
The lightning round a silent thunder-cloud;
And there were muttering crowds in the London streets,
And hurrying feet in the brooding Eastern ports.
All night, dark inns, gathering the country-side,
Reddened with clashing cups and talk of war.
All night, in the ships of Plymouth Sound, the soul
Of Francis Drake was England, and all night
Her singing seamen by the silver quays
Polished their guns and waited for the dawn.

But hour by hour that night grew deeper.   Spain
Watched, cloud by cloud, her huge Armadas grow,
Watched, tower by tower, and zone by zone, her fleets
Grapple the sky with a hundred hands and drag
Whole sea-horizons into her menacing ranks,
Joining her powers to those of night itself,
While Philip strove, with many a crafty word,
To lull the fears of England, till his plot
Were ripe, his armaments complete; and still
Elizabeth took her subtler woman's way,
Yet not without swift impulses to strike,
Swiftly recalled.   Blind, yet not blind, she smiled
On Mary of Scotland waiting for her throne.
Still with her agate smile, still she delayed,
Holding her pirate admiral in the leash;
Till Walsingham, nay, even the book-bowed Burghley,
That crafty king of statesmen, seeing the war
Inevitably approaching, ached to shatter
The tense tremendous hush that seemed to oppress
All hearts, compress all brows, load the broad night
With more than mortal menace.

                                        Only once
The night was traversed with one lightning flash,

One rapier stroke from England, at the heart
Of Spain, as swiftly parried, yet no less
A fiery challenge; for Philip's hate and scorn
Growing with his Armada's growth, he lured
With promises of just and friendly trade
A fleet of English corn-ships to relieve
His famine-stricken coast.   But as they lay
Within his ports he seized them all to feed
The Armada's maw.
                              Whereat Elizabeth,
Wickedly smiling, whispered to Walsingham,
"Unchain El Draque!"

                              A lightning flash indeed
Was this; for he whose little *Golden Hind*
With scarce a score of seamen late had scourged
The Spanish Main; he whose piratic neck
Hardly the Queen's most wily statecraft saved
From Spain's revenge; he, privateer to the eyes
Of Spain, but England to all English hearts,
Gathered together, in all good jollity,
All help and furtherance himself could wish,
Before that moon was out, a pirate fleet
Whereof the like old ocean had not seen—
Eighteen swift cruisers, two great battleships,
With pinnaces and store-ships and a force
Of nigh three thousand men, wherewith to singe
The beard of the King of Spain.
                              By night they gathered
In old dark wind-whipt inns nigh Plymouth Sound,
Not secretly as, ere the *Golden Hind*
Burst thro' the west, that small adventurous crew
Gathered beside the Thames, tossing the phrase
"Pieces of eight" from mouth to mouth, with tales
Of galleons crammed with hyacinths and gold,
Clouds in the sun, with mighty press of sail
Dragging the sunset out of the unknown world
And staining all the grey old seas of Time
With richer colour.   Pirates, or privateers,
Or Gloriana's men, no secret now!
For nightly round the glowing magic door
Of every inn the townsfolk grouped to hear
The storm-scarred seamen toasting Francis Drake.
And many a wide-eyed urchin face was pressed
On those red-curtained casements, ruby-bright

With wild reflection of the fires within,
The fires, the glasses, and the singing lips
Lifting defiance to the powers of Spain.

SONG

Sing we the Rose,
    The flower of flowers most glorious!
Never a storm that blows
    Across our English sea,
But its heart breaks out with the Rose
    On England's flag victorious,
The triumphing flag that flows
    Through the heavens of Liberty.

Sing we the Rose,
    The flower, the flower of love it is,
Which lovers aye shall sing
    And nightingales proclaim;
For oh, the heaven that glows,
    That glows and burns above it is
Freedom's perpetual Spring,
    Our England's faithful fame.

Sing we the Rose,
    That eastward still shall spread for us
Upon the dawn's bright breast,
    Her leaves with foam impearled;
And onward ever flows
    Till eventide make red for us
A Rose that sinks in the west
    And surges round the world;
        Sing we the Rose!

One night as, with his good vice-admiral,
Frobisher, his rear-admiral, Francis Knollys,
And Thomas Fenner, his flag-captain, Drake
Took counsel at his tavern, there came a knock,
The door opened, and cold as from the sea
The gloom rushed in, and there against the night
Glittered a courtier whom by face and form
All knew for the age's brilliant paladin,
Sidney, the king of courtesy, a star
Of chivalry.   The seamen stared at him,

Each with a hand upon the well-thumbed chart
Outspread before them.   Then all stared at Drake,
Who crouched like a great bloodhound over the table,
And rose with a strange light burning in his eyes;
For he remembered how, three years agone,
That other courtier came, with words and smiles
Copied from Sidney's self; and in his ears
Rang once again the sound of the two-edged sword
Upon the desolate Patagonian shore
Beneath Magellan's gallows.   With a voice
So harsh himself scarce knew it, he desired
This fair new courtier's errand.   With grim eyes
He scanned the silken knight from head to foot,
While Sidney, smiling graciously, besought
Some place in their adventure.   Drake's clenched fist
Crashed down on the black oak table like a rock,
Splintering the wood and dashing his rough wrist
With blood, as he thundered, "By the living God,
No!   We've no room for courtiers, now!   We leave
All that to Spain."
                              Whereat, seeing Sidney stood
Amazed, Drake, drawing nearer, said, "You ask
More than you think: I know you for a man
Most generous and most gentle and most true."
Then fiercely he outstretched his bleeding hand
And pointed through the door to where the gloom
Glimmered with bursting spray, and the thick night
Was all one wandering thunder of hidden seas.
"You'll find no fields of Arcady out there,
No lists of feudal chivalry, my friend.
Take you the word of one who has occupied
His business in great waters.   There's no room,
Meaning, or reason, office, or place, or name
For courtiers on the sea.   Does the sea flatter?
You cannot bribe it, torture it, or tame it!
Its laws are those of the moving universe,
Remorseless—listen to that!"—a mighty wave
Broke heavily down the coast.   "Your hands are white,
Your rapier jewelled, can you fence with that?
What part have you in all its flaming ways?
What share in its fierce gloom?   Has your heart broken
As those waves break out there?   Can you lie down
And sleep, as a lion-cub by the old lion,
When it shakes its mane out over you to hide you,
And leap out with the dawn as I have done?

103

These are big words; but, see, my hand is red.
You cannot torture me. I have borne all that;
And so I have some kinship with the sea,
Some sort of wild alliance with its storms,
At last, and power upon them. 'Tis the worse
For Spain. Be counselled well: come not between
My sea and its rich vengeance."
                                        Silently,
Bowing his head, Sidney withdrew. But Drake,
So fiercely the old grief rankled in his heart,
Summoned his swiftest horseman, bidding him ride,
Ride like the wind through the night, straight to the Queen,
Praying she would most instantly recall
Her truant courtier. Nay, to make all sure,
Drake sent a gang of seamen out to crouch
In ambush nigh the road, there to waylay
The Queen's reply, that she might never know
It reached him, if it proved against his will.

And still, in hourly dread of some new change
He knew no rest till out of Plymouth Sound
His pirate fleet shook out its sails again.
Then with the unfettered sea he mixed his soul
In great rejoicing union, while the ships
Crashing and soaring over the heart-free waves
Beat out once more for Spain.
                                    Water and food
They lacked; but the fierce fever of his mind
Had left no time for these. Right on he drove,
Determining, though the Queen's old officers
Beneath him stood appalled; to take in stores
Of all he needed, water, powder, food,
By plunder of Spain herself. In Vigo Bay,
Beneath the strong forts of Bayona town
He anchored, with the old sea-touch that wakes
Our England still. There, in the tingling ears
Of Spain he flung his challenge to her King.
There, ordering out his pinnaces in force,
While a great storm, as if indeed he held
Heaven's batteries in reserve, growled o'er the sea,
He landed. Ere one cumbrous limb of all
The monstrous armaments of Spain could move
His ships were stored; and ere the sword of Spain
Stirred in its crusted sheath, Bayona town
Beheld an empty sea; for like a dream

The pirate fleet had vanished, none knew whither.
But, in its visible stead, invisible fear
Filled the vast rondure of the sea and sky
As with Drake's threatening omnipresent soul.
For when Spain saw the small black anchored fleet
Ride in her bays, the sight set bounds to fear.
She knew at least the ships were oak, the guns
Of common range: nor did she dream that Drake
Could sail two seas at once.   But now, her coasts
Heard him all night in every bursting wave.
His top-sails gleamed in every moonlit cloud.
His battle-lanthorn glittered in the stars
That hung the low horizon.   He became
A universal menace; yet there followed
No sight or sound of him, unless the sea
Were that grim soul incarnate.   Did it not roar
His fierce commands?   The very spray that lashed
The cheeks of Spanish seamen lashed their hearts
To helpless hatred of him.   The wind sang
El Draque across the rattling blocks and sheets
When storms perplexed them; and when ships went down,
As under the fury of his onsetting battle,
The drowning sailors cursed him while they sank.

And onward over the great grey gleaming sea
Swept like a cloud of eagles that grim fleet
With vengeance in its heart.   Five years agone,
Young Hawkins, in the Cape Verde Islands, met—
At Santiago—with such treachery
As Drake burned to requite, and from that hour
Was Santiago doomed.   His chance had come;
Drake swooped upon it, plundered it, and was gone,
Leaving the treacherous isle a desolate heap
Of smoking ashes in the leaden sea.
Then all those pirate bowsprits plunged again
Along the sunset road.   "For I will show,"
Said Drake, "that Englishmen henceforth will sail
Old ocean where they will."   Onward they surged,
And the great glittering crests of the proud waves
Jubilantly rushed up to meet the keels,
Till there was nought around them but the grey
Ruin and roar of the huge Atlantic seas,
Grey mounded seas, pursuing and pursued,
That fly, hounded and hounding on for ever,
From empty marge to marge of the grey sky.

Over the wandering wilderness of foam,
Onward, through storm and death, Drake sailed.   A plague
Of deadly fever crept through all his ships;
And not by twos and threes as heretofore
His crews were minished; but in three black days
Three hundred seamen in their shotted shrouds
Were cast into the deep.   Onward he swept,
Implacably, having in mind to strike
Spain in the throat at San Domingo, port
Of Hispaniola, a city of far renown,
A jewel on the shores of old romance,
Palm-shadowed, gated with immortal gold,
Queen city of Spain's dominions over sea,
And guarded by great forts.   Out of the dawn
The pirate ships came leaping, grim and black,
And ere the Spaniards were awake, their heights
Blazed with the crackling banner of our St George.
But since he had not troops enough to hold
So great a city, Drake entrenched his men
Within the Plaza and held the batteries.
Thence he demanded ransom, and sent out
A boy with flag of truce.   The boy's return
Drake waited long.   Under a sheltering palm
He stood, watching the enemies' camp.   At noon,
Along the hot white purple-shadowed road
Tow'rd him, a crawling shape writhed through the dust
Up to his feet, a shape besmeared with blood,
A shape that moaned and lifted up a face
Hideously puckered, shrivelled like a monkey's
With lips drawn backward from its teeth.
                                        "Speak, speak,

In God's name, speak, what art thou?" whispered Drake,
And a sharp cry came, answering his dread,
A cry as of a sea-bird in the wind
Desolately astray from all earth's shores,
"See, see, my captain, see what they have done!"

Drake dropped upon his knees and gently strove
To pillow the blood-stained head upon his arm.
"What have they done to thee, what have they done?"
And at the touch the boy screamed, once, and died.

Drake rose to his feet.   His face was like a stone.
His grey lips quietly, as in slumber, spoke.

"Eternal God, be this the doom of Spain!
Bring up the Spanish prisoners."
                              Through their ranks
He strode.   "Is any here that speaks both tongues?"
A soldier caught his eye.   Drake led him out.
Like a cold wind his words went through their flesh:
"Go.   Take this message to the camp of Spain.
Tell them I have a hunger in my soul
To look upon the murderers of this boy,
To see what eyes they have, what manner of mouths,
To touch them and to take their hands in mine,
And draw them close to me and smile upon them
Until they know my soul as I know theirs.
Say that, until I get them, every day
I'll hang two Spaniards though I should dispeople
The Spanish Main.   Tell them that, every day,
I'll burn a portion of their city down,
Then find another city and burn that,
And then burn others till I burn away
Their empire from the world."

                    Across the Atlantic
The west wind bore the tale.   The gorgeous court
Of Philip shuddered away from the streaming coasts
As a wind-cuffed field of golden wheat.   The king,
Bidding his guests to a feast in his own ship
On that wind-darkened sea, was made a mock,
As one by one his ladies proffered excuse
For fear of that beyond.   Round Europe now
Ballad and story told how in the cabin
Of Francis Drake there hung a magic glass
Wherein he saw the fleets of every foe;
While darker legends told how Drake had bought,
Like old Norse wizards, power to loose or bind
The winds at will.

                    And soon a grimmer tale
Was whispered—of a distant blood-red dawn
At San Domingo, where his weather-stained crews
Met the proud troops of Spain—but not in fight—
Met in hushed awe, by his compelling will,
To offer up a sacrifice and slay
By Spain's own hand, the murderers of the boy
Who had borne his flag of truce.
                              And bitterer yet,

107

The mocking rumour spread of how Drake saw
A mighty scutcheon of the king of Spain,
Whereon was painted the terrestrial globe,
And on the globe a rampant steed, in act
To spring into the heavens, and from its mouth
A scroll of flame and fury—*non sufficit
Orbis;* and how Drake summoned the Spaniards round him,
And saying his seamen had but little Latin
Bade them translate. *"Earth is too small for Spain!"*
Quoth one; whereat Diego solemnly sneezed,
And echoes of hurricane laughter shook the world.

So, while at home the warrior eyes of Spain
Watched, every hour, her vast Armada grow
Readier to launch and strike, fear gripped her still;
For there came sounds across the heaving sea
Of rending chains. A stranger wilder tale
Shone like another dawn across the deep;
And, in that dawn, men saw the slaves of Spain,
The mutilated negroes of the mines,
With gaunt backs wealed and branded, scarred and seared
By whip and iron, in Spain's brute lust for gold;
Saw them, at Drake's great liberating word,
Burst from their chains, erect, uplifting hands
Of rapture to the blinding new-born light
In heaven, a light which, though from age to age
Clouds may obscure it, grows and still shall grow
Until that nobler commonwealth be born,
That Union which draws nigher with every day,
That turning of the wasteful strength of war
To accomplish large and fruitful tasks of peace,
A gathering up of one another's loads
Whereby the weak are strengthened and the strong
Made stronger in the increasing good of all.

Suddenly, it seemed, as he had gone,
A ship came stealing into Plymouth Sound
And Drake was home again, but not to rest;
For scarce had he cast anchor ere the road
To London rang beneath the flying hoofs
That bore his brief despatch to Burghley, saying,
"We have missed the Plate Fleet by but twelve hours' sail,
The reason being best known to God. No less
We have given a cooling to the King of Spain.
There is a great gap opened which, methinks.
Is little to his liking. We have sacked

The towns of his chief Indies, burnt their ships,
Captured great store of gold and precious stones,
Three hundred pieces of artillery,
The more part brass.   Our loss is heavy indeed,
Under the hand of God, eight hundred men,
Three parts of them by sickness.   Captain Moon,
My trusty old companion, he that struck
The first blow in the South Seas at a Spaniard,
Died of a grievous wound at Cartagena.
My fleet and I are ready to strike again
At once, wherever the Queen and England please.
I pray for her commands, and those with speed,
That I may strike again."   Outside the scroll
These words were writ once more, "My Queen's commands
I much desire, your servant, Francis Drake."
This terse despatch the brooding Burghley read
Thrice over, with the broad cliff of his brow
Bending among his books.   Thrice he assayed
To steel himself with caution as of old.
Thrice, as a glorious lightning running along
And flashing between the plain swift words, he saw
The great new power that lay at England's hand,
An ocean-sovereignty.   Could that power but grow
Before that army of thirty thousand men
Round Antwerp, under Parma, should be hurled
Across the seas, at England!   Thrice he assayed
To think of England's helplessness, her ships
Little and few.   Thrice he assayed to quench
With caution the high furnace in his soul
Which Drake had kindled.   As he read the last
Rough simple plea, *I wait my Queen's commands,*
His deep eyes flashed with glorious tears.

He leapt

To his feet and cried aloud, "Before my God,
I am proud, I am very proud for England's sake!
This Drake is a terrible man to the king of Spain."

And still, still, Gloriana, brooding darkly
On Mary of Scotland's doom, held back from war
And disavowed the deeds of Drake to Spain.
Philip, resolved at last never to swerve
By one digressive stroke, one ell or inch
From his own patient, sure, laborious path,
Accepted her suave plea, and with all speed
Pressed on his huge emprise.   His coasts grew dark

With cannon-foundries and grim hulks of war.
And, all round Antwerp, Parma still prepared
To fling such armies over the subject sea
As in all history hardly the earth herself
Felt shake with terror her own green hills and plains.
I wait my Queen's commands!   Despite the plea
Urged every hour upon her with the fire
That burned for action in the soul of Drake,
Still she delayed, till on one desperate eve
She gave him audience in that glimmering room
Where first he saw her.   Strangely sounded there
The seaman's rough strong passion as he poured
His heart before her, pleading—"Every hour
Is one more victory lost," and only heard
The bitter answer—"Nay, but every hour
A breath snatched from destruction.   Spain may forge
A sword, and yet its point may not be aimed
At England.   War would end us."   As she spake,
The winds, outside, clamoured with clash of bells.
There was a gleam of torches and a shout—
Mary, the traitress of the north, is dead!
God save the Queen!
                         "I like not this black news
From Fotheringay," said Drake.   "Fore God, I hope
The sins of Spain be blacker than our own."
Then that proud queen bent low her stately head,
And wept.   "Pity me, friend, though I be queen,
My heart is woman.   I am sorely pressed
On every side,—Scotland and France and Spain
Beset me, and I know not where to turn."
There came a hurried footstep.   Walsingham
Bowed low before her, offering her a letter.
"At last," he said, "your Majesty may read
The full intent of Spain.   Here, plainly writ
In black on white, is your own murder planned.
Blame not your Ministers who with such haste
Plucked out this Scottish peril from your breast!
Read here—how, with his thirty thousand men,
The pick of Europe, Parma joins the Scots,
While Ireland, grasped in their Armada's clutch,
And the Isle of Wight, against our west and south
Become their base."
                         "They count upon the power
Of Rome," Elizabeth muttered.   "Even here
In England she hath thousands.   Will she strike

Her curse out with pontific finger at me,
Curse me down and away to the bottomless pit?
A shadow like the shadow of clouds or sails,
The shadow of that huge event at hand,
Darkens the seas already, and the wind
Is on my cheek that shakes my kingdom down.
There are thousands, here in England, born and bred,
Who stand by Rome.   But will they stand by Spain?"

Even at the word, Lord Howard of Effingham
Entered and answered, "O, madam, you do us wrong!
There is another Rome—not this of Spain
Which lurks to pluck the world back into darkness
And stab it there for gold.   There is a City
Whose eyes are tow'rd the morning; on whose heights
Blazes the Cross of Christ above the world;
A Rome that shall wage warfare yet for God
In the dark days to come, even as she brought
Christ to our Saxon kings!   A strong-walled City
That hath foundations; a City whose very stones
Are all compact of thought, hewn by the toil
Of angels, from the intellectual hills.
Her deep creed cannot change, for all its roots
Are in the unchanging.   Therefore it endures.
Misjudge not those who love that City of God,
The folk who built the minsters of our kings,
From Canterbury to York, will not discrown you.
The folk whose dreams now live and breathe in stone
From Tintern to Melrose will not betray you.
From Winchester to Durham, all those towers,
All those lost arches, point to heaven, not Spain
This very day—and my heart burns with it—
I heard the Catholic gentlemen of England
Speaking in grave assembly.   At one breath
Of peril to our island, their clean swords
Leapt from their scabbards, and their cry went up
To split the heavens—*God save our English Queen!*"
He raised his head.   There passed the rushing gleam
Of torches once again and, as they stood
Silently listening, all the winds ran wild
With clamouring bells, and a great cry went up—
God save Elizabeth, our English Queen!

"I'll vouch for some five hundred Catholic throats
Among that thousand," whispered Walsingham
Eagerly, with his eyes on the Queen's face.

Then, seeing it brighten, fervently he cried,
Pressing the swift advantage home, "O, Madam,
The heart of England now is all on fire!
We are one people, as we have not been
In all our history.   You are beloved
As never yet was English king or queen!"
She looked at him, the tears in her keen eyes
Glittered—"And I am very proud," she said,
"But if our enemies command the world,
And we have one small island and no more . . ."
She ceased; and Drake, in a strange voice, hoarse and low,
Trembling with passion deeper than all speech,
Cried out—"No more than the great ocean-sea
Which makes the enemies' coast our frontier now;
No more than that dominion of the deep
Which rolls from Pole to Pole, washing the world
With thunder, that sea-kingdom whose command
This day is yours to take.   Hear me, my Queen,
This is a dream, a new dream, but a true;
For mightier days are dawning on the world
Than heart of man hath known.   If England hold
The sea, she holds the hundred thousand gates
That open to futurity.   She holds
The highway of all ages.   Argosies
Of unknown splendour set their sails this day
For England out of undiscovered worlds
If she but claim her heritage."

                              He ceased;
And the deep dream of that new realm, the sea,
Through all the soul of Gloriana surged,
A moment, then with splendid eyes that filled
With fire of sunsets far away, she cried
(Faith making her a child, yet queenlier still)
"Yea, claim it thou for me!"

                              A moment there
Trembling she stood.   Then, once again, there passed
A rush of torches through the gloom without,
And a great cry "God save Elizabeth,
God save our English Queen!"

                              "Yea, go, then, go,"
She said, "God speed you now, Sir Francis Drake,
Not as a privateer, but with full powers,
My Admiral-at-the-Seas!"

Without a word
Drake bent above her hand and, ere she knew it,
His eyes from the dark doorway flashed farewell,
And he was gone.   But, as he leapt to saddle,
Walsingham stood at his stirrup, muttering, "Ride,
Ride now like hell to Plymouth; for the Queen
Is hard beset, and ere ye are out at sea
Her mood will change.   The friends of Spain will move
Earth and the heavens for your recall.   They'll tempt her
With their false baits of peace again.   Be swift."
Fire flashed beneath the hoofs and Drake was gone.
Scarce had he vanished in the night than doubt
Once more assailed the Queen.   The death of Mary
Had brought even France against her.   Walsingham
And Burghley himself, prime mover of that death,
Being held in much disfavour for it, stood
As helpless.   Long ere Drake or human power,
They thought, could put to sea, a courier sped
To Plymouth bidding Drake forbear to strike.
The roadstead glittered empty.   Drake was gone.

Gone!   Though the friends of Spain had poured their gold
To thin his ranks, and every hour his crews
Deserted, he had laughed—"Let Spain buy scum!
Next to an honest seaman I love best
An honest landsman.   What more goodly task
Than teaching brave men seamanship?"   He had filled
His ships with soldiers!   Out in the teeth of the gale
That raged against him he had driven.   In vain,
Amid the boisterous laughter of the quays,
A pinnace dashed in hot pursuit and met
A roaring breaker and came hurtling back
With oars and spars all trailing in the foam,
A tangled mass of wreckage and despair.
Sky roared to stormy sky.   No sail could live
In that great yeast of waves; but Drake was gone!

Then, like wild winds, across the struggling sea
The rumours rushed, of how he had sacked the port
Of Cadiz, harrying all the enemy's coast
To Lisbon, where the whole Armada lay:
Had snapped up prizes under its very nose,
And taunted Santa Cruz, High Admiral
Of Spain, striving to draw him out for fight,
And offering, if his course should lie that way,

To convoy him to Britain, taunted him
So bitterly that for once, in the world's eyes,
A jest had power to kill; for Santa Cruz
Died with the spleen of it, since he could not move
Before the appointed season.   Then there came
Flying back home, the Queen's old Admiral
Borough, deserting Drake and all aghast
At Drake's temerity: "For," he said, "this man,
Thrust over my head, against all precedent,
Bade me follow him into a harbour mouth
'Cloaked,' quotha, 'by its own black cannon-smoke'
Whereat I much demurred; and straightway Drake
Clapped me in irons, me—an officer
And Admiral of the Queen; and, though my voice
Was all against it, plunged into the pit
Without me, muttering things that made me fear
The man was mad, some word of lonely seas,
A desert island and a mutineer
And dead Magellan's gallows.   Sirs, my life
Was hardly safe with him.   Why, he resolved
To storm the Castle of St Vincent, sirs,
A rock whose only loopholes were its guns
Well known impregnable!   The Spaniards fear
Drake; but to see him land below it and bid
Surrender, sirs, the strongest fort of Spain
Without a blow, they laughed!   And straightway he.
With all the fury of Satan, turned that cliff
To hell itself.   He sent down to the ships
For faggots, broken oars, beams, bowsprits, masts,
And piled them up against the outer gates,
Fired them, and smoked the wasps' nest out.   He stood
Amid the smoke and flame and cannon-shot,
This Admiral, like a fo'c'sle-hand, all black
With soot, besmeared with blood, his naked arms
Full of great faggots, labouring like a giant
And roaring like Apollyon.   Sirs, he is mad!
But did he take it, say you?   Ay, he took it,
The toughest stronghold on the coast of Spain.
Took it and tumbled all its big brass guns
Clattering over the cliffs into the sea.
But, sirs, ye need not raise a cheer so loud!
It is not warfare.   'Twas a madman's trick,
A devil's!"
                    Then the rumour of a storm
That scattered the fleet of Drake to the four winds

Disturbed the heart of England, as his ships
Came straggling into harbour, one by one,
Saying they could not find him.   Then, at last,
When the storm burst in its earth-shaking might
Along our coasts, one night of rolling gloom
His cannon woke old Plymouth.   In he came
Across the thunder and lightning of the sea
With his grim ship of war; and, hard behind,
A shadow like a mountain or a cloud
Torn from the heaven-high panoplies of Spain,
A captured galleon loomed, and round her prow
A blazoned scroll, whence (as she neared the quays
Which many a lanthorn swung from brawny fist
Yellowed) the sudden crimson of her name,
Flashed *San Filippe,* over the white cruddle of faces,
Packed on the quay.   Their sudden shout outroared
The galloping breakers—" 'Tis the heart of Spain!
The *San Filippe!"*   Overhead she towered,
The tallest ship afloat; and in her hold
The riches of a continent, a prize
Greater than earth had ever known; for there
Not only blood-rubines, like ocean-beaches
Heaped on a wizard coast, in that dim hull
Blazed to the lanthorn-light; not only gold
Gleamed, though of gold all London could not buy
Her store; but in her cabin lay the charts
And secrets of the wild unwhispered wealth
Of India, secrets that splashed London wharves
With coloured dreams and made her misty streets
Flame like an Eastern City.
                              But ever the seas
Darkened with growing menace; and ere that moon
Waned, a swift gunboat foamed into the Sound
With word that all the Invincible Fleet at last
Was hoisting sail for England.
                              Even yet,
Elizabeth, torn a thousand ways, withheld
The word for which Drake pleaded as for life,
That he might meet them ere they left their coasts,
Meet them before they reached the Channel, meet them
Now, or—"Too late!   Too late!"   At last his voice
Beat down all those that blindly dinned her ears
With chatter of meeting Spain on British soil;
And swiftly she commanded (seeing that light
In Drake's deep eyes) Lord Howard of Effingham,

High Admiral of England, straight to join him
At Plymouth Sound. "How many ships are wanted?"
She asked him, thinking, "we are few, indeed!"
"Give me but sixteen merchantmen," said Drake,
"And four good war-ships, by the mercy of God,
I'll answer for the Armada!"   Out to sea
They beat, in the teeth of a gale; but vainly Drake
Strove to impart the thought that filled his mind
With fire—to win command of the ocean-sea
By bursting on the fleets of Spain at once
Even as they left their ports, not as of old
To hover in a vain dream of defence
Round fifty threatened points of British coast.
But Howard, clinging to his old-world order,
Flung out his ships in a loose, long, straggling line
Across the Channel, waiting, wary, alert,
But powerless thus as a string of scattered sea-gulls
Beating against the storm.   Then, flying to meet them,
A merchantman brought amazement down the wind,
With news that she had seen that monstrous host
Stretching from sky to sky, great hulks of doom,
Dragging death's midnight with them o'er the sea.
Up to the Lord High Admiral's flag-ship Drake
Swirled thro' the swirling seas in his *Revenge*.
His pinnace dashed alongside.   On to the decks
Of the tossing flag-ship, like a very Viking
Shaking the flying rainbows of the spray
From sun-smit lion-like mane and beard he stood
Before Lord Howard in the escutcheoned poop
And poured his heart out like the rending sea
In passionate wave on wave:
                              "If yonder fleet
Once reach the Channel, hardly the mercy of God
Saves England!   I would pray with my last breath,
Let us beat up to windward of them now,
And handle them before they reach the Channel."—
"Nay; but we cannot bare the coast," cried Howard,
"Nor have we stores of powder or food enough!"—
"My lord," said Drake, with his great arm outstretched,
"There is food enough in yonder enemy's ships,
And powder enough and cannon-shot enough!
We must re-victual there.   Look!   look!" he cried,
And pointed to the heavens.   As for a soul
That by sheer force of will compels the world
To work his bidding, so it seemed the wind

That blew against them slowly veered.   The sails
Quivered, the skies revolved.   A northerly breeze
Awoke and now, behind the British ships,
Blew steadily tow'rds the unseen host of Spain.
"It is the breath of God," cried Drake; "they lie
Wind-bound, and we may work our will with them.
Signal the word, Lord Howard, and drive down!"
And as a man convinced by heaven itself
Lord Howard ordered, straightway, the whole fleet
To advance.

        The Armada lay beyond the mists
Wind-bound and helpless in Corunna bay,
At England's mercy, could her fleet but draw
Nigh enough, with its fire-ships and its guns
To windward.   Nearer, nearer, league by league
The ships of England came; till Ushant lay
Some seventy leagues behind.   Then, yet once more
The wind veered, straight against them.   To hold on,
Beating against it idly was to starve:
And, as a man whose power upon the world
Fails for one moment of exhausted will,
Drake, gathering up his forces as he went
For one more supreme struggle, turned his ship
Tow'rds Plymouth.

        There while axe and hammer rang
Re-fitting his worn fleet, one stormy day
When sunset turned the breakers' high-flung crests
To a riot of blazing wind-blown torches, Drake
Stood with old comrades on the close-cropped green
Of Plymouth Hoe, playing a game of bowls.

Far off unseen, a little barque, full-sail,
Noteless as any speckled herring-gull
Flickering between the white flakes of the waves,
Struggled and leapt and strove tow'rds Plymouth Sound.
A group of schoolboys with their satchels lay
Stretched on the green, gazing with great wide eyes
Upon their seamen heroes as, like gods
Disporting with the battles of the world,
They loomed, tossing black bowls like cannon-balls
Against the fiery west, or lounged at ease
With faces olive-dark against the sky,
Laughing, while from the neighbouring inn mine host,
White-aproned and blue-jerkined, hurried out

With foaming cups of ale, and they drank deep,
Tossing their heads back under the burning clouds
And burying their bearded lips.   The hues
That slashed their doublets, for the boys' bright eyes
(Even as the gleams of Grecian cloud or moon
Revealed the old gods) were here rich dusky streaks
Of splendour from the Spanish Main, that shone
But to proclaim these heroes.   There a boy
More bold crept nearer to a slouched hat thrown
Upon the green, and touched the silver plume,
And felt as if he had touched a sunset-isle
Of feathery palms beyond a crimson sea.
Another stared at the blue wreaths of smoke
A storm-scarred seaman puffed from a long pipe
Primed with the strange new herb they had lately found
Beyond the Atlantic.   But the little ship
Now plunging into Plymouth Bay none saw.
E'en when she had anchored and her straining boat
Had touched the land, and the boat's crew over the quays
Leapt with a shout, scarce was there one to heed.
A seaman, smiling, swaggered out of the inn
Swinging in one brown hand a gleaming cage
Wherein a big green parrot chattered and clung
Fluttering against the wires.   A troop of girls
With arms linked paused to watch the game of bowls;
And now they flocked around the cage, while one
With rosy finger tempted the horny beak
To bite.   Close overhead a sea-mew flashed
Seaward.   Once, from an open window, soft
Through trellised leaves, not far away, a voice
Floated, a voice that flushed the cheek of Drake,
The voice of Bess, bending her glossy head
Over the broidery frame, in a quiet song.

The song ceased.   Still, with rainbows in their eyes,
The schoolboys watched the bowls like cannon-balls
Roll from the hand of gods along the turf.

At last, up to the green, a little throng
Of seamen, shouting, stumbling, as they ran
Drew all eyes on them.   The game ceased.   A voice
Rough with the storms of many an ocean called,
"Drake! Cap'en Drake! The Armada! In the Channel!
We sighted them—war-galleons, in a line,
Stretching from north to south without an end.

They are coming like a storm.   They look like clouds
With little sparks of lightning, where the sun
Glints on the brasswork and the cannon-butts!"

All eyes were turned on Drake, as he stood there,
Looming against the sunset and the sea,
Stiller than bronze.   Far off, the first white star
Gleamed, as if motionless in heaven, a world
Of lonely light and wildering speed.
                              He tossed
A grim black ball in the lustrous air and laughed,—
"Come, lads," he said, "we've time to finish the game."

BOOK IX

FEW minutes, and well wasted those, were spent
On that great game of bowls; for well knew Drake
What panic threatened Plymouth, since his fleet
Lay trapped there by the fierce head-wind that blew
Straight up the Sound, and Plymouth town itself,
Unless the ships won seaward ere the dawn,
Lay at the Armada's mercy.   Never a seaman
Of all that thronged the wet wave-buffetted Hoe,
Hoped that one ship might win to the open sea.
At dawn, they thought, the Armada's rolling guns
To windward, in an hour, must shatter them,
Huddled in their red slaughter-house like sheep.

The sun had sunk.   The night was black as pitch.
Far off to westward, like a human soul
Fighting blind nature, a wild flare of red
High on a windy headland suddenly leapt
And vanished flickering into the clouds.   Again
It leapt and vanished.   Then, conquering, it streamed
Steadily as a crimson torch upheld
By Titan hands to heaven.   It was the first
Beacon!
              At once, along the quay there strode
The all-conquering power, the spirit of a man.

The voice of Drake bore down the thundering wind,
And ere men knew what new death-challenging might
Surged through them, his immortal little ship
Revenge had flung out cables to the quays.
And while the seamen, as he had commanded,

Knotted thick ropes together, he stood apart
(For well he knew what panic threatened still)
Whittling idly at a scrap of wood,
And carved a little boat out for the child
Of an old sea-companion.
So steady and calm a master of the world
Seemed Drake that, while he whittled, and the chips
Fluttered into the blackness over the quay,
Men said that in this hour of England's need
Each wind-blown flake turned to a ship of war.
For now began the lanthorns, one by one,
To glitter, and half-reveal the shadowy hulks
Before him.—So the huge old legend grew,
Not all unworthy the Homeric age
Of gods and god-like men.
                St Michael's Mount,
Answering the first wild beacon far away,
Licked at the flying clouds with a blood-red tongue.
The ropes were knotted.   Through the panting dark
Great heaving lines of seamen all together
Hauled with a shout, and all together again
Hauled with a shout against the roaring wind;
And slowly, slowly, onward tow'rds the sea
Moved the *Revenge*, and seaward ever heaved
The brawny backs together, and in their midst,
Wherever they slackened, Drake was always there
Hauling like any ten, and with his heart
Doubling the strength of all, giving them joy
Of battle against those odds, until they found
Delight in the burning tingle of the blood
That even their hardy hands must feel besmear
The harsh, rough, straining ropes.   And as they toiled,
Answering a score of hills, old Beachy Head
Streamed like a furnace to the streaming clouds.
Then all around the coast each windy ness
And craggy mountain kindled.   Peak from peak
Caught the tempestuous fire, and flung it on,
Round the bluff east and the black mouth of Thames,
Up, northward to the waste wild Yorkshire fells
And gloomy Cumberland, where, like a giant,
Grasping the red brand in his granite knuckles
Grim Skiddaw thrust it up to blind the stars.
Then all night long, inland, the wandering winds
Ran wild with clamour and clash of startled bells.

Down to the coasts with pike and halbert streamed
The trained bands, horse and foot, from every town
And every hamlet.   Many a shaggy hill
From Milford Haven to the downs of Kent,
And up to Humber, gleamed with naked steel.
Streaming through London forty thousand men,
In case the Invader should prevail, drew swords
Around their queen.   All night in dark St Paul's,
While all the thronged and fog-bound streets glanced red
With torch-lit harness, rose the passionate prayer
Of England's peril:
                    O Lord God of Hosts,
Let Thine enemies know that Thou hast taken
England into Thine hands!
                              The sea-deep sound
Billowed around the kneeling aisles, then died
Echoing up the heights.   A voice, far off,
As on some peak of vision, caught it up
And poured the prayer o'er that deep hush, alone:
We beseech Thee, O God, to go before our armies,
Bless and prosper them both by land and sea!
Grant unto them Thy victory, O God,
As Thou usedst to do to Thy children when they please **Thee!**
All power, all strength, all victory come from Thee!
Then from the unseen multitude arose
A sound as from the rent heart of an ocean,—
Some put their trust in chariots and some in horses;
But we will remember Thy name, O Lord our God!

So, while at Plymouth Sound her seamen toiled
Through those dark hours, and scarce a ship had won
Seaward, all night while mustering trumpets blared,
While torches flared behind the blazoned panes
And the quick tramp of troops went by like waves,
All night, amid that solemn pillared hush
From lips of kneeling thousands one deep prayer
Shook the strong Gates of Heaven!   *O Lord, our God,*
Heavenly Father, have mercy upon our Queen
To whom Thy far dispersèd flock do fly
In the anguish of their souls.   Behold, behold,
How many princes band themselves against her,
How long Thy servant hath laboured to them for ***peace,***
How proudly they prepare themselves for battle!
Arise, therefore!   Maintain Thine own cause,

Judge Thou between her and her enemies!
She seeketh not her own honour, but Thine,
Not the dominions of others, but Thy truth,
Not bloodshed but the saving of the afflicted!
Oh rend the heavens, therefore, and come down,
Deliver Thy people!
To vanquish is all one with Thee, by few
Or many, want or wealth, weakness or strength.
The cause is Thine, the enemies Thine, the afflicted
Thine! The honour, victory, and triumph
Thine! Grant her people now one heart, one mind,
One strength. Give unto her councils and her captains
Wisdom and courage strongly to withstand
The forces of her enemies, that the fame
And glory of Thy Kingdom may be spread
Unto the ends of the world. Father, we crave
This in Thy mercy, for the precious death
Of Thy dear Son, our Saviour, Jesus Christ!
Amen.
And as the dreadful dawn through mist-wreaths broke,
And out of Plymouth Sound at last there struggled
Six little ships, all that the night's long toil
Had warped down to the sea (but leading them
The ship of Drake) there rose one ocean-cry
From all those worshippers—*Let God arise,*
And let His enemies be scattered!

Empty and cold, indifferent as death,
The sea heaved strangely to the seamen's eyes,
Seeing all round them only the leaden surge
Wrapped in wet mist or flashing here and there
With crumbling white. Against the cold wet wind
Westward the struggling ships of England beat
With short tacks, close inshore, striving to win
The windward station of the threatening battle.
Close-hauled, with many a short tack, struggled and strained,
North-west, south-west, the ships; but westward gained
Some little way with every tack; and soon,
While the prows plunged beneath the grey-gold noon,
Lapped by the crackling waves, even as the wind
Died down a little, in the mists behind
There stole from Plymouth Sound the struggling score
Of ships that might not win last night to sea.
They followed; but the Six went on before,
Not knowing, to meet the invincible enemy.

Now, as they tacked north-west, the sullen roar
    Of reefs crept out, or some strange tinkling sound
Of sheep-bells on the hills.   South-west once more
    The bo'sun's whistle swung their bowsprits round.

And now the noon began to wane.   The west
    With slow rich colours filled and shadowy forms,
Dark curdling wreaths and fogs with crimsoned breast,
    And tangled zones of dusk, like frozen storms,

Motionless, flagged with sunset, hulled with doom!
    Motionless?   Nay, across the darkening deep
Surely the whole sky moved its gorgeous gloom
    Onward; and like the curtains of a sleep

The red fogs crumbled, mists dissolved away!
    There, like death's secret, dawning thro' a dream,
Great thrones of thunder dusked the dying day,
    And, higher, pale towers of cloud began to gleam.

There, in one heaven-wide storm, great masts and clouds
    Of sail crept slowly forth, the ships of Spain!
From north to south, their tangled spars and shrouds
    Controlled the slow wind as with bit and rein.
Onward they rode in insolent disdain
    Sighting the little fleet of England there,
While o'er the sullen splendour of the main
    Three solemn guns tolled all their host to prayer,
And their great ensign blazoned all the doom-fraught air.

The sacred standard of their proud crusade
    Up to the mast-head of their flag-ship soared.
On one side knelt the Holy Mother-maid.
    On one the crucified Redeemer poured
His blood, and all their kneeling hosts adored
    Their saints, and clouds of incense heavenward streamed
While pomp of cannonry and pike and sword
    Down long sea-lanes of mocking menace gleamed
Mocking the cross they bore, on seas that darkly dreamed.

Who comes to fight for England?   Is it ye,
    Six little straws that dance upon the foam?
Ay, sweeping o'er the sunset-crimsoned sea
    Let the proud pageant in its glory come,

Leaving the sunset like a hecatomb
    Of souls whose bodies yet endure the chain!
Let slaves, by thousands, branded, scarred and dumb,
    In those dark galleys grip their oars again,
And o'er the crouching deep bring on the pomp of Spain.

Bring on the pomp of royal paladins
    (For all the princedoms of the land are there!)
And for the gorgeous purple of their sins
    The papal pomp bring on with psalm and prayer.
Nearer the splendour heaves.   Can ye not hear
    The rushing foam, not see the blazoned arms,
And black-faced hosts thro' leagues of golden air
    Crowding the decks, muttering their beads and charms
To where, in furthest heaven, they thicken like locust swarms?

Bring on the pomp and pride of old Castille.
    Blazon the skies with royal Aragon.
Beneath Oquendo let old ocean reel.
    All Andalusia's armoured pride bring on.
And let her censers dusk the dying sun,
    The thunder of her banners on the breeze
Following Sidonia's glorious galleon
    Deride the sleeping thunder of the seas,
While sunset-smouldering armies chant her litanies.

Their gorgeous decks are kneeling!   Sky to sky
    Responds!   It is their solemn evening hour.
SALVE REGINA, though the daylight die,
    SALVE REGINA, though the darkness lour;
Have they not still the kingdom and the power?
    SALVE REGINA, all their thousands cry,
From where like clouds to where like mountains tower
    Their crowded galleons looming far or nigh.
SALVE REGINA CŒLI, what far seas reply!

What distant seas, what distant ages hear?
    Bring on the pomp!   The sun of Spain goes down.
The moon but swells the tide of praise and prayer.
    Bring on the world-wide pomp of her renown.
Let darkness crown her with a starrier crown,
    And let her watch the fierce waves crouch and fawn
Round those huge hulks from which her cannon frown,
    While close inshore the wet sea-mists are drawn
Round England's Drake: then wait, in triumph, for the dawn.

But through the misty darkness, close inshore,
North-west, south-west, and ever westward strained
The little ships of England.   All night long,
As down the coast the reddening beacons leapt,
The crackle and lapping splash of tacking keels,
The bo'suns' low sharp whistles and the whine
Of ropes, mixing with many a sea-bird's cry
Disturbed the darkness, waking vague swift fear
Among the turreted hulks of Spain that lay
Nearest, then fading through the mists inshore
North-west, then growing again, but farther down
Their ranks to westward with each dark return
And dark departure, till the rearmost rank
Of grim sea-castles heard the swish and creak
Pass plashing seaward thro' the wet sea-mists
To windward now of all that monstrous host,
Then heard no more than wandering sea-birds' cries
Wheeling around their leagues of lanthorn-light,
Or heave of waters, waiting for the dawn.

Dawn, everlasting and almighty dawn
   Walked on the waters.   The grey mists were fled.
From north to south, in menacing crescent drawn,
   The Armada's bannered spars and sails outspread,
Cloud upon cloud of darkness, drenched with red,
   Would still withstand the march of brightening skies,
Would still bring back the night, though night was dead,—
   While, out to windward, what bright sails arise,
What fearless morning burns in England's waking eyes!

There, on the glittering plains of open sea,
   To windward now, behind the fleet of Spain,
Two little files of ships are tossing free,
   Free of the winds and of the wind-swept main.
Were they not trapped?   Who led them forth again,
   To challenge the Unconquerable in war,
With sails like blossoms shining after rain,
   And guns that sparkle to the morning star?
Drake!—first upon the deep that rolls to Trafalgar!

And Spain knows well that flag of fiery fame.
   Spain knows by whom St George's cross is flown.
Low as the south-west wind his whispered name
   El Draque, across her crowded decks is blown.
But, here, the seas grow dark beneath her throne;

And, though the sea-wolves crouch, they dare not leap.
The might of heaven and hell is all her own.
    Her God hath given her all his keys to keep.
She sails in absolute power, upon her subject deep.

Yet—the sea-wolves draw nearer!   Nay, prepare,
    As even Goliath must, when fools draw nigh.
Madness itself would shrink; but Drake will dare
    Eternal hell!   Let the great signal fly,—
Close up your ranks.   El Draque comes down to die!
    El Draque is brave!   The vast sea-cities loom
Through heaven.   Spain spares one smile of chivalry,
    One wintry smile across her cannons' gloom
As that frail fleet, full-sail, comes rushing to its doom.

At once, as in the wild change of a dream,
Even as the Spaniards watched those daring prows
Leap straight at their huge hulks, watched well content,
Knowing their foe, once grappled, could but die;
Even as they caught the rush and hiss of foam
Across that narrow, dwindling gleam of sea,
And heard, abruptly close, the sharp commands
And drawled west-country answers, caught one glimpse
Of seamen crouching by their loaded guns,
The vision changed!   The ships of England swerved
Swiftly.   A volley of leaping flame and iron
From four full broadsides into a Spanish hulk
Crashed.   She reeled to leeward.   Before her guns
Could train upon her enemy, the thick smoke
Shrouding the sea, was rent by a redder volley
That stunned her, like a shattering hammer-blow.
She heeled.   Her cannon wounded the void air;
For, as by miracle, the ships of Drake
Vanished.   Behind the Spanish ships they flew
From north to south, raking them as they went
At close range, hardly a pistol-shot away.
Too near, too low, for the Spaniard's ponderous guns,
They sailed two knots to one.   Then swinging round
And volleying iron and death, from south to north,
Along the same fierce road, littered with spars,
Behind the fleet of Spain, their rushing sails
Returned in triumph, upon the south-west wind.

Then, then, from north to south, one mighty surge
    Of baleful pride, huge wrath, stormy disdain,

With shuddering clouds and towers of sail would urge
    Onward the heaving citadels of Spain,
    Which dragged earth's legions over the groaning main
    And held the panoplies of heaven in fee,
Beating against the wind, struggling in vain
    To close with that swift ocean-cavalry.
Spain had all earth in charge!   Had England, then, the sea?

Spain had the mountains—mountains flow like clouds.
    Spain had great kingdoms—kingdoms melt away!
Yet, in that crescent, army on army crowds.
    How shall *she* fear what seas or winds can say?—
The seas that leap and shine round earth's decay,
    The winds that mount and sing while empires fall,
And mountains pass like waves in the wind's way,
    And dying gods thro' shuddering twilights call.
Had England, then, the sea that sweeps o'er one and all?

See, in gigantic wrath the *Rata* hurls
    Her mighty prows round to the wild sea-wind:
The deep like one black maelstrom round her swirls
    While great Recalde follows hard behind:
Reeling, like Titans, lightning blasted, blind,
    They strive to bring the ships of Drake to bay,
Challenge them to the grapple, and only find
    Red broadsides bursting over the bursting spray,
And England sailing still, along her windward way!

To windward still *Revenge* and *Raleigh* flash
    And volley, and the sea flames red between.
In vain against the wind the galleons crash
    And plunge and pour blind volleys thro' the screen
Of drifting smoke at topsails dimly seen
    And ships that to and fro like sea-birds fly.
Ever to leeward the great hulks careen.
    Their thousand cannon can but wound the sky,
While England's little *Rainbow* foams and flashes by.

At last Recalde's flag-ship broke away
Alone, hoping this wild-cat foe would dare
To grapple her.   At once the little *Revenge*,
With Drake's flag flying, flashed at her throat,
And hardly a cable's-length away delivered
Broadside on broadside, under those grim guns,
Raking her shattered hull, four shots to one,

While Howard and the rest swept to and fro
Striving to keep at bay the hulks that plunged
Desperately against the freshening wind
To rescue their tall flag-ship from El Draque.

Sidonia comes!   Toledo comes!—proud ranks
    That rally against the storm from sky to sky,
As down the long blood-rusted chain-locked planks
    Of labouring galleys the dark slave-guards ply
Their knotted scourges, and the red flakes fly
    The bare scarred bodies that quiver and heave once more,
And slaves that heed not if they live or die
    Pull with numbed arms at many a red-stained oar,
Urging the might of Spain against the sea's deep roar.

Oquendo comes!   The seas are cloaked with gloom
    Of towering sails in arrogant array.
His haughty prows through heaven begin to loom.
    The ships of England flash and dart away:
Not England's heart can hold that host at bay.
    A swift light signal flutters down her line.
Her ships are scattered and driven in clouds of spray.
    A thousand cannon rake the spouting brine
And, round Recalde's wrath, Sidonia's bulwarks shine.

The wild sea-winds with golden trumpets blaze!
    One wave will wash away the crimson stain
That blots Recalde's decks.   Her first amaze
    Is over: down the Channel once again
Turns the triumphant pageantry of Spain
    In battle-order, now.   Behind her, far,
While the broad sun sinks to the western main
    The ships of Freedom form anew for war
And over them in heaven awakes the first white star.

The sun goes down.   The heart of Spain is proud.
    Her censers fume, her golden trumpets blow!
Into the darkening east with cloud on cloud
    Of broad-flung sail her tall sea-castles go.
Rich under blazoned poops like rose-flushed snow
    Tosses the foam.   Far off the sunset gleams.
Her banners like a thousand sunsets glow,
    As down the darkening east the pageant streams,
Full-fraught with doom for England, rigged with princely dreams.

Nay, "rigged with curses dark," as over the waves
Drake watched them slowly sweeping into the gloom
That thickened down the Channel, ranks compact
With Biscay's bristling broad-beamed squadron drawn
Behind for rear-guard.   As the sun went down
Drake flew the council-flag.   Across the sea,
Smoothed now to an oily surge of rose and green,
Up to the little *Revenge* the pinnaces foamed.

They gathered on Drake's powder-blackened ship,
Frobisher, Effingham, many a shining name,
And many a lean adventurer, gazing east
With faces dark as iron against the sky
And eyes that flashed like sword-flames as they turned
Against the setting sun, or deep as night
Followed the Armada where it slowly mixed
Its broad-flung sails with darkness.

                                        "My Lord Howard,"
Said Drake, "We have no more than pricked the skins
Of those bull-whales.   The hour grows late for England.
'Twere well to handle them at once."
                                        His voice
Carried the seamen with him; but Lord Howard
Coldly replied—"If we attack them now
We imperil our whole fleet.   The sport is good;
But if we lose, the price we pay is England.
I dare not risk it.   We have fought all day,
Accomplished nothing.   Food and powder are spent.
I think it best to hang upon their flanks
Till we be reinforced.
                            "My Lord," said Drake,
"Had we that week to spare for which I prayed,
And were we handling them in Spanish seas,
We might delay.   There is no choosing now.
In twelve more hours that Fleet Invincible
Will join its powers with Parma's thirty thousand.
If you would check that avalanche of arms
From overwhelming England, fight at sea.
There's powder enough in yonder enemy's fleet;
And shot enough we shall find, though we should pluck it
Out of our own ship's beams to feed our guns.
Blame not the Queen for aught that she withholds.
How could she trust this wide new realm of hers,
When even her seamen doubt.   She dreams of Crecy

And knights in armour still.   I think I see her
Riding upon her milk-white Barbary mare,
Before her pikes at Tilbury; hear her voice,
'My people, though this flesh of mine be woman,
My heart is of your kingly lion's breed,
I come myself to lead you!'   Blame her not;
But look not to the Queen.   This night, my friends,
Her seamen claim her kingdom.   We have known
Victories, never victory like to this;
When, in our England's darkest hour of need,
Her seamen, without wage, or arms, or food,
Are yet on fire to fight for her.   Your ships
Tossing in this great sunset of an Empire,
Dawn of a sovereign people, are all manned
By heroes, ragged, hungry, who will die
By scores ere long.   Their very food is carrion
Not fit for dogs.   They are half-naked, hopeless,
Living, of any reward; if they die
They die a dog's death.   We shall reap the fame
While they reap only famine.
                              They will be served
Six at the mess of four, eking it out
With what their own rude nets may catch at night.
They earn no silver but the herring scales
That I have seen so often, silvering their decks
Under the stars with silver past all price.
My Lord, it is a terrible thing for Spain
When poor men thus go out against her princes;
For so God whispers Victory in our ears,
I cannot dare to doubt it."

                       As he ceased
Hawkins cried out—"I stand by Francis Drake";
But Howard, clinging to his old-world order,
Sturdily shook his head.   "I dare not risk
A close attack.   Once grappled we are lost.
We'll follow hard upon their trail, with Drake
Leading.   Our oriflamme to-night shall be
His cresset and stern-lanthorn.   Where that shines
We follow."

                       Drake, still thinking in his heart,—
"And if Spain be not shattered here and now
We are lost no less," must even rest content
With that good vantage.

                    As the sunset died
Over the darkling emerald seas that swelled
Before the freshening wind, the pinnaces dashed
To their own ships; and into the mind of Drake
There stole a plot that twitched his lips to a smile.
Under the glimmer of firm and full-blown sails
He stared at his stern-cresset's crimson flare,
The star of all the shadowy ships that plunged
Like ghosts amid the grey stream of his wake.
High over him he heard the low keen song
Of hidden ropes above the wail and creak
Of blocks and long low swish of cloven foam,—
A keen rope-music in the formless night,
A harmony, a strong intent good sound,
Well-strung and taut, singing the will of man.
"Your oriflamme," he muttered,—"so you travail
With sea-speech in the tongue of old Poictiers—
Shall be my own stern-lanthorn.   Watch it well,
My good Lord Howard."

                    Eastward, one by one
Out of the gloom before them slowly crept,
Sinister gleam by gleam, like blood-red stars,
The rearmost lanthorns of the Spanish Fleet,
A shaggy purple sky of secret storm
Heaving from north to south.   Once more with lips
Twitched to a smile, Drake suddenly bade them crowd
All sail on his *Revenge*.   Smiling he watched
The widening gap, until he knew her light,
To all the ships behind, must be confused
With those of Spain.   Then, with a chuckle, he cried:
"Quick, master bo'sun, quench their oriflamme,
Dip their damned cresset in the good black sea
And let them follow the rearmost light of Spain.
Pray God they come to blows!"
                    The bo'sun grinned.
His cresset-flare went out in the thick night.
A fluttering as of blind bewildered moths
A moment seized upon the shadowy ships
Behind him, then with crowded sail they steered
Straight for the rearmost cresset-flare of Spain.

BOOK X

MEANWHILE, as in the dark Drake slipped aside
Waiting the crash of battle, he grew aware
Of strange sails bearing up into the wind
And thought, "Spain tries to weather us."   He gave chase
Until the moon rose, and the ghostly ships
With every block and spar cut sharp and black
As ebony on an opal-clouded sky
Stood out as Flemish merchantmen, amazed
With fears of Armageddon—such vast shrouds
Had lately passed them on the heaving sea.
Eastward, before the wind, the little *Revenge*
Leapt on the trail.   The beacons on the coast
Died.   The wind slackened.   The wide East turned grey,
And reddened, and he could not sight his fleet;
But, right in front, dark in the dazzle of dawn,
And helplessly becalmed in that light wind,
Drifted a tall ship, gloriously enscrolled
Señora del Rosario, the proud
Flag-ship of Andalusia.   On her poop,
Her two score officers clustered like a cloud
Of darker colour; great land-admirals they,
Doubleted in rich cramoisy, wreathed
With chains of gold, and sparkling when they moved
With little points of fire on breast and hand.
They challenged the *Revenge* as she drew near.
"What fool commands yon herring boat?—"

                                        "El Draque!
And in much haste!"

                    "El Draque!"   At that grim shout
A wild-eyed panic seized the Spanish crew.
They heard no more commands.   Down came their flag
Like a great smouldering fragment of the dawn
And lay in a crumpled cloud on their proud deck.

Into the soft bloom and Italian blue
Of sparkling ever-beautiful Torbay
Sailed the *Revenge* that noon with her new prize;
A prize indeed,—not for the gold moidores
Which Drake—that wicked pirate—tossed to his crew;
But for the powder and shot in her deep hold
More precious now than rubies.   Into the care
Of trusty Brixham fishermen he gave

All that could not be stowed in the *Revenge*.
Then, out to sea, they swooped in his white wake,
Sea-hawks, exultant at the sea-king's call,
To hunt their prey.
         'Twas sundown when he saw
The Armada's dusky fleet of phantoms, ranged
From north to south; with Howard's clustered ships
Drifting behind them, like small clouds becalmed.
The last breath of the wind, as Drake drew nigh,
Failed his own sails. The sun went down. The moon
Rose glittering. Hardly a cannon-shot apart
The two fleets floated on the silver tide.
Then—then—Spain thought her conquering hour had come.
For all those little ships, whose only strength
Was in their flying sails, helplessly drifted,
While Spain's great hulks, oared by their thousand slaves
Could turn at last and grapple them.
              On they came,
Swinging back suddenly in tremendous gloom
Over the silver calm. But even as Drake
With eyes on fire at last for his last fight
Measured the distance ere his guns could speak,
The sails all shivered and filled from the north-east.
His ships were on the wing. Out, out to sea
Like herring-gulls they flew before the wind
But not too swift; for in the mind of Drake
A fiercer plan was forming. He laughed low
As he looked back and heard a shout that rose
From twenty thousand throats, "They fly! They fly!"
And towering, crowding, plunging down the wind
The Spanish Fleet gave chase.
            The tempter, Drake,
Laughed low to watch them straggle, some swift, some slow,
And great gaps growing between them as they sailed.
All night the chase held on. When morning broke
Dazzling the Channel, it found the ships of Spain
Strung out like lonely islands, with broad seas
Roughening between them. Down, like a hawk, swooped Drake,
Where the *San Marcos*, that sea Titan, heaved
Her scutcheoned flanks alone, having out-sailed
All her companions. Then the sea-wind flared
With broadsides. Two long hours the sea flared red
While, one by one, the laggard ships beat up
To save her, and only met the buffeting blast

Of flame and iron, till huge Oquendo drove
His prows athwart the thunder.
                                    Then, once more,
Regathered into unshakeable battle order,
The whole Armada raked the reeling sea;
And up the wind the ships of England steered
Still holding Spain to leeward, but still foiled,
With little accomplished, half their powder spent,
While that Invincible Fleet—although three ships
Limped woundily,—turned, and moved on its grim path
Like destiny in doom— One heaven-wide zone
Of menacing storm—to join with Parma's host
And hurl half Europe on our little isle.
A little before sunset, once again
Drake flew the council flag. 'Twas growing dark
When Frobisher, Howard and Hawkins came aboard.
With face thrust close to Howard's, and out stretched arm
Under the stars, Drake pointed down the coast
Where the red beacons flared.
                                    "The shoals," he said,
"From Owers to Spithead! By the break of day
They'll lie to leeward of the Invincible Fleet.
And it may prove—not all Invincible!
We'll tempt the Armada down upon the shoals
And let the sea-wind shatter it.   Wind and sea
And the one Power that moves them, never our own,
Can win this war."   And, as he spoke, it seemed
The Power breathed through him.   Swiftly he bared his plan
Where plan before was none.   And so, at dawn,
The heart of Spain exulted, seeing the fleet
Of England now divided—as they hoped—
By jealousy or discord.   A fresh gale
Blew from the grey south-east.   Lord Howard's ships
To leeward, twixt the Armada and the shoals
Came out against the Spaniards, as though bent
To grapple them in blind fury, and make an end;
While, on the windward flank, the ships of Drake
Stood out to sea, as if in stark revolt
From that sheer madness.   Nearer the mad ships came.
Behind them gleamed, half-hidden in morning mist,
The menacing shark-white shoals.   The Spanish guns
Flashed out at Howard's onset; and still Drake
Stood out to sea.   Sidonia saw him go.
Rich was the omen of that day for Spain,
The feast-day of Sidonia's patron saint;

Victorious flags rose up, and trumpets blew,
And, like a moving mountain range his fleet
Bore down on Howard and the unseen shoals.
The lion's brood was in the imperial net
Of Spain at last.   Onward the mountains came
With all their dawn-flushed clouds of towering sail,
And flags like streaming cataracts in the sun,
And bugles echoing over glorious chasms
Calling and answering like the herald winds
That blow the silver trumpets of the morning
From Skiddaw to Helvellyn.   Howard's ships
Fell slowly back.   Their own thick smoke concealed
The mouse-trap of the shoals.   Their cannon drowned
The brawling of the surf.   On all their decks
The Spaniards made them ready with cold steel
And grappling irons.   Then like a thunder bolt,
To windward, Drake, returning, swooped and struck.
His cannon roared behind them, and the shoals
The menacing shark-white shoals crept out in front.
The ships of Howard, like sea-mews sheered away,
While Spain's deep-draughted galleons like a herd
Of Titan bullocks, with the foam of death
Flecking their desperate flanks, staggered and swerved
Careening towards that death-trap as they turned.
Then, in one wild stampede, seaward they swirled
With close-hauled sails, while all the grey sea plain
Smoked round them, and the cannonades of Drake
Raked them with chain-shot.
                                        Out, out, out to sea,
Narrowly weathering the grim banks they plunged.
Resolved at last, never to swerve again
From their dread path and solid end, to join
With Parma, and to hurl his armoured host
Against our isle.   With scarce a visible scar
The Invincible Fleet moved on.   And yet—strange fears
Were gathering in Sidonia's haughty soul,
As all day long the shadowy ships of Drake
Held steadily to his trail.
                                        By Calais cliffs,
Thinking to shake those blood hounds off, at dusk
The Armada anchored, hoping that the wind
Would carry our ships to leeward, unaware.
The grim, insistent watch of Drake was ready.
He, too, though hardly a cannon-shot away
Anchored, to windward still.

                              Stormily heaved
The ghostly chalk-grey seas in that great hour
While Hawkins, Howard, and Frobisher laid their plot
With Drake, on his *Revenge;* and, far away,
Through Spain, already, like a triumphing fire
The rumour flew that her Invincible Fleet
Had crushed its enemies, and "that great black dog
Sir Francis Drake" was writhing on the rack
Under the torturer's hands.
                              Dark on his deck
He stood, a granite rock, amid the throng
Of captains and the clashing waves of thought.
Silent, he gazed where now the increasing gale
Blew steadily to the north.   The dark North Sea,
Rolled into a darker night, unfathomable,
Under great flying clouds.   His lips moved, once,
As under a spell, murmuring inaudibly
The clouds, His chariot.
                              Pondering, he turned
And looked at many a ship, helpless in fight,
Weaponed with muskets, manned by the brave zeal
Of dwellers on the coast, who every hour
From every fishing-port raced to join his flag.
"They'll light our road to victory yet," he cried.
Then, once again, he drew his battle-plan:
"We'll set two hundred fishing-craft ablaze
With pitch, and loose them on the south-west wind,
To burn the Spaniard out of his anchorage.
A hurricane is coming, sirs.   He'll need
Seamen, not men-at-arms, in the North Sea;
He'll never ride it."   In the thickening gloom
They stared at his grim face, as at a man
Risen from the grave, with universal powers.
While, in a low deep voice that quietly blent
With the ebb and flow of the sea, his loaded words,
Aimed level as cannon, spoke the doom of Spain.

That night, on all her ships a cold fear crept;
   And, where the long dark sea-line met the sky,
Strange flickers, phantoms of the fires that leapt
   At Alva's bidding, lit the clouds on high!
And fearful wraiths of men arrayed to die
   In robes of yellow, writhing through the flame,
Wreathed with a redder smoke, drew slowly nigh:

Till, through the smoke, in wrath that none could tame
Borne on the south-west wind, the roaring fire-ships came!

Blazing with pitch, till all the blood-red foam
    To windward flares with shuddering witch-like fires.
On, on, across the lit strange waves they come
    With smoke-wreathed spars and masts like burning spires
Red hulks of fury, monstrous crackling pyres
    Fierce as the flames that Torquemada fed,
The flames that shrieked above the chanting choirs
    In old Madrid, when street and square shone red,
And, in the name of Christ, men smote the thorn-crowned head.

Thick as the ghosts that Dante saw in hell,
    Whirled on the livid air through leagues of pain,
Thick, thick as wind-blown leaves innumerable
    Pale twisted phantoms from the racks of Spain
Streamed through the flying cloud and fiery rain
    With bloodless hands outstretched upon the blast,
All pointing northward, as they shrieked again
    High over crackling spar and flame-licked mast,
We wait you in the North; and, like a storm, they passed.

And still the great wind hurls across the night
    The fierce pitch-furnace and the blood-red hail
Blinding and searing eyes and hands that fight
    Through smoke and fire to hoist a smouldering sail;
And still the blood-red furies ride the gale
    And laugh and shout in mockery—"Swift!   Cut free!
Cut your scorched cables!   Cry!   Reel backward!   Quail!
    Ay, huddled and driven like herded bullocks, flee!
Behind you roars the fire!   Before—the dark North Sea."

Dawn, staining all those myriads of white crests,
Tempestuously beautiful arose.
The ships of Spain, great ragged piles of gloom
And shaggy splendour, leaning to the North
In scattered squadrons, furiously plunged,
Wallowing like whales harpooned, or heaving high
Their giant bowsprits to the flying cloud,
Burying their mighty prows in the broad grey rush
Of smoking billowy seas, labouring in vain
To beat back southward, struggling in vain to lock
Their scattered ranks anew, but drifting still

Straight for the dark North Sea.

Hard by there lurched
One scutcheoned galleon on the ravening shoals,
Feeding the white maw of the famished waves
With gold and purple webs from kingly looms,
The spilth of a world's empire.

Howard still
Planning to pluck the Armada plume by plume,
Bore down upon that prey, and swiftly engaged
Her desperate guns; while Drake, our deep-sea king,
Knowing the full worth of that conquering hour,
Signalled the rest to follow his *Revenge*.
Unswervingly, with calm implacable face
Gazing as thro' all history, he steered
The crowded glory of his dawn-flushed sails
In superb onset, straight for the great Fleet
Invincible; and, after him, the main
Of England's fleet, knowing its captain now,
Followed, and with them rushed the storm's white waves.
For now, behind this war of nations, moved
The Might that moves the universe, a Power
Beyond man's thought; as, under the clash of waves
And flash of foam, huge glooms of ocean move,
Silent, invisible, undisturbed by storm,
But massed, controlled and drawn by darkling heavens
In rhythmic tides to their own timeless end.

But northward, northward still the storm's white waves
Rushed with Drake's ships, glittering companions,
And poured their volleys on the windward flanks
Of Spain, whose weltering galleons as they swirled
Heavily back before the sweeping seas
With all their grinding, wrenching cannon, worked
On rolling platforms by the helpless hands
Of twenty thousand soldiers, barked at clouds
Or crashed their broadsides into the black-troughed waves;
While all Drake's levelled guns, as he swooped nigh,
Pounded their great sea-castles, east and west,
Pounded their floating streets and timbered towns
To huddle them on their centre,—cities of shame
And havoc, in fiery forests of tangled wrath;
For, when a galleon sank, there came a cry
As if a distant kingdom had gone down
And earthquake-smitten palaces were engulfed
Beyond the sea-horizon.

One huge carved hulk,
Listing to sink, with all her swarthy crew,
A Devonshire privateer foamed up to save.
"Down arms, and come aboard," her captain cried.
A hail of bullets answered; and he fell
Paying in full for the old sea chivalry.
Sink or destroy! The deadly signal flew
From mast to mast of England. Once, twice, thrice,
A blind sea-fortress heaved her haggled bulk
And with one cry from all her crowded decks,
And one long muttering roar, as into the whirl
Of chaos yawning, sank. The slopes of the sea
A moment swarmed with struggling insect men,
Then scrambling surf and the great grey smoking waves
Hid them forever. Here a galleasse poured
Blood and green brine through scuppers and torn flanks;
And there a galleon, wrapped in creeping fire,
Suddenly like a great volcano flared
And shot to the sky a fountain of red flame,
Speckled with blocks and spars, like small black flies.
Hardly the thrust of a pike away, the ships
Of England flashed and swerved, till in one mass
Of wild death-stricken splendour and struggling gloom
The Armada shrank together. The pride that once
Had burned along the tempest of her banners
Withered, as on a murderer's face the light
Withers before the accuser. Its guns up-turned
Black helpless mouths.
                    Sink or Destroy! All day
The deadly signal flew, and ever the storm
Drove the grim battle northward, to the night
And Those who waited there. . . . At set of sun
That queenly ship so gloriously enscrolled
Santa Maria, uttering one wild cry,
Went down, with all hands, into the swallowing dark.
Hardly five rounds of shot were left to Drake.
Gun after gun fell silent, as the night
Deepened—"Yet we must follow them to the North,"
He cried, "or they'll return yet to shake hands
With Parma! Come, we'll put a brag upon it,
And harry them on as though we lacked for nought!"
So, when across the swinging smoking seas,
Grey and splendid and terrible broke the day
Once more, the flying Invincible Fleet beheld
Close on their weather-beam, steadily dogging them,

Like their own shadow, the dark ships of Drake,
Unswerving and implacable.   Ever the wind
And sea increased; till now the heaving waste
Swelled all around them into sulky hills,
Dark rolling mountains, whose majestic crests
Slowly and savagely crumbling into foam
Swept through the clouds; and, on their vanishing slopes,
Past the pursuing fleet began to swirl
Bodies of horses or mules, drowning or drowned,
That should have marched with Spain's victorious arms
Through England, now cast overboard to save
Her water-casks and lighten her flying ships,
A trail of utter terror.   And still the storm
Howled on her blind hulks, plunging to the North,
With all their splintered spars, like antlered stags
Chased by the wolves.   Off the dark Firth of Forth
At last, Drake signalled and lay head to wind,
Watching.   "The chariots of God are twenty thousand,"
He muttered, while, for a moment, close at hand,
Caught in a league-wide maelstrom of black water
Two weltering galleons crowded and towered and plunged
Above him, on a seething slope of sea
As if to trample him down into the night.
The next, a mile of surf had swept between,
And all those dwindling citadels were driven
With all their shrivelling scrolls of midget sail,
Away to the waiting North.
                              From sky to sky
The trampling, tossing tumult of the sea
Followed them—broad white cataracts, waves that grasped
With struggling Titan hands at reeling heavens,
And roared their doom-fraught greetings from Cape Wrath
Round to the Bloody Foreland.
                              There should the yeast
Of foam receive the purple of many kings,
And the grim gulfs devour the blood-bought gold
Of Aztecs and of Incas, and the reefs,
League after league, bristle with mangled spars;
While murderous kerns, on that wild sea-coast, stript
The silks and chains and jewel-encrusted rings
From thousands dead, and slaughtered thousands more
With gallow-glass axes, as they blindly crept
Out of the brawling surf.
                              To meet that end
Drake watched their sails go dwindling, till the last

Flicker of spars vanished as a skeleton leaf
Upon the blasts of winter, and there was nought
But one wild wilderness of splendour and gloom
Under the northern clouds.

                "Not unto us,"
Behind locked lips his inmost spirit cried
Silently, "unto Him who made the sea,
Belongs our England now!   Only to Him
Belongs this victory, whose ocean-fame
Shall wash the world with thunder till that day
When there is no more sea, and the strong cliffs
Pass like a smoke, and the last peal of it
Sounds through the trumpet."

                So, with close-hauled sails,
Over the rolling triumph of the deep,
Lifting their hearts to heaven, they turned back home.

THE ISLAND HAWK

HUSHED are the whimpering winds on the hill,
    Dumb is the shrinking plain,
And the songs that enchanted the woods are still
    As I shoot to the skies again!
Does the blood grow black on my fierce bent beak,
    Does the down still cling to my claw?
Who brightened these eyes for the prey they seek?
    Life, I follow thy law!
        For I am the hawk, the hawk, the hawk!
          Who knoweth my pitiless breast?
        Who watcheth me sway in the wild wind's way?
        Flee—flee—for I quest, I quest.

As I glide and glide with my peering head,
    Or swerve at a puff of smoke,
Who watcheth my wings on the wind outspread,
    Here—gone—with an instant stroke?
Who toucheth the glory of life I feel
    As I buffet this great glad gale,
Spire and spire to the cloud-world, wheel,
    Loosen my wings and sail?
        For I am the hawk, the island hawk,
          Who knoweth my pitiless breast?
        Who watcheth me sway in the sun's bright way?
        Flee—flee—for I quest, I quest.

My mate in the nest on the high bright tree
   Blazing with dawn and dew,
She knoweth the gleam of the world and the glee
   As I drop like a bolt from the blue.
She knoweth the fire of the level flight
   As I skim, close, close to the ground,
With the long grass lashing my breast and the bright
   Dew-drops flashing around.
         She watcheth the hawk, the hawk, the hawk
            (Oh, the red-blotched eggs in the nest!)
         Watcheth him sway in the sun's bright way.
         Flee—flee—for I quest, I quest.

She builded her nest on the high bright wold,
   She was taught in a world afar
The lore that is only an April old
   Yet old as the evening star.
Life of a far off ancient day
   In an hour unhooded her eyes.
In the time of the budding of one green spray
   She was wise as the stars are wise.
         An eyas in eyry, a yellow-eyed hawk,
            On the old elm's burgeoning breast,
         She watcheth me sway in the wild wind's way.
         Flee—flee—for I quest, I quest.

She hath ridden on white Arabian steeds
   Thro' the ringing English dells,
For the joy of a great queen, hunting in state,
   To the music of golden bells.
A queen's fair fingers have drawn the hood
   And tossed her aloft in the blue,
A white hand eager for needless blood.
   I hunt for the needs of two.
         A haggard in yarak, a hawk, a hawk!
            Who knoweth my pitiless breast?
         Who watcheth me sway in the sun's bright way?
         Flee—flee—for I quest, I quest.

Who fashioned her wide and splendid eyes
   That have stared in the eyes of kings?
With a silken twist she was looped to their wrist:
   She has clawed at their jewelled rings!
Who flung her first thro' the crimson dawn
   To pluck him a prey from the skies,

When the love-light shone upon lake and lawn
  In the valleys of Paradise?
    Who fashioned the hawk, the hawk, the hawk,
      Bent beak and pitiless breast?
    Who watcheth him sway in the wild wind's way?
    Flee—flee—for I quest, I quest.

Is there ever a song in all the world
  Shall say how the quest began
With the beak and the wings that have made us kings
  And cruel—almost—as man?
The wild wind whimpers across the heath
  Where the sad little tufts of blue
And the red-stained grey little feathers of death
  Flutter!   *Who fashioned us?   Who?*
    Who fashioned the scimitar wings of the hawk,
      Bent beak and arrowy breast?
    Who watcheth him sway in the sun's bright way?
    Flee—flee—for I quest, I quest.

THE TRAMP TRANSFIGURED

(AN EPISODE IN THE LIFE OF A CORN-FLOWER MILLIONAIRE.)

ALL the way to Fairyland across the thyme and heather,
  Round a little bank of fern that rustled on the sky,
Me and stick and bundle, sir, we jogged along together,—
  (Changeable the weather?   Well, it ain't all pie!)
Just about the sunset—Won't you listen to my story?—
  Look at me!   I'm only rags and tatters to your eye!
Sir, that blooming sunset crowned this battered hat with glory!
  Me that was a crawling worm became a butterfly,
      (Ain't it hot and dry?
  Thank you, sir, thank you, sir!) a blooming butterfly.

Well, it happened this way!   I was lying loose and lazy,
  Just as of a Sunday, you yourself might think no shame,
Puffing little clouds of smoke, and picking at a daisy,
  Dreaming of your dinner, p'raps, or wishful for the same:
Suddenly, around that ferny bank there slowly waddled—
  Slowly as the finger of a clock her shadow came—
Slowly as a tortoise down that winding path she toddled,

Leaning on a crookéd staff, a poor old crookéd dame,
   Limping, but not lame,
 Tick, tack, tick, tack, a poor old crookéd dame.

Slowly did I say, sir? Well, you've heard that funny fable
 Consekint the tortoise and the race it give an 'are?
This was curiouser than that! At first I wasn't able
 Quite to size the memory up that bristled thro' my hair:
Suddenly, I'd got it, with a nasty shivery feeling,
 While she walked and walked and yet was not a bit more near,—
Sir, it was the tread-mill earth beneath her feet a-wheeling
 Faster than her feet could trot to heaven or anywhere,
   Earth's revolvin' stair
 Wheeling, while my wayside clump was kind of anchored there.

Tick, tack, tick, tack, and just a little nearer,
 Inch and 'arf an inch she went, but never gained a yard.
Quiet as a fox I lay; I didn't wish to scare 'er,
 Watching thro' the ferns, and thinking "What a rum old card!"
Both her wrinkled tortoise eyes with yellow resin oozing,
 Both her poor old bony hands were red and seamed and scarred!
Lord, I felt as if myself was in a public boozing,
 While my own old woman went about and scrubbed and charred!
   Lord, it seemed so hard!
 Tick, tack, tick, tack, she never gained a yard.

Yus, and there in front of her—I hadn't seen it rightly—
 Lurked that little finger-post to point another road,
Just a tiny path of poppies twisting infi-nite-ly
 Through the whispering seas of wheat, a scarlet thread that showed
White with ox-eye daisies here and there and chalky cobbles,
 Blue with waving corn-flowers: far and far away it glowed,
Winding into heaven, I thinks; but, Lord, the way she hobbles,
 Lord, she'll never reach it, for she bears too great a load;
   Yus, and then I knowed,
 If she did, she couldn't, for the board was marked *No Road.*

Tick, tack, tick, tack, I couldn't wait no longer!
 Up I gets and bows polite and pleasant as a toff—
"Arternoon," I says, "I'm glad your boots are going stronger;
 Only thing I'm dreading is your feet 'ull both come off."
Tick, tack, tick, tack. She didn't stop to answer.
 "Arternoon," she says, and sort o' chokes a little cough,
"I must get to Piddinghoe to-morrow if I can, sir!"

"Demme, my good woman!   Haw!   Don't think I mean to loff,"
    Says I, like a toff,
"Where d'you mean to sleep to-night?   God made this grass for go'ff."

Tick, tack, tick, tack, and smilingly she eyed me.
    (Dreadful the low cunning of these creechars, don't you think?)
"That's all right!   The weather's bright.   Them bushes there 'ull hide
        me.
    Don't the gorse smell nice?"   I felt my derned old eyelids blink!
"Supper?   I've a crust of bread, a big one, and a bottle,"
    (Just as I expected!   Ah, these creechars always drink!)
"Sugar an' water an' half a pinch of tea to rinse my throttle,
    Then I'll curl up cosy!"—"If you're cotched it means the clink!"
        —"Yus, but don't you think
    If a star should see me, God 'ull tell that star to wink?"

"Now, look here," I says, "I don't know what your blooming age is!"
    "Three-score years and five," she says, "that's five more years to go
Tick, tack, tick, tack, before I gets my wages!"
    "Wages all be damned," I says, "there's one thing that I know—
Gals that stay out late o' nights are sure to meet wi' sorrow.
    Speaking as a toff," I says, "it isn't *comme il faut!*
Tell me why you want to get to Piddinghoe to-morrow."—
    "That was where my son worked, twenty years ago!"—
        "Twenty years ago?
    Never wrote?   May still be there?   Remember you? . . . Just so!"

Yus, it was a drama; but she weren't my long-lost parent!
    Tick, tack, tick, tack, she trotted all the while,
Never getting forrarder, and not the least aware on't,
    Though I stood beside her with a sort of silly smile
Stock-still!   *Tick, tack!*   This blooming world's a bubble:
    There I stood and stared at it, mile on flowery mile,
Chasing o' the sunset.—"Gals are sure to meet wi' trouble
    Staying out o' nights," I says, once more, and tries to smile,
        "Come, that ain't your style.
    Here's a shilling, mother, for to-day I've made my pile!"

Yus, a dozen coppers, all my capital, it fled, sir,
    Representin' twelve bokays that cost me nothink each,
Twelve bokays o' corn-flowers blue that grew beside my bed, sir,
    That same day, at sunrise, when the sky was like a peach:
Easy as a poet's dreams they blossomed round my head, sir,
    All I had to do was just to lift my hand and reach:

145

So, upon the roaring waves I cast my blooming bread, sir,
   Bread I'd earned with nose-gays on the bare-foot Brighton beach,
            Nose-gays *and* a speech,
   All about the bright blue eyes they matched on Brighton beach.

Still, you've only got to hear the bankers on the budget,
   Then you'll know the giving game is hardly "high finance";
Which no more it wasn't for that poor old dame to trudge it,
   Tick, tack, tick, tack, on such a devil's dance:
Crumbs, it took me quite aback to see her stop so humble,
   Casting up into my face a sort of shiny glance,
Bless you, bless you, that was what I thought I heard her mumble,
   Lord, a prayer for poor old Bill, a rummy sort of chance!
            Crumbs, that shiny glance
   Kinder made me king of all the sky from here to France.

Tick, tack, tick, tack, but now she toddled faster:
   Soon she'd reach the little twisted by-way through the wheat.
"Look 'ee here," I says, "young woman, don't you court disaster!
   Peepin' through yon poppies there's a cottage trim and neat,
White as chalk and sweet as turf: wot price a bed for sorrow,
   Sprigs of lavender between the pillow and the sheet?"
"No," she says, "I've got to get to Piddinghoe to-morrow!
   P'raps they'd tell the work'us!   And I've lashings here to eat:
            Don't the gorse smell sweet?" . . .
   Well, I turned and left her plodding on beside the wheat.

Every cent I'd given her like a hero in a story;
   Yet, alone with leagues of wheat I seemed to grow aware
Solomon himself, arrayed in all his golden glory,
   Couldn't vie with Me, the corn-flower king, the millionaire!
How to cash those bright blue cheques that night?   My trouser pockets
   Jingled sudden!   Six more pennies, crept from James knew where!
Crumbs!   I hurried back with eyes just bulging from their sockets,
   Pushed 'em in the old dame's fist and listened for the prayer,
            Shamming not to care,
   Bill—the blarsted chicken-thief, the corn-flower millionaire.

Tick, tack, tick, tack, and faster yet she clattered!
   Ay, she'd almost gained a yard!   I left her once again.
Feeling very warm inside and sort of 'ighly flattered,
   On I plodded, all alone, with hay-stacks in my brain.
Suddenly, with *chink—chink—chink,* the old sweet jingle
   Startled me!   'TWAS THRUPPENCE MORE! three coppers round and
      plain!

146

Lord, temptation struck me and I felt my gullet tingle.
  Then—I hurried back beside them seas of golden grain:
          No, I can't explain;
  There I thrust 'em in her fist, and left her once again.

Tinkle-chink! THREE HA'PENCE! If the vulgar fractions followed,
  Big fleas have little fleas! It flashed upon me there,—
Like the snakes of Pharaoh which the snakes of Moses swallowed
  All the world was playing at the tortoise and the hare:
Half the smallest atom is—my soul was getting tipsy—
  Heaven is one big circle and the centre's everywhere,
Yus, and that old woman was an angel and a gypsy,
  Yus, and Bill, the chicken-thief, the corn-flower millionaire,
          Shamming not to care,
  What was he? A seraph on the misty rainbow-stair!

Don't you make no doubt of it! The deeper that you look, sir,
  All your ancient poets tell you just the same as me,—
What about old Ovid and his most indecent book, sir,
  Morphosising females into flower and star and tree?
What about old Proteus and his 'ighly curious 'abits,
  Mixing of his old grey beard into the old grey sea?
What about old Darwin and the hat that brought forth rabbits,
  Mud and slime that growed into the pomp of Nineveh?
          What if there should be
  One great Power beneath it all, one God in you and me?

Anyway, it seemed to me I'd struck the world's pumphandle!
  "Back with that three ha'pence, Bill," I mutters, "or you're lost."
Back I hurries thro' the dusk where, shining like a candle,
  Pale before the sunset stood that fairy finger-post.
Sir, she wasn't there! I'd struck the place where all roads crost,
All the roads in all the world.
                    She couldn't yet have trotted
  Even to the . . . Hist! a stealthy step behind? A ghost?
Swish! A flying noose had caught me round the neck! Garotted!
  Back I staggered, clutching at the moonbeams, yus, almost
          Throttled! Sir, I boast
  Bill is tough, but . . . when it comes to throttling by a ghost!

  .   .   .   .

    Winged like a butterfly, tall and slender
      Out It steps with the rope on its arm.
    "Crumbs," I says, "all right! I surrender!
      When have I crossed you or done you harm?"

Ef you're a sperrit," I says, "O, crikey,
  Ef you're a sperrit, get hence, vamoose!"
Sweet as music, she spoke—"I'm Psyche!"—
  Choking me still with her silken noose.

Straight at the word from the ferns and blossoms
  Fretting the moon-rise over the downs,
Little blue wings and little white bosoms,
  Little white faces with golden crowns,
Peeped, and the colours came twinkling round me,
  Laughed, and the turf grew purple with thyme,
Danced, and the sweet crushed scents nigh drowned me,
  Sang, and the hare-bells rang in chime.

All around me, gliding and gleaming,
  Fair as a fallen sunset-sky,
Butterfly wings came drifting, dreaming,
  Clouds of the little folk clustered nigh,
Little white hands like pearls uplifted
  Cords of silk in shimmering skeins,
Cast them about me and dreamily drifted,
  Winding me round with their soft warm chains.

Round and round me they dizzily floated,
  Binding me faster with every turn:
Crumbs, my pals would have grinned and gloated
  Watching me over that fringe of fern,
Bill, with his battered old hat outstanding
  Black as a foam-swept rock to the moon,
Bill, like a rainbow of silks expanding
  Into a beautiful big cocoon,—

Big, as a cloud, though his hat still crowned him,
  Yus, and his old boots bulged below:
Seas of colour went shimmering round him,
  Dancing, glimmering, glancing, a-glow!
Bill knew well what them elves were at, sir,—
  Ain't you an en-to-mol-o-gist?
Well, despite of his old black hat, sir,
  Bill was *becoming—a chrysalist.*

. . . .

Muffled, smothered in a sea of emerald and opal,
  Down a dazzling gulf of dreams I sank and sank away,
Wound about with twenty thousand yards of silken rope, all

Shimmering into crimson, glimmering into grey,
Drowsing, waking, living, dying, just as you regards it,
  Buried in a sunset-cloud, or cloud of breaking day,
'Cording as from east or west yourself might look towards it,
  Losing, gaining, lost in darkness, raggéd, grimy, gay,
        'And-cuffed, not to say
  Gagged, but both my shoulders budding, sprouting white as may.

Sprouting like the milky buds o' hawthorn in the night-time,
  Pouting like the snowy buds o' roses in July,
Spreading in my chrysalist and waiting for the right time,
  When—I thought—they'd bust to wings and Bill would rise and fly.
Tick, tack, tick, tack, as if it came in answer,
  Sweeping o'er my head again the tide o' dreams went by,—
I must get to Piddinghoe to-morrow if I can, sir,
  Tick, tack, a crackle in my chrysalist, a cry!
       Then the warm blue sky
  Bust the shell, and out crept Bill—a blooming butterfly.

  .   .   .   .

Blue as a corn-flower, blazed the zenith: the deepening East, like a
    scarlet poppy,
  Burned while, dazzled with golden bloom, white clouds like daisies,
    green seas like wheat,
Gripping the sign-post, first, I climbs, to sun my wings, which were
    wrinkled and floppy,
  Spreading 'em white o'er the words *No Road,* and hanging fast by my
    six black feet.

Still on my head was the battered old beaver, but through it my clubbed
    antennæ slanted
  ("Feelers" yourself would probably call 'em), my battered old boots
    were hardly seen
Under the golden fluff of the tail!   It was Bill, sir, Bill, though highly
    enchanted,
  Spreading his beautiful snow-white pinions, tipped with orange, and
    veined with green.

Yus, old Bill was an Orange-tip, a spirit in glory, a blooming Psyche!
  New, it was new from East to West this rummy old world that I
    dreamed I knew.
How can I tell you the things that I saw with my—what shall *I* call 'em?
    —"feelers?"—O, crikey,
  "FEELERS?" You know how the man born blind described such col-
    ours as scarlet or blue.

"Scarlet," he says, "is the sound of a trumpet, blue is a flute," for he
hasn't a notion!
No, nor nobody living on earth can tell it him plain, if he hasn't the
sight!
That's how it stands with ragged old Bill, a-drift and a-dream on a
measureless ocean,
Gifted wi' fifteen new-born senses, and seeing you blind to their new
strange light.

How can I tell you?   Sir, you must wait, till you die like Bill, ere you
understand it!
Only—I saw—the same as a bee that strikes to his hive ten leagues
away—
Straight as a die, while I winked and blinked, on that sun-warmed wood,
and my wings expanded
(Whistler drawings that men call wings)—I saw—and I flew—that's
all I can say.

Flew over leagues of whispering wonder, fairy forests and flowery palaces,
Love-lorn casements, delicate kingdoms, beautiful flaming thoughts
of—Him;
Feasts of a million blue-mailed angels lifting their honey-and-wine-
brimmed chalices,
Throned upon clouds—(which *you'd* call white clover) down to the
world's most rosiest rim.

New and new and new and new, the white o' the cliffs and the wind in
the heather,
Yus, and the sea-gulls flying like flakes of the sea that flashed to the
new-born day!
Song, song, song, song, quivering up in the wild blue weather,
Thousands of seraphim singing together, and me just flying and—
knowing my way.

Straight as a die to Piddinghoe's dolphin, and there I drops in a cottage
garden.
There, on a sun-warmed window-sill, I winks and peeps, for the window was wide!
Crumbs, he was there, and fast in her arms, and a-begging his poor old
mother's pardon,
There with his lips on her old grey hair, and her head on his breast,
while she laughed and cried,—

*"One and nine-pence that old tramp gave me, or else I should never have
reached you, sonny,*

Never, and you just leaving the village to-day and meaning to cross
  the sea,
One and nine-pence he gave me, I paid for the farmer's lift with half o'
  the money!
  Here's the ten-pence halfpenny, sonny, 'twill pay for our little 'ouse-
  warming tea."

. . . .

Tick, tack, tick, tack, out into the garden
  Toddles that old Fairy with his arm about her—so,
Cuddling of her still, and still a-begging of her pardon,
  While she says "I wish the corn-flower king could only know!
Bless him, bless him, once again," she says and softly gazes
  Up to heaven, a-smiling in her mutch as white as snow,
All among her gilly-flowers and stocks and double daisies,
  Mignonette, forget-me-not, . . . *Twenty years ago,*
     All a rosy glow,
  This is how it was, she said, *twenty years ago.*

   . . . .

Once again I seemed to wake, the vision it had fled, sir.
  There I lay upon the downs: the sky was like a peach.
Yus, with twelve bokays of corn-flowers blue beside my bed, sir,
  More than usual 'andsome, so they'd bring me tuppence each.
Easy as a poet's dreams they blossomed round my head, sir.
  All I had to do was just to lift my hand and reach,
Tie 'em with a bit of string, and earn my blooming bread, sir,
  Selling little nose-gays on the bare-foot Brighton beach,
     Nose-gays *and* a speech,
  All about the bright blue eyes they matched on Brighton beach.

Overhead the singing lark and underfoot the heather,
  Far and blue in front of us the unplumbed sky,
Me and stick and bundle, oh, we jogs along together,
  (Changeable the weather? Well, it ain't all pie!)
Weather's like a woman, sir, and if she wants to quarrel,
  If her eyes begin to flash and hair begins to fly,
You've to wait a little, then—the story has a moral—
  Ain't the sunny kisses all the sweeter, by and by?—
     (Crumbs, it's 'ot and dry!
  Thank you, sir! Thank you, sir!) the sweeter by and by.

So the world's my sweetheart and I sort of want to squeeze 'er.
  Toffs 'ull get no chance of heaven, take 'em in the lump!
Never laid in hay-fields when the dawn came over-sea, sir?

Guess it's true that story 'bout the needle and the hump!
Never crept into a stack because the wind was blowing,
   Hollered out a nest and closed the door-way with a clump,
Laid and heard the whisper of the silence, growing, growing,
   Watched a thousand wheeling stars and wondered if they'd bump?
            What I say would stump
   Joshua!   But I've done it, sir.   Don't think I'm off my chump.

If you try and lay, sir, with your face turned up to wonder,
   Up to twenty million miles of stars that roll like one,
Right across to God knows where, and you just huddled under
   Like a little beetle with no business of his own,
There you'd hear—like growing grass—a funny silent sound, sir,
   Mixed with curious crackles in a steady undertone,
Just the sound of twenty billion stars a-going round, sir,
   Yus, and you beneath 'em like a wise old ant, alone,
            Ant upon a stone,
   Waving of his antlers, on the Sussex downs, alone.

BACCHUS AND THE PIRATES

HALF a hundred terrible pig-tails, pirates famous in song and story,
   Hoisting the old black flag once more, in a palmy harbour of Caribbee,
"Farewell" we waved to our brown-skinned lasses, and chorussing out to
      the billows of glory,
   Billows a-glitter with rum and gold, we followed the sunset over the
      sea.

         While earth goes round, let rum go round,
            Our capstan song we sung:
         Half a hundred broad-sheet pirates
            When the world was young!

Sea-roads plated with pieces of eight that rolled to a heaven by rum
      made mellow,
   Heaved and coloured our barque's black nose where the Lascar sang
      to a twinkling star,
And the tangled bow-sprit plunged and dipped its point in the west's
      wild red and yellow,
   Till the curved white moon crept out astern like a naked knife from
      a blue cymar.

         While earth goes round, let rum go round,
            Our capstan song we sung:

> *Half a hundred terrible pirates*
> *When the world was young!*

Half a hundred tarry pig-tails, Teach, the chewer of glass, had taught us,
  Taught us to balance the plank ye walk, your little plank-bridge to
    Kingdom Come:
Half a score had sailed with Flint, and a dozen or so the devil had
    brought us
  Back from the pit where Blackbeard lay, in Beelzebub's bosom,
    a-screech for rum.

> *While earth goes round, let rum go round,*
> *Our capstan song we sung:*
> *Half a hundred piping pirates*
> *When the world was young!*

There was Captain Hook (of whom ye have heard—so called from his
    terrible cold steel twister,
  His own right hand having gone to a shark with a taste for skippers on
    pirate-trips),
There was Silver himself, with his cruel crutch, and the blind man Pew,
    with a phiz like a blister,
  Gouged and white and dreadfully dried in the reek of a thousand
    burning ships.

> *While earth goes round, let rum go round,*
> *Our capstan song we sung:*
> *Half a hundred cut-throat pirates*
> *When the world was young!*

With our silver buckles and French cocked hats and our skirted coats
    (they were growing greener,
  But green and gold look well when spliced!   We'd trimmed 'em up
    wi' some fine fresh lace)
Bravely over the seas we danced to the horn-pipe tune of a concertina,
  Cutlasses jetting beneath our skirts and cambric handkerchiefs all in
    place.

> *While earth goes round, let rum go round,*
> *Our capstan song we sung:*
> *Half a hundred elegant pirates*
> *When the world was young!*

And our black prow grated, one golden noon, on the happiest isle of the
    Happy Islands,

An isle of Paradise, fair as a gem, on the sparkling breast of the wine-
   dark deep,
An isle of blossom and yellow sand, and enchanted vines on the purple
   highlands,
   With grapes like melons, nay clustering suns, a-sprawl over cliffs in
      their noonday sleep.

> *While earth goes round, let rum go round,*
>   *Our capstan song we sung:*
> *Half a hundred dream-struck pirates*
>   *When the world was young!*

And lo! on the soft warm edge of the sand, where the sea like wine in a
   golden noggin
   Creamed, and the rainbow-bubbles clung to his flame-red hair, a white
      youth lay,
Sleeping; and now, as his drowsy grip relaxed, the cup that he squeezed
   his grog in
   Slipped from his hand and its purple dregs were mixed with the flames
      and flakes of spray.

> *He'd only the pelt of a fawn to wear*
>   *And a sandal half unstrung;*
> *But he talked in his sleep of a queen at Naxos*
>   *When the world was young.*

And we suddenly saw (had we seen them before?   They were coloured
   like sand or the pelt on his shoulders)
   His head was pillowed on two great leopards, whose breathing rose
      and sank with his own;
Now a pirate is bold, but the vision was rum and would *call* for rum in
   the best of beholders,
   And it seemed we had seen Him before, in a dream, with that flame-
      red hair and that vine-leaf crown.

> *And the earth went round, and the rum went round,*
>   *And softlier now we sung:*
> *Half a hundred awe-struck pirates*
>   *When the world was young!*

Now Timothy Hook (of whom ye have heard with his talon of steel) our
   doughty skipper,
   A man that, in youth being brought up pious, had many a book on his
      cabin-shelf,

Suddenly caught at a comrade's hand with the tearing claws of his cold
   steel flipper
   And cried, "Great Thunder and Brimstone, boys, I've hit it at last!
   'Tis Bacchus himself."

   And the earth went round, and the rum went round,
   And never a word we sung:
   Half a hundred tottering pirates
   When the world was young!

He flung his French cocked hat i' the foam (though its lace was the best
   of his wearing apparel):
   We stared at him—Bacchus! the sea reeled round like a wine-vat
   splashing with purple dreams,
And the sunset-skies were dashed with blood of the grape as the sun like
   a new-staved barrel
   Flooded the tumbling west with wine and spattered the clouds with
   crimson gleams.

   And the earth went round, and our heads went round,
   And never a word we sung:
   Half a hundred staggering pirates
   When the world was young!

Down to the ship for a fishing-net our crafty Hook sent Silver leaping;
   Back he came on his pounding crutch, for all the world like a kan-
   garoo;
And we caught the net and up to the Sleeper on hands and knees we all
   went creeping,
   Flung it across him and staked it down!   'Twas the best of our dreams
   and the dream was true.

   And the earth went round, and the rum went round,
   And loudly now we sung:
   Half a hundred jubilant pirates
   When the world was young!

We had caught our god, and we got him aboard ere he woke (he was
   more than a little heavy);
   Glittering, beautiful, flushed he lay in the lurching bows of the old
   black barque,
As the sunset died and the white moon dawned, and we saw on the
   island a star-bright bevy

Of naked Bacchanals stealing to watch through the whispering vines
  in the purple dark!

> *While earth goes round, let rum go round,*
>   *Our capstan song we sung;*
> *Half a hundred innocent pirates*
> *When the world was young!*

Beautiful under the sailing moon, in the tangled net, with the leopards
  beside him,
  Snared like a wild young red-lipped merman, wilful, petulant, flushed
  he lay;
While Silver and Hook in their big sea-boots and their boat-cloaks
  guarded and gleefully eyed him,
  Thinking what Bacchus might do for a seaman, like standing him
  drinks, as a man might say.

> *While earth goes round, let rum go round,*
>   *We sailed away and sung:*
> *Half a hundred fanciful pirates*
> *When the world was young!*

All the grog that ever was heard of, gods, was it stowed in our sure
  possession?
  Oh, the pictures that broached the skies and poured their colours
  across our dreams!
Oh, the thoughts that tapped the sunset, and rolled like a great torch-
  light procession
  Down our throats in a glory of glories, a roaring splendour of golden
  streams!

> *And the earth went round, and the stars went round,*
>   *As we hauled the sheets and sung:*
> *Half a hundred infinite pirates*
> *When the world was young!*

Beautiful, white, at the break of day, He woke and, the net in a smoke
  dissolving,
  He rose like a flame, with his yellow-eyed pards and his flame-red
  hair like a windy dawn,
And the crew kept back, respectful like, till the leopards advanced with
  their eyes revolving,
  Then up the rigging went Silver and Hook, and the rest of us followed
  with case-knives drawn.

> *While earth goes round, let rum go round,*
>   *Our cross-tree song we sung:*
> *Half a hundred terrified pirates*
>   *When the world was young!*

And "Take me home to my happy island!" he says.   "Not I," sings
    Hook, "by thunder;
    We'll take you home to a happier isle, our palmy harbour of Carib-
    bee!"
"You won't!" says Bacchus, and quick as a dream the planks of the deck
    just heaved asunder,
    And a mighty Vine came straggling up that grew from the depths of
    the wine-dark sea.

> *And the sea went round, and the skies went round,*
>   *As our cross-tree song we sung:*
> *Half a hundred horrified pirates*
>   *When the world was young!*

We were anchored fast as an oak on land, and the branches clutched
    and the tendrils quickened,
    And bound us writhing like snakes to the spars!   Ay, we hacked with
    our knives at the boughs in vain,
And Bacchus laughed loud on the decks below, as ever the tough sprays
    tightened and thickened,
    And the blazing hours went by, and we gaped with thirst and our
    ribs were racked with pain.

> *And the skies went round, and the sea swam round,*
>   *And we knew not what we sung:*
> *Half a hundred lunatic pirates*
>   *When the world was young!*

Bunch upon bunch of sunlike grapes, as we writhed and struggled and
    raved and strangled,
    Bunch upon bunch of gold and purple daubed its bloom on our baked
    black lips.
Clustering grapes, O, bigger than pumpkins, just out of reach they
    bobbed and dangled
    Over the vine-entangled sails of that most dumbfounded of pirate
    ships!

> *And the sun went round, and the moon came round,*
>   *And mocked us where we hung:*
> *Half a hundred maniac pirates*
>   *When the world was young!*

Over the waters the white moon winked its bruised old eye at our
 bowery prison,
 When suddenly we were aware of a light such as never a moon or a
  ship's lamp throws,
And a shallop of pearl, like a Nautilus shell, came shimmering up as
 by magic arisen,
 With sails of silk and a glory around it that turned the sea to a
  rippling rose.

> And our heads went round, and the stars went round,
> At the song that cruiser sung:
> Half a hundred goggle-eyed pirates
> When the world was young!

Half a hundred rose-white Bacchanals .hauled the ropes of that rosy
 cruiser!
 Over the seas they came and laid their little white hands on the old
  black barque;
And Bacchus he ups and he steps aboard: "Hi, stop!" cries Hook, "you
 frantic old boozer!
 Belay, below there, don't you go and leave poor pirates to die in the
  dark!"

> And the moon went round, and the stars went round,
> As they all pushed off and sung:
> Half a hundred riotous Bacchanals
> When the world was young!

All around that rainbow Nautilus rippled the bloom of a thousand roses,
 Nay, but the sparkle of fairy sea-nymphs breasting a fairy-like sea of
  wine,
Swimming around it in murmuring thousands, with white arms tossing;
 till—all that we knows is
 The light went out, and the night was dark, and the grapes had burst
  and their juice was—brine!

> And the vines that bound our bodies round
> Were plain wet ropes that clung
> Squeezing the light out o' fifty pirates
> When the world was young!

. . . .

Over the seas in the pomp of dawn a king's ship came with her proud
 flag flying;
 Cloud upon cloud we watched her tower with her belts and her
  crowded zones of sail;

And an A.B. perched in a white crow's nest, with a brass-rimmed spy-
glass quietly spying,
As we swallowed the lumps in our choking throats and uttered our
last faint feeble hail!

> *And our heads went round as the ship came round,*
> *And we thought how coves had swung*
> *All for playing at broad-sheet pirates*
> *When the world was young!*

Half a hundred trembling corsairs, all cut loose, but a trifle giddy,
We lands on their trim white decks at last and the bo'sun he whistles
us good hot grog,
And we tries to confess, but there wasn't a soul from the Admiral's self
to the gold-laced middy
But says, "They're delirious still, poor chaps," and the Cap'n he enters
the fact in his log,

> *That his boat's crew found us well-nigh drowned*
> *In a barrel without a bung—*
> *Half a hundred suffering sea-cooks*
> *When the world was young!*

Ah, yet (if ye stand me a noggin of rum) shall the old Blue Dolphin
echo the story!
We'll hoist the white cross-bones again in our palmy harbour of
Caribbee!
We'll wave farewell to our brown-skinned lasses and, chorussing out to
the billows of glory,
Billows a-glitter with rum and gold, we'll follow the sunset over the
sea!

> *While earth goes round, let rum go round!*
> *Oh, sing it as we sung!*
> *Half a hundred terrible pirates*
> *When the world was young!*

APRIL AIR

THE happiest notes that ever he sung
— So let it be said on my latest day—
Leapt like the dew by a bird's wing flung
Over his page from a hawthorn spray.

They were never the work of his hand, they'll say,
 Those nine sweet syllables past compare.
They were breathed in his ear by his own true may:
 She sent him treading on April air.

He was plucking that day at a lyre unstrung.
 The tide was ebbing. The skies were grey.
A wan sea-mist to the downlands clung
 Where his thoughts went groping like ghosts astray,
And the burden he lacked went drifting away
 Till—a sunbeam danced in her eyes and hair,
And a sweet voice whispered it, blithe and gay:
 She sent him treading on April air.

O, love, we were happy, and poor, and young,
 And our clouds dispersed at a single ray;
And never a note so laughingly rung
 From a flower-crowned revel of elf and fay
As the one swift verse, like a swallow at play,
 That leapt to the heart of your lover's despair,
With a magical close to his laboured lay:
 She sent him treading on April air.

Once, memory, once, o'er the mire and clay
 Where the rest lies buried, O whisper it there,—
He met Love's eyes on the pilgrim's way:
 She sent, him treading on April air.

A MAY-DAY CAROL

What is the loveliest light that Spring,
 Rosily parting her robe of grey,
Girdled with leaflet green, can fling
 Over the fields where her white feet stray?
What is the merriest promise of May
 Flung o'er the dew-drenched April flowers?
Tell me, you on the pear-tree spray—
 Carol of birds between the showers.

What can life at its lightest bring
 Better than this on its brightest day?
How should we fetter the white-throat's wing
 Wild with joy of its woodland way?

Sweet, should love for an hour delay,
  Swift, while the primrose-time is ours!
What is the lover's royallest lay?—
  Carol of birds between the showers.

What is the murmur of bees a-swing?
  What is the laugh of a child at play?
What is the song that the angels sing?
  (Where were the tune could the sweet notes stay
Longer than this, to kiss and betray?)
  Nay, on the blue sky's topmost towers,
What is the song of the seraphim?   Say—
  Carol of birds between the showers.

Thread the stars on a silver string,
  (So did they sing in Bethlehem's bowers!)
Mirth for a little one, grief for a king,
  Carol of birds between the showers.

MOUNT IDA

[This poem commemorates an event of some years ago, when a young poet—still
remembered by many of his contemporaries at Oxford—went up into Mount Ida and
was never seen again.]

NOT cypress, but this warm pine-plumage now
  Fragrant with sap, I pluck; nor bid you weep,
Ye Muses that still haunt the heavenly brow
  Of Ida, though the ascent is hard and steep:
Weep not for him who left us wrapped in sleep
  At dawn beneath the holy mountain's breast
    And all alone from Ilion's gleaming shore
Clomb the high sea-ward glens, fain to drink deep
  Of earth's old glory from your silent crest,
        Take the cloud-conquering throne
        Of gods, and gaze alone
Thro' heaven.   Darkling we slept who saw his face no more.

But Lycidas had found in him a brother,
  And Adonaïs would not say him nay,
And Thyrsis to the breast of one sweet Mother
  Welcomed him, climbing by that wild hill way.
Quietly as a cloud at break of day
  Up the long glens of golden dew he stole

(And surely Bion called to him afar!)
The tearful hyacinths, and the greenwood spray
  Clinging to keep him from the sapphire goal,
          Kept of his path no trace!
          Upward the yearning face
Clomb the ethereal height, calm as the morning star.

Incline to earth, dear Sisters, or my song
  That with the light wings of the skimming swallow
Must range the reedy slopes, will work him wrong!
  And with some golden shaft do thou, Apollo,
Show the pine-shadowed path that none may follow;
  For, as the blue air shuts behind a bird,
      Round him closed Ida's cloudy woods and rills!
Day-long, night-long, by echoing height and hollow,
  We called him, but our tumult died unheard:
          Down from the scornful sky
          Our faint wing-broken cry
Fluttered and perished among the many-folded hills.

For though we clomb each faint-flushed peak of vision,
  Nought but our own sad faces we divined.
His radiant way still laughed us to derision,
  And still revengeful Echo proved unkind;
And oft our faithless hearts half feared to find
  A cold corse in some dark mist-drenched ravine
      Where the white foam flashed headlong to the sea.
How should we find thee, spirits deaf and blind
  Even to the things which we had heard and seen?
          Eyes that could see no more
          The old light on sea and shore,
What should they hope or fear to find?   They found not thee.

For thou wast ever alien to our skies,
  A wistful stray of radiance on this earth,
A changeling with deep memories in thine eyes
  Mistily gazing thro' our loud-voiced mirth
To some fair land beyond the gates of birth;
  Yet, as a star thro' clouds, thou still didst shed
      Through our dark world thy lovelier, rarer glow;
Time, like a picture of but little worth,
  Before thy young hand lifelessly outspread,
          At one light stroke from thee
          Gleamed with Eternity;
Thou gav'st the master's touch, and we—we did not know.

Not though we gazed from heaven o'er Ilion
   Dreaming on earth below, mistily crowned
With towering memories, and beyond her shone
   The wine-dark seas Achilles heard resound!
Only, and after many days, we found
   Dabbled with dew, at border of a wood
     Bedded in hyacinths, open and a-glow
Thy Homer's Iliad. . . . Dryad tears had drowned
   The rough Greek type and, as with honey or blood
       One crocus with crushed gold
       Stained the great page that told
Of gods that sighed their loves on Ida, long ago.

See—for a couch to their ambrosial limbs
   Even as their golden load of splendour presses
The fragrant thyme, a billowing cloud up-swims
   Of springing flowers beneath their deep caresses,
Hyacinth, lotus, crocus, wildernesses
   Of bloom . . . but clouds of sunlight and of dew
     Dropping rich balm, round the dark pine-woods curled
That the warm wonder of their inwoven tresses,
   And all the secret blisses that they knew,
       Where beauty kisses truth
       In heaven's deep heart of youth,
Might still be hidden, as thou art, from the heartless world.

Even as we found thy book, below these rocks
   Perchance that strange great eagle's feather lay,
When Ganymede, from feeding of his flocks
   On Ida, vanished thro' the morning grey.
Stranger it seemed, if thou couldst cast away
   Those golden musics as a thing of nought,
     A dream for which no longer thou hadst need!
Ah, was it here then that the break of day
   Brought thee the substance for the shadow, taught
       Thy soul a swifter road
       To ease it of its load
And watch this world of shadows as a dream recede?

We slept! Darkling we slept! Our busy schemes,
   Our cold mechanic world awhile was still;
But oh, their eyes are blinded even in dreams
   Who from the heavenlier Powers withdraw their will.
Here did the dawn with purer light fulfil
   Thy happier eyes than ours, here didst thou see

The quivering wonder-light in flower and dew,
The quickening glory of the haunted hill,
  The hamadryad beckoning from the tree,
      The naiad from the stream;
      While from her long dark dream
Earth woke, trembling with life, light, beauty, through and through.

And the everlasting miracle of things
  Flowed round thee, and this dark earth opposed no bar,
And radiant faces from the flowers and springs
  Dawned on thee, whispering, *Knowest thou whence* WE *are?*
Faintly thou heardst us calling thee afar
  As Hylas heard, sinking beneath the wave,
      Girdled with glowing arms, while wood and glen
Echoed his name beneath that rosy star;
  And thy farewell came faint as from the grave
      For very bliss; but we
      Could neither hear nor see;
And all the hill with *Hylas! Hylas!* rang again.

But there were deeper love-tales for thine ears
  Than mellow-tongued Theocritus could tell:
Over him like a sea two thousand years
  Had swept.   They solemnized his music well!
Farewell!   What word could answer but farewell,
  From thee, O happy spirit, that couldst steal
      So quietly from this world at break of day?
What voice of ours could break the silent spell
  Beauty had cast upon thee, or reveal
      The gates of sun and dew
      Which oped and let thee through
And led thee heavenward by that deep enchanted way?

Yet here thou mad'st thy choice: Love, Wisdom, Power,
  As once before young Paris, they stood here!
Beneath them Ida, like one full-blown flower,
  Shed her bloom earthward through the radiant air,
Leaving her rounded fruit, their beauty, bare
  To the everlasting dawn; and, in thy palm
      ·The golden apple of the Hesperian isle
Which thou must only yield to the Most Fair;
  But not to Juno's great luxurious calm,
      Nor Dian's curved white moon,
      Gav'st thou the sunset's boon,
Nor to foam-bosomed Aphrodite's rose-lipped smile.

Here didst thou make the eternal choice aright,
  Here, in this hallowed haunt of nymph and faun,
They stood before thee in that great new light,
  The three great splendours of the immortal dawn,
With all the cloudy veils of Time withdrawn
  Or only glistening round the firm white snows
    Of their pure beauty like the golden dew
Brushed from the feathery ferns below the lawn;
  But not to cold Diana's morning rose,
            Nor to great Juno's frown
            Was cast that apple down,
And, when the Paphian raised her lustrous eyes anew,

Thou from thy soul didst whisper—*in that heaven*
  Which yearns beyond us! Lead me up the height!
How should the golden fruit to one be given
  Till your three splendours in that Sun unite
Where each in each ye move like light in light?
  How should I judge the rapture till I know
    The pain? And like three waves of music there
They close thee round, blinding thy blissful sight
  With beauty and, like one roseate orb a-glow,
            They bore thee on their breasts
            Up the sun-smitten crests
And melted with thee smiling into the Most Fair.

Upward and onward, ever as ye went
  The cities of the world nestled beneath
Closer, as if in love, round Ida, blent
  With alien hills in one great bridal-wreath
Of dawn-flushed clouds; while, breathing with your breath
  New heavens mixed with your mounting bliss. Deep eyes,
    Beautiful eyes, imbrued with the world's tears
Dawned on you, beautiful gleams of Love and Death
  Flowed thro' your questioning with divine replies
            From that ineffable height
            Dark, dark to mortal sight,
Where the Ever-living dies and the All-loving hears.

For thou hadst seen what tears upon man's face
  Bled from the heart or burned from out the brain,
And not denied or cursed, but couldst embrace
  Infinite Paradise in the heart of pain,
And heardst those universal choirs again
  Wherein like waves of one harmonious sea

All our slight dreams of heaven are singing still,
And still the throned Olympians swell the strain,
    And, hark, the burden of all—*Come unto Me!*
                Sky into deepening sky
                Melts with that one great cry;
And the lost doves of Ida moan on Siloa's hill.

I gather all the ages in my song
    And send them singing up the heights to thee!
Chord by æonian chord the stars prolong
    Their passionate echoes to Eternity:
Earth wakes, and one orchestral symphony
    Sweeps o'er the quivering harp-strings of mankind;
        Grief modulates into heaven, hate drowns in love,
No strife now but of love in that great sea
    Of song!   I dream!   I dream, with eyes grown blind.
                Chords that I not command
                Escape the fainting hand;
Tears fall.   Thou canst not hear.   Thou art still too far above.

Farewell!   What word should answer but farewell
    From thee, O happy spirit, whose clear gaze
Discerned the path—clear, but unsearchable—
    Where Olivet sweetens, deepens, Ida's praise,
The path that strikes as through a sunlit haze
    Through Time to that clear reconciling height
        Where our commingling gleams of godhead dwell;
Strikes thro' the turmoil of our darkling days
    To that great harmony where, like light in light,
                Wisdom and Beauty still
                Haunt the thrice-holy hill,
And Love, immortal Love . . . what answer but farewell?

CREATION

In the beginning, there was nought
    But heaven, one Majesty of Light,
Beyond all speech, beyond all thought,
    Beyond all depth, beyond all height,
Consummate heaven, the first and last,
    Enfolding in its perfect prime
No future rushing to the past,
    But one rapt Now, that knew not Space or Time.

Formless it was, being gold on gold,
    And void—but with that complete Life
Where music could no wings unfold
    Until God smote the strings of strife.
"Myself unto Myself am Throne,
    Myself unto Myself am Thrall,
I that am All am all alone,"
    He said, "Yea, I have nothing, having all."

And, gathering round His mount of bliss
    The angel-squadrons of His will,
He said, "One battle yet there is
    To win, one vision to fulfil;
Since heaven where'er I gaze expands,
    And power that knows no strife or cry,
Weakness shall bind and pierce My hands
    And make a world for Me wherein to die.

All might, all vastness and all glory
    Being Mine, I must descend and make
Out of My heart a song, a story
    Of little hearts that burn and break.
Out of My passion without end
    I will make little azure seas,
And into small sad fields descend
    And make green grass, white daisies, rustling trees."

Then shrank His angels, knowing He thrust
    His arms out East and West and gave
For every little dream of dust
    Part of His Life as to a grave.
"*Enough O Father, for Thy words
    Have pierced Thy hands*"   But, low and sweet,
He said "Sunsets and streams and birds,
    And drifting clouds"—The purple stained His feet.—

"*Enough!*"   His angels moaned in fear,
    "*Father, Thy words have pierced Thy side!*"
He whispered, "Roses shall grow there,
    And there must be a hawthorn-tide.
And ferns, dewy at dawn," and still
    They moaned—"*Enough, the red drops bleed!*"
"And," low and clear, "on every hill,"
    He said, "I will have flocks and lambs to lead."

His angels bowed their heads beneath
　　Their wings till that great pang was gone.
"Pour not Thy soul out unto Death!"
　　They moaned, and still His Love flowed on:
"There shall be small white wings to stray
　　From bliss to bliss, from bloom to bloom,
And blue flowers in the wheat; and—" "Stay!
　　Speak not," they cried, "*the word that seals Thy tomb!*"

He spake—"I have thought of a little child
　　That I will have there to embark
On small adventures in the wild,
　　And front slight perils in the dark;
And I will hide from him and lure
　　His laughing eyes with suns and moons,
And rainbows that shall not endure;
　　And—when he is weary, sing him drowsy tunes."

His angels fell before Him weeping.
　　"Enough!　Tempt not the Gates of Hell!"
He said, "His soul is in his keeping
　　That we may love each other well;
And lest the dark too much affright him,
　　I will strow countless little stars
Across his childhood's skies to light him
　　That he may wage in peace his mimic wars;

And oft forget Me as he plays
　　With swords and childish merchandize,
Or with his elfin balance weighs,
　　Or with his foot-rule metes, the skies;
Or builds his castles by the deep,
　　Or tunnels through the rocks, and then—
Turn to Me as he falls asleep,
　　And, in his dreams, feel for My hand again.

And when he is older he shall be
　　My friend and walk here at My side;
Or—when he wills—grow young with Me,
　　And, to that happy world where once we died,
Descending through the calm blue weather,
　　Buy life once more with our immortal breath,
And wander through the little fields together,
　　And taste of Love and Death.'

168

HARBOUR LIGHTS

PILOT, how far from home?—
  Not far, not far to-night,
  A flight of spray, a sea-bird's flight,
A flight of tossing foam,
  And then the lights of home!—

And, yet again, how far?
  And seems the way so brief?
  Those lights beyond the roaring reef
Were lights of moon and star,
  Far, far, none knows how far!

Pilot, how far from home?—
  The great stars pass away
  Before Him as a flight of spray,
Moons as a flight of foam!
  I see the lights of home.

TALES OF THE MERMAID TAVERN

1

A KNIGHT OF THE OCEAN-SEA

UNDER that foggy sunset London glowed,
Like one huge cob-webbed flagon of old wine;
And, as I walked down Fleet Street, the soft sky
Flowed thro' the roaring thoroughfares, transfused
Their hard sharp outlines, blurred the throngs of black
On either pavement, blurred the rolling stream
Of red and yellow busses, till the town
Turned to a golden suburb of the clouds.
And, round that mighty bubble of St. Paul's,
Over the up-turned faces of the street,
An air-ship slowly sailed, with whirring fans,
A voyager in the new-found realms of gold,
A shadowy silken chrysalis whence should break
What radiant wings in centuries to be.

So, wandering on, while all the shores of Time
Softened into Eternity, it seemed

A dead man touched me with his living hand,
A flaming legend passed me in the streets
Of London—laugh who will—that City of Clouds,
Where what a dreamer yet, in spite of all,
Is man, that splendid visionary child
Who sent his fairy beacon through the dusk,
On a blue bus before the moon was risen,—
This Night, at eight, The Tempest!

                            Dreaming thus,
(Small wonder that my footsteps went astray!)
I found myself within a narrow street,
Alone.   There was no rumour, near or far,
Of the long tides of traffic.   In my doubt
I turned and knocked upon an old inn-door,
Hard by, an ancient inn of mullioned panes,
And crazy beams and over-hanging eaves.
And, as I knocked, the slowly changing west
Seemed to change all the world with it and leave
Only that old inn steadfast and unchanged,
A rock in the rich-coloured tides of time.

And, suddenly, as a song that wholly escapes
Remembrance, at one note, wholly returns,
There, as I knocked, memory returned to me.
I knew it all—the little twisted street,
The rough wet cobbles gleaming, far away,
Like opals, where it ended on the sky;
And, overhead, the darkly smiling face
Of that old wizard inn; I knew by rote
The smooth sun-bubbles in the worn green paint
Upon the doors and shutters.

                            There was one
Myself had idly scratched away one dawn,
One mad May-dawn, three hundred years ago,
When out of the woods we came with hawthorn boughs
And found the doors locked, as they seemed to-night.
Three hundred years ago—nay, Time was dead!
No need to scan the sign-board any more
Where that white-breasted siren of the sea
Curled her moon-silvered tail among such rocks
As never in the merriest seaman's tale
Broke the blue-bliss of fabulous lagoons
Beyond the Spanish Main.

And, through the dream,

Even as I stood and listened, came a sound
Of clashing wine-cups: then a deep-voiced song
Made the old timbers of the Mermaid Inn
Shake as a galleon shakes in a gale of wind
When she rolls glorying through the Ocean-sea.

SONG

Marchaunt Adventurers, chanting at the windlass,
   Early in the morning, we slipped from Plymouth Sound,
All for Adventure in the great New Regions,
   All for Eldorado and to sail the world around!
Sing! the red of sun-rise ripples round the bows again.
   Marchaunt Adventurers, O sing, we're outward bound,
All to stuff the sunset in our old black galleon,
   All to seek the merchandise that no man ever found.

Chorus: Marchaunt Adventurers!
                  Marchaunt Adventurers!

Marchaunt Adventurers, O, whither are ye bound?—
All for Eldorado and the great new Sky-line,
   All to seek the merchandize that no man ever found.

Marchaunt Adventurers, O, what'ull ye bring home again?—
   Wonders and works and the thunder of the sea!
Whom will ye traffic with?—The King of the Sunset!
   What shall be your pilot then?—A wind from Galilee.
Nay, but ye be marchaunts, will ye come back empty-handed?—
   Ay, we be marchaunts, though our gain we ne'er shall see.
Cast we now our bread upon the waste wild waters.
   After many days, it shall return with usury.

Chorus: Marchaunt Adventurers!
                  Marchaunt Adventurers!

What shall be your profit in the mighty days to be?—
Englande!—Englande!—Englande!—Englande!—
   Glory everlasting and the lordship of the sea!

And there, framed in the lilac patch of sky
That ended the steep street, dark on its light,
And standing on those glistering cobblestones

171

Just where they took the sunset's kiss, I saw
A figure like foot-feathered Mercury,
Tall, straight, and splendid as a sunset-cloud.
Clad in a crimson doublet and trunk-hose,
A rapier at his side; and, as he paused,
His long fantastic shadow swayed and swept
Against my feet.
                        A moment he looked back,
Then swaggered down as if he owned a world
Which had forgotten—did I wake or dream?—
Even his gracious ghost!
                        Over his arm
He swung a gorgeous murrey-coloured cloak
Of Ciprus velvet, caked and smeared with mud
As on the day when—did I dream or wake?
And had not all this happened once before?—
When he had laid that cloak before the feet
Of Gloriana!   By that mud-stained cloak,
'Twas he!   Our Ocean-Shepherd!   Walter Raleigh!
He brushed me passing, and with one vigorous thrust
Opened the door and entered.   At his heels
I followed—into the Mermaid!—through three yards
Of pitch-black gloom, then into an old inn-parlour
Swimming with faces in a mist of smoke
That up-curled, blue, from long Winchester pipes,
While—like some rare old picture, in a dream
Recalled—quietly listening, laughing, watching,
Pale on that old black oaken wainscot floated
One bearded oval face, young, with deep eyes,
Whom Raleigh hailed as "Will!"
                        But as I stared
A sudden buffet from a brawny hand
Made all my senses swim, and the room rang
With laughter as upon the rush-strewn floor
My feet slipped and I fell.   Then a gruff voice
Growled over me—"Get up now, John-a-dreams,
Or else mine host must find another drawer!
Hast thou not heard us calling all this while?"
And, as I scrambled up, the rafters rang
With cries of "Sack!   Bring me a cup of sack!
Canary!   Sack!   Malmsey! and Muscadel!"
I understood and flew.   I was awake,
A leather-jerkined pot-boy to these gods,
A prentice Ganymede to the Mermaid Inn!
There, flitting to and fro with cups of wine,

I heard them toss the Chrysomelan names
From mouth to mouth—Lyly and Peele and Lodge,
Kit Marlowe, Michael Drayton, and the rest,
With Ben, rare Ben, brick-layer Ben, who rolled
Like a great galleon on his ingle-bench.
Some twenty years of age he seemed; and yet
This young Gargantua with the bull-dog jaws,
The T, for Tyburn, branded on his thumb,
And grim pock-pitted face, was growling tales
To Dekker that would fright a buccaneer,—
How in the fierce Low Countries he had killed
His man, and won that scar on his bronzed fist;
Was taken prisoner, and turned Catholick;
And, now returned to London, was resolved
To blast away the vapours of the town
With Boreas-throated plays of thunderous mirth.
"I'll thwack their Tribulation-Wholesomes, lad,
Their Yellow-faced Envies and lean Thorns-i'-the-Flesh,
At the *Black-friars Theatre,* or *The Rose,*
Or else *The Curtain.* Failing these, I'll find
Some good square inn-yard with wide galleries,
And windows level with the stage. 'Twill serve
My Comedy of Vapours; though, I grant,
For Tragedy a private House is best;
Or, just as Burbage tip-toes to a deed
Of blood, or, over your stable's black half-door,
Marked *Battlements* in white chalk, your breathless David
Glowers at the whiter Bathsheba within,
Some humorous coach-horse neighs a 'hallelujah'!
And the pit splits its doublets. Over goes
The whole damned apple-barrel, and the yard
Is all one rough and tumble, scramble and scratch
Of prentices, green madams, and cut-purses
For half-chewed Norfolk pippins. Never mind!
We'll build the perfect stage in Shoreditch yet;
And Will, there, hath half promised I shall write
A piece for his own company! What d'ye think
Of *Venus and Adonis,* his first heir,
Printed last week? A bouncing boy, my lad!
And he's at work on a Midsummer's Dream
That turns the world to fairyland!"
                                        All these
And many more were there, and all were young!
There, as I brimmed their cups, I heard the voice
Of Raleigh ringing across the smoke-wreathed room,—

"Ben, could you put a frigate on the stage,
I've found a tragedy for you.   Have you heard
The true tale of Sir Humphrey Gilbert?"

                                        "No!"

"Why, Ben, of all the tragical affairs
Of the Ocean-sea, and of that other Ocean
Where all men sail so blindly, and misjudge
Their friends, their charts, their storms, their stars, their God,
If there be truth in the blind crowder's song
I bought in Bread Street for a penny, this
Is the brief type and chronicle of them all.
Listen!"   Then Raleigh sent these rugged rhymes
Of some blind crowder rolling in great waves
Of passion across the gloom.   At each refrain
He sank his voice to a broad deep undertone,
As if the distant roar of breaking surf
Or the low thunder of eternal tides
Filled up the pauses of the nearer storm,
Storm against storm, a soul against the sea:—

A KNIGHT OF THE OCEAN-SEA

Sir Humphrey Gilbert, hard of hand,
    Knight-in-chief of the Ocean-sea,
Gazed from the rocks of his New Found Land
    And thought of the home where his heart would be.

He gazed across the wintry waste
    That weltered and hissed like molten lead,—
"He saileth twice who saileth in haste!
    I'll wait the favour of Spring," he said.

        Ever the more, ever the more,
        He heard the winds and the waves roar!
        Thunder on thunder shook the shore.

The yellow clots of foam went by
    Like shavings that curl from a ship-wright's plane,
Clinging and flying, afar and nigh,
    Shuddering, flying and clinging again.

A thousand bubbles in every one
    Shifted and shimmered with rainbow gleams;

174

But—had they been planets and stars that spun
   He had let them drift by his feet like dreams:

Heavy of heart was our Admirall,
   For, out of his ships—and they were but three!—
He had lost the fairest and most tall,
   And—he was a Knight of the Ocean-sea.

Ever the more, ever the more,
He heard the winds and the waves roar!
Thunder on thunder shook the shore.

Heavy of heart, heavy of heart,
   For she was a galleon mighty as May,
And the storm that ripped her glory apart
   Had stripped his soul for the winter's way;

And he was aware of a whisper blown
   From fo'c'sle to poop, from windward to lee,
That the fault was his, and his alone,
   And—he was a Knight of the Ocean-sea.

"Had he done that!   Had he done this!"
   And yet his mariners loved him well;
But an idle word is hard to miss,
   And the foam hides more than the deep can tell.

And the deep had buried his best-loved books,
   With many a hard-worn chart and plan:
And a king that is conquered must see strange looks,
   So bitter a thing is the heart of man!

And—"Whom will you find to pay your debt?
   For a venture like this is a costly thing!
Will they stake yet more, tho' your heart be set
   On the mightier voyage you planned for the Spring?"

He raised his head like a Viking crowned,—
   "I'll take my old flag to her Majestie,
And she will lend me ten thousand pound
   To make her Queen of the Ocean-sea!"

Ever the more, ever the more,
He heard the winds and the waves roar!
Thunder on thunder shook the shore.

Outside—they heard the great winds blow!
  Outside—the blustering surf they heard,
And the bravest there would ha' blenched to know
  That they must be taken at their own word.

For the great grim waves were as molten lead
  —And he had two ships who sailed with three!—
"And I sail not home till the Spring," he said,
  "They are all too frail for the Ocean-sea."

But the trumpeter thought of an ale-house bench,
  And the cabin-boy longed for a Devonshire lane,
And the gunner remembered a green-gowned wench,
  And the fo'c'sle whisper went round again,—

"Sir Humphrey Gilbert is hard of hand,
  But his courage went down with the ship, may-be,
And we wait for the Spring in a desert land,
  For—*he is afraid of the Ocean-sea.*"

> *Ever the more, ever the more,*
> *He heard the winds and the waves roar!*
> *Thunder on thunder shook the shore.*

He knew, he knew how the whisper went!
  He knew he must master it, last or first!
He knew not how much or how little it meant;
  But his heart was heavy and like to burst.

"Up with your sails, my sea-dogs all!
  The wind has veered!   And my ships," quoth he,
"They will serve for a British Admirall
  Who is Knight-in-chief of the Ocean-sea!"

His will was like a north-east wind
  That swept along our helmless crew;
But he would not stay on the *Golden Hynde,*
  For that was the stronger ship of the two.

"My little ship's-company, lads, hath passed
  Perils and storms a-many with me!
Would ye have me forsake them at the last?
  They'll need a Knight of the Ocean-sea!"

Ever the more, ever the more,
We heard the winds and the waves roar!
Thunder on thunder shook the shore.

Beyond Cape Race, the pale sun splashed
    The grim grey waves with silver light
Where, ever in front, his frigate crashed
    Eastward, for England and the night.

And still as the dark began to fall,
    Ever in front of us, running free,
We saw the sails of our Admirall
    Leading us home through the Ocean-sea.

Ever the more, ever the more,
We heard the winds and the waves roar!
But he sailed on, sailed on before.

On Monday, at noon of the third fierce day
    A-board our *Golden Hynde* he came,
With a trail of blood, marking his way
    On the salt wet decks as he walked half-lame.

For a rusty nail thro' his foot had pierced.
    "Come, master-surgeon, mend it for me;
Though I would it were changed for the nails that amerced
    The dying thief upon Calvary."

The surgeon bathed and bound his foot,
    And the master entreated him sore to stay;
But roughly he pulled on his great sea-boot
    With—"The wind is rising and I must away!"

I know not why so little a thing,
    When into his pinnace we helped him down,
Should make our eyelids prick and sting
    As the salt spray were into them blown,

But he called as he went—"Keep watch and steer
    By my lanthorn at night!"   Then he waved his hand
With a kinglier watch-word, "We are as near
    To heaven, my lads, by sea as by land!"

Ever the more, ever the more,
We heard the gathering tempest roar!
But he sailed on, sailed on before.

Three hundred leagues on our homeward road,
  We strove to signal him, swooping nigh,
That he would ease his decks of their load
  Of nettings and fights and artillery.

And dark and dark that night 'gan fall,
  And high the muttering breakers swelled,
Till that strange fire which seamen call
  "Castor and Pollux," we beheld,

An evil sign of peril and death,
  Burning pale on the high main-mast;
But calm with the might of Gennesareth
  Our Admirall's voice went ringing past.

Clear thro' the thunders, far and clear,
  Mighty to counsel, clear to command,
Joyfully ringing, "We are as near
  To heaven, my lads, by sea as by land!"

    Ever the more, ever the more,
    We heard the rising hurricane roar!
    But he sailed on, sailed on before.

And over us fled the fleet of the stars,
  And, ever in front of us, far or nigh,
The lanthorn on his cross-tree spars
  Dipped to the Pit or soared to the Sky!

'Twould sweep to the lights of Charles's Wain,
  As the hills of the deep 'ud mount and flee,
Then swoop down vanishing cliffs again
  To the thundering gulfs of the Ocean-sea.

We saw it shine as it swooped from the height,
  With ruining breakers on every hand,
Then—a cry came out of the black mid-night,
"As near to heaven by sea as by land!"

And the light was out! Like a wind-blown spark,
  All in a moment! And we—and we—
Prayed for his soul as we swept thro' the dark;
  For he was a Knight of the Ocean-sea.

Over our fleets for evermore
The winds 'ull triumph and the waves roar!
But he sails on, sails on before!

Silence a moment held the Mermaid Inn,
Then Michael Drayton, raising a cup of wine,
Stood up and said,—"Since many have obtained
Absolute glory that have done great deeds,
But fortune is not in the power of man,
So they that, truly attempting, nobly fail,
Deserve great honour of the common-wealth.
Such glory did the Greeks and Romans give
To those that in great enterprises fell
Seeking the true commodity of their country
And profit to all mankind; for, though they failed,
Being by war, death, or some other chance,
Hindered, their images were set up in brass,
Marble and silver, gold and ivory,
In solemn temples and great palace-halls,
No less to make men emulate their virtues
Than to give honour to their just deserts.
God, from the time that He first made the world,
Hath kept the knowledge of His Ocean-sea
And the huge Æquinoctiall Continents
Reserved unto this day. Wherefore I think
No high exploit of Greece and Rome but seems
A little thing to these Discoveries
Which our adventurous captains even now
Are making, out there, westward, in the night,
Captains most worthy of commendation,
Hugh Willoughby—God send him home again
Safe to the Mermaid!—and Dick Chauncellor,
That excellent pilot. Doubtless this man, too,
Sir Humphrey Gilbert, was worthy to be made
Knight of the Ocean-sea. I bid you all
Stand up, and drink to his immortal fame!"

II

A COINER OF ANGELS

SOME three nights later, thro' the thick brown fog,
A link-boy, dropping flakes of crimson fire,
Flared to the door and, through its glowing frame,
Ben Jonson and Kit Marlowe, arm in arm,

Swaggered into the Mermaid Inn and called
For red-deer pies.
                        There, as they supped, I caught
Scraps of ambrosial talk concerning Will,
His *Venus and Adonis.*
                        "Gabriel thought
'Twas wrong to change the old writers and create
A cold Adonis."
                        —"Laws were made for Will,
Not Will for laws, since first he stole a buck
In Charlecote woods."
                        —"Where never a buck chewed fern,"
Laughed Kit, "unless it chewed the fern seed, too,
And walked invisible."
                        "Bring me some wine," called Ben,
And, with his knife thrumming upon the board,
He chanted, while his comrade munched and smiled.

> Will Shakespeare's out like Robin Hood
>   With his merry men all in green,
> To steal a deer in Charlecote wood
>   Where never a deer was seen.
>
> He's hunted all a night of June,
>   He's followed a phantom horn,
> He's killed a buck by the light of the moon,
>   . Under a fairy thorn.
>
> He's carried it home with his merry, merry band,
>   There never was haunch so fine;
> For this buck was born in Elfin-land
>   And fed upon sops-in-wine.
>
> This buck had browsed on elfin boughs
>   Of rose-marie and bay,
> And he's carried it home to the little white house
>   Of sweet Anne Hathaway.
>
> "The dawn above your thatch is red!
>   Slip out of your bed, sweet Anne!
> I have stolen a fairy buck," he said,
>   "The first since the world began.
>
> "Roast it on a golden spit,
>   And see that it do not burn;

180

For we never shall feather the like of it
  Out of the fairy fern."

She scarce had donned her long white gown
  And given him kisses four,
When the surly Sheriff of Stratford-town
  Knocked at the little green door.

They have jailed sweet Will for a poacher;
  But squarely he fronts the squire,
With "When did you hear in your woods of a deer?
  Was it under a fairy briar?"

Sir Thomas he puffs,—"If God thought good
  My water-butt ran with wine,
Or He dropt me a buck in Charlecote wood.
  I wot it is mine, not thine!"

"If you would eat of elfin meat,"
  Says Will, "you must blow up your horn!
Take your bow, and feather the doe
  That's under the fairy thorn!

"If you would feast on elfin food,
  You've only the way to learn!
Take your bow and feather the doe
  That's under the fairy fern!"

They're hunting high, they're hunting low,
  They're all away, away,
With horse and hound to feather the doe
  That's under the fairy spray!

Sir Thomas he raged!   Sir Thomas he swore!
  But all and all in vain;
For there never was deer in his woods before,
  And there never would be again!

And, as I brought the wine—"This is my grace,"
Laughed Kit, "Diana grant the jolly buck
That Shakespeare stole were toothsome as this pie."

He suddenly sank his voice,—"Hist, who comes here?
Look—Richard Bame, the Puritan!   O, Ben, Ben,
Your Mermaid Inn's the study for the stage,

Your only teacher of exits, entrances,
And all the shifting comedy.   Be grave!
Bame is the godliest hypocrite on earth!
Remember I'm an atheist, black as coal.
He has called me Wormall in an anagram.
Help me to bait him; but be very grave.
We'll talk of Venus."
                              As he whispered thus,
A long white face with small black-beaded eyes
Peered at him through the doorway.   All too well,
Afterwards, I recalled that scene, when Bame,
Out of revenge for this same night, I guessed,
Penned his foul tract on Marlowe's tragic fate;
And, twelve months later, I watched our Puritan
Riding to Tyburn in the hangman's cart
For thieving from an old bed-ridden dame
With whom he prayed, at supper-time, on Sundays.

Like a conspirator he sidled in,
Clasping a little pamphlet to his breast,
While, feigning not to see him, Ben began:—

"Will's *Venus and Adonis,* Kit, is rare,
A round, sound, full-blown piece of thorough work,
On a great canvas, coloured like one I saw
In Italy, by one—Titian!   None of the toys
Of artistry your lank-haired losels turn,
Your Phyllida—Love-lies-bleeding—Kiss-me-Quicks,
Your fluttering Sighs and Mark-how-I-break-my-beats.
Begotten like this, whenever and how you list,
Your Moths of verse that shrivel in every taper;
But a sound piece of craftsmanship to last
Until the stars are out.   'Tis twice the length
Of Vergil's books—he's listening!   Nay, don't look!—
Two hundred solid stanzas, think of that;
But each a square celestial brick of gold
Laid level and splendid.   I've laid bricks and know
What thorough work is.   If a storm should shake
The Tower of London down, Will's house would stand.
Look at his picture of the stallion,
Nostril to croup, that's thorough finished work!"

" 'Twill shock our Tribulation-Wholesomes, Ben!
Think of that kiss of Venus!   Deep, sweet, slow,
As the dawn breaking to its perfect flower

And golden moon of bliss; then slow, sweet, deep,
Like a great honeyed sunset it dissolves
Away!"
              A hollow groan, like a bass viol,
Resounded thro' the room.   Up started Kit
In feigned alarm—"What, Master Richard Bame!
Quick, Ben, the good man's ill.   Bring him some wine!
Red wine for Master Bame, the blood of Venus
That stained the rose!"
              "White wine for Master Bame,"
Ben echoed, "Juno's cream that" . . . Both at once
They thrust a wine-cup to the sallow lips
And smote him on the back.
"Sirs, you mistake!" coughed Bame, waving his hand
And struggling to his feet,
              "Sirs, I have brought
A message from a youth who walked with you
In wantonness, aforetime, and is now
Groaning in sulphurous fires!"
              "Kit, that means hell!"
"Yea, sirs, a pamphlet from the pit of hell,
Written by Robert Greene before he died.
Mark what he styles it—*A Groatsworth of Wit
Bought with a Million of Repentance!*"
              "Ah,
Poor Rob was all his life-time either drunk,
Wenching, or penitent, Ben!   Poor lad, he died
Young.   Let me see now, Master Bame, you say
Rob Greene wrote this on earth before he died,
And then you printed it yourself in hell!"
"Stay, sir, I came not to this haunt of sin
To make mirth for Beëlzebub!"
              "O, Ben,
That's you!"
              " 'Swounds, sir, am I Beëlzebub?
Ogs-gogs!" roared Ben, his hand upon his hilt!
"Nay, sir, I signified the god of flies!
I spake out of the scriptures!" snuffled Bame
With deprecating eye.
              "I come to save
A brand that you have kindled at your fire,
But not yet charred, not yet so far consumed,
One Richard Cholmeley, who declares to all
He was persuaded to turn atheist
By Marlowe's reasoning.   I have wrestled with him,

But find him still so constant to your words
That only you can save him from the fire."
"Why, Master Bame," said Kit, "had I the keys
To hell, the damned should all come out and dance
A morrice round the Mermaid Inn to-night."
"Nay, sir, the damned are damned!"

                    "Come, sit you down!
Take some more wine!   You'd have them all be damned
Except Dick Cholmeley.   What must I unsay
To save him?"   A quick eyelid dropt at Ben.
"Now tell me, Master Bame!"

                    "Sir, he derides
The books of Moses!"

                  "Bame, do you believe:—
There's none to hear us but Beëlzebub—
Do you believe that we must taste of death
Because God set a foolish naked wench
Too near an apple-tree, how long ago?
Five thousand years?   But there were men on earth
Long before that!"   "Nay, nay, sir, if you read
The books of Moses . . ."   "Moses was a juggler!"
"A juggler, sir, how, what!"   "Nay, sir, be calm!
Take some more wine—the white, if that's too red!
I never cared for Moses!   Help yourself
To red-deer pie.   Good!

                  All the miracles
You say that he performed—why, what are they?
I know one Heriots, lives in Friday Street,
Can do much more than Moses!   Eat your pie
In patience, friend, the mouth of man performs
One good work at a time.   What says he, Ben?
The red-deer stops his—what?   Sticks in his gizzard?
O—*led them through the wilderness!*   No doubt
He did—for forty years, and might have made
The journey in six months.   Believe me, sir,
That is no miracle.   Moses gulled the Jews!
Skilled in the sly tricks of the Egyptians,
Only one art betrayed him.   Sir, his books
Are filthily written.   I would undertake—
If I were put to write a new religion—
A method far more admirable.   Eh, what?
Gruel in the vestibule?   Interpret, Ben!
His mouth's too full!   *O, the New Testament!*
Why, there, consider, were not all the Apostles
Fishermen and base fellows, without wit

Or worth?"—again his eyelid dropt at Ben—
"The Apostle Paul alone had wit, and he
Was a most timorous fellow in bidding us
Prostrate ourselves to worldly magistrates
Against our conscience!   I shall fry for this?
I fear no bugbears or hobgoblins, sir,
And would have all men not to be afraid
Of roasting, toasting, pitch-forks, or the threats
Of earthly ministers, tho' their mouths be stuffed
With curses or with crusts of red-deer pie!
One thing I will confess—if I must choose—
Give me the Papists that can serve their God
Not with your scraps, but solemn ceremonies,
Organs, and singing men, and shaven crowns.
Your protestant is a hypocritical ass!"

"Profligate!   You blaspheme!"   Up started Bame,
A little unsteady now upon his feet,
And shaking his crumpled pamphlet over his head!

"Nay—if your pie be done, you shall partake
A second course.   Be seated, sir, I pray.
We atheists will pay the reckoning!
I had forgotten that a Puritan
Will swallow Moses like a red-deer pie
Yet choke at a wax-candle!   Let me read
Your pamphlet.   What, 'tis half addressed to me!
Ogs-gogs!   Ben!   Hark to this—the Testament
Of poor Rob Greene would cut Will Shakespeare off
With less than his own groatsworth!   Hark to this!"
And there, unseen by them, a quiet figure
Entered the room and beckoning me for wine
Seated himself to listen, Will himself,
While Marlowe read aloud with knitted brows.
" 'Trust them not; for there is an upstart crow
Beautified with our feathers!'
                                        —O, he bids
All green eyes open:—'And, being an absolute
Johannes fac-totum is in his own conceit
The only Shake-scene in a country!' "
                                        "Feathers!"
Exploded Ben.   "Why, come to that, he pouched
Your eagle's feather of blank verse, and lit
His Friar Bacon's little magic lamp
At the Promethean fire of Faustus.   Jove,

It was a faery buck, indeed, that Will
Poached in that greenwood."

        "Ben, see that you walk
Like Adam, naked! Nay, in nakedness
Adam was first. Trust me, you'll not escape
This calumny! Vergil is damned—he wears
A hen-coop round his waist, nicked in the night
From Homer! Plato is branded for a thief,
Why, he wrote Greek! And old Prometheus, too,
Who stole his fire from heaven!"

         "Who printed it?"
"Chettle! I know not why, unless he too
Be one of these same dwarfs that find the world
Too narrow for their jealousies. Ben, Ben,
I tell thee 'tis the dwarfs that find no world
Wide enough for their jostling, while the giants,
The gods themselves, can in one tavern find
Room wide enough to swallow the wide heaven
With all its crowded solitary stars."

"Why, then, the Mermaid Inn should swallow this,"
The voice of Shakespeare quietly broke in,
As laying a hand on either shoulder of Kit
He stood behind him in the gloom and smiled
Across the table at Ben, whose eyes still blazed
With boyhood's generous wrath. "Rob was a poet.
And had I known . . . no matter! I am sorry
He thought I wronged him. His heart's blood beats in this.
Look, where he says he dies forsaken, Kit!"
"Died drunk, more like," growled Ben. "And if he did,"
Will answered, "none was there to help him home,
Had not a poor old cobbler chanced upon him,
Dying in the streets, and taken him to his house,
And let him break his heart on his own bed.
Read his last words. You know he left his wife
And played the moth at tavern tapers, burnt
His wings and dropt into the mud. Read here,
His dying words to his forsaken wife,
Written in blood, Ben, blood. Read it, *'I charge thee,*
Doll, by the love of our youth, by my soul's rest,
See this man paid! Had he not succoured me
I had died in the streets.' How young he was to call
Thus on their poor dead youth, this withered shadow
That once was Robin Greene. He left a child—
See—in its face he prays her not to find

The father's, but her own. '*He is yet green*
And may grow straight,' so flickers his last jest,
Then out for ever. At the last he begged
A penny-pott of malmsey. In the bill,
All's printed now for crows and daws to peck,
You'll find four shillings for his winding sheet.
He had the poet's heart and God help all
Who have that heart and somehow lose their way
For lack of helm, souls that are blown abroad
By the great winds of passion, without power
To sway them, chartless captains. Multitudes ply
Trimly enough from bank to bank of Thames
Like shallow wherries, while tall galleons,
Out of their very beauty driven to dare
The uncompassed sea, founder in starless nights,
And all that we can say is—'They died drunk!' "

"I have it from veracious witnesses,"
Bame snuffled, "that the death of Robert Greene
Was caused by a surfeit, sir, of Rhenish wine
And pickled herrings. Also, sir, that his shirt
Was very foul, and while it was at wash
He lay i' the cobbler's old blue smock, sir!"

                                         "Gods,"
The voice of Raleigh muttered nigh mine ear,
"I had a dirty cloak once on my arm;
But a Queen's feet had trodden it! Drawer, take
Yon pamphlet, have it fried in cod-fish oil
And bring it hither. Bring a candle, too,
And sealing-wax! Be quick. The rogue shall eat it,
And then I'll seal his lips."

                          "No—not to-night,"
Kit whispered, laughing, "I've a prettier plan
For Master Bame."

                          "As for that scrap of paper,"
The voice of Shakespeare quietly resumed,
"Why, which of us could send his heart and soul
Thro' Caxton's printing-press and hope to find
The pretty pair unmangled. I'll not trust
The spoken word, no, not of my own lips,
Before the Judgment Throne against myself
Or on my own defence; and I'll not trust
The printed word to mirror Robert Greene.
See—here's another Testament, in blood,
Written, not printed, for the Mermaid Inn.

Rob sent it from his death-bed straight to me.
Read it. 'Tis for the Mermaid Inn alone;
And when 'tis read, we'll burn it, as he asks."

Then, from the hands of Shakespeare, Marlowe took
A little scroll, and, while the winds without
Rattled the shutters with their ghostly hands
And wailed among the chimney-tops, he read:—

> Greeting to all the Mermaid Inn
> From their old Vice and Slip of Sin,
> Greeting, Ben, to you, and you,
> Will Shakespeare and Kit Marlowe, too.
> Greeting from your Might-have-been,
> Your broken sapling, Robert Greene.
>
> Read my letter 'tis my last,
> Then let Memory blot me out,   .
> I would not make my maudlin past
> A trough for every swinish snout.
> First, I leave a debt unpaid,
> It's all chalked up, not much all told,
> For Bread and Sack.   When I am cold,
> Doll can pawn my Spanish blade
> And pay mine host.   She'll pay mine host!
> But . . . I have chalked up other scores
> In your own hearts, behind the doors,
> Not to be paid so quickly.   Yet,
> O, if you would not have my ghost
> Creeping in at dead of night,
> Out of the cold wind, out of the wet,
> With weeping face and helpless fingers
> Trying to wipe the marks away,
> Read what I can write, still write,
> While this life within them lingers.
> Let me pay, lads, let me pay.
>
> *Item,* for a peacock phrase,
> Flung out in a sudden blaze,
> Flung out at his friend Shake-scene,
> By this ragged Might-have-been,
> This poor Jackdaw, Robert Greene.
>
> Will, I knew it all the while!
> And you know it—and you smile!

My quill was but a Jackdaw's feather,
While the quill that Ben, there, wields,
Fluttered down thro' azure fields,
From an eagle in the sun;
And yours, Will, yours, no earth-born thing,
A plume of rainbow-tinctured grain,
Dropt out of an angel's wing.
Only a Jackdaw's feather mine,
And mine ran ink, and Ben's ran wine,
And yours the pure Pierian streams.

But I had dreams, O, I had dreams!
Dreams, you understand me, Will;
And I fretted at the tether
That bound me to the lowly plain,
Gnawed my heart out, for I knew
Once, tho' that was long ago,
I might have risen with Ben and you
Somewhere near that Holy Hill
Whence the living rivers flow.
Let it pass.   I did not know
One bitter phrase could ever fly
So far through that immortal sky
—Seeing all my songs had flown so low—
One envious phrase that cannot die
From century to century.

Kit Marlowe ceased a moment, and the wind,
As if indeed the night were all one ghost,
Wailed round the Mermaid Inn, then sent once more
Its desolate passion through the reader's voice:—

Some truth there was in what I said:
Kit Marlowe taught you half your trade;
And something of the rest you learned
From me,—but all you took you earned.
You took the best I had to give,
You took my clay and made it live;
And that—why that's what God must do!—
My music made for mortal ears
You flung to all the listening spheres.
You took my dreams and made them true;
And, if I claimed them, the blank air
Might claim the breath I shape to prayer.
I do not claim them!   Let the earth

Claim the thrones she brings to birth.
Let the first shapers of our tongue
Claim whate'er is said or sung,
Till the doom repeal that debt
And cancel the first alphabet.
Yet when, like a god, you scaled
The shining crags where my foot failed;
When I saw my fruit of the vine
Foam in the Olympian cup,
Or in that broader chalice shine
Blood-red, a sacramental drink,
With stars for bubbles, lifted up,
Through the universal night,
Up to the celestial brink,
Up to that quintessential Light
Where God acclaimed you for the wine
Crushed from those poor grapes of mine;
O, you'll understand, no doubt,
How the poor vine-dresser fell,
How a pin-prick can let out
All the bannered hosts of hell,
Nay, a knife-thrust, the sharp truth—
I had spilt my wine of youth,
The Temple was not mine to build.
My place in the world's march was filled.

Yet—through all the years to come—
Men to whom my songs are dumb
Will remember them and me
For that one cry of jealousy,
That curse where I had come to bless,
That harsh voice of unhappiness.
They'll note the curse, but not the pang,
Not the torment whence it sprang,
They'll note the blow at my friend's back,
But not the soul stretched on the rack.
They'll note the weak convulsive sting,
Not the crushed body and broken wing.

Item, for my thirty years,
Dashed with sun and splashed with tears,
Wan with revel, red with wine,
This Jack-o-lanthorn life of mine.
Other wiser, happier men,
Take the full three-score-and-ten,

Climb slow, and seek the sun.
Dancing down is soon done.
Golden boys, beware, beware,—
The ambiguous oracles declare
Loving gods for those that die
Young, as old men may; but I,
Quick as was my pilgrimage,
Wither in mine April age.

Item, one groatsworth of wit,
Bought at an exceeding price,
Ay, a million of repentance.
Let me pay the whole of it.
Lying here these deadly nights,
Lads, for me the Mermaid lights
Gleam as for a castaway
Swept along a midnight sea
The harbour-lanthorns, each a spark,
A pin-prick in the solid dark,
That lets trickle through a ray
Glorious out of Paradise,
To stab him with new agony.
Let me pay, lads, let me pay!
Let the Mermaid pass the sentence:
I am pleading guilty now,
A dead leaf on the laurel-bough,
And the storm whirls me away.

Kit Marlowe ceased; but not the wailing wind
That round and round the silent Mermaid Inn
Wandered, with helpless fingers trying the doors,
Like a most desolate ghost.
                                A sudden throng
Of players bustled in, shaking the rain
From their plumed hats.   "Veracious witnesses,"
The snuffle of Bame arose anew, "declare
It was a surfeit killed him, Rhenish wine
And pickled herrings.   His shirt was very foul.
He had but one.   His doublet, too, was frayed,
And his boots broken . . ."
                                "What! Gonzago, you!"
A short fat player called in a deep voice
Across the room and, throwing aside his cloak
To show the woman's robe he wore beneath,
Minced up to Bame and bellowed—" 'Tis such men

As you that tempt us women to our fall!"
And all the throng of players rocked and roared,
Till at a nod and wink from Kit a hush
Held them again.

              "Look to the door," he said,
"Is any listening?"   The young player crept,
A mask of mystery, to the door and peeped.
"All's well! The coast is clear!"

                     "Then shall we tell
Our plan to Master Bame?"

                       Round the hushed room
Went Kit, a pen and paper in his hand,
Whispering each to read, digest, and sign,
While Ben re-filled the glass of Master Bame.
"And now," said Kit aloud, "what think you, lads?
Shall he be told?"   Solemnly one or two
'Gan shake their heads with "Safety! safety, Kit!"
"O, Bame can keep a secret! Come, we'll tell him!
He can advise us how a righteous man
Should act! We'll let him share an he approve.
Now, Master Bame,—come closer—my good friend,
Ben Jonson here, hath lately found a way
Of—hush! Come closer!—coining money, Bame."
"Coining!" "Ay, hush, now! Hearken! A certain sure
And indiscoverable method, sir!
He is acquainted with one Poole, a felon
Lately released from Newgate, hath great skill
In mixture of metals—hush!—and, by the help
Of a right cunning maker of stamps, we mean
To coin French crowns, rose-nobles, pistolettes,
Angels and English shillings."

                     For one breath
Bame stared at him with bulging beetle-eyes,
Then murmured shyly as a country maid
In her first wooing, "Is't not against the law?"
"Why, sir, who makes the law? Why should not Bame
Coin his own crowns like Queen Elizabeth?
She is but mortal! And consider, too,
The good works it should prosper in your hands,
Without regard to red-deer pies and wine
White as the Milky Way. Such secrets, Bame,
Were not good for the general; but a few
Discreet and righteous palms, your own, my friend,
And mine,—what think you?"

                   With a hesitant glance

Of well-nigh child-like cunning, screwing his eyes,
Bame laughed a little huskily and looked round
At that grave ring of anxious faces, all
Holding their breath and thrilling his blunt nerves
With their stage-practice.   "And no risk?" breathed Bame,
"No risk at all?"   "O, sir, no risk at all!
We make the very coins.   Besides, that part
Touches not you.   Yours is the honest face,
That's all we want."
                    "Why, sir, if you be sure
There is no risk . . ."
                    "You'll help to spend it.   Good!
We'll talk anon of this, and you shall carry
More angels in your pocket, Master Bame,
Than e'er you'll meet in heaven.   Set hand on seal
To this now, Master Bame, to prove your faith.
Come, all have signed it.   Here's the quill, dip, write.
Good!"
            And Kit, pocketing the paper, bowed
The gull to the inn-door, saying as he went,—
"You shall hear further when the plan's complete.
But there's one great condition—not one word,
One breath of scandal more on Robert Greene.
He's dead; but he was one of us.   The day
You air his shirt, I air this paper, too."
No gleam of understanding, even then,
Illumed that long white face: no stage, indeed,
Has known such acting as the Mermaid Inn
That night, and Bame but sniggered, "Why, of course,
There's good in all men; and the best of us
Will make mistakes."
                    "But no mistakes in this,"
Said Kit, "or all together we shall swing
At Tyburn—who knows what may leap to light?
You understand?   No scandal!"   "Not a breath!"
So, in dead silence, Master Richard Bame
Went out into the darkness and the night,
To ask, as I have heard, for many a moon,
The price of malmsey-butts and silken hose,
And doublets slashed with satin.
                                As the door
Slammed on his back, the pent-up laughter burst
With echo and re-echo round the room,
But ceased as Will tossed on the glowing hearth
The last poor Testament of Robert Greene.

All watched it burn. The black wind wailed and moaned
Around the Mermaid as the sparks flew up.
"God, what a night for ships upon the sea,"
Said Raleigh, peering through the wet black panes,
"Well—we may thank Him for the Little Red Ring!"
"*The Little Red Ring*," cried Kit, "*the Little Red Ring!*"
Then up stood Dekker on the old black settle.
"Give it a thumping chorus, lads," he called,
And sang this brave song of the Mermaid Inn:—

> Seven wise men on an old black settle,
>   Seven wise men of the Mermaid Inn,
> Ringing blades of the one right metal,
>   What is the best that a blade can win?
> Bread and cheese, and a few small kisses?
>   Ha! ha! ha!   Would you take them—you?
> —Ay, if Dame Venus would add to her blisses
>   A roaring fire and a friend or two!

Chorus: Up now, answer me, tell me true!—
>   —Ay, if the hussy would add to her blisses
>   A roaring fire and a friend or two!

> What will you say when the world is dying?
>   What, when the last wild midnight falls
> Dark, too dark for the bat to be flying
>   Round the ruins of old St. Paul's?
> What will be last of the lights to perish?
>   What but the little red ring we knew,
> Lighting the hands and the hearts that cherish
>   A fire, a fire, and a friend or two!

Chorus: Up now, answer me, tell me true!
>   What will be last of the stars to perish?
>   —The fire that lighteth a friend or two!

> Up now, answer me, on your mettle
>   Wisest man of the Mermaid Inn,
> Soberest man on the old black settle,
>   Out with the truth!   It was never a sin.—
> Well, if God saved me alone of the seven,
>   Telling me *you* must be damned, or *you*,
> "This," I would say, "This is hell, not heaven!
>   Give me the fire and a friend or two!"

Chorus: Steel was never so ringing true:
          "God," we would say, "this is hell, not heaven!
          Give us the fire, and a friend or two!"

III

BLACK BILL'S HONEY-MOON

THE garlands of a Whitsun ale were strewn
About our rushes, the night that Raleigh brought
Bacon to sup with us.   There, on that night,
I saw the singer of the *Faërie Queen*
Quietly spreading out his latest cantos
For Shakespeare's eye, like white sheets in the sun.
Marlowe, our morning-star, and Michael Drayton
Talked in that ingle-nook.   And Ben was there,
Humming a song upon that old black settle:
          "Or leave a kiss but in the cup
          And I'll not ask for wine."
But, meanwhile, he drank malmsey.
                              Francis Bacon
Straddled before the fire; and, all at once,
He said to Shakespeare, in a voice that gripped
The Mermaid Tavern like an arctic frost:
*"There are no poets in this age of ours,
Not to compare with Plautus.   They are all
Dead, the men that were famous in old days."*
"Why—so they are," said Will.   The humming stopped.
I saw poor Spenser, a shy gentle soul,
With haunted eyes like starlit forest pools,
Smuggling his cantos under his cloak again.
"There's verse enough, no doubt," Bacon went on,
"But English is no language for the Muse.
Whom would you call our best?   There's Gabriel Harvey,
And Edward, Earl of Oxford.   Then there's Dyer,
And Doctor Golding; while, for tragedy,
Thomas, Lord Buckhurst, hath a lofty vein.
And, in a lighter prettier vein, why, Will,
There is *thyself!*   But—where's Euripides?"

"Dead," echoed Ben, in a deep ghost-like voice.
And drip—drip—drip—outside we heard the rain
Miserably dropping round the Mermaid Inn.

195

"Thy Summer's Night—eh, Will?   Midsummer's Night?—
That's a quaint fancy," Bacon droned anew,
"But—Athens was an error, Will!   Not Athens!
Titania knew not Athens!   Those wild elves
Of thy Midsummer's Dream—eh?   Midnight's Dream?—
Are English all.   Thy woods, too, smack of England;
They never grew round Athens.   Bottom, too,
He is not Greek!"
                          "Greek?" Will said, with a chuckle,
"Bottom a Greek?   Why, no, he was the son
Of Marian Hacket, the fat wife that kept
An ale-house, Wincot-way.   I lodged with her
Walking from Stratford.   You have never tramped
Along that countryside?   By Burton Heath?
Ah, well, you would not know my fairylands.
It warms my blood to let my home-spuns play
Around your cold white Athens.   There's a joy
In jumping time and space."
                          But, as he took
The cup of sack I proffered, solemnly
The lawyer shook his head.   "Will, couldst thou use
Thy talents with discretion, and obey
Classic examples, thou mightst match old Plautus,
In all except priority of the tongue.
This English tongue is only for an age,
But Latin for all time.   So I propose
To embalm in Latin my philosophies.
Well seize your hour!   But, ere you die, you'll sail
A British galleon to the golden courts
Of Cleopatra."
                          "Sail it!" Marlowe roared,
Mimicking in a fit of thunderous glee
The drums and trumpets of his Tamburlaine:
"And let her buccaneers bestride the sphinx,
And play at bowls with Pharaoh's pyramids,
And hale white Egypt with their tarry hands
Home to the Mermaid!   Lift the good old song
That Rob Greene loved.   Gods, how the lad would shout it!
Stand up and sing, John Davis!"
                          "Up!" called Raleigh,
"Lift the chanty of Black Bill's Honey-moon, Jack!
We'll keep the chorus going!"
                          "Silence, all!"
Ben Jonson echoed, rolling on his bench:
"This gentle lawyer hath a longing, lads,

To hear a right Homeric hymn.   Now, Jack!
But wet your whistle, first!   A cup of sack
For the first canto!   Muscadel, the next!
Canary for the last!"   I brought the cup.
John Davis emptied it at one mighty draught,
Leapt on a table, stamped with either foot,
And straight began to troll this mad sea-tale:

CANTO THE FIRST

Let Martin Parker at hawthorn-tide
  Prattle in Devonshire lanes,
Let all his pedlar poets beside
  Rattle their gallows-chains,
A tale like mine they never shall tell
  Or a merrier ballad sing,
Till the Man in the Moon pipe up the tune
  And the stars play Kiss-in-the-Ring!

Chorus: Till Philip of Spain in England reign,
  And the stars play Kiss-in-the-Ring!

All in the gorgeous dawn of day
  From grey old Plymouth Sound
Our galleon crashed thro' the crimson spray
  To sail the world around:
Cloud i' the Sun was her white-scrolled name,—
  There was never a lovelier lass
For sailing in state after pieces of eight
  With her bombards all of brass.

Chorus: Culverins, robinets, iron may-be;
  But her bombards all of brass!

Now, they that go down to the sea in ships,
  Though piracy be their trade,
For all that they pray not much with their lips
  They know where the storms are made:
With the stars above and the sharks below,
  They need not parson or clerk;
But our bo'sun Bill was an atheist still,
  Except—sometimes—in the dark!

Chorus: Now let Kit Marlowe mark!
  Our bo'sun Bill was an atheist still,
    Except—sometimes—in the dark!

197

All we adventured for, who shall say,
   Nor yet what our port might be?—
A magical city of old Cathay,
   Or a castle of Muscovy,
With our atheist bo'sun, Bill, Black Bill,
   Under the swinging Bear,
Whistling at night for a seaman to light
   His little poop-lanthorns there.

Chorus:　On the deep, in the night, for a seaman to light
   His little lost lanthorns there.

But, as over the Ocean-sea we swept,
   We chanced on a strange new land
Where a valley of tall white lilies slept
   With a forest on either hand;
A valley of white in a purple wood
   And, behind it, faint and far,
Breathless and bright o'er the last rich height
   Floated the sunset-star.

Chorus:　Fair and bright o'er the rose-red height,
   Venus, the sunset-star.

'Twas a marvel to see, as we beached our boat,
   Black Bill, in that peach-bloom air,
With the great white lilies that reached to his throat
   Like a stained-glass bo'sun there,
And our little ship's chaplain, puffing and red,
   A-starn as we onward stole,
With the disk of a lily behind his head
   Like a cherubin's aureole.

Chorus:　He was round and red and behind his head
   He'd a cherubin's aureole.

"Hyrcania, land of honey and bees,
   We have found thee at last," he said,
"Where the honey-comb swells in the hollow trees."
   (O, the lily behind his head!)
"The honey-comb swells in the purple wood!
   'Tis the swette which the heavens distil,
Saith Pliny himself, on my little book-shelf!
   Is the world not sweet to thee, Bill?"

Chorus: "Saith Pliny himself, on my little book-shelf!
              Is the world not sweet to thee, Bill?"

Now a man may taste of the devil's hot spice,
   And yet if his mind run back
To the honey of childhood's Paradise
   His heart is not wholly black;
And Bill, Black Bill, from the days of his youth
   Tho' his chest was broad as an oak,
Had cherished one innocent little sweet tooth,
   And it itched as our chaplain spoke.

Chorus: He had kept one perilous little tooth,
              And it itched as our chaplain spoke.

All around was a mutter of bees,
   And Bill 'gan muttering too,—
"If the honey-comb swells in the hollow trees,
   (What else can a Didymus do?)
I'll steer to the purple woods myself
   And see if this thing be so,
Which the chaplain found on his little book-shelf,
   For Pliny lived long ago."

Chorus: There's a platter of delf on his little book-shelf,
              And Pliny lived long ago.

Scarce had he spoken when, out of the wood,
   And buffeting all around,
Rooting our sea-boots where we stood,
   There rumbled a marvellous sound,
As a mountain of honey were crumbling asunder,
   Or a sunset-avalanche hurled
Honey-comb boulders of golden thunder
   To smother the old black world.

Chorus: Honey-comb boulders of musical thunder
              To mellow this old black world.

And the chaplain he whispered—"This honey, one saith,
   On my camphired cabin-shelf,
None may harvest on pain of death;
   For the bee would eat it himself!
None walketh those woods but him whose voice

In the dingles you then did hear!"
"A Voice?" growls Bill.   "Ay, Bill, r-r-rejoice!
'Twas the great Hyrcanian Bear!"

Chorus: Give thanks!   *Re*-joice!   'Twas the glor-r-r-ious Voice
Of the great Hyrcanian Bear!

But, marking that Bill looked bitter indeed,
For his sweet tooth hungered sore,
"Consider," he saith, "that the Sweet hath need
Of the Sour, as the Sea of the Shore!
As the night to the day is our grief to our joy,
And each for its brother prepares
A banquet, Bill, that would otherwise cloy
Thus is it with honey and bears."

Chorus: Roses and honey and laughter would cloy!
Give us thorns, too, and sorrow and bears!

"Consider," he saith, "how by fretting a string
The lutanist maketh sweet moan,
And a bird ere it fly must have air for its wing
To buffet or fall like a stone:
Tho' you blacken like Pluto you make but more white
These blooms which not Enna could yield!
Consider, Black Bill, ere the coming of night,
The lilies," he saith, "of the field."

Chorus: "Consider, Black Bill, in this beautiful light,
The lilies," he saith, "of the field."

"Consider the claws of a Bear," said Bill,
"That can rip off the flesh from your bones,
While his belly could cabin the skipper and still
Accommodate Timothy Jones!
Why, that's where a seaman who cares for his grog
Perspires how this world isn't square!
If there's *cause* for a *cow,* if there's *use* for a *dog,*
By Pope John, there's no *Sense* in a *Bear!*"

Chorus: Cause for a cow, use for a dog,
By'r Lakin, no *Sense* in a *Bear!*

But our little ship's chaplain—"Sense," quoth he,
"Hath the Bear tho' his making have none;

For, my little book saith, by the sting of this bee
　　Would Ursus be wholly foredone,
But, or ever the hive he adventureth nigh
　　And its crisp gold-crusted dome,
He lardeth his nose and he greaseth his eye
　　With a piece of an honey-comb."

Chorus:　His velvety nose and his sensitive eye
　　With a piece of an honey-comb.

Black Bill at the word of that golden crust
—For his ears had forgotten the roar,
And his eyes grew soft with their innocent lust—
　　'Gan licking his lips once more:
"Be it bound like a missal and printed as fair,
　　With capitals blue and red,
'Tis a lie; for what honey could comfort a bear,
　　Till the bear win the honey?" he said.

Chorus:　"Ay, *whence* the first honey wherewith the first bear
　　First larded his nose?" he said.

"Thou first metaphysical bo'sun, Bill,"
　　Our chaplain quizzingly cried,
"Wilt thou riddle me redes of a dumpling still
　　With thy 'how came the apple inside'?"
"Nay," answered Bill, "but I quest for truth,
　　And I find it not on your shelf!
I will face your Hyrcanian bear, forsooth,
　　And look at his nose myself."

Chorus:　For truth, for truth, or a little sweet tooth—
　　I will into the woods myself.

Breast-high thro' that foam-white ocean of bloom
　　With its wonderful spokes of gold,
Our sun-burnt crew in the rose-red gloom
　　Like buccaneer galleons rolled:
Breast-high, breast-high in the lilies we stood,
　　And before we could say "good-night,"
Out of the valley and into the wood
　　He plunged thro' the last rich light.

Chorus:　Out of the lilies and into the wood,
　　Where the Great Bear walks all night!

And our little ship's chaplain he piped thro' the trees
   As the moon rose, white and still,
"Hylas, return to thy Heracles!"
   And we helped him with "Come back, Bill!"
Thrice he piped it, thrice we halloo'd,
   And thrice we were dumb to hark;
But never an answer came from the wood,
   So—we turned to our ship in the dark.

Chorus: Good-bye, Bill! you're a Didymus still;
      But—you're all alone in the dark.

"This honey now"—as the first canto ceased,
The great young Bacon pompously began—
"Which Pliny calleth, as it were, the swette
Of heaven, or spettle of the stars, is found
In Muscovy. Now . . ." "Bring the muscadel,"
Ben Jonson roared—" 'Tis a more purple drink,
And suits with the next canto!"
                        At one draught
John Davis drained the cup, and with one hand
Beating the measure, rapidly trolled again.

CANTO THE SECOND

Now, Rabelais, art thou quite foredone,
Dan Chaucer, Drayton, Every One!
Leave we aboard our *Cloud i' the Sun*
   This crew of pirates dreaming—
Of Angels, minted in the blue
Like golden moons, Rose-nobles, too,
As under the silver-sliding dew
   Our emerald creek lay gleaming!

Chorus: Under the stars lay gleaming!

And mailed with scales of gold and green
The high star-lilied banks between,
Nosing our old black hulk unseen,
   Great alligators shimmered:
Blood-red jaws i' the blue-black ooze,
Where all the long warm day they snooze,
Chewing old cuds of pirate-crews,
   Around us grimly glimmered.

Chorus: Their eyes like rubies glimmered.

Let us now sing of Bill, good sirs!
Follow him, all green forestéres,
Fearless of Hyrcanian bears
   As of these ghostly lilies!
For Oh, not Drayton there could sing
  Of wild Pigwiggen and his King
  So merry a jest, so jolly a thing
   As this my tale of Bill is.

Chorus: Into the woods where Bill is!

Now starts he as a white owl hoots,
And now he stumbles over roots,
And now beneath his big sea-boots
   In yon deep glade he crunches
Black cakes of honey-comb that were
So elfin-sweet, perchance, last year;
But neither Bo'sun, now, nor Bear
   At that dark banquet munches.

Chorus: Onward still he crunches!

Black cakes of honey-comb he sees
Above him in the forks of trees,
Filled by stars instead of bees,
   With brimming silver glisten:
But ah, such food of gnome and fay
Could neither Bear nor Bill delay
Till where yon ferns and moonbeams play
   He starts and stands to listen!

Chorus: What melody doth he listen?

Is it the Night-Wind as it comes
Through the wood and softly thrums
Silvery tabors, purple drums,
   To speed some wild-wood revel?
Nay, Didymus, what faint sweet din
Of viol and flute and violin
Makes all the forest round thee spin,
   The Night-Wind or the Devil?

Chorus: No doubt at all—the Devil!

He stares, with naked knife in hand,
This buccaneer in fairyland!
Dancing in a saraband
　　The red ferns reel about him!
Dancing in a morrice-ring
The green ferns curtsey, kiss and cling!
Their Marians flirt, their Robins fling
　　Their feathery heels to flout him!

Chorus:　　The whole wood reels about him.

Dance, ye shadows!　O'er the glade,
Bill, the Bo'sun, undismayed,
Pigeon-toes with glittering blade!
　　Drake was never bolder!
Devil or Spaniard, what cares he
Whence your eerie music be?
Till—lo, against yon old oak-tree
　　He leans his brawny shoulder!

Chorus:　　He lists and leans his shoulder!

Ah, what melody doth he hear
As to that gnarled old tree-trunk there
He lays his wind-bit brass-ringed ear,
　　And steals his arm about it?
What Dryad could this Bo'sun win
To that slow-rippling amorous grin?—
'Twas full of singing bees within!
　　Not Didymus could doubt it!

Chorus:　　So loud they buzzed about it!

Straight, o'er a bough one leg he throws,
And up that oaken main-mast goes
With reckless red unlarded nose
　　And gooseberry eyes of wonder!
Till now, as in a galleon's hold,
Below, he sees great cells of gold
Whence all the hollow trunk up-rolled
　　A low melodious thunder.

Chorus:　　A sweet and perilous thunder!

Ay, there, within that hollow tree,
Will Shakespeare, mightst thou truly see

The Imperial City of the Bee,
     In Chrysomelan splendour!
And, in the midst, one eight-foot dome
Swells o'er that Titan honey-comb
Where the Bee-Empress hath her home,
     With such as do attend her.

Chorus: Weaponed with stings attend her!

But now her singing sentinels
Have turned to sleep in waxen cells,
And Bill leans down his face and smells
     The whole sweet summer's cargo—
In one deep breath, the whole year's bloom,
Lily and thyme and rose and broom,
One Golden Fleece of flower-perfume
     In that old oaken Argo.

Chorus: That green and golden Argo!

And now he hangs with dangling feet
Over that dark abyss of sweet,
Striving to reach such wild gold meat
     As none could buy for money:
His left hand grips a swinging branch
When—crack!   Our Bo'sun, stout and stanch
Falls like an Alpine avalanche,
     Feet first into the honey!

Chorus: Up to his ears in honey!

And now his red unlarded nose
And bulging eyes are all that shows
Above it, as he puffs and blows!
     And now—to 'scape the scathing
Of that black host of furious bees
His nose and eyes he fain would grease
And bobs below those golden seas
     Like an old woman bathing.

Chorus: Old Mother Hubbard bathing!

And now he struggles, all in vain,
To reach some little bough again;
But, though he heaves with might and main,

This honey holds his ribs, sirs,
So tight, a barque might sooner try
To steer a cargo through the sky
Than Bill, thus honey-logged, to fly
    By flopping of his jib, sirs!

Chorus: His tops'l and his jib, sirs!

Like Oberon in the hive his beard
With wax and honey all besmeared
Would make the crescent moon afeard
    That now is sailing brightly
Right o'er his leafy donjon-keep!
But that she knows him sunken deep,
And that his tower is straight and steep,
    She would not smile so lightly.

Chorus: Look down and smile so lightly.

She smiles in that small heavenly space,
Ringed with the tree-trunk's leafy grace,
While upward grins his ghastly face
    As if some wild-wood Satyr,
Some gnomish Ptolemy should dare
Up that dark optic tube to stare,
As all unveiled she floated there,
    Poor maiden moon, straight at her!

Chorus: The buccaneering Satyr!

But there, till some one help him out,
Black Bill must stay, without a doubt.
"Help!   Help!" he gives a muffled shout!
    None but the white owls hear it!
Who?   Whoo? they cry: Bill answers "ME!
*I am stuck fast in this great tree!
Bring me a rope, good Timothy!
    There's honey, lads, we'll share it!"*

Chorus: Ay, now he wants to share it.

Then, thinking help may come with morn,
He sinks, half-famished and out-worn,
And scarce his nose exalts its horn
    Above that sea of glory!

But, even as he owns defeat,
His belly saith, "A man must eat,
And since there is none other meat,
   Come, lap this mess before 'ee!"

Chorus: This glorious mess before 'ee.

Then Dian sees a right strange sight
As, bidding him a fond good-night,
She flings a silvery kiss to light
   In that deep oak-tree hollow,
And finds that gold and crimson nose
A moving, munching, ravenous rose
That up and down unceasing goes,
   Save when he stops to swallow!

Chorus: He finds it hard to swallow!

Ay, now his best becomes his worst,
For honey cannot quench his thirst,
Though he should eat until he burst;
   But, ah, the skies are kindly,
And from their tender depths of blue
They send their silver-sliding dew.
So Bill thrusts out his tongue anew
   And waits to catch it—blindly!

Chorus: For ah, the stars are kindly!

And sometimes, with a shower of rain,
They strive to ease their prisoner's pain:
Then Bill thrusts out his tongue again
   With never a grace, the sinner!
And day and night and day goes by,
And never a comrade comes anigh,
And still the honey swells as high
   For supper, breakfast, dinner!

Chorus: Yet Bill has grown no thinner!

The young moon grows to full and throws
Her buxom kiss upon his nose,
As nightly over the tree she goes,
   And peeps and smiles and passes,
Then with her fickle silver flecks

Our old black galleon's dreaming decks;
And then her face, with nods and becks,
    In midmost ocean glasses.

Chorus: 'Twas ever the way with lasses!

Ah, Didymus, hast thou won indeed
That Paradise which is thy meed?
(Thy tale not all that run may read!)
    Thy sweet hath now no leaven!
Now, like an onion in a cup
Of mead, thou liest for Jove to sup,
Could Polyphemus lift thee up
    With Titan hands to heaven!

Chorus: This great oak-cup to heaven!

The second canto ceased; and, as they raised
Their wine-cups with the last triumphant note,
Bacon, undaunted, raised his grating voice—
"This honey which, in some sort, may be styled
The Spettle of the Stars . . ."   "Bring the Canary!"
Ben Jonson roared.   "It is a moral wine
And suits the third, last canto!"   At one draught
John Davis drained it and began anew.

CANTO THE THIRD

A month went by.   We were hoisting sail!
    We had lost all hope of Bill;
Though, laugh as you may at a seaman's tale,
    He was fast in his honey-comb still!
And often he thinks of the chaplain's word
    In the days he shall see no more,—
How the Sweet, indeed, of the Sour hath need;
    And the Sea, likewise, of the Shore.

Chorus: The chaplain's word of the Air and a Bird;
    Of the Sea, likewise, and the Shore!

"O, had I the wings of a dove, I would fly
    To a heaven, of aloes and gall!
I have honeyed," he yammers, "my nose and mine eye,
    And the bees cannot sting me at all!

And it's O, for the sting of a little brown bee,
   Or to blister my hands on a rope,
Or to buffet a thundering broad-side sea
   On a deck like a mountain-slope!"

Chorus: With her mast snapt short, and a list to port
   And a deck like a mountain-slope.

But alas, and he thinks of the chaplain's voice
   When that roar from the woods out-break—
R-r-re-joice! *R-r-re-joice!* "Now, wherefore rejoice
   In the music a bear could make?
'Tis a judgment, maybe, that I stick in this tree;
   Yet in this I out-argued him fair!
Though I live, though I die, in this honey-comb pie,
   By Pope Joan, there's no sense in a bear!"

Chorus: Notes in a nightingale, plums in a pie,
   By'r Lakin, no *Sense* in a *Bear!*

He knew not our anchor was heaved from the mud:
   He was growling it over again,
When—a strange sound suddenly froze his blood,
   And curdled his big slow brain!—
A marvellous sound, as of great steel claws
   Gripping the bark of his tree,
Softly ascended!   Like lightning ended
   His honey-comb reverie!

Chorus: The honey-comb quivered!   The little leaves shivered!
   Something was climbing the tree!

Something that breathed like a fat sea-cook,
   Or a pirate of fourteen ton!
But it clomb like a cat (tho' the whole tree shook)
   Stealthily tow'rds the sun,
Till, as Black Bill gapes at the little blue ring
   Overhead, which he calls the sky,
It is clean blotted out by a monstrous Thing
   Which—*hath larded its nose and its eye.*

Chorus: O, well for thee, Bill, that this monstrous Thing
   Hath blinkered its little red eye.

Still as a mouse lies Bill with his face
   Low down in the dark sweet gold,

While this monster turns round in the leaf-fringed space
   Then—taking a good firm hold,
As the skipper descending the cabin-stair,
   Tail-first with a vast slow tread,
Solemnly, softly, cometh this Bear
   Straight down o'er the Bo'sun's head.

Chorus: Solemnly—slowly—cometh this Bear,
     Tail-first o'er the Bo'sun's head.

Nearer—nearer—then all Bill's breath
   Out-bursts in one leap and yell!
And this Bear thinks, "Now am I gripped from beneath
   By a roaring devil from hell!"
And madly Bill clutches his brown bow-legs,
   And madly this Bear doth hale,
With his little red eyes fear-mad for the skies
   And Bill's teeth fast in his tail!

Chorus: Small wonder a Bear should quail!
    To have larded his nose, to have greased his eyes,
     And be stung at the last in his tail.

Pull, Bo'sun! Pull, Bear! In the hot sweet gloom,
   Pull Bruin, pull Bill, for the skies!
Pull—out of their gold with a bombard's boom
   Come Black Bill's honeyed thighs!
Pull! Up! Up! Up! with a scuffle and scramble,
   To that little blue ring of bliss,
This Bear doth go with our Bo'sun in tow
   Stinging his tail, I wis.

Chorus: And this Bear thinks—"Many great bees I know,
    But there never was Bee like this!"

   .   .   .   .

All in the gorgeous death of day
   We had slipped from our emerald creek,
And our *Cloud i' the Sun* was careening away
   With the old gay flag at the peak,
When, suddenly, out of the purple wood,
   Breast-high thro' the lilies there danced
A tall lean figure, black as a nigger,
   That shouted and waved and pranced!

Chorus: A gold-greased figure, but black as a nigger,
      Waving his shirt as he pranced!

    " 'Tis Hylas!   'Tis Hylas!" our chaplain flutes,
      And our skipper he looses a shout!
    " 'Tis Bill!   Black Bill, in his old sea-boots!
      Stand by to bring her about!
    Har-r-rd a-starboard!"   And round we came,
      With a lurch and a dip and a roll,
    And a banging boom thro' the rose-red gloom
      For our old Black Bo'sun's soul!

Chorus: Alive!   Not dead!   Tho' behind his head
      He'd a seraphin's aureole!

.   .   .   .

    And our chaplain he sniffs, as Bill finished his tale,
      (With the honey still scenting his hair!)
    O'er a plate of salt beef and a mug of old ale—
      "By Pope Joan, there's no sense in a bear!"
    And we laughed, but our Bo'sun he solemnly growls
      —"Till the sails of yon heavens be furled,
    It taketh—now, mark!—all the beasts in the Ark,
      Teeth and claws, too, to make a good world!"

Chorus: Till the great—blue—sails—be—furled,
     It taketh—now, mark!—all the beasts in the Ark,
     Teeth and claws, too, to make a good world!

    "Sack!   Sack!   Canary!   Malmsey!   Muscadel!"—
    As the last canto ceased, the Mermaid Inn
    Chorussed.   I flew from laughing voice to voice;
    But, over all the hubbub, rose the drone
    Of Francis Bacon,—"Now, this Muscovy
    Is a cold clime, not favourable to bees
    (Or love, which is a weakness of the south)
    As well might be supposed.   Yet, as hot lands
    Gender hot fruits and odoriferous spice,
    In this case we may think that honey and flowers
    Are comparable with the light airs of May
    And a more temperate region.   Also we see,
    As Pliny saith, this honey being a swette
    Of heaven, a certain spettle of the stars,
    Which, gathering unclean vapours as it falls,

Hangs as a fat dew on the boughs, the bees
Obtain it partly thus, and afterwards
Corrupt it in their stomachs, and at last
Expel it through their mouths and harvest it
In hives; yet, of its heavenly source it keeps
A great part.   Thus, by various principles
Of natural philosophy we observe—"
And, as he leaned to Drayton, droning thus,
I saw a light gleam of celestial mirth
Flit o'er the face of Shakespeare—scarce a smile—
A swift irradiation from within
As of a cloud that softly veils the sun.

IV

THE SIGN OF THE GOLDEN SHOE

WE had just set our brazier smouldering,
To keep the Plague away.   Many a house
Was marked with the red cross.   The bells tolled
Incessantly.   Nash crept into the room
Shivering like a fragment of the night,
His face yellow as parchment, and his eyes
Burning.

   "The Plague!   He has taken it!" voices cried.
"That's not the Plague!   The old carrion-crow is drunk;
But stand away.   What ails you, Nash my lad?"
Then, through the clamour, as through a storm at sea,
The master's voice, the voice of Ben, rang out,
"Nash!"

   Ben leapt to his feet, and like a ship
Shouldering the waves, he shouldered the throng aside.
"What ails you, man?   What's that upon your breast?
Blood?"

   "Marlowe is dead," said Nash,
And stunned the room to silence . . .

       "Marlowe—dead!"
Ben caught him by the shoulders.   "Nash!   Awake!
What do you mean?   Marlowe?   Kit Marlowe?   Dead?
I supped with him—why—not three nights ago!
You are drunk!   You are dazed!   There's blood upon your coat!"
"That's—where he died," said Nash, and suddenly sank
Sidelong across a bench, bowing his head
Between his hands . . .

Wept, I believe.   Then, like a whip of steel,
His lean black figure sprang erect again.
"Marlowe!" he cried, "Kit Marlowe, killed for a punk,
A taffeta petticoat!   Killed by an apple-squire!
Drunk!   I was drunk; but I am sober now,
Sober enough, by God!   Poor Kit is dead."

.   .   .   .

The Mermaid Inn was thronged for many a night
With startled faces.   Voices rose and fell,
As I recall them, in a great vague dream,
Curious, pitiful, angry, thrashing out
The tragic truth.   Then, all along the Cheape,
The ballad-mongers waved their sheets of rhyme,
Croaking: *Come buy!   Come buy!   The bloody death
Of Wormall, writ by Master Richard Bame!
Come buy!   Come buy!   The Atheist's Tragedy.*
And, even in Bread Street, at our very door,
The crowder to his cracked old fiddle sang:—

> *"He was a poet of proud repute
> And wrote full many a play,
> Now strutting in a silken suit,
> Now begging by the way."*

Then, out of the hubbub and the clash of tongues,
The bawdy tales and scraps of balladry,
(As out of chaos rose the slow round world)
At last, though for the Mermaid Inn alone,
Emerged some tragic semblance of a soul,
Some semblance of the rounded truth, a world
Glimpsed only through great mists of blood and tears,
Yet smitten, here and there, with dreadful light,
As I believe, from heaven.
                              Strangely enough,
(Though Ben forgot his pipe and Will's deep eyes
Deepened and softened, when they spoke of Kit,
For many a month thereafter) it was Nash
That took the blow like steel into his heart.
Nash, our "Piers Penniless," whom Rob Greene had called
"Young Juvenal," the first satirist of our age,
Nash, of the biting tongue and subtle sneer,
Brooded upon it, till his grief became
Sharp as a rapier, ready to lunge in hate
At all the lies of shallower hearts.

                              One night,
The night he raised the mists from that wild world,
He talked with Chapman in the Mermaid Inn
Of Marlowe's poem that was left half-sung,
His *Hero and Leander*.
                         "Kit desired,
If he died first, that you should finish it,"
Said Nash.
                 A loaded silence filled the room
As with the imminent spirit of the dead
Listening.   And long that picture haunted me:
Nash, like a lithe young Mephistopheles
Leaning between the silver candle-sticks,
Across the oak table, with his keen white face,
Dark smouldering eyes, and black, dishevelled hair;
Chapman, with something of the steady strength
That helms our ships, and something the Greek,
The cool clear passion of Platonic thought
Behind the fringe of his Olympian beard
And broad Homeric brows, confronting him
Gravely.
               There was a burden of mystery
Brooding on all that night; and, when at last
Chapman replied, I knew he felt it, too.
The curious pedantry of his wonted speech
Was charged with living undertones, like truths
Too strange and too tremendous to be breathed
Save thro' a mask.   And though, in lines that flamed
Once with strange rivalry, Shakespeare himself defied
Chapman, that spirit "by spirits taught to write
Above a mortal pitch," Will's nimbler sense
Was quick to breathings from beyond our world
And could not hold them lightly.
                                 "Ah, then Kit,"
Said Chapman, "had some prescience of his end,
Like many another dreamer.   What strange hints
Of things past, present, and to come, there lie
Sealed in the magic pages of that music
Which, laying strong hold on universal laws,
Ranges beyond these mud-walls of the flesh,
Though dull wits fail to follow.   It was this
That made men find an oracle in the books
Of Vergil, and an everlasting fount
Of science in the prophets."

Once again

That haunted silence filled the shadowy room;
And, far away up Bread Street, we could hear
The crowder, piping of black Wormall still:—

> *"He had a friend, once gay and green,*
> *Who died of want alone,*
> *In whose black fate he might have seen*
> *The warning of his own."*

"Strange he should ask a hod-man like myself
To crown that miracle of his April age,"
Said Chapman, murmuring softly under breath,
"Amorous Leander, beautiful and young . . .
Why, Nash, had I been only charged to raise
Out of its grave in the green Hellespont
The body of that boy,
To make him sparkle and leap thro' the cold waves
And fold young Hero to his heart again,
The task were scarce as hard.

But . . . stranger still,"—

And his next words, although I hardly knew
All that he meant, went tingling through my flesh—
"Before you spoke, before I knew his wish,
I had begun to write!

I knew and loved

His work.   Himself I hardly knew at all;
And yet—I know him now!   I have heard him now
And, since he pledged me in so rare a cup,
I'll lift and drink to him, though lightnings fall
From envious gods to scourge me.   I will lift
This cup in darkness to the soul that reigns
In light on Helicon.   Who knows how near?
For I have thought, sometimes, when I have tried
To work his will, the hand that moved my pen
Was mine, and yet—not mine.   The bodily mask
Is mine, and sometimes, dull as clay, it sleeps
With old Musæus.   Then strange flashes come,
Oracular glories, visionary gleams,
And the mask moves, not of itself, and sings."
  "I know that thought," said Nash.   "A mighty ship,
A lightning-shattered wreck, out in that night,
Unseen, has foundered thundering.   We sit here
Snug on the shore, and feel the wash of it,

215

The widening circles running to our feet.
Can such a soul go down to glut the sharks
Without one ripple?   Here comes one sprinkle of spray.
Listen!"   And through that night, quick and intense,
And hushed for thunder, tingled once again,
Like a thin wire, the crowder's distant tune:—

> "Had he been prenticed to the trade
>   His father followed still,
> This exit he had never made,
>   Nor played a part so ill."

"Here is another," said Nash, "I know not why;
But like a weed in the long wash, I too
Was moved, not of myself, to a tune like this.
O, I can play the crowder, fiddle a song
On a dead friend, with any the best of you;
Lie and kick heels in the sun on a dead man's grave,
And yet—God knows—it is the best we can;
And better than the world's way, to forget."
So saying, like one that murmurs happy words
To torture his own grief, half in self-scorn,
He breathed a scrap of balladry that raised
The mists a moment from that Paradise,
That primal world of innocence, where Kit
In childhood played, outside his father's shop,
Under the sign of the *Golden Shoe,* as thus:—

> A cobbler lived in Canterbury
> —He is dead now, poor soul!—
> He sat at his door and stitched in the sun,
> Nodding and smiling at everyone;
> For St. Hugh makes all good cobblers merry,
> And often he sang as the pilgrims passed,
> "I can hammer a soldier's boot,
> And daintily glove a dainty foot.
> Many a sandal from my hand
> Has walked the road to Holy Land.
> Knights may fight for me, priests may pray for me,
> Pilgrims walk the pilgrim's way for me,
> I have a work in the world to do!
> —*Trowl the bowl, the nut-brown bowl,*
>   *To good St. Hugh!*—
> The cobbler must stick to his last."

And anon he would cry
"Kit! Kit! Kit!" to his little son,
"Look at the pilgrims riding by!
Dance down, hop down, after them, run!"
Then, like an unfledged linnet, out
Would tumble the brave little lad,
With a piping shout,—
"O, look at them, look at them, look at them, **Dad!**
Priest and prioress, abbot and friar,
Soldier and seaman, knight and squire!
How many countries have they seen?
Is there a king there, is there a queen?
Dad, one day,
Thou and I must ride like this,
All along the Pilgrim's Way,
By Glastonbury and Samarcand,
El Dorado and Cathay,
London and Persepolis,
All the way to Holy Land!"

   Then, shaking his head as if he knew,
Under the sign of the *Golden Shoe*,
Touched by the glow of the setting sun,
While the pilgrims passed,
The little cobbler would laugh and say:
"When you are old you will understand
'Tis a very long way
To Samarcand!
Why, largely to exaggerate
Befits not men of small estate,
But—I should say, yes, I should say,
'Tis a hundred miles from where you stand;
And a hundred more, my little son,
A hundred more, to Holy Land! . . .
I have a work in the world to do
—*Trowl the bowl, the nut-brown bowl,*
        To good St. Hugh!—
The cobbler must stick to his last."

"Which last," said Nash, breaking his rhyme off short,
"The crowder, after his kind, would seem to approve.
Well—all the waves from that great wreck out there
Break, and are lost in one withdrawing sigh:

The little lad that used to play
    Around the cobbler's door,
    We shall not see him more.
Kit Marlowe, Kit Marlowe,

But—could I tell you how that galleon sank,
Could I but bring you to that hollow whirl,
The black gulf in mid-ocean, where that wreck
Went thundering down, and round it hell still roars,
That were a tale to snap all fiddle-strings."
"Tell me," said Chapman.

                                "Ah, you wondered why,"
Said Nash, "you wondered why he asked your help
To crown that work of his.   Why, Chapman, think,
Think of the cobbler's awl—there's a stout lance
To couch at London, there's a conquering point
To carry in triumph through Persepolis!
I tell you Kit was nothing but a child,
When some rich patron of the *Golden Shoe*
Beheld him riding into Samarcand
Upon a broken chair, the which he said
Was a white steed, splashed with the blood of kings.
    When, on that patron's bounty, he did ride
So far as Cambridge, he was a brave lad,
Untamed, adventurous, but still innocent,
O, innocent as the cobbler's little self!
He brought to London just a bundle and stick,
A slender purse, an Ovid, a few scraps
Of song, and all unshielded, all unarmed
A child's heart, packed with splendid hopes and dreams.
I say a child's heart, Chapman, and that phrase
Crowns, not dis-crowns, his manhood.

                                Well—he turned
An honest penny, taking some small part
In plays at the *Red Bull*.   And, all the while,
Beyond the paint and tinsel of the stage,
Beyond the greasy cock-pit with its reek
Of orange-peel and civet, as all of these
Were but the clay churned by the glorious rush
Of his white chariots and his burning steeds,
Nay, as the clay were a shadow, his great dreams,
Like bannered legions on some proud crusade,
Empurpling all the deserts of the world.
Swept on in triumph to the glittering towers
Of his abiding City.

Then—he met
That damned blood-sucking cockatrice, the pug
Of some fine strutting mummer, one of those plagues
Bred by our stage, a puff-ball on the hill
Of Helicon.   As for his wench—she too
Had played so many parts that she forgot
The cue for truth.   King Puff had taught her well.
He was the vainer and more foolish thing,
She the more poisonous.

                           One dark day, to spite
Archer, her latest paramour, a friend
And apple-squire to Puff, she set her eyes
On Marlowe . . . feigned a joy in his young art,
Murmured his songs, used all her London tricks
To coney-catch the country greenhorn.   Man,
Kit never even *saw* her painted face!
He pored on books by candle-light and saw
Everything thro' a mist.   O, I could laugh
To think of it, only—his up-turned skull
There, in the dark, now that the flesh drops off,
Has laughed enough, a horrible silent laugh,
To think his Angel of Light was, after all,
Only the red-lipped Angel of the Plague.
He was no better than the rest of us,
No worse.   He felt the heat.   He felt the cold.
He took her down to Deptford to escape
Contagion, and the crashing of sextons' spades
On dead men's bones in every churchyard round;
The jangling bell and the cry, *Bring out your dead.*
And there she told him of her luckless life,
Wedded, deserted, both against her will,
A luckless Eve that never knew the snake.
True and half-true she mixed in one wild lie,
And then—she caught him by the hand and wept.
No death-cart passed to warn him with its bell.
Her eyes, her perfumed hair, and her red mouth,
Her warm white breast, her civet-scented skin,
Swimming before him, in a piteous mist,
Made the lad drunk, and—she was in his arms;
And all that God had meant to wake one day
Under the Sun of Love, suddenly woke
By candle-light and cried, 'The Sun; The Sun!'
And he believed it, Chapman, he believed it!
He was a cobbler's son, and he believed

In Love!   Blind, through that mist, he caught at Love,
The everlasting King of all this world.

Kit was not clever.   Clever men—like Pomp—
Might jest.   And fools might laugh.   But when a man,
Simple as all great elemental things,
Makes his whole heart a sacrificial fire
To one whose love is in her supple skin,
There comes a laughter in which jests break up
Like icebergs in a sea of burning marl.
Then dreamers turn to murderers in an hour.
Then topless towers are burnt, and the Ocean-sea
Tramples the proud fleet, down, into the dark,
And sweeps over it, laughing.   Come and see,
The heart now of this darkness—no more waves,
But the black central hollow where that wreck
Went down for ever.
                    How should Piers Penniless
Brand that wild picture on the world's black heart?—
Last night I tried the way of the Florentine,
And bruised myself; but we are friends together
Mourning a dead friend, none will ever know!—
Kit, do you smile at poor Piers Penniless,
Measuring it out?   Ah, boy, it is my best!
Since hearts must beat, let it be *terza rima*,
A ladder of rhyme that two sad friends alone
May let down, thus, to the last circle of hell."

So saying, and motionless as a man in trance,
Nash breathed the words that raised the veil anew,
Strange intervolving words which, as he spake them,
Moved like the huge slow whirlpool of that pit
Where the wreck sank, the serpentine slow folds
Of the lewd Kraken that sucked it, shuddering, down:—

This is the Deptford Inn.   Climb the dark stair.
   Come, come and see Kit Marlowe lying dead!
See, on the table, by that broken chair,

The little phials of paint—the white and red.
   A cut-lawn kerchief hangs behind the door,
Left by his punk, even as the tapster said.

There is the gold-fringed taffeta gown she wore,
   And, on that wine-stained bed, as is most meet,
He lies alone, never to waken more.

O, still as chiselled marble, the frayed sheet
  Folds the still form on that sepulchral bed,
Hides the dead face, and peaks the rigid feet.

Come, come and see Kit Marlowe lying dead!
  Draw back the sheet, ah, tenderly lay bare
The splendour of that Apollonian head;

The gloriole of his flame-coloured hair;
  The lean athletic body, deftly planned
To carry that swift soul of fire and air;

The long thin flanks, the broad breast, and the grand
  Heroic shoulders!   Look, what lost dreams lie
Cold in the fingers of that delicate hand;

And, shut within those lyric lips, what cry
  Of unborn beauty, sunk in utter night,
Lost worlds of song, sealed in an unknown sky,

Never to be brought forth, clothed on with light.
  Was this, then, this the secret of his song?—
Who ever loved that loved not at first sight?

It was not Love, not Love, that wrought this wrong;
  And yet—what evil shadow of this dark town
Could quench a soul so flame-like clean and strong,

Strike the young glory of his manhood down,
  Dead, like a dog, dead in a drunken brawl,
Dead for a phial of paint, a taffeta gown?

What if his blood were hot?   High over all
  He heard, as in his song the world still hears,
Those angels on the burning heavenly wall

Who chant the thunder-music of the spheres.
  Yet—through the glory of his own young dream
Here did he meet that face, wet with strange tears,

Andromeda, with piteous face astream,
  Hailing him, Perseus.   In her treacherous eyes
As in dark pools the mirrored stars will gleam,

Here did he see his own eternal skies;
    And here—she laughed, nor found the dream amiss;
But bade him pluck and eat—in Paradise.

Here did she hold him, broken up with bliss,
    Here, like a supple snake, around him coiled,
Here did she pluck his heart out with a kiss,

Here were the wings clipped and the glory soiled,
    Here adders coupled in the pure white shrine.
Here was the Wine spilt, and the Shew-bread spoiled.

Black was that feast, though he who poured the Wine
    Dreamed that he poured it in high sacrament.
Deep in her eyes he saw his own eyes shine,

Beheld Love's god-head and was well content.
    Subtly her hand struck the pure silver note,
The throbbing chord of passion that God meant

To swell the bliss of heaven.   Round his young throat
    She wound her swarthy tresses; then, with eyes
Half mad to see their power, half mad to gloat,

Half mad to batten on their own devilries,
    And mark what heaven-born splendours they could quell,
She held him quivering in a mesh of lies,

And in soft broken speech began to tell—
    There as, against her heart, throbbing he lay—
The truth that hurled his soul from heaven to hell.

Quivering, she watched the subtle whip-lash flay
    The white flesh of the dreams of his pure youth;
Then sucked the blood and left them cold as clay.

Luxuriously she lashed him with the truth.
    Against his mouth her subtle mouth she set
To show, as through a mask, O, without ruth,

As through a cold clay mask (brackish and wet
    With what strange tears!) it was not his, not his,
The kiss that through his quivering lips she met.

Kissing him, *"Thus,"* she whispered, *"did he kiss.*
  Ah, is the sweetness like a sword, then, sweet?
Last night—ah, kiss again—aching with bliss,

Thus was I made his own, from head to feet."
  —A sudden agony thro' his body swept
Tempestuously.—*"Our wedded pulses beat*

Like this and this; and then, at dawn, he slept."
  She laughed, pouting her lips against his cheek
To drink; and, as in answer, Marlowe wept.

As a dead man in dreams, he heard her speak.
  Clasped in the bitter grave of that sweet clay,
Wedded and one with it, he moaned.   Too weak

Even to lift his head, sobbing, he lay.
  Then, slowly, as their breathings rose and fell,
He felt the storm of passion, far away,

Gather.   The shuddering waves began to swell.
  And, through the menace of the thunder-roll,
The thin quick lightnings, thrilling through his hell,

Lightnings that hell itself could not control
  (Even while she strove to bow his neck anew)
Woke the great slumbering legions of his soul.

Sharp was that severance of the false and true,
  Sharp as a sword drawn from a shuddering wound,
But they, that were one flesh, were cloven in two.

Flesh leapt from clasping flesh, without a sound.
  He plucked his body from her white embrace,
And cast him down, and grovelled on the ground.

Yet, ere he went, he strove once more to trace,
  Deep in her eyes, the loveliness he knew;
Then—spat his hatred into her smiling face.

She clung to him.   He flung her off.   He drew
  His dagger, thumbed the blade, and laughed—"Poor punk!
What?   Would you make me your own murderer, too?"

  ·   ·   ·   ·   ·   ·   ·   ·   ·   ·   ·   ·

"That was the day of our great feast," said Nash,
"Aboard the *Golden Hynde*. The grand old hulk
Was drawn up for the citizens' wonderment
At Deptford.   Ay, Piers Penniless was there!
Soaked and besotted as I was, I saw
Everything.   On her poop the minstrels played,
And round her sea-worn keel, like meadow-sweet
Curtseying round a lightning-blackened oak,
Prentices and their sweethearts, heel and toe,
Danced the brave English dances, clean and fresh
As May.
          But in her broad gun-guarded waist
Once red with British blood, long tables groaned
For revellers not so worthy.   Where her guns
Had raked the seas, barrels of ale were sprung,
Bestrid by roaring tipplers.   Where at night
The storm-beat crew silently bowed their heads
With Drake before the King of Life and Death,
A strumpet wrestled with a mountebank
For pence, a loose-limbed Lais with a clown
Of Cherry Hilton.   Leering at their lewd twists,
Cross-legged upon the deck, sluggish with sack,
Like a squat toad sat Puff . . .
Propped up against the bulwarks, at his side,
Archer, his apple-squire, hiccoughed a bawdy song.

Suddenly, through that orgy, with wild eyes,
Yet with her customary smile, O, there
I saw in daylight what Kit Marlowe saw
Through blinding mists, the face of his first love.
She stood before her paramour on the deck,
Cocking her painted head to right and left,
Her white teeth smiling, but her voice a hiss:
'Quickly,' she said to Archer, 'come away,
Or there'll be blood spilt!'
                              'Better blood than wine,'
Said Archer, struggling to his feet, 'but who,
Who would spill blood?'
                          'Marlowe!' she said.
                                        Then Puff
Reeled to his feet.   'What, Kit, the cobbler's son?
The lad that broke his leg at the *Red Bull*,
Tamburlaine-Marlowe, he that would chain kings
To's chariot-wheel?   What, is he rushing hither?
He would spill blood for Gloriana, hey?

O, my Belphœbe, you will crack my sides!
Was this the wench that shipped a thousand squires?
O, ho!   But here he comes.   Now, solemnly, lads,—
Now walk the angels on the walls of heaven
To entertain divine Zenocrate!'
And there stood Kit, high on the storm-scarred poop,
Against the sky, bare-headed.   I saw his face,
Pale, innocent, just the clear face of that boy
Who walked to Cambridge with a bundle and stick,—
The little cobbler's son.   Yet—there I caught
My only glimpse of how the sun-god looked,
And only for one moment.
                                              When he saw
His mistress, his face whitened, and he shook.
Down to the deck he came, a poor weak man;
And yet—by God—the only man that day
In all our drunken crew.
                                       'Come along, Kit,'
Cried Puff, 'we'll all be friends now, all take hands,
And dance—ha! ha!—the shaking of the sheets!'
Then Archer, shuffling a step, raised his cracked voice
In Kit's own song to a falsetto tune,
Snapping one hand, thus, over his head as he danced:—

          'Come, live with me, and be my love,
           And we will all the pleasures prove!' . . .

Puff reeled between, laughing.   'Damn you,' cried Kit,
And, catching the fat swine by his round soft throat,
Hurled him headlong, crashing across the tables,
To lie and groan in the red bilge of wine
That washed the scuppers.
                                          Kit gave him not one glance.
'Archer,' he said in a whisper.
                                            Instantly
A long thin rapier flashed in Archer's hand.
The ship was one wild uproar.   Women screamed
And huddled together.   A drunken clamorous ring
Seethed around Marlowe and his enemy.
Kit drew his dagger, slowly, and I knew
Blood would be spilt.
                                 'Here, take my rapier, Kit!'
I cried across the crowd, seeing the lad
Was armed so slightly.   But he did not hear.
I could not reach him.

                        All at once he leapt
Like a wounded tiger, past the rapier point
Straight at his enemy's throat.   I saw his hand
Up-raised to strike!   I heard a harlot's scream,
And, in mid-air, the hand stayed, quivering, white,
A frozen menace.
                        I saw a yellow claw
Twisting the dagger out of that frozen hand;
I saw his own steel in that yellow grip,
His own lost lightning raised to strike at him!
I saw it flash!   I heard the driving grunt
Of him that struck!   Then, with a shout, the crowd
Sundered, and through the gap, a blank red thing
Streaming with blood, came the blind face of Kit,
Reeling, to me!   And I, poor drunken I,
Held my arms wide for him.   Here, on my breast,
With one great sob, he burst his heart and died."

.   .   .   .

Nash ceased.   And, far away down Friday Street,
The crowder with his fiddle wailed again:

            "Blaspheming Tambolin must die
              And Faustus meet his end.
            Repent, repent, or presentlie
              To hell ye must descend."

And, as in answer, Chapman slowly breathed
Those mightiest lines of Marlowe's own despair:

            "Think'st thou that I who saw the face of God,
            And tasted the eternal joys of heaven,
            Am not tormented with ten thousand hells?"

"Ah, you have said it," said Nash, "and there you know
Why Kit desired your hand to crown his work.
He reverenced you as one whose temperate eyes,
Austere and grave, could look him through and through;
One whose firm hand could grasp the reins of law
And guide those furious horses of the sun,
As Ben and Will can guide them, where you will.
His were, perchance, the noblest steeds of all,
And from their nostrils blew a fierier dawn
Above the world.   That glory is his own;

But where he fell, he fell.   Before his hand
Had learned to quell them, he was dashed to the earth.
'Tis yours to show that good men honoured him.
For, mark this, Chapman, since Kit Marlowe fell,
There will be fools that, in the name of Art,
Will wallow in the mire, crying 'I fall,
I fall from heaven!'—fools that have only heard
From earth, the rumour of those golden hooves
Far, far above them.   Yes, you know the kind,
The fools that scorn Will for his lack of fire
Because he quells the storms they never knew,
And rides above the thunder; fools of Art
That skip and vex, like little vicious fleas,
Their only Helicon some green madam's breast.
Art!   Art!   O, God, that I could send my soul,
In one last wave, from that night-hidden wreck,
Across the shores of all the years to be;
O, God, that like a crowder I might shake
Their blind dark casements with the pity of it,
Piers Penniless his ballad, a poor scrap,
That but for lack of time, and hope, and pence,
He might have bettered!   For a dead man's sake,
Thus would the wave break, thus the crowder cry:—

    Dead, like a dog upon the road;
      Dead, for a harlot's kiss;
    The Apollonian throat and brow,
    The lyric lips, so silent now,
    The flaming wings that heaven bestowed
      For loftier airs than this!

    The sun-like eyes whose light and life
      Had gazed an angel's down,
    That burning heart of honey and fire,
    Quenched and dead for an apple-squire,
    Quenched at the thrust of a mummer's knife,
      Dead—for a taffeta gown!

    The wine that God had set apart,
      The noblest wine of all,
    Wine of the grapes that angels trod,
    The vintage of the glory of God,
    The crimson wine of that rich heart,
      Spilt in a drunken brawl,

Poured out to make a steaming bath
  That night in the Devil's Inn,
A steaming bath of living wine
Poured out for Circe and her swine,
A bath of blood for a harlot
  To supple and sleek her skin.

And many a fool that finds it sweet
  Through all the years to be,
Crowning a lie with Marlowe's fame,
Will ape the sin, will ape the shame,
Will ape our captain in defeat;
  But—not in victory;

Till Art become a leaping-house,
  And Death be crowned as Life,
And one wild jest outshine the soul
Of Truth . . . O, fool, is this your goal?
You are not our Kit Marlowe,
  But the drunkard with the knife;

Not Marlowe, but the Jack-o'-Lent
  That lured him o'er the fen!
O, ay, the tavern is in its place,
And the punk's painted smiling face,
But where is our Kit Marlowe
  The man, the king of men?

Passion?   You kiss the painted mouth,
  The hand that clipped his wings,
The hand that into his heart she thrust
And tuned him to her whimpering lust,
And played upon his quivering youth
  As a crowder plucks the strings.

But he who dared the thunder-roll,
  Whose eagle-wings could soar,
Buffeting down the clouds of night,
To beat against the Light of Light,
That great God-blinded eagle-soul,
  We shall not see him more."

V

THE COMPANION OF A MILE

THWACK! *Thwack!* One early dawn upon our door
I heard the bauble of some motley fool
Bouncing, and all the dusk of London shook
With bells! I leapt from bed,—had I forgotten?—
I flung my casement wide and craned my neck
Over the painted Mermaid. There he stood,
His right leg yellow and his left leg blue,
With jingling cap, a sheep-bell at his tail,
Wielding his eel-skin bladder,—*bang! thwack! bang!*—
Catching a comrade's head with the recoil
And skipping away! All Bread Street dimly burned
Like a reflected sky, green, red and white
With littered branches, ferns and hawthorn-clouds;
For, round Sir Fool, a frolic morrice-troop
Of players, poets, prentices, mad-cap queans,
Robins and Marians, coloured like the dawn,
And sparkling like the greenwood whence they came
With their fresh boughs all dewy from the dark,
Clamoured, *Come down! Come down, and let us in!*
High over these, I suddenly saw Sir Fool
Leap to a sign-board, swing to a conduit-head,
And perch there, gorgeous on the morning sky,
Tossing his crimson cockscomb to the blue
And crowing like Chanticleer, *Give them a rouse!*
Tickle it, tabourer! Nimbly, lasses, nimbly!
Tuck up your russet petticoats and dance!
Let the Cheape know it is the first of May!
And as I seized shirt, doublet and trunk-hose,
I saw the hobby-horse come cantering down,
A pasteboard steed, dappled a rosy white
Like peach-bloom, bridled with purple, bitted with gold,
A crimson foot-cloth on his royal flanks,
And, riding him, His Majesty of the May!
Round him the whole crowd frolicked with a shout,
And as I stumbled down the crooked stair
I heard them break into a dance and sing:—

SONG

Into the wood we'll trip and go,
Up and down and to and fro,

Under the moon to fetch in May,
And two by two till break of day,
        A-maying,
        A-playing,
For Love knows no gain-saying!
Wisdom trips not?   Even so—
Come, young lovers, trip and go,
        Trip and go.

Out of the woods we'll dance and sing
Under the morning-star of Spring,
Into the town with our fresh boughs
And knock at every sleeping house,
        Not sighing,
        Or crying,
Though Love knows no denying!
Then, round your summer queen and king,
Come, young lovers, dance and sing,
        Dance and sing!

"*Chorus,*" the great Fool tossed his gorgeous crest,
And lustily crew against the deepening dawn,
"*Chorus,*" till all the Cheape caught the refrain,
And, with a double thunder of frolic feet,
Its ancient nut-brown tabors woke the Strand:—

        A-maying,
        A-playing,
For Love knows no gain-saying!
Wisdom trips not?   Even so,—
Come, young lovers, trip and go,
        Trip and go.

Into the Mermaid with a shout they rushed
As I shot back the bolts, and *bang, thwack, bang,*
The bladder bounced about me.   What cared I?
This was all England's holy-day!   "Come in,
My yellow-hammers," roared the Friar Tuck
Of this mad morrice, "come you into church,
My nightingales, my scraps of Lincoln green,
And hear my sermon!"   On a window-seat
He stood, against the diamonded rich panes
In the old oak parlour and, throwing back his hood,
Who should it be but Ben, rare Ben himself?
The wild troup laughed around him, some a-sprawl

On tables, kicking parti-coloured heels,
Some with their Marians jigging on their knees,
And, in the front of all, the motley fool
Cross-legged upon the rushes.
                                        O, I knew him,—
Will Kemp, the player, who danced from London town
To Norwich in nine days and was proclaimed
Freeman of Marchaunt Venturers and hedge-king
Of English morrice-dancery for ever!
His nine-days' wonder, through the countryside
Was hawked by every ballad-monger.   Kemp
Raged at their shake-rag Muses.   None but I
Guessed ever for what reason, since he chose
His anticks for himself and, in his games,
Was more than most May-fools fantastical.
I watched his thin face, as he rocked and crooned,
Shaking the squirrels' tails around his ears;
And, out of all the players I had seen,
His face was quickest through its clay to flash
The passing mood.   Though not a muscle stirred,
The very skin of it seemed to flicker and gleam
With little summer lightnings of the soul
At every fleeting fancy.   For a man
So quick to bleed at a pin-prick or to leap
Laughing through hell to save a butterfly,
This world was difficult; and perchance he found
In his fantastic games that open road
Which even Will Shakespeare only found at last
In motley and with some wild straws in his hair.
But "Drawer! drawer!" bellowed Friar Ben,
"Make ready a righteous breakfast while I preach;—
Tankards of nut-brown ale, and cold roast beef,
Cracknels, old cheese, flaunes, tarts and clotted cream.
Hath any a wish not circumscribed by these?"

"A white-pot custard, for my white-pot queen,"
Cried Kemp, waving his bauble, "mark this, boy,
A white-pot custard for my queen of May,—
She is not here, but that concerns not thee!—
A white-pot Mermaid custard, with a crust,
Lashings of cream, eggs, apple-pulse and spice,
A little sugar and manchet bread.   Away!
Be swift!"
                        And as I bustled to and fro,
The Friar raised his big brown fists again

231

And preached in mockery of the Puritans
Who thought to strip the moonshine wings from Mab,
Tear down the May-poles, rout our English games,
And drive all beauty back into the sea.

Then laughter and chatter and clashing tankards drowned
All but their May-day jollity a-while.
But, as their breakfast ended, and I sank
Gasping upon a bench, there came still more
Poets and players crowding into the room;
And one—I only knew him as Sir John—
Waved a great ballad at Will Kemp and laughed,
"Atonement, Will, atonement!"
                              "What," groaned Kemp,
"Another penny poet?   How many lies
Does *this* rogue tell?   Sir, I have suffered much
From these Melpomenes and strawberry quills,
And think them better at their bloody lines
On *The Blue Lady*.   Sir, they set to work
At seven o'clock in the morning, the same hour
That I, myself, that's *Cavaliero* Kemp,
With heels of feather and heart of cork, began
Frolickly footing, from the great Lord Mayor
Of London, tow'rds the worshipful Master Mayor
Of Norwich."
                  "Nay, Kemp, this is a May-day tune,
A morrice of country rhymes, made by a poet
Who thought it shame so worthy an act as thine
Should wither in oblivion if the Muse
With her Castalian showers could keep it green.
And while the fool nid-nodded all in time,
Sir John, in swinging measure, trolled this tale:—

With Georgie Sprat, my overseer, and Thomas Slye, my tabourer,
    And William Bee, my courier, when dawn emblazed the skies,
I met a tall young pedlar as I danced by little Sudbury,
    Head-master o' morrice-dancers all, high headborough of hyes.

By Sudbury, by Sudbury, by little red-roofed Sudbury,
    He wished to dance a mile with me!   I made a courtly bow:
I fitted him with morrice-bells, with treble, bass and tenor bells,
    And *"Tickle your tabor, Tom,"* I cried, *"we're going to market now."*

And rollicking down the lanes we dashed, and frolicking up the hills we
    clashed,

And like a sail behind me flapped his great white frock a-while,
Till, with a gasp, he sank and swore that he could dance with me no
    more;
And—over the hedge a milk-maid laughed, *Not dance with him a*
    mile?

"You lout!" she laughed, "I'll leave my pail, and dance with him for
    cakes and ale!
I'll dance a mile for love," she laughed, "and win my wager, too.
Your feet are shod and mine are bare; but when could leather dance
    on air?
A milk-maid's feet can fall as fair and light as falling dew."

I fitted her with morrice-bells, with treble, bass and tenor bells:
    The fore-bells, as I linked them at her throat, how soft they sang!
Green linnets in a golden nest, they chirped and trembled on her breast,
    And, faint as elfin blue-bells, at her nut-brown ankles rang.

I fitted her with morrice-bells that sweetened into woodbine bells,
    And trembled as I hung them there and crowned her sunny brow:
"Strike up," she laughed, "my summer king!" And all her bells began
    to ring,
    And *"Tickle your tabor, Tom,"* I cried, *"we're going to Sherwood*
    now!"

When cocks were crowing, and light was growing, and horns were blow-
    ing, and milk-pails flowing,
    We swam thro' waves of emerald gloom along a chestnut aisle,
Then, up a shining hawthorn-lane, we sailed into the sun again,
    Will Kemp and his companion, his companion of a mile.

      "Truer than most," snarled Kemp, "but mostly lies!
      And why does he forget the miry lanes
      By Brainford with thick woods on either side,
      And the deep holes, where I could find no ease
      But skipped up to my waist?" A crackling laugh
      Broke from his lips which, if he had not worn
      The cap and bells, would scarce have roused the mirth
      Of good Sir John, who roundly echoed it,
      Then waved his hand and said, "Nay, but he treats
      Your morrice in the spirit of Lucian, Will,
      Who thought that dancing was no mushroom growth,
      But sprung from the beginning of the world
      When Love persuaded earth, air, water, fire,
      And all the jarring elements to move

In measure.   Right to the heart of it, my lad,
The song goes, though the skin mislike you so."
"Nay, an there's more of it, I'll sing it, too!
'Tis a fine tale, Sir John, I have it by heart,
Although 'tis lies throughout."   Up leapt Will Kemp,
And crouched and swayed, and swung his bauble round,
Making the measure as they trolled the tale,
Chanting alternately, each answering each.

The Fool

The tabor fainted far behind us, but her feet that day
  They beat a rosier morrice o'er the fairy-circled green.

Sir John

And o'er a field of buttercups, a field of lambs and buttercups,
  We danced along a cloth of gold, a summer king and queen!

The Fool

And straying we went, and swaying we went, with lambkins round us
        playing we went;
  Her face uplift to drink the sun, and not for me her smile;
We danced, a king and queen of May, upon a fleeting holy-day,
  But O, she'd won her wager, my companion of a mile!

Sir John

Her rosy lips they never spoke, though every rosy foot-fall broke
  The dust, the dust to Eden-bloom; and, past the throbbing blue,
All ordered to her rhythmic feet, the stars were dancing with my sweet,
  And all the world a morrice-dance!

The Fool

                        She knew not; but I knew!
Love like Amphion with his lyre, made all the elements conspire
  To build His world of music.   All in rhythmic rank and file,
I saw them in their cosmic dance, catch hands across, retire, advance,
  For me and my companion, my companion of a mile!

Sir John

The little leaves on every tree, the rivers winding to the sea,
  The swinging tides, the wheeling winds, the rolling heavens above,
Around the May-pole Igdrasil, they worked the Morrice-master's will,
  Persuaded into measure by the all-creative Love.

That hour I saw, from depth to height, this wildering universe unite!
  The lambs of God around us and His passion in every flower!

The Fool

His grandeur in the dust, His dust a blaze of blinding majesty,
  And all His immortality in one poor mortal hour.

And Death was but a change of key in Life the golden melody,
  And Time became Eternity, and Heaven a fleeting smile;
For all was each and each was all, and all a wedded unity,
  Her heart in mine, and mine in my companion of a mile.

Thwack! Thwack!   He whirled his bauble round about,
  "This fellow beats them all," he cried, "the worst
Those others wrote was that I hopped from York
To Paris with a mortar on my head.
This fellow sends me leaping through the clouds
To buss the moon!   The best is yet to come;
Strike up, Sir John!   Ha! ha!   You know no more?"
Kemp leapt upon a table.   "Clear the way,"
He cried, and with a great stamp of his foot
And a wild crackling laugh, drew all to hark.
          "With hey and ho, through thick and thin,
              The hobby-horse is forgotten.
          But I must finish what I begin,
              Tho' all the roads be rotten.
  "By all those twenty thousand chariots, Ben,
Hear this true tale they shall!   Now, let me see,
Where was Will Kemp?   Bussing the moon's pale mouth?
Ah, yes!"   He crouched above the listening throng,—
"*Good as a play*," I heard one whispering quean,—
And, waving his bauble, shuffling with his feet
In a dance that marked the time, he sank his voice
As if to breathe great secrets, and so sang:—

At Melford town, at Melford town, at little grey-roofed Melford town,
  A long mile from Sudbury, upon the village green,
We danced into a merry rout of country-folk that skipt about
  A hobby-horse, a May-pole, and a laughing white-pot queen.

They thronged about us as we stayed, and there I gave my sunshine maid
  An English crown for cakes and ale—her dancing was so true!
And "Nay," she said, "I danced my mile for love!"   I answered with a
      smile,
  " 'Tis but a silver token, lass, thou'st won that wager, too."

I took my leash of morrice-bells, my treble, bass and tenor bells,
  They pealed like distant marriage-bells!   And up came William Bee
With Georgie Sprat, my overseer, and Thomas Slye, my tabourer,
  "Farewell," she laughed, and vanished with a Suffolk courtesie.
I leapt away to Rockland, and from Rockland on to Hingham,
  From Hingham on to Norwich, sirs!   I hardly heard a-while
The throngs that followed after, with their shouting and their laughter,
  For a shadow danced beside me, my companion of a mile!

At Norwich, by St. Giles his gate, I entered, and the Mayor in state,
  With all the rosy knights and squires for twenty miles about,
With trumpets and with minstrelsy, was waiting there to welcome me;
  And, as I skipt into the street, the City raised a shout.

They gave me what I did not seek.   I fed on roasted swans a week!
  They pledged me in their malmsey, and they lined me warm with ale!
They sleeked my skin with red-deer pies, and all that runs and swims and
    flies;
  But, through the clashing wine-cups, O, I heard her clanking pail.

And, rising from his crimson chair, the worshipful and portly Mayor
  Bequeathed me forty shillings every year that I should live,
With five good angels in my hand that I might drink while I could stand!
  They gave me golden angels!   What I lacked they could not give.

They made Will Kemp, thenceforward, sirs, Freeman of Marchaunt
    Venturers!
  They hoped that I would dance again from Norwich up to York;
Then they asked me, all together, had I met with right May weather,
  And they praised my heels of feather, and my heart, my heart of cork.

    .   .   .   .

As I came home by Sudbury, by little red-roofed Sudbury,
  I waited for my bare-foot maid, among her satin kine!
I heard a peal of wedding-bells, of treble, bass and tenor bells:
  "Ring well," I cried, "this bridal morn!   You soon shall ring for
    mine!"

I found her foot-prints in the grass, just where she stood and saw me pass.
  I stood within her own sweet field and waited for my may.
I laughed.   The dance has turned about!   I stand within: she'll pass
    without,
  And—*down the road the wedding came, the road I danced that day!*

I saw the wedding-folk go by, with laughter and with minstrelsy,
  I gazed across her own sweet hedge, I caught her happy smile,

I saw the tall young pedlar pass to little red-roofed Sudbury,
  His bride upon his arm, my lost companion of a mile.

Down from his table leapt the motley Fool.
His bladder bounced from head to ducking head,
His crackling laugh rang high,—"Sir John, I danced
In February, and the song says May!
A fig for all your poets, liars all!
Away to Fenchurch Street, lasses and lads,
They hold high revel there this May-day morn.
Away!" The mad-cap throng echoed the cry.
He drove them with his bauble through the door;
Then, as the last gay kerchief fluttered out
He gave one little sharp sad lingering cry
As of a lute-string breaking. He turned back
And threw himself along a low dark bench;
His jingling cap was crumpled in his fist,
And, as he lay there, all along Cheapside
The happy voices of his comrades rang:—

    Out of the woods we'll dance and sing
    Under the morning-star of Spring,
    Into the town with our fresh boughs
    And knock at every sleeping house,
        Not sighing,
        Or crying,
    Though Love knows no denying!
    Then, round your summer queen and king,
    Come, young lovers, dance and sing,
        Dance and sing!

His motley shoulders heaved. I touched his arm,
"What ails you, sir?" He raised his thin white face,
Wet with the May-dew still. A few stray petals
Clung in his tangled hair. He leapt to his feet,
" 'Twas February, but I danced, boy, danced
In May! Can you do this?" Forward he bent
Over his feet, and shuffled it, heel and toe,
Out of the Mermaid, singing his old song—

        A-maying,
        A-playing,
    For Love knows no gain-saying!
    Wisdom trips not? Even so,—

> Come, young lovers, trip and go,
>   Trip and go.

Five minutes later, over the roaring Strand,
"Chorus!" I heard him crow, and half the town
Reeled into music under his crimson comb.

VI

BIG BEN

GODS, what a hubbub shook our cobwebs out
The day that Chapman, Marston and our Ben
Waited in Newgate for the hangman's hands.
Chapman and Marston had been flung there first
For some imagined insult to the Scots
In *Eastward Ho,* the play they wrote with Ben.
But Ben was famous now, and our brave law
Would fain have winked and passed the big man by.
The lesser men had straightway been condemned
To have their ears cut off, their noses slit,
With other tortures.
                    Ben had risen at that!
He gripped his cudgel, called for a quart of ale,
Then like Helvellyn with his rocky face
And mountain-belly, he surged along Cheapside,
Snorting with wrath, and rolled into the gaol,
To share the punishment.
                    "There is my mark!
'Tis not the first time you have branded me,"
Said our big Ben, and thrust his broad left thumb
Branded with T for Tyburn, into the face
Of every protest.   "That's the mark you gave me
Because I killed my man in Spitalfields,
A duel honest as any your courtiers fight.
But I was no Fitzdotterel, bore no gules
And azure, robbed no silk-worms for my hose,
I was Ben Jonson, out of Annandale,
Bricklayer in common to the good Lord God.
You branded me.   I am Ben Jonson still.
You cannot rub it out."
                    The Mermaid Inn
Buzzed like a hornet's nest, upon the day
Fixed for their mutilation.   And the stings
Were ready, too; for rapiers flashed and clashed

238

Among the tankards.   Dekker was there, and Nash,
Brome (Jonson's body-servant, whom he taught
His art of verse and, more than that, to love him,)
And half a dozen more.   They planned to meet
The prisoners going to Tyburn, and attempt
A desperate rescue.
                    All at once we heard
A great gay song come marching down the street,
A single voice, and twenty marching men,
Then the full chorus, twenty voices strong:—

            The prentice whistles at break of day
                All under fair roofs and towers,
            When the old Cheape openeth every way
                Her little sweet inns like flowers;
            And he sings like a lark, both early and late,
                To think, if his house take fire,
            At the good *Green Dragon* in Bishopsgate
                He may drink to his heart's desire.

Chorus: Or sit at his ease in the old *Cross Keys*
                And drink to his heart's desire.

            But I, as I walk by *Red Rose Lane,*
                Tho' it warmeth my heart to see
            The Swan, The Golden Hynde, and *The Crane,*
                With the door set wide for me;
            Tho' Signs like daffodils paint the strand
                When the thirsty bees begin,
            Of all the good taverns in Engeland
                My choice is—*The Mermaid Inn.*

Chorus: There is much to be said for *The Saracen's Head,*
                But my choice is *The Mermaid Inn.*

Into the tavern they rushed, these roaring boys.
"Now broach your ripest and your best," they cried.
    "All's well!   They are all released!   They are on the way!
Old Camden and young Selden worked the trick.
Where is Dame Dimpling?   Where's our jolly hostess?
Tell her the Mermaid Tavern will have guests:
We are sent to warn her.   She must raid Cook's Row,
And make their ovens roar.   Nobody dines
This day with old Duke Humphrey.   Red-deer pies,
Castles of almond crust, a shield of brawn
Big as the nether millstone, barrels of wine,

Three roasted peacocks!   Ben is on the way!"
Then all the rafters rang with song again:—

> There was a Prince—long since, long since!—
>   To East Cheape did resort,
> For that he loved *The Blue Boar's Head*
>   Far better than Crown or Court;
> But old King Harry in Westminster
>   Hung up, for all to see,
> Three bells of power in St. Stephen's Tower,
>   Yea, bells of a thousand and three.

Chorus: Three bells of power in a timber tower,
             Thirty thousand and three.

> For Harry the Fourth was a godly king
>   And loved great godly bells!
> He bade them ring and he bade them swing
>   Till a man might hear nought else.
> In every tavern it soured the sack
>   With discord and with din;
> But they drowned it all in a madrigal
>   Like this, at *The Mermaid Inn.*

Chorus: They drowned it all in a madrigal
             Like this, at *The Mermaid Inn.*

   "But how did Selden work it?"—"Nobody knows.
They will be here anon.   Better ask Will.
He's the magician!"—"Ah, here comes Dame Dimpling!"
And, into the rollicking chaos our good Dame
—A Dame of only two and thirty springs—
All lavender and roses and white kerchief,
Bustled, to lay the tables.
                    Fletcher flung
His arm around her waist and kissed her cheek.
But all she said was, *"One—two—three—four—five—*
Six at a pinch, in yonder window-seat."
"A health to our Dame Dimpling," Beaumont cried,
And Dekker, leaping on the old black settle,
Led all their tumult into a song again:—

What is the Mermaid's merriest toast?
   Our hostess—good Dame Dimpling!
Who is it rules the Mermaid roast?

Who is it bangs the Mermaid host,
Tho' her hands be soft as her heart almost?
      Dame Dimpling!

She stands at the board in her fresh blue gown
   With the sleeves tucked up—Dame Dimpling!
She rolls the white dough up and down
And her pies are crisp, and her eyes are brown.
So—she is the Queen of all this town,—
      Dame Dimpling!

Her sheets are white as black-thorn bloom,
   White as her neck, Dame Dimpling!
Her lavender sprigs in the London gloom
Make every little bridal-room
A country nook of fresh perfume,—
      Dame Dimpling!

She wears white lace on her dark brown hair:
   And a rose on her breast, Dame Dimpling!
And who can show you a foot as fair
Or an ankle as neat when she climbs the stair,
Taper in hand, and head in the air,
And a rose in her cheek?—O, past compare,
      Dame Dimpling!

"But don't forget those oyster-pies," cried Lyly.
"Nor the roast beef," roared Dekker.   "Prove yourself
The Muse of meat and drink."
                  There was a shout
In Bread Street, and our windows all swung wide,
Six heads at each.
           Nat Field bestrode our sign
And kissed the painted Mermaid on her lips,
Then waved his tankard.
            "Here they come," he cried.
"Camden and Selden, Chapman and Marston, too,
And half Will's company with our big Ben
Riding upon their shoulders."
            "Look!" cried Dekker,
"But where is Atlas now?   O, let them have it!
A thumping chorus, lads!   Let the roof crack!"
And all the Mermaid clashed and banged again
In thunderous measure to the marching tune
That rolled down Bread Street, forty voices strong:—

At *Ypres Inn,* by *Wring-wren Lane,*
   Old John of Gaunt would dine:
He scarce had opened an oyster or twain,
   Or drunk one flagon of wine,
When, all along the Vintry Ward,
   He heard the trumpets blow,
And a voice that roared—"If thou love thy lord,
   Tell John of Gaunt to go!"

Chorus: A great voice roared—"If thou love thy lord,
   Tell John of Gaunt to go!"

Then into the room rushed Haviland
   That fair fat Flemish host,
"They are marching hither with sword and brand,
   Ten thousand men—almost!
It is these oysters or thy sweet life,
   Thy blood or the best of the bin!"—
"Proud Pump, avaunt!" quoth John of Gaunt,
   "I will dine at *The Mermaid Inn!*"

Chorus: "Proud Pump, avaunt!" quoth John of Gaunt,
   "There is wine at *The Mermaid Inn!*"

And in came Ben like a great galleon poised
High on the white crest of a shouting wave,
And then the feast began.   The fragrant steam
As from the kitchens of Olympus drew
A throng of ragged urchins to our doors.
Ben ordered them a castellated pie
That rolled a cloud around them where they sat
Munching upon the cobblestones.   Our casements
Dripped with the golden dews of Helicon;
And, under the warm feast our cellarage
Gurgled and foamed in the delicious cool
With crimson freshets—
             "Tell us," cried Nat Field,
When pipes began to puff.   "How did you work it?"
Camden chuckled and tugged his long white beard.
"Out of the mouth of babes," he said and shook
His head at Selden!   "O, young man, young man,
There's a career before you!   Selden did it.
Take my advice, my children.   Make young Selden
Solicitor-general to the Mermaid Inn.

That rosy silken smile of his conceals
A scholar!   Yes, that suckling lawyer there
Puts my grey beard to shame.   His courteous airs
And silken manners hide the nimblest wit
That ever trimmed a sail to catch the wind
Of courtly favour.   Mark my words now, Ben,
That youth will sail right up against the wind
By skilful tacking.   But you run it fine,
Selden, you run it fine.   Take my advice
And don't be too ironical, my boy,
Or even the King will see it."
                              He chuckled again.
"But tell them of your tractate!"
                              "Here it is,"
Quoth Selden, twisting a lighted paper spill,
Then, with his round cherubic face aglow
Lit his long silver pipe,
                        "Why, first," he said,
"Camden being Clarencieux King-at-arms,
He read the King this little tract I wrote
Against tobacco."   And the Mermaid roared
With laughter.   "Well, you went the way to hang
All three of them," cried Lyly, "and, as for Ben,
His Trinidado goes to bed with him."
"Green gosling, quack no more," Selden replied,
Smiling that rosy silken smile anew.
"The King's a *critic!*   When have critics known
The poet from his creatures, God from me?
How many cite Polonius to their sons
And call it Shakespeare?   Well, I took my text
From sundry creatures of our great big Ben,
And called it 'Jonson.'
                        Camden read it out
Without the flicker of an eye.   His beard
Saved us, I think.   The King admired his text.
'There is a man,' he read, *'lies at death's door
Thro' taking of tobacco.   Yesterday
He voided a bushel of soot.'*
                              'God bless my soul,
A bushel of soot!   Think of it!' said the King.
'The man who wrote those great and splendid words,'
Camden replied,—I had prepared his case
Carefully—'lies in Newgate prison, sire.
His nose and ears await the hangman's knife.'

'Ah,' said the shrewd King, goggling his great eyes
Cannily.   'Did he not defame the Scots?'
'That's true,' said Camden, like a man that hears
Truth for the first time.   'O ay, he defamed 'em,'
The King said, very wisely, once again.
'Ah, but,' says Camden, like a man that strives
With more than mortal wit, 'only such Scots
As flout your majesty, and take tobacco.
He is a Scot, himself, and hath the gift
Of preaching.'   Then we gave him Jonson's lines
Against Virginia.   *'Neither do thou lust
After that tawny weed; for who can tell,
Before the gathering and the making up,
What alligarta may have spawned thereon,'*
Or words to that effect.

                    'Magneeficent!'
Spluttered the King—'who knows?   Who knows, indeed?
That's a grand touch, that Alligarta, Camden!'
'The Scot who wrote those great and splendid words,'
Said Camden, 'languishes in Newgate, sire.
His ears and nose—'

                    And there, as we arranged
With Inigo Jones, the ladies of the court
Assailed the King in tears.   Their masque and ball
Would all be ruined.   All their Grecian robes,
Procured at vast expense, were wasted now.
The masque was not half-written.   Master Jones
Had lost his poets.   They were all in gaol.
Their noses and their ears . . . .
                              'God bless my soul,'
Spluttered the King, goggling his eyes again,
'What d'you make of it, Camden?'—
                              'I should say
A Puritan plot, sire; for these justices—
Who love tobacco—use their law, it seems,
To flout your Majesty at every turn.
If this continue, sire, there'll not be left
A loyal ear or nose in all your realm.'
At that, our noble monarch well-nigh swooned.
He hunched his body, padded as it was
Against the assassin's knife, six inches deep
With great green quilts, wagged his enormous head,
Then, in a dozen words, he wooed destruction:

'It is presumption and a high contempt
In subjects to dispute what kings can do,'
He whimpered.   'Even as it is blasphemy
To thwart the will of God.'
                          He waved his hand,
And rose.   'These men must be released, at once!'
Then, as I think, to seek a safer place,
He waddled from the room, his rickety legs
Doubling beneath that great green feather-bed
He calls his 'person.'—I shall dream to-night
Of spiders, Camden.—But in half an hour,
Inigo Jones was armed with Right Divine
To save such ears and noses as the ball
Required for its perfection.   Think of that!
And let this earthly ball remember, too,
That Chapman, Marston, and our great big Ben
Owe their poor adjuncts to—ten Grecian robes
And 'Jonson' on tobacco!   England loves
Her poets, O, supremely, when they're dead."
"But Ben has narrowly escaped her love,"
Said Chapman gravely.
                          "What do you mean?" said Lodge.
And, as he spoke, there was a sudden hush.
A tall gaunt woman with great burning eyes,
And white hair blown back softly from a face
Ethereally fierce, as might have looked
Cassandra in old age, stood at the door.
"Where is my Ben?" she said.
                          "Mother!" cried Ben.
He rose and caught her in his mighty arms.
Her labour-reddened, long-boned hands entwined
Behind his neck.
                          "She brought this to the gaol,"
Said Chapman quietly, tossing a phial across
To Camden.   "And he meant to take it, too,
Before the hangman touched him.   Half an hour
And you'd have been too late to save big Ben.
He has lived too much in ancient Rome to love
A slit nose and the pillory.   He'd have wrapped
His purple round him like an emperor.
I think she had another for herself."
"There's Roman blood in both of them," said Dekker,
"Don't look.   She is weeping now."   And, while Ben held
That gaunt old body sobbing against his heart,
Dekker, to make her think they paid no heed,

I*   245

Began to sing; and very softly now,
Full forty voices echoed the refrain:—

> The Cardinal's Hat is a very good inn,
>   And so is The Puritan's Head;
> But I know a sign of a Wine, a Wine
>   That is better when all is said.
> It is whiter than Venus, redder than Mars,
>   It was old when the world begun;
> For all good inns are moons or stars
>   But The Mermaid is their Sun.

Chorus: They are all alight like moons in the night,
            But The Mermaid is their Sun.

> Therefore, when priest or parson cries
>   That inns like flowers increase,
> I say that mine inn is a church likewise,
>   And I say to them "Be at peace!"
> An host may gather in dark St. Paul's
>   To salve their souls from sin;
> But the Light may be where "two or three"
>   Drink Wine in The Mermaid Inn.

Chorus: The Light may be where "two or three"
            Drink Wine in The Mermaid Inn.

VII

THE BURIAL OF A QUEEN

'Twas on an All Souls' Eve that our good Inn
—Whereof, for ten years now, myself was host—
Heard and took part in its most eerie tale.
    It was a bitter night, and master Ben,
—His hair now flecked with grey, though youth still fired
His deep and ageless eyes,—in the old oak-chair,
Over the roaring hearth, puffed at his pipe;
A little sad, as often I found him now
Remembering vanished faces.   Yet the years
Brought others round him.   Wreaths of Heliochrise
Gleamed still in that great tribe of Benjamin,
Burned still across the malmsey and muscadel.
Chapman and Browne, Herrick,—a name like thyme

Crushed into sweetness by a bare-foot maid
Milking, at dewy dawn, in Elfin-land,—
These three came late, and sat in a little room
Aside, supping together, on one great pie,
Whereof both crust and coffin were prepared
By master Herrick's receipt, and all washed down
With mighty cups of sack.   This left with Ben,
John Ford, wrapped in his cloak, brooding aloof,
Drayton and Lodge and Drummond of Hawthornden.
   Suddenly, in the porch, I heard a sound
Of iron that grated on the flags.   A spade
And pick came edging through the door.

                      "O, room!
Room for the master-craftsman," muttered Ford,
And grey old sexton Scarlet hobbled in.
   He shuffled off the snow that clogged his boots,
—On my clean rushes!—brushed it from his cloak
Of northern russet, wiped his rheumatic knees,
Blew out his lanthorn, hung it on a nail,
Leaned his rude pick and spade against the wall,
Flung back his rough frieze hood, flapped his gaunt arms,
And called for ale.   "Come to the fire," said Lodge.
"Room for the wisest counsellor of kings,
The kindly sage that puts us all to bed,
And tucks us up beneath the grass-green quilt."
   "Plenty of work, eh Timothy?" said Ben.
"Work?   Where's my liquor?   O, ay, there's work to spare,"
Old Scarlet croaked, then quaffed his creaming stoup,
While Ben said softly—"Pity you could not spare,
You and your Scythe-man, some of the golden lads
That I have seen here in the Mermaid Inn!"
Then, with a quiet smile he shook his head
And turned to master Drummond of Hawthornden.
"Well, songs are good; but flesh and blood are better.
The grey old tomb of Horace glows for me
Across the centuries, with one little fire
Lit by a girl's light hand."   Then, under breath,
Yet with some passion, he murmured this brief rhyme:—

Dulce ridentem, laughing through the ages,
   Dulce loquentem, O, fairer far to me,
Rarer than the wisdom of all his golden pages
   Floats the happy laughter of his vanished Lalage.

Dulce loquentem,—we hear it and we know it.
   Dulce ridentem,—so musical and low.
"Mightier than marble is my song!"   Ah, did the poet
   Know why little Lalage was mightier even so?

Dulce ridentem,—through all the years that sever,
   Clear as o'er yon hawthorn hedge we heard her passing by,—
Lalagen amabo,—a song may live for ever
   Dulce loquentem,—but Lalage must die.

"I'd like to learn that rhyme," the sexton said.
"I've a fine memory too.   You start me now,
I'd keep it up all night with ancient ballads."
   And then—a strange thing happened.   I saw John Ford
"With folded arms and melancholy hat"
(As in our Mermaid jest he still would sit)
Watching old Scarlet like a man in trance.
The sexton gulped his ale and smacked his lips,
Then croaked again—"O, ay, there's work to spare,
We fills 'em faster than the spades can dig,"
And, all at once, the lights burned low and blue.
Ford leaned right forward, with his grim black eyes
Widening.
            "Why, that's a marvellous ring!" he said,
And pointed to the sexton's gnarled old hand
Spread on the black oak-table like the claw
Of some great bird of prey.   "A ruby worth
The ransom of a queen!"   The fire leapt up!
The sexton stared at him;
Then stretched his hand out, with its blue-black nails,
Full in the light, a grim earth-coloured hand,
But bare as it was born.
                        "There was a ring!
I could have sworn it!   Red as blood!" cried Ford.
And Ben and Lodge and Drummond of Hawthornden
All stared at him.   For such a silent soul
Was master Ford that, when he suddenly spake,
It struck the rest as dumb as if the Sphinx
Had opened its cold stone lips.   He would sit mute
Brooding, aloof, for hours, his cloak around him,
A staff between his knees, as if prepared
For a long journey, a lonely pilgrimage
To some dark tomb; a strange and sorrowful soul,
Yet not—as many thought him—harsh or hard,
But of a most kind patience.   Though he wrote

In blood, they say, the blood came from his heart;
And all the sufferings of this world he took
To his own soul, and bade them pasture there;
Till out of his compassion, he became
A monument of bitterness.   He rebelled;
And so fell short of that celestial height
Whereto the greatest only climb, who stand
By Shakespeare, and accept the Eternal Law.
These find, in law, firm footing for the soul,
The strength that binds the stars, and reins the sea,
The base of being, the pillars of the world,
The pledge of honour, the pure cord of love,
The form of truth, the golden floors of heaven.
These men discern a height beyond all heights,
A depth below all depths, and never an end
Without a pang beyond it, and a hope;
Without a heaven beyond it, and a hell.
For these, despair is like a bubble pricked,
An old romance to make young lovers weep.
For these, the law becomes a fiery road,
A Jacob's ladder through that vast abyss
Lacking no rung from realm to loftier realm,
Nor wanting one degree from dust to wings.
These, at the last, radiant with victory,
Lay their strong hands upon the wingèd steeds
And fiery chariots, and exult to hold,
Themselves, the throbbing reins, whereby they steer
The stormy splendours.
                        He, being less, rebelled,
Cried out for unreined steeds, and unruled stars,
An unprohibited ocean and a truth
Untrue; and the equal thunder of the law
Hurled him to night and chaos, who was born
To shine upon the forehead of the day.
And yet—the voice of darkness and despair
May speak for heaven where heaven would not be heard,
May fight for heaven where heaven would not prevail,
And the consummate splendour of that strife,
Swallowing up all discords, all defeat,
In one huge victory, harmonising all,
Make Lucifer, at last, at one with God.

  There,—on that All Souls Eve, you might have thought
A dead man spoke, to see how Drayton stared,
And Drummond started.

                    "You saw no ruby ring,"
The old sexton muttered sullenly.   "If you did,
The worse for me, by all accounts.   The lights
Burned low.   You caught the firelight on my fist.
What was it like, this ring?"

                    "A band of gold,
And a great ruby, heart-shaped, fit to burn
Between the breasts of Laïs.   Am I awake
Or dreaming?"

                    "Well,—that makes the second time!
There's many have said they saw it, out of jest,
To scare me.   For the astrologer did say
The third time I should die.   Now, did you see it?
Most likely someone's told you that old tale!
You hadn't heard it, now?"

                    Ford shook his head.
"What tale?" said Ben.

                    "O, you could make a book
About my life.   I've talked with quick and dead,
And neither ghost nor flesh can fright me now!
I wish it was a ring, so's I could catch him,
And sell him; but I've never seen him yet.
A white witch told me, if I did, I'd go
Clink, just like that, to heaven or t'other place,
Whirled in a fiery chariot with ten steeds
The way Elijah went.   For I have seen
So many mighty things that I must die
Mightily.

                    Well,—I came, sirs, to my craft
The day mine uncle Robert dug the grave
For good Queen Katharine, she whose heart was broke
By old King Harry, a very great while ago.
Maybe you've heard about my uncle, sirs?
He was far-famous for his grave-digging.
In depth, in speed, in neatness, he'd no match!
They've put a fine slab to his memory
In Peterborough Cathedral—*Robert Scarlet,*
Sexton for half a century, it says,
In Peterborough Cathedral, where he built
The last sad habitation for two queens,
And many hundreds of the common sort.
And now himself, who for so many built
Eternal habitations, others have buried.
Obiit anno œtatis, ninety-eight,
July the second, fifteen ninety-four.

We should do well, sir, with a slab like that,
Shouldn't we?"   And the sexton leered at Lodge.
"Not many boasts a finer slab than that.
There's many a king done worse.   Ah, well, you see,
He'd a fine record.   Living to ninety-eight,
He buried generations of the poor,
A countless host, and thought no more of it
Than digging potatoes.   He'd a lofty mind
That found no satisfaction in small deeds.
But from his burying of two queens he drew
A lively pleasure.   Could he have buried a third,
It would indeed have crowned his old white hairs.
But he was famous, and he thought, perchance,
A third were mere vain-glory.   So he died.
I helped him with the second."
                                    The old man leered
To see the shaft go home.
                                    Ben filled the stoup
With ale.   "So that," quoth he, "began the tale
About this ruby ring?"   "But who," said Lodge,
"Who was the second queen?"
                                    "A famous queen,
And a great lover!   When you hear her name,
Your hearts will leap.   Her beauty passed the bounds
Of modesty, men say, yet—she died young!
We buried her at midnight.   There were few
That knew it; for the high State Funeral
Was held upon the morrow, Lammas morn.
Anon you shall hear why.   A strange thing that,—
To see the mourners weeping round a hearse
That held a dummy coffin.   Stranger still
To see us lowering the true coffin down
By torchlight, with some few of her true friends,
In Peterborough Cathedral, all alone."
"Old as the world," said Ford.   "It is the way
Of princes.   Their true tears and smiles are seen
At dead of night, like ghosts raised from the grave!
And all the luxury of their brief, bright noon,
Cloaks but a dummy throne, a mask of life;
And, at the last, drapes a false catafalque,
Holding a vacant urn, a mask of death.
But tell, tell on!"
                                    The sexton took a draught
Of ale and smacked his lips.
                                    "Mine uncle lived

251

A mile or more from Peterborough, then.
And, past his cottage, in the dead of night,
Her royal coach came creeping through the lanes,
With scutcheons round it and no crowd to see,
And heralds carrying torches in their hands,
And none to admire, but him and me, and one,
A pedlar-poet, who lodged with us that week
And paid his lodging with a bunch of rhymes.
By these, he said, my uncle Robert's fame
Should live, as in a picture, till the crack
Of doom.   My uncle thought that he should pay
Four-pence beside; but, when the man declared
The thought unworthy of these august events,
My uncle was abashed.

              And, truth to tell,
The rhymes were mellow, though here and there he swerved
From truth to make them so.   Nor would he change
'June' to 'July' for all that we could say.
'I never said the month was June,' he cried,
'And if I did, Shakespeare hath jumped an age!
Gods, will you hedge me round with thirty nights?
"June" rhymes with "moon"!'   With that, he flung them down
And strode away like Lucifer, and was gone,
Before old Scarlet could approach again
The matter of that four-pence.

                  Yet his rhymes
Have caught the very colours of that night!
I can see through them,
Ay, just as through our cottage window-panes,
Can see the great black coach,
Carrying the dead queen past our garden-gate.
The roses bobbing and fluttering to and fro,
Hide, and yet show the more by hiding, half.
And, like smoked glass through which you see the sun,
The song shows truest when it blurs the truth.
This is the way it goes."

             He rose to his feet,
Picked up his spade, and struck an attitude,
Leaning upon it.   "I've got to feel my spade,
Or I'll forget it.   This is the way I speak it,
Always."   And, with a schoolboy's rigid face,
And eyes fixed on the rafters, he began,
Sing-song, the pedlar-poet's bunch of rhymes:—

As I went by the cattle-shed
  The grey dew dimmed the grass,

And, under a twisted apple-tree,
Old Robin Scarlet stood by me.
"Keep watch!   Keep watch to-night," he said,
   "There's things 'ull come to pass.

"Keep watch until the moon has cleared
   The thatch of yonder rick;
Then I'll come out of my cottage-door
To wait for the coach of a queen once more;
And—you'll say nothing of what you've heard,
   But rise and follow me quick."

"And what 'ull I see if I keep your trust,
   And wait and watch so late?"
"Pride," he said, "and Pomp," he said,
"Beauty to haunt you till you're dead,
And Glorious Dust that goes to dust,
   Passing the white farm-gate.

"You are young and all for adventure, lad,
   And the great tales to be told:
This night, before the clock strike one,
Your lordliest hour will all be done;
But you'll remember it and be glad,
   In the days when you are old!"

All in the middle of the night,
   My face was at the pane;
When, creeping out of his cottage-door,
To wait for the coach of a queen once more,
Old Scarlet, in the moon-light,
   Beckoned to me again.

He stood beneath a lilac-spray,
   Like Father Time for dole,
In Reading tawny cloak and hood,
With mattock and with spade he stood,
And, far away to southward,
   A bell began to toll.

He stood beneath a lilac-spray,
   And never a word he said;
But, as I stole out of the house,
He pointed over the orchard boughs,
Where, not with dawn or sunset,
   The Northern sky grew red.

I followed him, and half in fear,
  To the old farm-gate again;
And, round the curve of the long white road,
I saw that the dew-dashed hedges glowed
Red with the grandeur drawing near,
  And the torches of her train.

They carried her down with singing,
  With singing soft and low,
Slowly round the curve they came,
Twenty torches dropping flame,
The heralds that were bringing her
  The way we all must go.

'Twas master William Dethick,
  The Garter King of Arms,
Before her royal coach did ride,
With none to see his Coat of Pride,
For peace was on the countryside,
  And sleep upon the farms;

Peace upon the red farm,
  Peace upon the grey,
Peace on the heavy orchard trees,
And little white-walled cottages,
Peace upon the wayside,
  And sleep upon the way.

So master William Dethick,
  With forty horse and men,
Like any common man and mean
Rode on before the Queen, the Queen,
And—only a wandering pedlar
  Could tell the tale again.

How, like a cloud of darkness,
  Between the torches moved
Four black steeds and a velvet pall
Crowned with the Crown Imperiall
And—on her shield—the lilies,
  The lilies that she loved.

Ah, stained and ever stainless
  Ah, white as her own hand,
White as the wonder of that brow,

Crowned with colder lilies now,
White on the velvet darkness,
   The lilies of her land!

The witch from over the water,
   The fay from over the foam,
The bride that rode thro' Edinbro' town
With satin shoes and a silken gown,
A queen, and a great king's daughter,—
   Thus they carried her home,

With torches and with scutcheons,
   Unhonoured and unseen,
With the lilies of France in the wind a-stir,
And the Lion of Scotland over her,
Darkly, in the dead of night,
   They carried the Queen, the Queen.

The sexton paused and took a draught of ale.
" 'Twas there," he said, "I joined 'em at the gate,
My uncle and the pedlar.   What they sang,
The little shadowy throng of men that walked
Behind the scutcheoned coach with bare bent heads
I know not; but 'twas very soft and low.
They walked behind the rest, like shadows flung
Behind the torch-light, from that strange dark hearse;
And, some said, afterwards, they were the ghosts
Of lovers that this queen had brought to death.
A foolish thought it seemed to me, and yet
Like the night-wind they sang.   And there was one
An olive-coloured man,—the pedlar said
Was like a certain foreigner that she loved,
One Chastelard, a wild French poet of hers.
Also the pedlar thought they sang 'farewell'
In words like this, and that the words in French
Were written by the hapless Queen herself,
When as a girl she left the vines of France
For Scotland and the halls of Holyrood:—

      Though thy hands have plied their trade
        Eighty years without a rest,
    Robin Scarlet, never thy spade
        Built a house for such a guest!
    Carry her where, in earliest June,
        All the whitest hawthorns blow:

Carry her under the midnight moon,
   Singing very soft and low.
Slow between the low green larches, carry the lovely lady sleeping,
   Past the low white moon-lit farms, along the lilac-shadowed way!
Carry her through the summer darkness, weeping, weeping, weeping,
   weeping!
   Answering only, to any that ask you, whence ye carry her,—*Fothering-
   hay!*

   She was gayer than a child!
   —*Let your torches droop for sorrow.*—
   Laughter in her eyes ran wild!
   —*Carry her down to Peterboro'.*—
   Words were kisses in her mouth!
   —*Let no word of blame be spoken.*—
   She was Queen of all the South!
   —*In the North, her heart was broken.*—
They should have left her in her vineyards, left her heart to her land's
   own keeping,
   Left her white breast room to breathe, and left her light foot free to
   dance.
Out of the cold grey Northern mists, we carry her weeping, weeping,
   weeping,—

   O, ma patrie,
   La plus chérie,
   Adieu, plaisant pays de France!

   Many a red heart died to beat
   —*Music swelled in Holyrood!*—
   Once, beneath her fair white feet.
   —*Now the floors may rot with blood*—
   She was young and her deep hair—
   —*Wind and rain were all her fate!*—
   Trapped young Love as in a snare.
   —*And the wind's a sword in the Canongate!*—
   Edinboro'!
   Edinboro'!
Music built the towers of Troy, but thy grey walls are built of sorrow!
Wind-swept hills, and sorrowful glens, of thrifty sowing and iron reap-
   ing,
   What if her foot were fair as a sunbeam, how should it touch or melt
   your snows?
   What if her hair were a silken mesh?
   Hands of steel can deal hard blows,

256

Iron breast-plates bruise fair flesh!
Carry her southward, palled in purple,
Weeping, weeping, weeping, weeping,
What had their rocks to do with roses?   Body and soul she was all one
rose.

Thus, through the summer night, slowly they went,
We three behind,—the pedlar-poet and I,
And Robin Scarlet.   The moving flare that ringed
The escutcheoned hearse, lit every leaf distinct
Along the hedges and woke the sleeping birds,
But drew no watchers from the drowsier farms.
Thus, through a world of innocence and sleep,
We brought her to the doors of her last home,
In Peterborough Cathedral.   Round her tomb
They stood, in the huge gloom of those old aisles,
The heralds with their torches, but their light
Struggled in vain with that tremendous dark.
Their ring of smoky red could only show
A few sad faces round the purple pall,
The wings of a stone angel overhead,
The base of three great pillars, and, fitfully,
Faint as the phosphorus glowing in some old vault,
One little slab of marble, far away.
   Yet, or the darkness, or the pedlar's words
Had made me fanciful, I thought I saw
Bowed shadows praying in those unplumbed aisles,
Nay, dimly heard them weeping, in a grief
That still was built of silence, like the drip
Of water from a frozen fountain-head.
   We laid her in her grave.   We closed the tomb.
With echoing footsteps all the funeral went;
And I went last to close and lock the doors;
Last, and half frightened of the enormous gloom
That rolled along behind me as one by one
The torches vanished.   O, I was glad to see
The moonlight on the kind turf-mounds again.
   But, as I turned the key, a quivering hand
Was laid upon my arm.   I turned and saw
That foreigner with the olive-coloured face.
   From head to foot he shivered, as with cold.
He drew me into the shadows of the porch.
'Come back with me,' he whispered, and slid his hand
—Like ice it was!—along my wrist, and slipped

A ring upon my finger, muttering quick,
As in a burning fever, 'All the wealth
Of Eldorado for one hour!   Come back!
I must go back and see her face again!
I was not there, not there, the day she—died.
You'll help me with the coffin.   Not a soul
Will know.   Come back!   One moment, only one!'
   I thought the man was mad, and plucked my hand
Away from him.   He caught me by the sleeve,
And sank upon his knees, lifting his face
Most piteously to mine.   'One moment!   See!
I loved her!'
I saw the moonlight glisten on his tears,
Great, long, slow tears they were; and then—my God—
As his face lifted and his head sank back
Beseeching me—I saw a crimson thread
Circling his throat, as though the headsman's axe
Had cloven it with one blow, so shrewd, so keen,
The head had slipped not from the trunk.
                                        I gasped;
And, as he pleaded, stretching his head back,
The wound, O like a second awful mouth,
The wound began to gape.
                           I tore my cloak
Out of his clutch.   My keys fell with a clash.
I left them where they lay, and with a shout
I dashed into the broad white empty road.
There was no soul in sight.   Sweating with fear
I hastened home, not daring to look back;
But as I turned the corner, I heard the clang
Of those great doors, and knew he had entered in.

Not till I saw before me in the lane
The pedlar and my uncle did I halt
And look at that which clasped my finger still
As with a band of ice.
                       My hand was bare!
I stared at it and rubbed it.   Then I thought
I had been dreaming.   There had been no ring!
The poor man I had left there in the porch,
Being a Frenchman, talked a little wild;
But only wished to look upon her grave.
And I—I was the madman!   So I said
Nothing.   But all the same, for all my thoughts,
I'd not go back that night to find the keys,

No, not for all the rubies in the crown
Of Prester John.

.   .   .   .

                    The high State Funeral
Was held on Lammas Day.   A wondrous sight
For Peterborough!   For myself, I found
Small satisfaction in a catafalque
That carried a dummy coffin.   None the less,
The pedlar thought that as a Solemn Masque,
Or Piece of Purple Pomp, the thing was good,
And worthy of a picture in his rhymes;
The more because he said it shadowed forth
The ironic face of Death.
                         The Masque, indeed
Began before we buried her.   For a host
Of Mourners—Lords and Ladies—on Lammas eve
Panting with eagerness of pride and place,
Arrived in readiness for the morrow's pomp,
And at the Bishop's Palace they found prepared
A mighty supper for them, where they sat
All at one table.   In a Chamber hung
With scutcheons and black cloth, they drank red wine
And feasted, while the torches and the Queen
Crept through the darkness of Northampton lanes.

At seven o'clock on Lammas Morn they woke,
After the Queen was buried; and at eight
The Masque set forth, thus pictured in the rhymes
With tolling bells, which on the pedlar's lips
Had more than paid his lodging.   Thus he spake it,
Slowly, sounding the rhymes like solemn bells,
And tolling, in between, with lingering tongue:—

Toll!—From the Palace the Releevants creep,—
   A hundred poor old women, nigh their end,
Wearing their black cloth gowns, and on each head
An ell of snow-white holland which, some said,
                    Afterwards they might keep,
—*Ah, Toll!*—with nine new shillings each to spend,
   For all the trouble that they had, and all
   The sorrow of walking to this funeral.

Toll!—And the Mourning Cloaks in purple streamed
   Following, a long procession, two by two,

Her Household first.   With these, Monsieur du Preau.
Her French Confessor, unafraid to show
                    The golden Cross that gleamed
About his neck, warned what the crowd might do
    Said *"I will wear it, though I die for it!"*
So subtle in malice was that Jesuit.

Toll!—Sir George Savile in his Mourner's Gown
    Carried the solemn Cross upon a field
Azure, and under it by a streamer borne
Upon a field of Gules, an Unicorn
                    Argent and, lower down,
A scrolled device upon a blazoned shield,
    Which seemed to say—I AM SILENT TILL THE END!—
    Toll! Toll!—IN MY DEFENCE, GOD ME DEFEND!

Toll!—and a hundred poor old men went by,
    Followed by two great Bishops.—*Toll, ah toll!*—
Then, with White Staves and Gowns, four noble lords;
Then sixteen Scots and Frenchmen with drawn swords;
                    Then, with a Bannerol,
Sir Andrew Noel, lifting to the sky
    The Great Red Lion.   Then the Crown and Crest
    Borne by a Herald on his glittering breast.

And now—ah now, indeed, the deep bell tolls—
    That empty Coffin, with its velvet pall,
Borne by six Gentlemen, under a canopy
Of purple, lifted by four knights, goes by.
                    The Crown Imperial
Burns on the Coffin-head.   Four Bannerols
    On either side, uplifted by four squires,
    Roll on the wind their rich heraldic fires.
Toll!   The Chief Mourner—the fair Russell!—*toll!*—
    Countess of Bedford—*toll!*—they bring her now,
Weeping under a purple Cloth of State,
Till, halting there before the Minster Gate,
                    Having in her control
The fair White Staves of office, with a bow
    She gives them to her two great Earls again,
    And then sweeps on with all her mournful train.

Toll!   At the high Cathedral door the Quires
    Meet them and lead them, singing all the while
A mighty *Miserere* for her soul!

Then, as the rolling organ—*toll, ah toll!*—
            Floods every glimmering aisle
With ocean-thunders, all those knights and squires
  Bring the false Coffin to the central nave
  And set it in the Catafalque o'er her grave.

The Catafalque was made in Field-bed wise
  Valanced with midnight purple, fringed with gold:
All the Chief Mourners on dark thrones were set
Within it, as jewels in some huge carcanet:
            Above was this device
IN MY DEFENCE, GOD ME DEFEND, inscrolled
  Round the rich Arms of Scotland, as to say
  "Man judged me.   I abide the Judgment Day."

The sexton paused anew.   All looked at him,
And at his wrinkled, grim, earth-coloured hand,
As if, in that dim light, beclouded now
With blue tobacco-smoke, they thought to see
The smouldering ruby again.
                "Ye know," he said,
"How master William Wickham preached that day?"
Ford nodded.   "I have heard of it.   He showed
Subtly, O very subtly, after his kind,
That the white Body of Beauty such as hers
Was in itself Papistical, a feast,
A fast, an incense, a burnt-offering,
And an Abomination in the sight
Of all true Protestants.   Why, her very name
Was Mary!"
        "Ay, that's true, that's very true!"
The sexton mused.   "Now that's a strange deep thought!
The Bishop missed a text in missing that.
Her name, indeed, was Mary!"
                "Did you find
Your keys again?"   "Ay, sir, I found them!"   "Where?"
"Strange you should ask me that!   After the throng
Departed, and the Nobles were at feast,
All in the Bishop's Palace—a great feast
And worthy of their sorrow—I came back
Carrying my uncle's second bunch of keys
To lock the doors and search, too, for mine own.
'Twas growing dusk already, and as I thrust
The key into the lock, the great grey porch
Grew cold upon me, like a tomb.

                                        I pushed
Hard at the key—then stopped—with all my flesh
Freezing, and half in mind to fly; for, sirs,
The door was locked already, and—*from within!*
I drew the key forth quietly and stepped back
Into the Churchyard, where the graves were warm
With sunset still, and the blunt carven stones
Lengthened their homely shadows, out and out,
To Everlasting.   Then I plucked up heart,
Seeing the footprints of that mighty Masque
Along the pebbled path.   A queer thought came
Into my head that all the world without
Was but a Masque, and I was creeping back,
Back from the Mourner's Feast to Truth again.
Yet—I grew bold, and tried the Southern door.
   'Twas locked, but held no key on the inner side
To foil my own, and softly, softly, click,
I turned it, and with heart, sirs, in my mouth,
Pushed back the studded door and entered in . . .
   Stepped straight out of the world, I might have said,
Out of the dusk into a night so deep,
So dark, I trembled like a child. . . .
                                        And then
I was aware, sirs, of a great sweet wave
Of incense.   All the gloom was heavy with it,
As if her Papist Household had returned
To pray for her poor soul; and, my fear went.
But either that strange incense weighed me down,
Or else from being sorely over-tasked,
A languor came upon me, and sitting there
To breathe a moment, in a velvet stall,
I closed mine eyes.
                        A moment, and no more,
For then I heard a rustling in the nave,
And opened them; and, very far away,
As if across the world, in Rome herself,
I saw twelve tapers in the solemn East,
And saw, or thought I saw, cowled figures kneel
Before them, in an incense-cloud.
                                        And then,
Maybe the sunset deepened in the world
Of masques without—clear proof that I had closed
Mine eyes but for a moment, sirs, I saw
As if across a world-without-end tomb,
A tiny jewelled glow of crimson panes

Darkening and brightening with the West.
                                        And then,
Then I saw something more—Queen Mary's vault,
And—it was open! . . .
                        Then, I heard a voice,
A strange deep broken voice, whispering love
In soft French words, that clasped and clung like hands;
And then—two shadows passed against the West,
Two blurs of black against that crimson stain,
Slowly, O very slowly, with bowed heads,
Leaning together, and vanished into the dark
Beyond the Catafalque.
                        Then—I heard him pray,—
And knew him for the man that prayed to me,—
Pray as a man prays for his love's last breath!
And then, O sirs, it caught me by the throat,
And I, too, dropped upon my knees and prayed;
For, as in answer to his prayer, there came
A moan of music, a mighty shuddering sound
From the great organ, a sound that rose and fell
Like seas in anger, very far away;
And then a peal of thunder, and then it seemed,
As if the graves were giving up their dead,
A great cowled host of shadows rose and sang:—

            Dies iræ, dies illa
            Solvet sæclum in favilla,
            Teste David cum Sibylla.

I heard her sad, sad, little broken voice,
Out in the darkness.   'Ay, and David, too,
His blood is on the floors of Holyrood,
To speak for me.'   Then that great ocean-sound
Swelled to a thunder again, and heaven and earth
Shrivelled away; and in that huge slow hymn
Chariots were driven forth in flaming rows,
And terrible trumpets blown from deep to deep.

And then, ah then, the heart of heaven was hushed,
And—in the hush—it seemed an angel wept,
Another Mary wept, and gathering up
All our poor wounded, weary, way-worn world,
Even as a Mother gathers up her babe,
Soothed it against her breast, and rained her tears
On the pierced feet of God, and melted Him

To pity, and over His feet poured her deep hair.
The music died away.   The shadows knelt.
And then—I heard a rustling nigh the tomb,
And heard—and heard—or dreamed I heard—farewells,
Farewells for everlasting, deep farewells,
Bitter as blood, darker than any death.
And, at the last, as in a kiss, one breath,
One agony of sweetness, like a sword
For sharpness, drawn along a soft white throat;
And, for its terrible sweetness, like a sigh
Across great waters, very far away,—
Sweetheart!
And then, like doors, like world-without-end doors
That shut for Everlasting, came a clang,
And ringing, echoing, through the echo of it,
One terrible cry that plucked my heart-strings out,
Mary!   And on the closed and silent tomb,
Where there were two, one shuddering shadow lay,
And then—I, too,—reeled, swooned and knew no more.

Sirs, when I woke, there was a broad bright shaft
Of moonlight, slanting through an Eastern pane
Full on her tomb and that black Catafalque.
And on the tomb there lay—my bunch of keys!
I struggled to my feet,
Ashamed of my wild fancies, like a man
Awakening from a drunken dream.   And yet,
When I picked up the keys, although that storm
Of terror had all blown by and left me calm,
I lifted up mine eyes to see the scroll
Round the rich crest of that dark canopy,
IN MY DEFENCE, GOD ME DEFEND.   The moon
Struck full upon it; and, as I turned and went,
God help me, sirs, though I were loyal enough
To good Queen Bess, I could not help but say,
Amen!
And yet, methought it was not I that spake,
But some deep soul that used me for a mask,
A soul that rose up in this hollow shell
Like dark sea-tides flooding an empty cave.
I could not help but say with my poor lips,
Amen!   Amen!
                    Sirs, 'tis a terrible thing
To move in great events.   Since that strange night
I have not been as other men.   The tides

Would rise in this dark cave"—he tapped his skull—
"Deep tides, I know not whence; and when they rose
My friends looked strangely upon me and stood aloof
And once, my uncle said to me—indeed,
It troubled me strangely,—'Timothy,' he said,
'Thou art translated!   I could well believe
Thou art two men, whereof the one's a fool,
The other a prophet.   Or else, beneath thy skin
There lurks a changeling!   What hath come to thee?'
And then, sirs, then—well I remember it!
'Twas on a summer eve, and we walked home
Between high ghostly hedges white with may—
And uncle Robin, in his holy-day suit
Of Reading tawny, felt his old heart swell
With pride in his great memories.   He began
Chanting the pedlar's tune, keeping the time
Thus, jingle, jingle, slowly, with his keys:—

Douglas, in the moonless night
   —*Muffled oars on blue Loch Leven!*—
Took her hand, a flake of white
   —*Beauty slides the bolts of heaven.*—
Little white hand, like a flake of snow,
   When they saw it, his Highland crew
Swung together and murmured low,
   'Douglas, wilt *thou* die then, too?'
And the pine trees whispered, weeping,
   '*Douglas, Douglas, tender and true!*'
Little white hand like a tender moonbeam, soon shall you set the broad-
      swords leaping.
   'It is the Queen, the Queen!' they whispered, watching her soar to the
      saddle anew.
'There will be trumpets blown in the mountains, a mist of blood on the
      heather, and weeping,
   Weeping, weeping, and *thou*, too, dead for her, Douglas, Douglas,
   tender and true.'

Carry the queenly lass along!
   —*Cold she lies, cold and dead,*—
She whose laughter was a song,
   —*Lapped around with sheets of lead!*—
She whose blood was wine of the South,
   —*Light her down to a couch of clay!*—
And a royal rose her mouth,
   And her body made of may!

265

     —Lift your torches, weeping, weeping,
        Light her down to a couch of clay.
They should have left her in her vineyards, left her heart to her land's
    own keeping,
  Left her white breast room to breathe, and left her light foot free to
    dance!

Hush! Between the solemn pinewoods, carry the lovely lady sleeping,
  Out of the cold grey Northern mists, with banner and scutcheon,
    plume, and lance,
Carry her southward, palled in purple, weeping, weeping, weeping,
    weeping,—
        O, ma patrie,
        La plus chérie,
    Adieu, plaisant pays de France!

Well, sirs, that dark tide rose within my brain!
I snatched his keys and flung them over the hedge,
Then flung myself down on a bank of ferns
And wept and wept and wept.
                 It puzzled him.
Perchance he feared my mind was going and yet,
O, sirs, if you consider it rightly now,
With all those ages knocking at his doors,
With all that custom clamouring for his care,
Is it so strange a grave-digger should weep?
Well—he was kind enough and heaped my plate
That night at supper.
But I could never dig my graves at ease
In Peterborough Churchyard. So I came
To London—to St. Mary Magdalen's.
And thus, I chanced to drink my ale one night
Here in the Mermaid Inn. 'Twas All Souls' Eve,
And, on that bench, where master Ford now sits
Was master Shakespeare—
Well, the lights burned low,
And just like master Ford to-night he leaned
Suddenly forward. 'Timothy,' he said,
'That's a most marvellous ruby!'
                 My blood froze!
I stretched my hand out bare as it was born;
And he said nothing, only looked at me.
Then, seeing my pipe was empty, he bade me fill
And lit it for me.
          Peach, the astrologer,

Was living then; and that same night I went
And told him all my trouble about this ring.
He took my hand in his, and held it—thus—
Then looked into my face and said this rhyme:—

    The ruby ring, that only three
    While Time and Tide go by, shall see,
    Weds your hand to history.

    Honour and pride the first shall lend;
    The second shall give you gold to spend;
    The third—shall warn you of your end.

Peach was a rogue, some say, and yet he spake
Most truly about the first," the sexton mused,
"For master Shakespeare, though they say in youth
Outside the theatres, he would hold your horse
For pence, prospered at last, bought a fine house
In Stratford, lived there like a squire, they say.
And here, here he would sit, for all the world
As he were but a poet, God bless us all,
And then—to think!—he rose to be a squire!
A deep one, masters!   Well, he lit my pipe!"
"Why did they bury such a queen by night?"
Said Ford.   "Kings might have wept for her.   Did Death
Play epicure and glutton that so few
Were bidden to such a feast.   Once on a time,
I could have wept, myself, to hear a tale
Of beauty buried in the dark.   And hers
Was loveliness, far, far beyond the common!
Such beauty should be marble to the touch
Of time, and clad in purple to amaze
The moth.   But she was kind and soft and fair,
A woman, and so she died.   But, why the dark?"
"Sir, they gave out the coffin was too heavy
For gentlemen to bear!"—"For kings to bear?"
Ford flashed at him.   The sexton shook his head,—
"Nay!   Gentlemen to bear!   But—the true cause—
Ah, sir, 'tis unbelievable, even to me,
A sexton, for a queen so fair of face!
And all her beds, even as the pedlar said,
Breathing Arabia, sirs, her walls all hung
With woven purple wonders and great tales
Of amorous gods and mighty mirrors, too,
Imaging her own softness, night and dawn,

When through her sumptuous hair she drew the combs;
And like one great white rose-leaf half her breast
Shone through it, firm as ivory."

       "Ay," said Lodge,
Murmuring his own rich music under breath,
"*About her neck did all the graces throng,*
And lay such baits as did entangle death."
"Well, sir, the weather being hot, they feared
She would not hold the burying!" . . .

       "In some sort,"
Ford answered slowly, "if your tale be true,
She did not hold it. Many a knightly crest
Will bend yet o'er the ghost of that small hand."

There was a hush, broken by Ben at last,
Who turned to Ford—"How now, my golden lad?
The astrologer's dead hand is on thy purse!"

Ford laughed, grimly, and flung an angel down.
"Well, cause or consequence, rhyme or no rhyme,
There is thy gold. I will not break the spell,
Or thou mayst live to bury us one and all!"
 "And, if I live so long," the old man replied,
Lighting his lanthorn, "you may trust me, sirs,
Mine Inn is quiet, and I can find you beds
Where Queens might sleep all night and never move.
Good-night, sirs, and God bless you, one and all."
 He shouldered pick and spade. I opened the door.
The snow blew in, and, as he shuffled out,
There, in the strait dark passage, I could swear
I saw a spark of red upon his hand,
Like a great smouldering ruby.

      I gasped. He stopped.
He peered at me.

     "Twice in a night," he said.
"Nothing," I answered, "only the lanthorn-light."
He shook his head. "I'll tell you something more!
There's nothing, nothing now in life or death
That frightens me. Ah, things used to frighten me.
But never now. I thought I had ten years;
But if the warning comes and says '*Thou fool,*
This night!' Why, then, I'm ready."

       I watched him go,
With glimmering lanthorn up the narrow street,

Like one that walked upon the clouds, through snow
That seemed to mix the City with the skies.

On Christmas Eve we heard that he was dead.

FLOS MERCATORUM

FLOS MERCATORUM!   On that night of nights
We drew from out our Mermaid cellarage
All the old glory of London in one cask
Of magic vintage.   Never a city on earth—
Rome, Paris, Florence, Bagdad—held for Ben
The colours of old London; and, that night,
We staved them like a wine, and drank, drank deep!

'Twas Master Heywood, whom the Mermaid Inn
Had dubbed our London laureate, hauled the cask
Out of its ancient harbourage.   "Ben," he cried,
Bustling into the room with Dekker and Brome,
"The prentices are up!"   Ben raised his head
Out of the chimney-corner where he drowsed,
And listened, reaching slowly for his pipe.

"*Clerk of the Bow Bell,*" all along the Cheape
There came a shout that swelled into a roar.
   "What!   Will they storm the Mermaid?"   Heywood laughed,
"They are turning into Bread Street!"
                                                        Down they came!
We heard them hooting round the poor old Clerk—
"Clubs! Clubs!   The rogue would have us work all night!
He rang ten minutes late!   Fifteen, by Paul's!"
And over the hubbub rose, like a thin bell,
The Clerk's entreaty—"Now, good boys, good boys,
Children of Cheape, be still, I do beseech you!
I took some forty winks, but then . . ."   A roar
Of wrathful laughter drowned him—"Forty winks!
Remember Black May-day!   We'll make you wink!"
There was a scuffle, and into the tavern rushed
Gregory Clopton, Clerk of the Bow Bell,—
A tall thin man, with yellow hair a-stream,
And blazing eyes.
                          "Hide me," he clamoured, "quick!
These picaroons will murder me!"
                                                      I closed

269

The thick oak doors against the coloured storm
Of prentices in red and green and ray,
Saffron and Reading tawny.   Twenty clubs
Drubbed on the panels as I barred them out;
And even our walls and shutters could not drown
Their song that, like a mocking peal of bells,
Under our windows, made all Bread Street ring:—

> *"Clerk of the Bow Bell,*
> *With the yellow locks,*
> *For thy late ringing*
> *Thy head shall have knocks!"*

Then Heywood, seeing the Clerk was all a-quake,
Went to an upper casement that o'er-looked
The whole of Bread Street.   Heywood knew their ways,
And parleyed with them till their anger turned
To shouts of merriment.   Then, like one deep bell
His voice rang out, in answer to their peal:—

> *"Children of Cheape,*
> *Hold you all still!*
> *You shall have Bow Bell*
> *Rung at your will!"*

Loudly they cheered him.   Courteously he bowed,
Then firmly shut the window; and, ere I filled
His cup with sack again, the crowd had gone.

"My clochard, sirs, is warm," quavered the Clerk.
"I do confess I took some forty winks!
They are good lads, our prentices of Cheape,
But hasty!"
            "Wine!" said Ben.   He filled a cup
And thrust it into Gregory's trembling hands.
"Yours is a task," said Dekker, "a great task!
You sit among the gods, a lord of time,
Measuring out the pulse of London's heart."
   "Yea, sir, above the hours and days and years,
I sometimes think.   'Tis a great Bell—the Bow!
And hath been, since the days of Whittington."
   "The good old days," growled Ben.   "Both good and bad
Were measured by my Bell," the Clerk replied.
And, while he spoke, warmed by the wine, his voice
Mellowed and floated up and down the scale

As if the music of the London bells
Lingered upon his tongue.   "I know them all,
And love them, all the voices of the bells.

FLOS MERCATORUM!   That's the Bell of Bow
Remembering Richard Whittington.   You should hear
The bells of London when they tell his tale.
Once, after hearing them, I wrote it down.
I know the tale by heart now, every turn."
    "Then ring it out," said Heywood.
                                Gregory smiled
And cleared his throat.
                        "You must imagine, sirs,
The Clerk, sitting on high, among the clouds,
With London spread beneath him like a map.
Under his tower, a flock of prentices
Calling like bells, of little size or weight,
But bells no less, ask that the Bell of Bow
Shall tell the tale of Richard Whittington,
As thus."
            Then Gregory Clopton, mellowing all
The chiming vowels, and dwelling on every tone
In rhythm or rhyme that helped to swell the peal
Or keep the ringing measure, beat for beat,
Chanted this legend of the London bells:—

Clerk of the Bow Bell, four and twenty prentices,
    All upon a Hallowe'en, we prithee, for our joy,
Ring a little turn again for sweet Dick Whittington,
    Flos Mercatorum, and a barefoot boy!—

"Children of Cheape," did that old Clerk answer,
    "You will have a peal, then, for well may you know,
All the bells of London remember Richard Whittington
    When they hear the voice of the big Bell of Bow!"—

Clerk with the yellow locks, mellow be thy malmsey!
    He was once a prentice, and carolled in the Strand!
Ay, and we are all, too, Marchaunt Adventurers,
    Prentices of London, and lords of Engeland.

"Children of Cheape," did that old Clerk answer,
    "Hold you, ah hold you, ah hold you all still!
Souling if you come to the glory of a Prentice,
    You shall have the Bow Bell rung at your will!"

"Whittington! Whittington! O, turn again, Whittington,
 Lord Mayor of London," the big Bell began:
"Where was he born?   O, at Pauntley in Gloucestershire
 Hard by Cold Ashton, Cold Ashton," it ran.

"*Flos Mercatorum,*" moaned the bell of All Hollowes,
 "There was he an orphan, O, a little lad alone!"
"Then we all sang," echoed happy St. Saviour's,
 "Called him, and lured him, and made him our own.

Told him a tale as he lay upon the hillside,
 Looking on his home in the meadow-lands below!"
"Told him a tale," clanged the bell of Cold Abbey;
 "Told him the truth," boomed the big Bell of Bow!

Sang of a City that was like a blazoned missal-book,
 Black with oaken gables, carven and inscrolled;
Every street a coloured page, and every sign a hieroglyph,
 Dusky with enchantments, a City paved with gold;

"Younger son, younger son, up with stick and bundle!"—
 Even so we rung for him—"But—kneel before you go;
Watch by your shield, lad, in little Pauntley Chancel,
 Look upon the painted panes that hold your Arms a-glow,—

Coat of Gules and Azure; but the proud will not remember it!
 And the Crest a Lion's Head, until the new be won!
Far away, remember it!   And O, remember this, too,—
 Every barefoot boy on earth is but a younger son."

Proudly he answered us, beneath the painted window,—
 "Though I be a younger son, the glory falls to me:
While my brother bideth by a little land in Gloucestershire,
 All the open Earth is mine, and all the Ocean-sea.

Yet will I remember, yet will I remember,
 By the chivalry of God, until my day be done,
When I meet a gentle heart, lonely and unshielded,
 Every barefoot boy on earth is but a younger son!"

Then he looked to northward for the tall ships of Bristol;
 Far away, and cold as death, he saw the Severn shine:
Then he looked to eastward, and he saw a string of colours
 Trickling through the grey hills, like elfin drops of wine;

Down along the Mendip dale, the chapmen and their horses,
  Far away, and carrying each its little coloured load,
Winding like a fairy-tale, with pack and corded bundle,
  Trickled like a crimson thread along the silver road.

Quick he ran to meet them, stick and bundle on his shoulder!
  Over by Cold Ashton, he met them trampling down,—
White shaggy horses with their packs of purple spicery,
  Crimson kegs of malmsey, and the silks of London town.

When the chapmen asked of him the bridle-path to Dorset,
  Blithely he showed them, and he led them on their way,
Led them through the fern with their bales of breathing Araby,
  Led them to a bridle-path that saved them half a day.

Merrily shook the silver bells that hung the broidered bridle rein,
  Chiming to his hand, as he led them through the fern,
Down to deep Dorset, and the wooded Isle of Purbeck,
  Then—by little Kimmeridge—they led him turn for turn.

Down by little Kimmeridge, and up by Hampshire forest roads,
  Round by Sussex violets, and apple-bloom of Kent,
Singing songs of London, telling tales of London,
  All the way to London, with packs of wool they went.

"London was London, then! A clean, clear moat
Girdled her walls that measured, round about,
Three miles or less. She is big and dirty now,"
Said Dekker.
            "Call it a silver moat," growled Ben,
"That's the new poetry! Call it crystal, lad!
But, till you kiss the Beast, you'll never find
Your Fairy Prince. Why, all those crowded streets,
Flung all their filth, their refuse, rags and bones,
Dead cats and dogs, into your clean clear moat,
And made it sluggish as old Acheron.
Fevers and plagues, death in a thousand shapes
Crawled out of it. London was dirty, lad;
And till you kiss that fact, you'll never see
The glory of this old Jerusalem!"
          "Ay, 'tis the fogs that make the sunset red,"
Answered Tom Heywood. "London is earthy, coarse,
Grimy and grand. You must make dirt the ground,
Or lose the colours of friend Clopton's tale.
Ring on!" And, nothing loth, the Clerk resumed:—

Bravely swelled his heart to see the moat of London glittering
  Round her mighty wall—they told him—two miles long!
Then—he gasped as, echoing in by grim black Aldgate,
  Suddenly their shaggy nags were nodding through a throng:

Prentices in red and ray, marchaunts in their saffron,
  Aldermen in violet, and minstrels in white,
Clerks in homely hoods of budge, and wives with crimson wimples,
  Thronging as to welcome him that happy summer night.

"Back," they cried, and "Clear the way," and caught he ringing bridle
    reins:
  "Wait! the Watch is going by, this vigil of St. John!"
Merrily laughed the chapmen then, reining their great white horses back,
  "When the pageant passes, lad, we'll up and follow on!"

There, as thick the crowd surged, beneath the blossomed ale-poles,
  Lifting up to Whittington a fair face afraid,
Swept against his horse by a billow of madcap prentices,
  Hard against the stirrup breathed a green-gowned maid.

Swift he drew her up and up, and throned her there before him,
  High above the throng with her laughing April eyes,
Like a Queen of Faërie on the great pack-saddle.
  "Hey!" laughed the chapmen, "the prentice wins the prize!"

"Whittington! Whittington! the world is all before you!"
  Blithely rang the bells and the steeples rocked and reeled!
Then—he saw her eyes grow wide, and, all along by Leaden Hall,
  Drums rolled, earth shook, and shattering trumpets pealed.

Like a marching sunset, there, from Leaden Hall to Aldgate,
  Flared the crimson cressets—O, her brows were haloed then!—
Then the stirring steeds went by with all their mounted trumpeters
  Then, in ringing harness, a thousand marching men.

Marching—marching—his heart and all the halberdiers,
  And his pulses throbbing with the throbbing of the drums;
Marching—marching—his blood and all the burganets!
  "Look," she cried, "O, look," she cried, "and now the morrice comes!"

Dancing—dancing—her eyes and all the Lincoln Green,
  Robin Hood and Friar Tuck, dancing through the town!
"Where is Marian?"   Laughingly she turned to Richard Whittington.
  "Here," he said, and pointed to her own green gown.

Dancing—dancing—her heart and all the morrice-bells!
  Then there burst a mighty shout from thrice a thousand throats!
Then, with all their bows bent, and sheaves of peacock arrows,
  Marched the tall archers in their white silk coats,

White silk coats, with the crest of London City
  Crimson on the shoulder, a sign for all to read,—
Marching—marching—and then the sworded henchmen,
  Then, William Walworth, on his great stirring steed.

Flos Mercatorum, ay, the fish-monger, Walworth,—
  He whose nets of silk drew the silver from the tide,
He who saved the king when the king was but a prentice,—
  Lord Mayor of London, with his sword at his side!

Burned with magic changes, his blood and all the pageantry;
  Burned with deep sea-changes, the wonder in her eyes;
Flos Mercatorum! 'Twas the rose marie of Paphos,
  Reddening all the City for the prentice and his prize!

All the book of London, the pages of adventure,
  Passed before the prentice on that vigil of St. John:
Then the chapmen shook their reins,—"We'll ride behind the revelry,
  Round again to Cornhill!   Up, and follow on!"

Riding on his pack-horse, above the shouting multitude,
  There she turned and smiled at him, and thanked him for his grace:
"Let me down by *Red Rose Lane*," and, like a wave of twilight
  While she spoke, her shadowy hair—touched his tingling face.

When they came to *Red Rose Lane,* beneath the blossomed ale-poles,
  Light along his arm she lay, a moment, leaping down:
Then she waved "farewell" to him, and down the Lane he watched her
  Flitting through the darkness in her gay green gown.

All along the Cheape, as he rode among the chapmen,
  Round by *Black Friars,* to the *Two-Necked Swan*
Coloured like the sunset, prentices and maidens
  Danced for red roses on the vigil of St. John.

Over them were jewelled lamps in great black galleries,
  Garlanded with beauty, and burning all the night;
All the doors were shadowy with orpin and St. John's wort,
  Long fennel, green birch, and lilies of delight.

"He should have slept here at the Mermaid Inn,"
Said Heywood as the chanter paused for breath.
"What? Has our Mermaid sung so long?" cried Ben.
"Her beams are black enough. There was an Inn,"
Said Tom, "that bore the name; and through its heart
There flowed the right old purple. I like to think
It was the same, where Lydgate took his ease
After his hood was stolen; and Gower, perchance;
And, though he loved the *Tabard* for a-while,
I like to think the Father of us all,
The old Adam of English minstrelsy caroused
Here in the Mermaid Tavern. I like to think
Jolly Dan Chaucer, with his kind shrewd face
Fresh as an apple above his fur-fringed gown,
One plump hand sporting with his golden chain,
Looked out from that old casement over the sign,
And saw the pageant, and the shaggy nags,
With Whittington, and his green-gowned maid, go by.
    "O, very like," said Clopton, "for the bells
Left not a head indoors that night." He drank
A draught of malmsey—and thus renewed his tale:—

"*Flos Mercatorum,*" mourned the bell of All Hallowes,
    "There was he an orphan, O, a little lad alone,
Rubbing down the great white horses for a supper!"
    "True," boomed the Bow Bell, "his hands were his own!"

Where did he sleep? On a plump white wool-pack,
    Open to the moon on that vigil of St. John,
Sheltered from the dew, where the black-timbered gallery
    Frowned above the yard of the *Two-Necked Swan.*

Early in the morning, clanged the bell of St. Martin's,
    Early in the morning, with a groat in his hand,
Mournfully he parted with the jolly-hearted chapmen,
    Shouldered his bundle and walked into the *Strand;*

Walked into the *Strand,* and back again to *West Cheape,*
    Staring at the wizardry of every painted sign,
Dazed with the steeples and the rich heraldic cornices
    Drinking in the colours of the Cheape like wine.

All about the booths now, the parti-coloured prentices
    Fluted like a flock of birds along a summer lane,
Green linnets, red caps, and gay gold finches,—
    What d'ye lack, and what d'ye lack, and what d'ye lack again?

"Buy my dainty doublets, cut on double taffetas,
  Buy my Paris thread," they cried, and caught him by the hand,
"Laces for your Heart's-Delight, and lawns to make her love you,
  Cambric for her wimple, O, the finest in the land."

Ah, but he was hungry, foot-sore, weary,
  Knocking at the doors of the armourers that day!
What d'ye lack? they asked of him; but no man lacked a prentice:
  When he told them what he lacked, they frowned and turned away.

Hard was his bed that night, beneath a cruel archway,
  Down among the hulks, with his heart growing cold!
London is a rare town, but O, the streets of London,
  Red though their flints be, they are not red with gold.

Pale in the dawn, ere he marched on his adventure,
  Starving for a crust, did he kneel a-while again,
Then, upon the fourth night, he cried, O, like a wounded bird
  "Let me die, if die I must, in *Red Rose Lane.*"

Like a little wounded bird he trailed through the darkness,
  Laid him on a door-step, and then—O, like a breath
Pitifully blowing out his life's little rushlight,
  Came a gush of blackness, a swoon deep as death.

Then he heard a rough voice!   Then he saw a lanthorn!
  Then he saw a bearded face, and blindly wondered whose:
Then—a marchaunt's portly legs, with great Rose-Windows,
  Bigger than St. Paul's, he thought, embroidered on his shoes.

"Alice!" roared the voice, and then, O like a lilied angel,
  Leaning from the lighted door a fair face afraid,
Leaning over *Red Rose Lane,* O, leaning out of Paradise,
  Drooped the sudden glory of his green-gowned maid!

      .   .   .   .

"O, mellow be thy malmsey," grunted Ben,
Filling the Clerk another cup.
                            "The peal,"
Quoth Clopton, "is not ended, but the pause
In ringing, chimes to a deep inward ear
And tells its own deep tale.   Silence and sound,
Darkness and light, mourning and mirth,—no tale,
No painting, and no music, nay, no world,
If God should cut their fruitful marriage-knot.

K*   277

A shallow sort to-day would fain deny
A hell, sirs, to this boundless universe.
To such I say 'no hell, no Paradise!'
Others would fain deny the topless towers
Of heaven, and make this earth a hell indeed.
To such I say, 'the unplumbed gulfs of grief
Are only theirs for whom the blissful chimes
Ring from those unseen heights.' This earth, mid-way,
Hangs like a belfry where the ringers grasp
Their ropes in darkness, each in his own place,
Each knowing, by the tune in his own heart,
Never by sight, when he must toss through heaven
The tone of his own bell. Those bounded souls
Have never heard our chimes! Why, sirs, myself
Simply by running up and down the scale
Descend to hell or soar to heaven. My bells
Height above height, deep below deep, respond!
Their scale is infinite. Dare I, for one breath,
Dream that one note hath crowned and ended all,
Sudden I hear, far, far above those clouds,
Like laughing angels, peal on golden peal,
Innumerable as drops of April rain,
Yet every note distinct, round as a pearl,
And perfect in its place, a chime of law,
Whose pure and boundless mere arithmetic
Climbs with my soul to God."

                                Ben looked at him,
Gently. "Resume, old moralist," he said.
"On to thy marriage-bells!"

                                "The fairy-tales
Are wiser than they know, sirs. All our woes
Lead on to those celestial marriage-bells.
The world's a-wooing; and the pure City of God
Peals for the wedding of our joy and pain!

This was well seen of Richard Whittington;
For only he that finds the London streets
Paved with red flints, at last shall find them paved
Like to the Perfect City, with pure gold.
Ye know the world! what was a London waif
To Hugh Fitzwarren's daughter? He was fed
And harboured; and the cook declared she lacked
A scullion. So, in Hugh Fitzwarren's house,
He turned the jack, and scoured the dripping-pan.
How could he hope for more?

                              This marchaunt's house
Was builded like a great high-gabled inn,
Square, with a galleried courtyard, such as now
The players use.   Its rooms were rich and dim
With deep-set coloured panes and massy beams.
Its ancient eaves jutted o'er *Red Rose Lane*
Darkly, like eyebrows of a mage asleep.
Its oaken stair coiled upward through a dusk
Heavy with fume of scented woods that burned
To keep the Plague away,—a gloom to embalm
A Pharaoh, but to dull the cheek and eye
Of country lads like Whittington.
                                        He pined
For wind and sunlight.   Yet he plied his task
Patient as in old tales of Elfin-land,
The young knight would unhelm his golden locks
And play the scullion, so that he might watch
His lady's eyes unknown, and oftener hear
Her brook-like laughter rippling overhead;
Her green gown, like the breath of Eden boughs,
Rustling nigh him.   And all day long he found
Sunshine enough in this.   But when at night
He crept into the low dark vaulted den,
The cobwebbed cellar, where the cook had strewn
The scullion's bed of straw (and none too thick
Lest he should sleep too long), he choked for breath;
And, like an old man hoarding up his life,
Fostered his glimmering rushlight as he sate
Bolt upright, while a horrible scurry heaved
His rustling bed, and bright black-beaded eyes
Peered at him from the crannies of the wall.
Then darkness whelmed him, and perchance he slept,—
Only to fight with nightmares and to fly
Down endless tunnels in a ghastly dream,
Hunted by horrible human souls that took
The shape of monstrous rats, great chattering snouts,
Vile shapes of shadowy cunning and grey greed,
That gnaw through beams, and undermine tall towns,
And carry the seeds of plague and ruin and death
Under the careless homes of sleeping men.
    Thus, in the darkness, did he wage a war
With all the powers of darkness.   'If the light
Do break upon me, by the grace of God,'
So did he vow, 'O, then will I remember,.
Then, then, will I remember, ay, and help

                        279

To build that lovelier City which is paved
For rich and poor alike, with purest gold.'

Ah, sirs, he kept his vow.   Ye will not smile
If, at the first, the best that he could do
Was with his first poor penny-piece to buy
A cat, and bring her home, under his coat
By stealth (or else that termagant, the cook,
Had drowned it in the water-butt, nor deemed
The water worse to drink).   So did he quell
First his own plague, but bettered others, too.
Now, in those days, Marchaunt Adventurers
Shared with their prentices the happy chance
Of each new venture.   Each might have his stake,
Little or great, upon the glowing tides
Of high romance that washed the wharfs of Thames;
And every lad in London had his groat
Or splendid shilling on some fair ship at sea.

So, on an April eve, Fitzwarren called
His prentices together; for, ere long,
The *Unicorn*, his tall new ship, must sail
Beyond the world to gather gorgeous webs
From Eastern looms, great miracles of silk
Dipt in the dawn by wizard hands of Ind;
Or, if they chanced upon that fabled coast
Where Sydon, river of jewels, like a snake
Slides down the gorge its coils of crimson fire,
Perchance a richer cargo,—rubies, pearls,
Or gold bars from the Gates of Paradise.
And many a moon, at least, a faërie foam
Would lap Blackfriars wharf, where London lads
Gazed in the sunset down that misty reach
For old black battered hulks and tattered sails
Bringing their dreams home from the uncharted sea.

And one flung down a groat—he had no more.
One staked a shilling, one a good French crown;
And one an angel, O, light-winged enough
To reach Cathay; and not a lad but bought
His pennyworth of wonder,
                              So they thought,
Till all at once Fitzwarren's daughter cried
'Father, you have forgot poor Whittington!'
'Snails,' laughed the rosy marchaunt, 'but that's true!

Fetch Whittington!   The lad must stake his groat!
'Twill bring us luck!'
                        'Whittington!   Whittington!'
Down the dark stair, like a gold-headed bird,
Fluttered sweet Alice.   'Whittington!   Richard!   Quick!
Quick with your groat now for the *Unicorn!'*

'A groat!' cried Whittington, standing there aghast,
With brown bare arms, still coloured by the sun,
Among his pots and pans.   'Where should I find
A groat?   I staked my last groat in a cat!'
—'What!   Have you nothing?   Nothing but a cat?
Then stake the cat,' she said; and the quick fire
That in a woman's mind out-runs the thought
Of man, lit her grey eyes.
                            Whittington laughed
And opened the cellar-door.   Out sailed his wealth,
Waving its tail, purring, and rubbing its head
Now on his boots, now on the dainty shoe
Of Alice, who straightway, deaf to his laughing prayers,
Caught up the cat, whispered it, hugged it close,
Against its grey fur leaned her glowing cheek,
And carried it off in triumph.
                        Red Rose Lane
Echoed with laughter as, with amber eyes
Blinking, the grey cat in a seaman's arms
Went to the wharf.   'Ay, but we need a cat,'
The captain said.   So, when the painted ship
Sailed through a golden sunrise down the Thames,
A grey tail waved upon the misty poop,
And Whittington had his venture on the seas.

It was a nine days' jest, and soon forgot.
But, all that year,—ah, sirs, ye know the world,
For all the foolish boasting of the proud,
Looks not beneath the coat of Taunton serge
For Gules and Azure.   A prince that comes in rags
To clean your shoes and, out of his own pride,
Waits for the world to paint his shield again
Must wait for ever and a day.
                        The world
Is a great hypocrite, hypocrite most of all
When thus it boasts its purple pride of race,
Then with eyes blind to all but pride of place
Tramples the scullion's heraldry underfoot,

Nay, never sees it, never dreams of it,
Content to know that, here and now, his coat
Is greasy . . .
                    So did Whittington find at last
Such nearness was most distant; that to see her,
Talk with her, serve her thus, was but to lose
True sight, true hearing.   He must save his life
By losing it; forsake, to win, his love;
Go out into the world to bring her home.
It was but labour lost to clean the shoes,
And turn the jack, and scour the dripping-pan.
For every scolding blown about her ears
The cook's great ladle fell upon the head
Of Whittington; who, beneath her rule, became
The scullery's general scapegoat.   It was he
That burned the pie-crust, drank the hippocras,
Dinted the silver beaker. . . .
                         Many a month
He chafed, till his resolve took sudden shape
And, out of the dark house at the peep of day,
Shouldering bundle and stick again, he stole
To seek his freedom, and to shake the dust
Of London from his shoes. . . .
                         You know the stone
On Highgate, where he sate awhile to rest,
With aching heart, and thought 'I shall not see
Her face again.'   There, as the coloured dawn
Over the sleeping City slowly bloomed,
A small black battered ship with tattered sails
Blurring the burnished glamour of the Thames
Crept, side-long to a wharf.
                         Then, all at once,
The London bells rang out a welcome home;
And, over them all, tossing the tenor on high,
The Bell of Bow, a sun among the stars,
Flooded the morning air with this refrain:—

'Turn again, Whittington!   Turn again, Whittington!
  Flos Mercatorum, thy ship hath come home!
Trailing from her cross-trees the crimson of the sunrise,
    Dragging all the glory of the sunset thro' the foam.
            Turn again, Whittington.
            Turn again, Whittington,
              Lord Mayor of London!

Turn again, Whittington!   When thy hope was darkest,
  Far beyond the sky-line a ship sailed for thee.
Flos Mercatorum, O, when thy faith was blindest,
  Even then thy sails were set beyond the Ocean-sea.'

So he heard and heeded us, and turned again to London,
  Stick and bundle on his back, he turned to *Red Rose Lane*,
Hardly hearing as he went the chatter of the prentices,—
  What d'ye lack, and what d'ye lack, and what d'ye lack again?

Back into the scullery, before the cook had missed him,
  Early in the morning his labours he began:
Once again to clean the shoes and clatter with the water-pail,
  Once again to scrub the jack and scour the dripping-pan.

All the bells of London were pealing as he laboured.
  Wildly beat his heart, and his blood began to race.
Then—there came a light step and, suddenly, beside him
  Stood his lady Alice, with a light upon her face.

'Quick,' she said, 'O, quick,' she said, 'they want you, Richard Whitting-
  ton!'
  'Quick,' she said; and, while she spoke, her lighted eyes betrayed
All that she had hidden long, and all she still would hide from him.
  So—he turned and followed her, his green-gowned maid.

          .   .   .   .

There, in a broad dark oaken-panelled room
Rich with black carvings and great gleaming cups
Of silver, sirs, and massy halpace built
Half over *Red Rose Lane*, Fitzwarren sat;
And, at his side, O, like an old romance
That suddenly comes true and fills the world
With April colours, two bronzed seamen stood,
Tattered and scarred, and stained with sun and brine.
'*Flos Mercatorum*,' Hugh Fitzwarren cried,
Holding both hands out to the pale-faced boy,
'The prentice wins the prize!   Why, Whittington,
Thy cat hath caught the biggest mouse of all!'
And, on to the table, tilting a heavy sack,
One of the seamen poured a glittering stream
Of rubies, emeralds, opals, amethysts,
That turned the room to an Aladdin's cave,
Or magic goblet brimmed with dusky wine

Where clustering rainbow-coloured bubbles clung
And sparkled, in the halls of Prester John.

'And that,' said Hugh Fitzwarren, 'is the price
Paid for your cat in Barbary, by a King
Whose house was rich in gems, but sorely plagued
With rats and mice.   Gather it up, my lad,
And praise your master for his honesty;
For, though my cargo prospered, yours outshines
The best of it.   Take it, my lad, and go;
You're a rich man; and, if you use it well,
Riches will make you richer, and the world
Will prosper in your own prosperity.
The miser, like the cold and barren moon,
Shines with a fruitless light.   The spendthrift fool
Flits like a Jack-o-Lent over quags and fens;
But he that's wisely rich gathers his gold
Into a fruitful and unwasting sun
That spends its glory on a thousand fields
And blesses all the world.   Take it and go.'

Blankly, as in a dream, Whittington stared.
'How should I take it, sir?   The ship was yours,
And . . .'
              'Ay, the ship was mine; but in that ship
Your stake was richer than we knew.   'Tis yours.'
   'Then,' answered Whittington, 'if this wealth be mine,
Who but an hour ago was all so poor,
I know one way to make me richer still.'
He gathered up the glittering sack of gems,
Turned to the halpace, where his green-gowned maid
Stood in the glory of the coloured panes.
He thrust the splendid load into her arms,
Muttering—'Take it, lady!   Let me be poor!
But rich, at least, in that you not despise
The waif you saved.'
                  —'Despise you, Whittington?'—
'O, no, not in the sight of God!   But I
Grow tired of waiting for the Judgment Day!
I am but a man.   I am a scullion now;
But I would like, only for half an hour,
To stand upright and say "I am a king!"
Take it!'
              And, as they stood, a little apart,

Their eyes were married in one swift level look,
Silent, but all that souls could say was said.

.   .   .   .

And
'I know a way,' said the Bell of St. Martin's.
    'Tell it, and be quick,' laughed the prentices below!
'Whittington shall marry her, marry her, marry her!
    Peal for a wedding,' said the big Bell of Bow.

He shall take a kingdom up, and cast it on the sea again;
    He shall have his caravels to traffic for him now;
He shall see his royal sails rolling up from Araby,
    And the crest—a honey-bee—golden at the prow.

Whittington! Whittington! The world is all a fairy tale!—
    Even so we sang for him.—But O, the tale is true!
Whittington he married her, and on his merry marriage-day,
    O, we sang, we sang for him, like lavrocks in the blue.

Far away from London, these happy prentice lovers
    Wandered through the fern to his western home again,
Down by deep Dorset to the wooded isle of Purbeck,
    Round to little Kimmeridge, by many a lover's lane.

There did they abide as in a dove-cote hidden
    Deep in happy woods until the bells of duty rang;
Then they rode the way he went, a barefoot boy to London,
    Round by Hampshire forest-roads, but as they rode he sang:—

Kimmeridge in Dorset is the happiest of places!
    All the little homesteads are thatched with beauty there!
All the old ploughmen, there, have happy smiling faces,
    Christmas roses in their cheeks, and crowns of silver hair.

Blue as are the eggs in the nest of the hedge-sparrow,
    Gleam the little rooms in the homestead that I know:
Death, I think, has lost the way to Kimmeridge in Dorset;
    Sorrow never knew it, or forgot it long ago!

Kimmeridge in Dorset, Kimmeridge in Dorset,
    Though I may not see you more thro' all the years to be,
Yet will I remember the little happy homestead
    Hidden in that Paradise where God was good to me.

.   .   .   .

So they turned to London, and with mind and soul he laboured,
  Flos Mercatorum, for the mighty years to be,
Fashioning, for profit—to the years that should forget him!—
  This, our sacred City that must shine upon the sea.

London was a City when the Poulters ruled the Poultry!
  Rosaries of prayer were hung in Paternoster Row,
Gutter Lane was Guthrun's, then; and, bright with painted missal-books
  Ave Mary Corner, sirs, was fairer than ye know.

London was mighty when her marchaunts loved their merchandise,
  Bales of Eastern magic that empurpled wharf and quay:
London was mighty when her booths were a dream-market,
  Loaded with the colours of the sunset and the sea.

There, in all their glory, with the Virgin on their bannerols,
  Glory out of Genoa, the Mercers might be seen,
Walking to their Company of Marchaunt Adventurers;—
  Gallantly they jetted it in scarlet and in green.

There, in all the glory of the lordly Linen Armourers,
  Walked the Marchaunt Taylors with the Pilgrim of their trade,
Fresh from adventuring in Italy and Flanders,
  Flos Mercatorum, for a green-gowned maid.

Flos Mercatorum!   Can a good thing come of Nazareth?
  High above the darkness, where our duller senses drown,
Lifts the splendid Vision of a City, built on merchandize,
  Fairer than that City of Light that wore the violet crown,

Lifts the sacred vision of a far-resplendent City,
  Flashing, like the heart of heaven, its messages afar,
Trafficking, as God Himself through all His interchanging worlds,
  Holding up the scales of law, weighing star by star,

Stern as Justice, in one hand the sword of Truth and Righteousness;
  Blind as Justice, in one hand the everlasting scales,
Lifts the sacred Vision of that City from the darkness,
  Whence the thoughts of men break out, like blossoms, or like sails!

Ordered and harmonious, a City built to music,
  Lifting, out of chaos, the shining towers of law,—
Ay, a sacred City, and a City built of merchandize,
  Flos Mercatorum, was the City that he saw.

286

And by that light," quoth Clopton, "did he keep
His promise.   He was rich; but in his will
He wrote those words which should be blazed with gold
In London's *Liber Albus:*—

> *The desire*
> *And busy intention of a man, devout*
> *And wise, should be to forecast and secure*
> *The state and end of this short life with deeds*
> *Of mercy and pity, especially to provide*
> *For those whom poverty insulteth, those*
> *To whom the power of labouring for the needs*
> *Of life, is interdicted.*

He became
The Father of the City.   Felons died
Of fever in old Newgate.   He rebuilt
The prison.   London sickened from the lack
Of water, and he made fresh fountains flow.
He heard the cry of suffering and disease,
And built the stately hospital that still
Shines like an angel's lanthorn through the night,
The stately halls of St. Bartholomew.
He saw men wrapt in ignorance, and he raised
Schools, colleges, and libraries.   He heard
The cry of the old and weary, and he built
Houses of refuge.

Even so he kept
His prentice vows of Duty, Industry,
Obedience, words contemned of every fool
Who shrinks from law; yet were those ancient vows
The adamantine pillars of the State.
Let all who play their Samson be well warned
That Samsons perish, too!

His monument
Is London!"

"True," quoth Dekker, "and he deserves
Well of the Mermaid Inn for one good law,
Rightly enforced.   He pilloried that rogue
Will Horold, who in Whittington's third year
Of office, as Lord Mayor, placed certain gums
And spices in great casks, and filled them up
With feeble Spanish wine, to have the taste
And smell of Romeney,—Malmsey!"

"Honest wine,
Indeed," replied the Clerk, "concerns the State,
That solemn structure touched with light from heaven.

Which he, our merchant, helped to build on earth.
And, while he laboured for it, all things else
Were added unto him, until the bells
More than fulfilled their prophecy.

                           One great eve,
Fair Alice, leaning from her casement, saw
Another Watch, and mightier than the first,
Billowing past the newly painted doors
Of Whittington Palace—so men called his house
In Hart Street, fifteen yards from old Mark Lane,—
A thousand burganets and halberdiers,
A thousand archers in their white silk coats,
A thousand mounted men in ringing mail,
A thousand sworded henchmen; then, his Guild,
Advancing, on their splendid bannerols
The Virgin, glorious in gold; and then,
Flos Mercatorum, on his great stirring steed
Whittington!   On that night he made a feast
For London and the King.   His feasting hall
Gleamed like the magic cave that Prester John
Wrought out of one huge opal.   East and West
Lavished their wealth on that great Citizen
Who, when the King from Agincourt returned
Victorious, but with empty coffers, lent
Three times the ransom of an Emperor
To fill them—on the royal bond, and said,
When the King questioned him of how and whence,
'I am the steward of your City, sire!
There is a sea, and who shall drain it dry?'

   Over the roasted swans and peacock pies,
The minstrels in the great black gallery tuned
All hearts to mirth, until it seemed their cups
Were brimmed with dawn and sunset, and they drank
The wine of gods.   Lord of a hundred ships,
Under the feet of England, Whittington flung
The purple of the seas.   And when the Queen,
Catharine, wondered at the costly woods
That burned upon his hearth, the Marchaunt rose,
He drew the great sealed parchments from his breast,
The bonds the King had given him on his loans,
Loans that might drain the Mediterranean dry.
'They call us hucksters, madam, we that love
Our City,' and, into the red-hot heart of the fire,

He tossed the bonds of sixty thousand pounds.
'The fire burns low,' said Richard Whittington.
Then, overhead, the minstrels plucked their strings;
And, over the clash of wine-cups, rose a song
That made the old timbers of their feasting-hall
Shake, as a galleon shakes in a gale of wind,
When she rolls glorying through the Ocean-sea:—

Marchaunt Adventurers, O, what shall it profit you
   Thus to seek your kingdom in the dream-destroying sun?
Ask us why the hawthorn brightens on the sky-line:
   Even so our sails break out when Spring is well begun!
Flos Mercatorum! Blossom wide, ye sails of Englande,
   Hasten ye the kingdom, now the bitter days are done!
Ay, for we be members, one of another,
   'Each for all and all for each,' quoth Richard Whittington!

Chorus:—   Marchaunt Adventurers,
                  Marchaunt Adventurers,
  Marchaunt Adventurers, the Spring is well begun!
Break, break out on every sea, O, fair white sails of Englande!
  'Each for all, and all for each,' quoth Richard Whittington.

Marchaunt Adventurers, O what 'ull ye bring home again?
   Woonders and works and the thunder of the sea!
Whom will ye traffic with? The King of the sunset!—
   What shall be your pilot, then?—A wind from Galilee!
Nay, but ye be marchaunts, will ye come back empty-handed?—
   Ay, we be marchaunts, though our gain we ne'er shall see!
Cast we now our bread upon the waste wild waters;
   After many days it shall return with usury.

Chorus:—   Marchaunt Adventurers,
                  Marchaunt Adventurers,
  What shall be your profit in the mighty days to be?
Englande! Englande! Englande! Englande!
  Glory everlasting and the lordship of the sea.

    What need to tell you, sirs, how Whittington
    Remembered? Night and morning, as he knelt
    In those old days, O, like two children still,
    Whittington and his Alice bowed their heads
    Together, praying.
                From such simple hearts,

O never doubt it, though the whole world doubt
The God that made it, came the steadfast strength
Of England, all that once was her strong soul,
The soul that laughed and shook away defeat
As her strong cliffs hurl back the streaming seas.
Sirs, in his old age Whittington returned,
And stood with Alice, by the silent tomb
In little Pauntley church.
                              There, to his Arms,
The Gules and Azure, and the Lion's Head
So proudly blazoned on the painted panes;
(O, sirs, the simple wistfulness of it
Might move hard hearts to laughter, but I think
Tears tremble through it, for the Mermaid Inn)
He added his new crest, the hard-won sign
And lowly prize of his own industry,
The Honey-bee.   And, far away, the bells
Peal softly from the pure white City of God:—

> *Ut fragrans nardus*
> *Fama fuit iste Ricardus.*

With folded hands he waits the Judgment now.
Slowly our dark bells toll across the world,
For him who waits the reckoning, his accompt
Secure, his conscience clear, his ledger spread
A *Liber Albus* flooded with pure light.

> *Flos Mercatorum,*
> *Fundator presbyterorum, . . .*

Slowly the dark bells toll for him who asks
No more of men, but that they may sometimes
Pray for the souls of Richard Whittington,
Alice, his wife, and (as themselves of old
Had prayed) the father and mother of each of them.
Slowly the great notes fall and float away:—

> *Omnibus exemplum*
> *Barathrum vincendo morosum*
> *Condidit hoc templum . . .*
> *Pauperibus pater . . . . .*
> *Finiit ipse dies*
> *Sis sibi Christe quies.   Amen."*

RALEIGH

BEN was our only guest that day.   His tribe
Had flown to their new shrine—the Apollo Room,
To which, though they enscrolled his golden verse
Above their doors like some great-fruited vine,
Ben still preferred our *Mermaid,* and to smoke
Alone in his old nook; perhaps to hear
The voices of the dead,
The voices of his old companions,
Hovering near him,—Will and Kit and Rob.

"Our Ocean-shepherd from the Main-deep sea,
Raleigh," he muttered, as I brimmed his cup,
"Last of the men that broke the fleets of Spain,
'Twas not enough to cage him, sixteen years,
Rotting his heart out in the Bloody Tower,
But they must fling him forth in his old age
To hunt for El Dorado.   Then, mine host,
Because his poor old ship *The Destiny*
Smashes the Spaniard, but comes tottering home
Without the Spanish gold, our gracious king,
To please a catamite,
Sends the old lion back to the Tower again.
The friends of Spain will send him to the block
This time.   That male Salome, Buckingham,
Is dancing for his head.   Raleigh is doomed."
A shadow stood in the doorway.   We looked up;
And there, but O, how changed, how worn and grey,
Sir Walter Raleigh, like a hunted thing,
Stared at us.
           "Ben," he said, and glanced behind him.
Ben took a step towards him.
                      "O, my God,
Ben," whispered the old man in a husky voice,
Half timorous and half cunning, so unlike
His old heroic self that one might weep
To hear it, "Ben, I have given them all the slip!
I may be followed.   Can you hide me here
Till it grows dark?"
Ben drew him quickly in, and motioned me
To lock the door.   "Till it grows dark," he cried,
"My God, that you should ask it!"

                                    "Do not think,
Do not believe that I am quite disgraced,"
The old man faltered, "for they'll say it, Ben;
And when my boy grows up, they'll tell him, too,
His father was a coward.   I do cling
To life for many reasons, not from fear
Of death.   No, Ben, I can disdain that still;
But—there's my boy!"
                           Then all his face went blind.
He dropt upon Ben's shoulder and sobbed outright,
"They are trying to break my pride, to break my pride!"
The window darkened, and I saw a face
Blurring the panes.   Ben gripped the old man's arm,
And led him gently to a room within,
Out of the way of guests.
                              "Your pride," he said,
"That is the pride of England!"
                                 At that name—

England!—
As at a signal-gun, heard in the night
Far out at sea, the weather-and-world-worn man,
That once was Raleigh, lifted up his head.
Old age and weakness, weariness and fear
Fell from him like a cloak.   He stood erect.
His eager eyes, full of great sea-washed dawns,
Burned for a moment with immortal youth,
While tears blurred mine to see him.
                                       "You do think
That England will remember?   You do think it?"
He asked with a great light upon his face.
Ben bowed his head in silence.

   .   .   .   .

                              "I have wronged
My cause by this," said Raleigh.   "Well they know it
Who left this way for me.   I have flung myself
Like a blind moth into this deadly light
Of freedom.   Now, at the eleventh hour,
Is it too late?   I might return and—"
                                       "No!
Not now!" Ben interrupted.   "I'd have said
Laugh at the headsman sixteen years ago,
When England was awake.   She will awake
Again.   But now, while our most gracious king,
Who hates tobacco, dedicates his prayers

To Buckingham—
This is no land for men that, under God,
Shattered the Fleet Invincible."
                              A knock
Startled us, at the outer door.   "My friend
Stukeley," said Raleigh, "if I know his hand.
He has a ketch will carry me to France,
Waiting at Tilbury."
                    I let him in,—
A lean and stealthy fellow, Sir Lewis Stukeley,—
I liked him little.   He thought much of his health,
More of his money bags, and most of all
On how to run with all men all at once
For his own profit.   At the *Mermaid Inn*
Men disagreed in friendship and in truth;
But he agreed with all men, and his life
Was one soft quag of falsehood.   Fugitives
Must use false keys, I thought; and there was hope
For Raleigh if such a man would walk one mile
To serve him now.   Yet my throat moved to see him
Usurping, with one hand on Raleigh's arm,
A kind of ownership.   *"Lend me ten pounds,"*
Were the first words he breathed in the old man's ear,
And Raleigh slipped his purse into his hand.

.   .   .   .

Just over Bread Street hung the bruised white moon
When they crept out.   Sir Lewis Stukeley's watch-dog,
A derelict bo'sun, with a mulberry face,
Met them outside.   "The coast quite clear, eh, Hart?"
Said Stukeley.   "Ah, that's good.   Lead on, then, quick."
And there, framed in the cruddle of moonlit clouds
That ended the steep street, dark on its light,
And standing on those glistening cobblestones
Just where they turned to silver, Raleigh looked back
Before he turned the corner.   He stood there.
A figure like foot-feathered Mercury,
Tall, straight and splendid, waving his plumed hat
To Ben, and taking his last look, I felt,
Upon our *Mermaid Tavern*.   As he paused,
His long fantastic shadow swayed and swept
Against our feet.   Then, like a shadow, he passed.

"It is not right," said Ben, "it is not right.
Why did they give the old man so much grace?

Witness and evidence are what they lack.
Would you trust Stukeley—not to draw him out?
Raleigh was always rash.   A phrase or two
Will turn their murderous axe into a sword
Of righteousness—

                    Why, come to think of it,
Blackfriar's Wharf, last night, I landed there,
And—no, by God!—Raleigh is not himself,
The tide will never serve beyond Gravesend.
It is a trap!   Come on!   We'll follow them!
Quick!   To the river side!"—

                              We reached the wharf
Only to see their wherry, a small black cloud
Dwindling far down that running silver road.
Ben touched my arm.
"Look there," he said, pointing up-stream.

                                        The moon
Glanced on a cluster of pikes, like silver thorns,
Three hundred yards away, a little troop
Of weaponed men, embarking hurriedly.
Their great black wherry clumsily swung about,
Then, with twelve oars for legs, came striding down,
An armoured beetle on the glittering trail
Of some small victim.

                    Just below our wharf
A little dinghy waddled.
Ben cut the painter, and without one word
Drew her up crackling thro' the lapping water,
Motioned me to the tiller, thrust her off,
And, pulling with one oar, backing with the other,
Swirled her round and down, hard on the track
Of Raleigh.   Ben was an old man now but tough,
O tough as a buccaneer.   We distanced them.
His oar blades drove the silver boiling back.
By Broken Wharf the beetle was a speck.
It dwindled by Queen Hythe and the Three Cranes.
By Bellyn's Gate we had left it, out of sight.
By Custom House and Galley Keye we shot
Thro' silver all the way, without one glimpse
Of Raleigh.   Then a dreadful shadow fell
And over us the Tower of London rose
Like ebony; and, on the glittering reach
Beyond it, I could see the small black cloud
That carried the great old seaman slowly down
Between the dark shores whence in happier years

The throng had cheered his golden galleons out,
And watched his proud sails filling for Cathay.
There, as through lead, we dragged by Traitor's Gate,
There, in the darkness, under the Bloody Tower,
There, on the very verge of victory,
Ben gasped and dropped his oars.
"Take one and row," he said, "my arms are numbed.
We'll overtake him yet!"   I clambered past him,
And took the bow oar.
                           Once, as the pace flagged,
Over his shoulder he turned his great scarred face
And snarled, with a trickle of blood on his coarse lips,
"Hard!"—
And blood and fire ran through my veins again,
For half a minute more.
                           Yet we fell back.
Our course was crookèd now.   And suddenly
A grim black speck began to grow behind us,
Grow like the threat of death upon old age.
Then, thickening, blackening, sharpening, foaming, swept
Up the bright line of bubbles in our wake,
That armoured wherry, with its long twelve oars
All well together now.
                           "Too late," gasped Ben,
His ash-grey face uplifted to the moon,
One quivering hand upon the thwart behind him,
A moment.   Then he bowed over his knees
Coughing.   "But we'll delay them.   We'll be drunk,
And hold the catch-polls up!"
                           We drifted down
Before them, broadside on.   They sheered aside.
Then, feigning a clumsy stroke, Ben drove our craft
As they drew level, right in among their blades.
There was a shout, an oath.   They thrust us off;
And then we swung our nose against their bows
And pulled them round with every well-meant stroke,
A full half minute, ere they won quite free,
Cursing us for a pair of drunken fools.

We drifted down behind them.
                           "There's no doubt,"
Said Ben, "the headsman waits behind all this
For Raleigh.   This is a play to cheat the soul
Of England, teach the people to applaud
The red fifth act."

Without another word we drifted down,
For centuries it seemed, until we came
To Greenwich.
Then up the long white burnished reach there crept
Like little sooty clouds the two black boats
To meet us.
            "He is in the trap," said Ben,
"And does not know it yet.   See, where he sits
By Stukeley as by a friend."
                        Long after this,
We heard how Raleigh, simply as a child,
Seeing the tide would never serve him now,
And they must turn, had taken from his neck
Some trinkets that he wore.   "Keep them," he said
To Stukeley, "in remembrance of this night."

He had no doubts of Stukeley when he saw
The wherry close beside them.   He but wrapped
His cloak a little closer round his face.
Our boat rocked in their wash when Stukeley dropped
The mask.   We saw him give the sign, and heard
His high-pitched quavering voice—"IN THE KING'S NAME!"
Raleigh rose to his feet.   "I am under arrest?"
He said, like a dazed man.
                        And Stukeley laughed.
Then, as he bore himself to the grim end,
All doubt being over, the old sea-king stood
Among those glittering points, a king indeed.
The black boats rocked.   We heard his level voice,
*"Sir Lewis, these actions never will turn out
To your good credit."*   Across the moonlit Thames
It rang contemptuously, cold as cold steel,
And passionless as the judgment that ends all.

.   .   .   .

Some three months later, Raleigh's widow came
To lodge a se'nnight at the Mermaid Inn.
His house in Bread Street was no more her own,
But in the hands of Stukeley, who had reaped
A pretty harvest . . .
She kept close to her room, and that same night,
Being ill and with some fever, sent her maid
To fetch the apothecary from Friday Street,
Old "Galen" as the Mermaid christened him.
At that same moment, as the maid went out,

Stukeley came in.   He met her at the door;
And, chucking her under the chin, gave her a letter.
"Take this up to your mistress.   It concerns
Her property," he said.   "Say that I wait,
And would be glad to speak with her."
                                        The wench
Looked pertly in his face, and tripped upstairs.
I scarce could trust my hands.
                              "Sir Lewis," I said,
"This is no time to trouble her.   She is ill."
"Let her decide," he answered, with a sneer.
Before I found another word to say
The maid tripped down again.   I scarce believed
My senses, when she beckoned him up the stair.
Shaking from head to foot, I blocked the way.
"Property!"   Could the crux of mine and thine
Bring widow and murderer into one small room?
"Sir Lewis," I said, "she is ill.   It is not right!
She never would consent."
                          He·sneered again,
"You are her doctor?   Out of the way, old fool!
She has decided!"
                  "Go," I said to the maid,
"Fetch the apothecary.   Let it rest
With him!"
            She tossed her head.   Her quick eyes glanced,
Showing the white, like the eyes of a vicious mare.
She laughed at Stukeley, loitered, then obeyed.

And so we waited, till the wench returned,
With Galen at her heels.   His wholesome face,
Russet and wrinkled like an apple, peered
Shrewdly at Stukeley, twinkled once at me,
And passed in silence, leaving a whiff of herbs
Behind him on the stair.
                          Five minutes later,
To my amazement, that same wholesome face
Leaned from the lighted door above, and called
"Sir Lewis Stukeley!"
                        Sir Judas hastened up.
The apothecary followed him within.
The door shut.   I was left there in the dark
Bewildered; for my heart was hot with thoughts
Of those last months.   Our Summer's Nightingale,
Our Ocean-Shepherd from the Main-deep Sea,

The Founder of our Mermaid Fellowship,
Was this his guerdon—at the Mermaid Inn?
Was this that maid-of-honour whose romance
With Raleigh, once, had been a kingdom's talk?
Could Bess Throckmorton slight his memory thus?
"It is not right," I said, "it is not right.
She wrongs him deeply."
                I leaned against the porch
Staring into the night.   A ghostly ray
Above me, from her window, bridged the street,
And rested on the goldsmith's painted sign
Opposite.
              I could hear the muffled voice
Of Stukeley overhead, persuasive, bland;
And then, her own, cooing, soft as a dove
Calling her mate from Eden cedar-boughs,
Flowed on and on; and then—all my flesh crept
At something worse than either, a long space
Of silence that stretched threatening and cold,
Cold as a dagger-point pricking the skin
Over my heart.
             Then came a stifled cry,
A crashing door, a footstep on the stair
Blundering like a drunkard's, heavily down;
And with his gasping face one tragic mask
Of horror,—may God help me to forget
Some day the frozen awful eyes of one
Who, fearing neither hell nor heaven, has met
That ultimate weapon of the gods, the face
And serpent-tresses that turn flesh to stone—
Stukeley stumbled, groping his way out,
Blindly, past me, into the sheltering night.

.   .   .   .

It was the last night of another year
Before I understood what punishment
Had overtaken Stukeley. Ben, and Brome—
Ben's ancient servant, but turned poet now—
Sat by the fire with the old apothecary
To see the New Year in.
               The starry night
Had drawn me to the door. Could it be true
That our poor earth no longer was the hub
Of those white wheeling orbs? I scarce believed
The strange new dreams; but I had seen the veils

298

Rent from vast oceans and huge continents,
Till what was once our comfortable fire,
Our cosy tavern, and our earthly home
With heaven beyond the next turn in the road,
All the resplendent fabric of our world
Shrank to a glow-worm, lighting up one leaf
In one small forest, in one little land,
Among those wild infinitudes of God.
A tattered wastrel wandered down the street,
Clad in a seaman's jersey, staring hard
At every sign.   Beneath our own, the light
Fell on his red carbuncled face.   I knew him—
The bo'sun, Hart.

                        He pointed to our sign
And leered at me.   "That's her," he said, "no doubt,
The sea-witch with the shiny mackerel tail
Swishing in wine.   That's what Sir Lewis meant.
He called it blood.   Blood is his craze, you see.
This is the Mermaid Tavern, sir, no doubt?"
I nodded.   "Ah, I thought as much," he said.
"Well—happen this is worth a cup of ale."
He thrust his hand under his jersey and lugged
A greasy letter out.   It was inscribed
THE APOTHECARY AT THE MERMAID TAVERN.
I led him in.   "I knew it, sir," he said,
While Galen broke the seal.   "Soon as I saw
That sweet young naked wench curling her tail
In those red waves.—The old man called it blood.
Blood is his craze, you see.—But you can tell
'Tis wine, sir, by the foam.   Malmsey, no doubt.
And that sweet wench to make you smack your lips
Like oysters, with her slippery tail and all!
Why, sir, no doubt, this was the Mermaid Inn."

"But this," said Galen, lifting his grave face
To Ben, "this letter is from all that's left
Of Stukeley.   The good host, there, thinks I wronged
Your Ocean-shepherd's memory.   From this letter,
I think I helped to avenge him.   Do not wrong
His widow, even in thought.   She loved him dearly.
You know she keeps his poor grey severed head
Embalmed; and so will keep it till she dies;
Weeps over it alone.   I have heard such things
In wild Italian tales.   But *this* was true.
Had I refused to let her speak with Stukeley

I feared she would go mad.   This letter proves
That I—and she perhaps—were instruments,
Of some more terrible chirurgery
Than either knew."
                    "Ah, when I saw your sign,"
The bo'sun interjected, "I'd no doubt
That letter was well worth a cup of ale."
  "Go—paint your bows with hell-fire somewhere else,
Not at this inn," said Ben, tossing the rogue
A good French crown.   "Pickle yourself in hell."
And Hart lurched out into the night again,
Muttering "Thank you, sirs.   'Twas worth all that.
No doubt at all."
                 "There are some men," said Galen,
Spreading the letter out on his plump knees,
"Will heap up wrong on wrong; and, at the last,
Wonder because the world will not forget
Just when it suits them, cancel all they owe,
And, like a mother, hold its arms out wide
At their first cry.   And, sirs, I do believe
That Stukeley, on that night, had some such wish
To reconcile himself.   What else had passed
Between the widow and himself I know not;
But she had lured him on until he thought
That words and smiles, perhaps a tear or two,
Might make the widow take the murderer's hand
In friendship, since it might advantage both.
Indeed, he came prepared for even more.
Villains are always fools.   A wicked act,
What is it but a false move in the game,
A blind man's blunder, a deaf man's reply,
The wrong drug taken in the dead of night?
I always pity villains.
                         I mistook
The avenger for the victim.   There she lay
Panting, that night, her eyes like summer stars,
Her pale gold hair upon the pillows tossed
Dishevelled, while the fever in her face
Brought back the lost wild roses of her youth
For half an hour.   Against a breast as pure
And smooth as any maid's, her soft arms pressed
A bundle wrapped in a white embroidered cloth.
She crooned over it as a mother croons
Over her suckling child.   I stood beside her.

—That was her wish, and mine, while Stukeley stayed.—
And, over against me, on the other side,
Stood Stukeley, gnawing his nether lip to find
She could not, or she would not, speak one word
In answer to his letter.

    'Lady Raleigh,
You wrong me, and you wrong yourself,' he cried,
'To play like a green girl when great affairs
Are laid before you. Let me speak with you
Alone.'

   'But I am all alone,' she said,
'Far more alone than I have ever been
In all my life before. This is my doctor.
He must not leave me.'

    Then she lured him on,
Played on his brain as a musician plays
Upon the lute.

    'Forgive me, dear Sir Lewis,
If I am grown too gay for widowhood.
But I have pondered for a long, long time
On all these matters. I know the world was right;
And Spain was right, Sir Lewis. Yes, and you,
You too, were right; and my poor husband wrong.
You see I knew his mind so very well.
I knew his every gesture, every smile.
I lived with him. I think I died with him.
It is a strange thing, marriage. For my soul
(As if myself were present in this flesh)
Beside him, slept in his grey prison-cell
On that last dreadful dawn. I heard the throng
Murmuring round the scaffold far away;
And, with the smell of sawdust in my nostrils,
I woke, bewildered as himself, to see
That tall black-cassocked figure by his bed.
I heard the words that made him understand:
The Body of our Lord—take and eat this!
I rolled the small sour flakes beneath my tongue
With him. I caught, with him, the gleam of tears,
Far off, on some strange face of sickly dread.
The Blood—and the cold cup was in my hand,
Cold as an axe-heft washed with waterish red.
I heard his last poor cry to wife and child.—
Could any that heard forget it?—*My true God,
Hold you both in His arms, both in His arms.*

L

And then—that last poor wish, a thing to raise
A smile in some.   I have smiled at it myself
A thousand times.

              "Give me my pipe," he said,
"My old Winchester clay, with the long stem,
And half an hour alone.   The crowd can wait.
They have not waited half so long as I."
And then, O then, I know what soft blue clouds,
What wavering rings, fragrant ascending wreaths
Melted his prison walls to a summer haze,
Through which I think he saw the little port
Of Budleigh Salterton, like a sea-bird's nest
Among the Devon cliffs—the tarry quay
Whence in his boyhood he had flung a line
For bass or whiting-pollock.   I remembered
(Had he not told me, on some summer night,
His arm about my neck, kissing my hair)
He used to sit there, gazing out to sea;
Fish, and for what?   Not all for what he caught
And handled; but for rainbow-coloured things,
The water-drops that jewelled his thin line,
Flotsam and jetsam of the sunset-clouds;
While the green water, gurgling through the piles,
Heaving and sinking, helped him to believe
The fast-bound quay a galleon plunging out
Superbly for Cathay   There would he sit
Listening, a radiant boy, child of the sea,
Listening to some old seaman's glowing tales,
His grey eyes rich with pictures—

                        Then he saw,
And I with him, that gathering in the West,
To break the Fleet Invincible.   O, I heard
The trumpets and the neighings and the drums.
I watched the beacons on a hundred hills.
I drank that wine of battle from *his* cup,
And gloried in it, lying against his heart.
I sailed with him and saw the unknown worlds!
The slender ivory towers of old Cathay
Rose for us over lilac-coloured seas
That crumbled a sky-blue foam on long shores
Of shining sand, shores of so clear a glass
They drew the sunset-clouds into their bosom
And hung that City of Vision in mid-air
Girdling it round, as with a moat of sky,
Hopelessly beautiful.   O, yet I heard,

Heard from his blazoned poops the trumpeters
Blowing proud calls, while overhead the flag
Of England floated from white towers of sail—
And yet, and yet, I knew that he was wrong,
And soon he knew it, too.

                     I saw the cloud
Of doubt assail him, in the Bloody Tower,
When, being withheld from sailing the high seas
For sixteen years, he spread a prouder sail,
Took up his pen, and, walled about with stone,
Began to write—his *History of the World.*
And emperors came like Lazarus from the grave
To wear his purple. And the night disgorged
Its empires, till, O, like the swirl of dust
Around their marching legions, that dim cloud
Of doubt closed round him. Was there any man
So sure of heart and brain as to record
The simple truth of things himself had seen?
Then who could plumb that night? The work broke off!
He knew that he was wrong. I knew it, too!
Once more that stately structure of his dreams
Melted like mist. His eagles perished like clouds.
Death wound a thin horn through the centuries.
The grave resumed his forlorn emperors.
His empires crumbled back to a little ash
Knocked from his pipe.—
He dropped his pen in homage to the truth.
The truth? *O, eloquent, just and mighty Death!*

Then, when he forged, out of one golden thought,
A key to open his prison; when the King
Released him for a tale of faërie gold
Under the tropic palms; when those grey walls
Melted before his passion; do you think
The gold that lured the King was quite the same
As that which Raleigh saw? You know the song:

> "Say to the King," quoth Raleigh,
>   "I have a tale to tell him;
>   Wealth beyond derision,
>   Veils to lift from the sky,
> Seas to sail for England,
>   And a little dream to sell him,
>   Gold, the gold of a vision
>   That angels cannot buy."

Ah, no!   For all the beauty and the pride,
Raleigh was wrong; but not so wrong, I think,
As those for whom his kingdoms oversea
Meant only glittering dust.   The fight he waged
Was not with them.   They never worsted him.
It was *The Destiny* that brought him home
Without the Spanish gold.—   O, he was wrong,
But such a wrong, in Gloriana's day,
Was more than right, was immortality.
He had just half an hour to put all this
Into his pipe and smoke it.—

                  The red fire,
The red heroic fire that filled his veins
When the proud flag of England floated out
Its challenge to the world—all gone to ash?
What!   Was the great red wine that Drake had quaffed
Vinegar?   He must fawn, haul down his flag,
And count all nations nobler than his own,
Tear out the lions from the painted shields
That hung his poop, for fear that he offend
The pride of Spain?   Treason to sack the ships
Of Spain?   The wounds of slaughtered Englishmen
Cried out—*there is no law beyond the line!*
Treason to sweep the seas with Francis Drake?
Treason to fight for England?

                  If it were so,
The times had changed and quickly.   He had been
A schoolboy in the morning of the world
Playing with wooden swords and winning crowns
Of tinsel; but his comrades had outgrown
Their morning-game, and gathered round to mock
His battles in the sunset.   Yet he knew
That all his life had passed in that brief day;
And he was old, too old to understand
The smile upon the face of Buckingham,
The smile on Cobham's face, at that great word
England!

           He knew the solid earth was changed
To something less than dust among the stars—
And, O, be sure he knew that he was wrong,
That gleams would come,
Gleams of a happier world for younger men,
That Commonwealth, far off.   This was a time
Of sadder things, destruction of the old
Before the new was born.   At least he knew

It was his own way that had brought the world
Thus far, England thus far!   How could he change,
Who had loved England as a man might love
His mistress, change from year to fickle year?
For the new years would change, even as the old.
No—he was wedded to that old first love,
Crude flesh and blood, and coarse as meat and drink,
The woman—England; no fine angel-isle,
Ruled by that male Salome—Buckingham!
Better the axe than to live on and wage
These new and silent and more deadly wars
That play at friendship with our enemies.
Such times are evil.   Not of their own desire
They lead to good, blind agents of that Hand
Which now had hewed him down, down to his knees,
But in a prouder battle than men knew.

His pipe was out, the guard was at the door.
Raleigh was not a god.   But, when he climbed
The scaffold, I believe he looked a man.
And when the axe fell, I believe that God
'Set on his shoulders that immortal head
Which he desired on earth.

                          O, he was wrong!
But when that axe fell, not one shout was raised.
That mighty throng around that crimson block
Stood silent—like the hushed black cloud that holds
The thunder.   You might hear the headsman's breath.
Stillness like that is dangerous, being charged,
Sometimes, with thought, Sir Lewis!   England sleeps!
What if, one day, the Stewart should be called
To know that England wakes?   What if a shout
Should thunder-strike Whitehall, and the dogs lift
Their heads along the fringes of the crowd
To catch a certain savour that I know,
The smell of blood and sawdust?—

                          Ah, Sir Lewis,
'Tis hard to find one little seed of right
Among so many wrongs.   Raleigh was wrong,
And yet—it was because he loved his country
Next to himself, Sir Lewis, by your leave,
His country butchered him.   You did not know
That I was only third in his affections?
The night I told him—we were parting then—
I had begged the last disposal of his body,

Did he not say, with O, so gentle a smile,
"Thou hadst not always the disposal of it
In life, dear Bess. 'Tis well it should be thine
In death!"'
      'The jest was bitter at such an hour,
And somewhat coarse in grain,' Stukeley replied.
'Indeed I thought him kinder.'
        'Kinder,' she said,
Laughing bitterly.
      Stukeley looked at her.
She whispered something, and his lewd old eyes
Fastened upon her own. He knelt by her.
'Perhaps,' he said, 'your woman's wit has found
A better way to solve this bitter business.'
Her head moved on the pillow with little tossings.
He touched her hand. It leapt quickly away.
She hugged that strange white bundle to her breast,
And writhed back, smiling at him, across the bed.

'Ah, Bess,' he whispered huskily, pressing his lips
To that warm hollow where her head had lain,
'There is one way to close the long dispute,
Keep the estates unbroken in your hands
And stop all slanderous tongues, one happy way.
We have some years to live; and why alone?'
'Alone?' she sighed. 'My husband thought of that.
He wrote a letter to me long ago,
When he was first condemned. He said—he said—
Now let me think—what was it that he said?—
I had it all by heart. *"Beseech you, Bess,*
Hide not yourself for many days", he said.'
'True wisdom that,' quoth Stukeley, 'for the love
That seeks to chain the living to the dead
Is but self-love at best!'
        'And yet,' she said,
'How his poor heart was torn between two cares,
Love of himself and care for me, as thus:
Love God! Begin to repose yourself on Him!
Therein you shall find true and lasting riches;
But all the rest is nothing. When you have tired
Your thoughts on earthly things, when you have travelled
Through all the glittering pomps of this proud world
You shall sit down by Sorrow in the end.
Begin betimes, and teach your little son

To serve and fear God also.
Then God will be a husband unto you,
And unto him a father; nor can Death
Bereave you any more.   When I am gone,
No doubt you shall be sought unto by many
For the world thinks that I was very rich.
No greater misery can befall you, Bess,
Than to become a prey, and, afterwards,
To be despised.'

             'Human enough,' said Stukeley,
'And yet—self-love, self-love!'

                      'Ah no,' quoth she,
'You have not heard the end: *God knows, I speak it*
Not to dissuade you—not to dissuade you, mark—
From marriage.   That will be the best for you,
Both in respect of God and of the world.
Was *that* self-love, Sir Lewis?   Ah, not all.
And thus he ended: *For his father's sake*
That chose and loved you in his happiest times,
Remember your poor child!   The Everlasting,
Infinite, powerful, and inscrutable God,
Keep you and yours, have mercy upon me,
And teach me to forgive my false accusers—
Wrong, even in death, you see.   Then—*My true wife,*
Farewell!
Bless my poor boy!   Pray for me!   My true God,
Hold you both in His arms, both in His arms!
I know that he was wrong.   You did not know,
Sir Lewis, that he had left me a little child.
Come closer.   You shall see its orphaned face,
The sad, sad relict of a man that loved
His country—all that's left to me.   Come, look!'
She beckoned Stukeley nearer.   He bent down
Curiously.   Her feverish fingers drew
The white wrap from the bundle in her arms,
And, with a smile that would make angels weep,
She showed him, pressed against her naked breast,
Terrible as Medusa, the grey flesh
And shrivelled face, embalmed, the thing that dropped
Into the headsman's basket, months agone,—
The head of Raleigh.

               Half her body lay
Bare, while she held that grey babe to her heart;
But Judas hid his face. . . .

'Living,' she said, 'he was not always mine;
But—dead—I shall not wean him'—
                              Then, I too
Covered my face—   I cannot tell you more.
There was a dreadful silence in that room,
Silence that, as I know, shattered the brain
Of Stukeley.—   When I dared to raise my head
Beneath that silent thunder of our God,
The man had gone—
                        This is his letter, sirs,
Written from Lundy Island: *For God's love,
Tell them it is a cruel thing to say
That I drink blood.   I have no secret sin.
A thousand pound is not so great a sum;
And that is all they paid me, every penny.
Salt water, that is all the drink I taste
On this rough island.   Somebody has taught
The sea-gulls how to wail around my hut
All night, like lost souls.   And there is a face,
A dead man's face that laughs in every storm,
And sleeps in every pool along the coast.
I thought it was my own, once.   But I know
These actions never, never, on God's earth,
Will turn out to their credit, who believe
That I drink blood.*"
                        He crumpled up the letter
And tossed it into the fire.
                        "Galen," said Ben,
"I think you are right—that one should pity villains."

.   .   .   .

The clock struck twelve.   The bells began to peal.
We drank a cup of sack to the New Year.
"New songs, new voices, all as fresh as may,"
Said Ben to Brome, "but I shall never live
To hear them."
                        All was not so well, indeed,
With Ben, as hitherto.   Age had come upon him.
He dragged one foot as in paralysis.
The critics bayed against the old lion, now,
And called him arrogant.   "My brain," he said,
"Is yet unhurt although, set round with pain,
It cannot long hold out."   He never stooped,
Never once pandered to that brainless hour.
His coat was thread-bare.   Weeks had passed of late
Without his voice resounding in our inn.

"The statues are defiled, the gods dethroned,
The Ionian movement reigns, not the free soul.
And, as for me, I have lived too long," he said.
"Well—I can weave the old threnodies anew."
And, filling his cup, he murmured, soft and low,
A new song, breaking on an ancient shore:

Marlowe is dead, and Greene is in his grave,
    And sweet Will Shakespeare long ago is gone!
Our Ocean-shepherd sleeps beneath the wave;
Robin is dead, and Marlowe in his grave.
Why should I stay to chant an idle stave,
    And in my Mermaid Tavern drink alone?
For Kit is dead and Greene is in his grave,
    And sweet Will Shakespeare long ago is gone.

Where is the singer of the Faërie Queen?
    Where are the lyric lips of Astrophel?
Long, long ago, their quiet graves were green;
Ay, and the grave, too, of their Faërie Queen!
And yet their faces, hovering here unseen,
    Call me to taste their new-found œnomel;
To sup with him who sang the Faërie Queen;
    To drink with him whose name was Astrophel.

I drink to that great Inn beyond the grave!
    —If there be none, the gods have done us wrong.—
Ere long I hope to chant a better stave,
In some great Mermaid Inn beyond the grave;
And quaff the best of earth that heaven can save,
    Red wine like blood, deep love of friends and song.
I drink to that great Inn beyond the grave;
    And hope to greet my golden lads ere long.

He raised his cup and drank in silence.   Brome
Drank with him, too.   The bells had ceased to peal.
Galen shook hands, and bade us all good-night.
Then Brome, a little wistfully, I thought,
Looked at his old-time master, and prepared
To follow.
              "Good-night—Ben," he said, a pause
Before he spoke the name.   "Good-night!   Good-night!
My dear old Brome," said Ben.
                              And, at the door,
Brome whispered to me, "He is lonely now.

There are not many left of his old friends.
We all go out—like this—into the night.
But what a fleet of stars!" he said, and shook
My hand, and smiled, and pointed to the sky.
And, when I looked into the room again,
The lights were very dim, and I believed
That Ben had fallen asleep.   His great grey head
Was bowed across the table, on his arms.
Then, all at once, I knew that he was weeping;
And like a shadow I crept back again,
And stole into the night.
                              There as I stood
Under the painted sign, I could have vowed
That I, too, heard the voices of the dead,
The voices of his old companions,
Gathering round him in that lonely room,
Till all the timbers of the Mermaid Inn
Trembled above me with their ghostly song:

"Say to the King," quoth Raleigh,
   "I have a tale to tell him,
      Wealth beyond derision,
         Veils to lift from the sky,
Seas to sail for England,
   And a little dream to sell him,
      Gold, the gold of a vision,
         That angels cannot buy."

Fair thro' the walls of his dungeon,
   —What were the stones but a shadow?—
      Streamed the light of the rapture,
         The lure that he followed of old,
The dream of his old companions,
   The vision of El Dorado,
      The fleet that they never could capture,
         The City of Sunset-gold.

Yet did they sail the seas
   And, dazed with exceeding wonder,
      Straight through the sunset-glory
         Plunge into the dawn:
Leaving their home behind them,
   By a road of splendour and thunder,
      They came to their home in amazement
         Simply by sailing on.

310

THE LORD OF MISRULE

"On May days the wild heads of the parish would choose a Lord of Misrule, whom they would follow even into the church, though the minister were at prayer or preaching, dancing and swinging their may-boughs about like devils incarnate."—OLD PURITAN WRITER.

ALL on a fresh May morning, I took my love to church,
To see if Parson Primrose were safely on his perch.
He scarce had got to *Thirdly*, or squire begun to snore,
   When, like a sun-lit sea-wave,
    A green and crimson sea-wave,
A frolic of madcap May-folk came whooping through the door:—

   Come up, come in with streamers!
    Come in, with boughs of may!
   Come up and thump the sexton,
    And carry the clerk away.
   Now skip like rams, ye mountains,
    Ye little hills, like sheep!
   Come up and wake the people
    That parson puts to sleep.

They tickled their nut-brown tabors. Their garlands flew in showers,
And lasses and lads came after them, with feet like dancing flowers.
Their queen had torn her green gown, and bared a shoulder as white,
   O, white as the may that crowned her,
    While all the minstrels round her
Tilted back their crimson hats and sang for sheer delight:

   Come up, come in with streamers!
    Come in, with boughs of may!
   Now by the gold upon your toe
    You walked the primrose way.
   Come up, with white and crimson!
    O, shake your bells and sing;
   Let the porch bend, the pillars bow,
    Before our Lord, the Spring!

The dusty velvet hassocks were dabbled with fragrant dew.
The font grew white with hawthorn. It frothed in every pew.
Three petals clung to the sexton's beard as he mopped and mowed at
   the clerk,
   And "Take that sexton away," they cried;
    "Did Nebuchadnezzar eat may?" they cried.
"Nay, that was a prize from Betty," they cried, "for kissing her in the
   dark."

Come up, come in with streamers!
  Come in, with boughs of may!
Who knows but old Methuselah
  May hobble the green-wood way?
If Betty could kiss the sexton,
  If Kitty could kiss the clerk,
Who knows how Parson Primrose
  Might blossom in the dark?

The congregation spluttered.   The squire grew purple and all,
And every little chorister bestrode his carven stall.
The parson flapped like a magpie, but none could hear his prayers;
    For Tom Fool flourished his tabor,
    Flourished his nut-brown tabor,
Bashed the head of the sexton, and stormed the pulpit stairs.

    High in the old oak pulpit
      This Lord of all misrule—
    I think it was Will Summers
      That once was Shakespeare's fool—
    Held up his hand for silence,
      And all the church grew still:
    "And are you snoring yet," he said,
      "Or have you slept your fill?

"Your God still walks in Eden, between the ancient trees,
Where Youth and Love go wading through pools of primroses.
And this is the sign we bring you, before the darkness fall,
    That Spring is risen, is risen again,
    That Life is risen, is risen again,
That Love is risen, is risen again, and Love is Lord of all.

    "At Paske began our morrice
      And, ere Pentecost, our May;
    Because, albeit your words be true,
      You know not what you say.
    You chatter in church like jackdaws,
      Words that would wake the dead,
    Were there one breath of life in you,
      One drop of blood," he said.

"*He died and He went down to hell!*   You know not what you mean.
Our rafters were of green fir.   Also our beds were green.
But out of the mouth of a fool, a fool, before the darkness fall,
    We tell you He is risen again,

The Lord of Life is risen again,
The boughs put forth their tender buds, and Love is Lord of all!"

He bowed his head.   He stood so still,
    They bowed their heads as well.
And softly from the organ-loft
    The song began to swell.
Come up with blood-red streamers,
    The reeds began the strain.
The *vox humana* pealed on high,
    The Spring is risen again!

The *vox angelica* replied—*The shadows flee away!*
Our house-beams were of cedar.   Come in, with boughs of may!
The *diapason* deepened it—*Before the darkness fall,*
    We tell you He is risen again!
    Our God hath burst His prison again!
The Lord of Life is risen again; and Love is Lord of all.

BLIND MOONE OF LONDON

Blind Moone of London
    He fiddled up and down,
Once for an angel,
    And twice for a crown.
He fiddled at the *Green Man,*
    He fiddled at the *Rose;*
And where they have buried him
    Not a soul knows.

All his tunes are dead and gone, dead as yesterday;
    And his lanthorn flits no more
    Round the *Devil Tavern* door,
Waiting till the gallants come, singing from the play;
    Waiting in the wet and cold!
    All his Whitsun tales are told.
He is dead and gone, sirs, very far away.

He would not give a silver groat
    For good or evil weather.
He carried in his white cap
    A long red feather.
He wore a long coat

Of the Reading tawny kind,
And darned white hosen
With a blue patch behind.

So—one night—he shuffled past, in his buckled shoon.
We shall never see his face,
Twisted to that queer grimace,
Waiting in the wind and rain, till we called his tune;
Very whimsical and white,
Waiting on a blue Twelfth Night!
He is grown too proud at last—old blind Moone.

Yet, when May was at the door,
And Moone was wont to sing,
Many a maid and bachelor
Whirled into the ring:
Standing on a tilted wain
He played so sweet and loud
The Mayor forgot his golden chain
And jigged it with the crowd.

Old blind Moone, his fiddle scattered flowers along the street;
Into the dust of Brookfield Fair
Carried a shining primrose air,
Crooning like a poor mad maid, O, very low and sweet,
Drew us close, and held us bound,
Then— to the tune *of Pedlar's Pound,*
Caught us up, and whirled us round, a thousand frolic feet.

Master Shakespeare was his host.
The tribe of Benjamin
Used to call him Merlin's Ghost
At the *Mermaid Inn.*
He was only a crowder,
Fiddling at the door.
Death has made him prouder.
We shall not see him more.

Only—if you listen, please—through the master's themes,
You shall hear a wizard strain,
Blind and bright as wind and rain,
Shaken out of willow-trees, and shot with elfin gleams.
How should I your true love know?
Scraps and snatches—even so!
That is old blind Moone again, fiddling in your dreams.

Once, when Will had called for sack
　　And bidden him up and play,
Old blind Moone, he turned his back,
　　Growled, and walked away,
Sailed into a thunder-cloud,
　　Snapped his fiddle-string,
And hobbled from *The Mermaid*
　　Sulky as a king.

Only from the darkness now, steals the strain we knew:
　　　　No one even knows his grave!
　　　　Only here and there a stave,
Out of all his hedge-row flock, be-drips the may with dew.
　　　　And I know not what wild bird
　　　　Carried us his parting word:—
Master Shakespeare needn't take the crowder's fiddle, too.

　　　　Will has wealth and wealth to spare.
　　　　　Give him back his own.
　　　　At his head a grass-green turf,
　　　　　At his heels a stone.
　　　　See his little lanthorn-spark.
　　　　　Hear his ghostly tune,
　　　　Glimmering past you, in the dark,
　　　　　Old blind Moone!

All the little crazy brooks, where love and sorrow run
　　　　Crowned with sedge and singing wild,
　　　　Like a sky-lark—or a child!—
Old blind Moone, he knew their springs, and played 'em every one;
　　　　Stood there in the darkness, blind,
　　　　And sang them into Shakespeare's mind . . .
Old blind Moone of London, O now his songs are done,
The light upon his lost white face, they say it was the sun!

The light upon his poor old face, they say it was the sun!

MOVING THROUGH THE DEW

I

Moving through the dew, moving through the dew,
Ere I waken in the city—Life, thy dawn makes all things new!
And up a fir-clad glen, far from all the haunts of men,
Up a glen among the mountains, oh my feet are wings again!

Moving through the dew, moving through the dew,
O mountains of my boyhood, I come again to you,
By the little path I know, with the sea far below,
And above, the great cloud-galleons with their sails of rose and snow;

As of old, when all was young, and the earth a song unsung
And the heather through the crimson dawn its Eden incense flung
From the mountain-heights of joy, for a careless-hearted boy,
And the lavrocks rose like fountain sprays of bliss that ne'er could cloy,

From their little beds of bloom, from the golden gorse and broom,
With a song to God the Giver, o'er that waste of wild perfume;
Blowing from height to height, in a glory of great light,
While the cottage-clustered valleys held the lilac last of night,

So, when dawn is in the skies, in a dream, a dream, I rise,
And I follow my lost boyhood to the heights of Paradise.
Life, thy dawn makes all things new!   Hills of Youth, I come to you,
Moving through the dew, moving through the dew.

II

Moving through the dew, moving through the dew,
Floats a brother's face to meet me!   Is it you?   Is it you?
For the night I leave behind keeps these dazzled eyes still blind!
But oh, the little hill-flowers, their scent is wise and kind;

And I shall not lose the way from the darkness to the day,
While dust can cling as their scent clings to memory for aye;
And the least link in the chain can recall the whole again,
And heaven at last resume its far-flung harvests, grain by grain.

To the hill-flowers clings my dust, and tho' eyeless Death may thrust
All else into the darkness, in their heaven I put my trust;
And a dawn shall bid me climb to the little spread of thyme
Where first I heard the ripple of the fountain-heads of rhyme.

And a fir-wood that I know, from dawn to sunset-glow,
Shall whisper to a lonely sea, that swings far, far below.
Death, thy dawn makes all things new.   Hills of Youth, I come to you,
Moving through the dew, moving through the dew.

THE INN OF APOLLO

Have you supped at the Inn of Apollo,
   While the last light fades from the West?
Has the Lord of the sun, at the world's end,
   Poured you his ripest and best?
O, there's wine in that Inn of Apollo;

Wine, mellow and deep as the sunset,
   With mirth in it, singing as loud
As the skylark sings in a high wind,
   High over a crisp white cloud.
Have you laughed in that Inn of Apollo?

Was the whole world molten in music
   At once, by the heat of that wine?
Did the stars and the tides and your own heart
   Dance with the heavenly Nine?
For they dance in that Inn of Apollo.

Was their poetry croaked by the sages,
   Or born in a whisper of wings?
For the music that masters the ages,
   Be sure, is the music that sings!
Yes, they sing in that Inn of Apollo.

HELICON

I climbed to Helicon's height and found you,
   Daughters of Memory, heavenly Nine.
Though the dawn-mist flowed like a veil around you,
   I drank your glory again like wine.

I saw how the cold clear morning glances
   Through peaks of pine on your breasts of snow,
Where, slowly wreathing your stately dances,
   You drift through the glens of delight and go;

With scents of the wild thyme round you blowing,
   And limbs that burn in the rising sun,
And the golden law of the measure showing
   The way that the many are woven in one;

How the pulse of life dictates your pleasure
   To hearts and tides and the stars on high;
For all the universe moves in measure,
   And even the gods, if they break it, die.

Long since, in music, this law was spoken
   To all that wander on Helicon hill.
By wrong and death though the song be broken,
   The stars are working the Muses' will.

This law runs deeper than all earth's dreaming.
   Who follows it, walks in a heaven unseen.
He has passed all veils of thinking and seeming,
   Who drinks one cup of this Hippocrene.

EUTERPE

THE witchery of her voice from far blue hills
   At sunset, called me on,
With exquisite echoes of all those bird-like rills
   That warble on Helicon.
Once, over a cloud of thyme, I saw her gleam.
   I touched her snowy side.
She vanished, into the dusk, a moth-like dream;
   And all that music died.

Farewell, Euterpe.   Turn to your own skies.
   Few dreams are half so fair
As those that lit the mutiny of your eyes
   And crowned your fragrant hair;
Yet, if the lyric Muse like mist can go,
   I, too, can go like rain;
For I've a tryst to keep on earth below,
   A troth to plight again.

Let all those proud immortals, then, betray
   The hopes they brought to birth;
But I will crown, with violets of a day,
   A love that walks on earth;
Though never a Muse on Helicon may wear
   More sweetness on her brow
Then lives and breathes in my dear lady's hair
   Like April blossoms now.

318

Then, as I looked into my true love's face,
    Thinking all dreams had gone,
Clear, through her own deep eyes, with mocking grace,
    The lost Immortal shone.
Low from her lips the sweet lost music flowed,—
    "Euterpe left your sky
Only to be your comrade on the road.
    Look closely.   It is I."

THE SONG-TREE

Grow, my song, like a tree,
    As thou hast ever grown,
Since first, a wondering child,
    Long since, I cherished thee.
It was at break of day,
    Well I remember it,—
The first note that I heard,
    A magical undertone,
Sweeter than any bird
    —Or so it seemed to me—
And my tears ran wild.
    This tale, this tale is true.
The light was growing gray;
    And the rhymes ran so sweet
(For I was only a child)
    That I knelt down to pray.

Grow, my song, like a tree.
    Since then I have forgot
    A thousand dreams, but not
The song that set me free,
    So that to thee I gave
My hopes and my despairs,
    My boyhood's ecstasy,
My manhood's prayers.
    In dreams I have watched thee grow,
A ladder of sweet boughs,
    Where angels come and go,
And birds keep house.
    In dreams, I have seen thee wave
Over a distant land,
    And watched thy roots expand,

And given my life to thee,
  As I would give my grave.

Grow, my song, like a tree,
  And when I am grown old,
Let me die under thee,
  Die to enrich thy mould;
Die at thy roots, and so
  Help thee to grow.
Make of this body and blood
  Thy sempiternal food.
Then let some little child,
  Some friend I shall not see,
When the great dawn is gray,
  Some lover I have not known,
In summers far away,
  Sit listening under thee.
And in thy rustling hear
  That mystical undertone,
Which made my tears run wild,
  And made thee, O, how dear.

In the great years to be?
  I am proud then?   Ah, not so.
I have lived and died for thee.
  Be patient.   Grow.
Grow, my song, like a tree.

BALLAD OF BOYHOOD

Ships long salted with the spray
  Welter at our tarry quays.
Younger hands their anchors weigh
  Now, for the unaltering seas.
Masts that tower like redwood trees
  Creak; the windlass cranks the chain.
Then—that rush of memories—
  Would I were a boy again.

Blue as Hybla, blithe as May,
  Hills of thyme, alive with bees,
Lift above the land-locked bay
  Cliffs for boyhood's tattered knees,
Crags where eaglets crouch at ease
  Watching, off the Spanish Main,

Skulls and cross-bones on the breeze.
   Would I were a boy again!

Hoist your sails! Away! Away!
   Steer for any cloud you please;
Lost Atlantis, far Cathay,
   Isles of the Hesperides.
All their whispering wizardries
   Waste like foam to one refrain.
Nothing shall your hearts appease.
   Would I were a boy again.

Prince, the heaven that none could seize
   Lies before us. Not in vain
Every moment as it flees
   Brings us nearer heaven again.

PHANTOM SAILS

WHERE dark pines framed a silvery gleam of sea,
   With all sail set, faint thro' the brooding haze,
Like a grey ghost there crept—O, memory!—
   A tall three-masted ship of other days.
I watched as one who knew that her deep hold
Was fraught with treasure, youth's re-captured gold,
Boyhood's delight. . . . She bore them, and passed by,
A phantom ship, against a phantom sky.

THE NEW SIRENS AND ULYSSES

IT is the isle—not we!
   It is the Spring in the land,
And the soft foam of the sea,
   And the palms, and the shining sand
Swept by the dusk of your sail
   As the black ship welters by;
And the smell of flowers on the gale,
   And the birds with their April cry:
It is all these things—not we!

Why do you strain at your cords?
   You have bound yourself to the mast!
It is no wild honey of words

That shall loose your bonds at the last.
It is not the red of our lips
    Or the light on a sun-lit breast
That has wrecked so many ships
    And robbed your heart of its rest.
'Tis the soft white foam of the sea.

It is not our shining eyes,
    Or the song you strain to hear
That drain the strength from the skies
    And fill your heart with fear.
It is only a sunset-breath
    That rustles along the glade.
It is not our voice that saith,
    "Why are you so afraid?"
'Tis the wandering air—not we!

Do we melt in the dusk like snow?
    We have left no print on the sand!
Odysseus, listen and know.
    (You shall see no beckoning hand!)
Why do you labour in vain
    For the truth that none can learn?
There is no more sorrow or pain,
    Where we hide ourselves in the fern—
Saith the whispering fern—not we!

CARDUCCI TO HOMER

"E se tu ritornassi al nostro mondo"
ALWAYS when Spring returns, I turn to you,
    Old man divine, whose youth shall never fail;
    I turn to you and that enduring tale
Of sunset isles and Circe's magic brew.
Tell me, Olympian, of that sunburnt crew,
    The black ship, and the long bright westward trail,
    The wreck, the raft, the sea-witch, and the sail
That brings men home. Tell—tell it all anew.

But no—tell nothing, blind one! Go your way!
    The swineherd has cut down your olive-tree.
    We have rounded earth. There is no light beyond!
Homer, if you came tapping back to-day,

You'd find **our** sewage in your wine-dark sea,
And none to chuck you a penny, old vagabond.

THE BURNING BOUGHS

HE pipes to himself alone,
The child of Pan, where the woods are mellowing now;
   For his echo, the thrush, is flown;
And the clouds of the sunset burn on the maple-bough.
See, stained with a golden tan,
   Like the smooth-skinned sun-kissed pear,
The young god shines thro' the shadows. O, little god Pan,
   What song are you piping there?

The wild grape purples the glen,
But the lovers that followed the lilt of his pipes are fled.
   Are they lost in the cities of men?
Does he call through the soft blue tendrils now to the dead?
Does he summon the Oread throng?
   Or, leashed and lashed with the vine,
Do the panthers of Bacchus approach to the pulse of his song,
   And the white feet splashed with wine?

I sing of immortal joy,—
The warbling pipes of the young god cried like a bird,—
   The laughter of girl and boy,
And all the kisses and whispers that once I heard;
For the oak may darken and turn
   To a smouldering crimson pyre;
And the golden birch in her own bright tresses may burn;
   But I sing of the world's desire.

Though the wild grape shrivel and fall,
Under boughs that are flaring like funeral torches here,
   My joy shall outlive them all,
As the bare bright seed that endures till the youth of the year.
As I sang when the world began,
   I shall sing when the world grows old;
For I am the fruit and the berry, the little god Pan,
   The green leaf under the gold.

I am the lamp in the tomb;
The little gold acorn alive in the drifts of decay;

The heart in the crumbling bloom;
The hope that abides when the petals are winnowed away.
The roses of life, at a breath,
  Break; and your memories wane;
But I am the magic insurgent! Through darkness and death
  I shall lead you to April again.

The sumach burns in the brake.
The hills are a furnace of colour and mellowing light,
  Where junipers flame and flake,
And the blueberry dreams like a faint blue smoke on the height.
The pine-cones fall below
  On the sweet red-needled earth;
But wilder and sweeter the pipes of the child-god blow
  In a song of the world's re-birth.

"When the Phœnix fires her nest
I sing as the rose-red feathers consume and change,
  And the rainbow plumes of her breast
Kindle with beauty and shine, transfigured and strange;
For the world and your heart's desire
  And the spice of a thousand springs
Awake with the bird reborn from the heart of the fire,
  And mount on her radiant wings!"

It is all October now;
But he sings of a mellower harvest than any of ours.
  He laughs at the burning bough,
And pipes till the withering leaves grow brighter than flowers.
While the pomp of the world goes by,
  As age upon age it has gone,
Though the sun-swarms perish like leaves on the boughs of the sky,
  The youth of the world sings on.

THE BUTTERFLY GARDEN

" Then there is that more capricious close of happy surprises—the butterfly garden. By keeping a sheltered corner for the colours and scents that they like best, you may have not only the anchored sort of flowers, but what our forefathers would have called a pretty pleasance of winged flowers, flowers that have cut their stalky cables, and sail as they please upon the sunlit air."—ORCHARD'S BAY.

HERE, by this crumbling wall
  We'll spread the feast, then watch what guests it brings.
  Earth-rooted flowers to flowers of heaven shall call,
    And all the gorgeous air shall wink with wings.

We'll choose what they love most
    As all men must whose guests are of the sky;
Not lavender, of lost gardens the sweet ghost;
    But heliotrope, young Psyche's cherry-pie.

Be sure she does not pine
    For any phantom feast, that heavenly Maid!
'Tis we that make a wraith of things divine,
    And think the very soul into a shade.

The Chilian orange-ball
    First of the shrubs that Tortoise-shells prefer,
Must hang its honeyed clusters over all
    And tempt the freckled blues to flutter near;

With globes of fragrant gold
    Luring the Green-veined White from near and far,
While faultless Painted Ladies here unfold
    Their pearly fans, inlaid with moon and star;

Till later buddleias trail
    Their long racemes of violet and rose,
Round which the glorious Admirals dip and sail,
    And swarthy Peacocks flit and sip and doze.

Hedging them closely round
    Veronica must spread her spikes of blue,
That sun and flowers may in one sleep be drowned
    Yet keep her own Fritillaries fluttering, too.

Blue is their heart's delight.
    Therefore, though crimson petals also please,
And soft white wings will sail to bridal white
    Like yachts with orange tips on blossoming seas,

We'll make them doubly blest
    With this, the deepening blue of children's eyes;
For wingèd creatures love that colour best,
    Which smiled upon them, once, in Paradise.

BIRD OF DELIGHT

BIRD of delight,
    Sing on your topmost bough.

Gather all heaven into your tiny heart
  And utter it now.

Lift your soft throat;
  And as the dawn shines in each drop of dew
Let the pure glory of each rounded note
  Tell of His infinite love who sings in you.

How else could He
  Who is all beauty see or hear His own?
Dying, He shares your mortal ecstasy
  And makes new heavens to sing and share His throne.

For men on earth,
  They also hear what else were all unheard,—
Their own lost Aprils, in divine re-birth,
  Singing to heaven through one unweeting bird.

WESTWARD

In Devon, whose red cliffs and rock-bound trees
  Bred hawks that scoured the seas,
Deep lanes are narrowing with their clouds of may,
  And, on dark moors to-day,
Bridal whitethorns are breathing everywhere
  A Paradisal air.

Tavistock, Bideford, Budleigh Salterton
  Are shining in the sun.
Grey Plymouth Sound, whence all those sea-dogs hailed,
  Is quiet as when they sailed
Across the Atlantic with a trawler's crew
  And shaped the world anew.

Somewhere, in town to-night, proud banqueteers
  Explain, amid loud cheers,
The important things that made and keep us great;
  And the rotund orate;
And party leaders, hair brushed back and sleek,
  Talk blandly, tongue in cheek,

As mummers talk, with mobile mouths and eyes,
  And smiles that fit all lies,
Denying all that they affirmed last night,
  Or proving black is white.
Silence! For Mr. Glibbery Slick, the Bore,
  The tall toast-masters roar.
"Your excellencies, my lords . . ." Then, round and round,
  Drones the old hollow sound.

But here, O here in Devon, listen long
  To England's own deep song:
Streams in the steep-down valley, and wild birds
  That, clearer far than words,
Make even the listening stranger understand
  Our love for this dear land.

Love looks askance at majesty and power;
  But kneels here, to a flower.
One cottage-lamp can hold a star for him
  Bright as the skies are dim.
For all his boundless kingdom, he likes well
  In one green glen to dwell,
Knowing that he who loves his own home best
  Cares most for all the rest.

So these things please him,—nooks where Spring may hide
  To make young earth his bride;
Sprays of wild fern along an old stone wall;
  A wood where white owls call;
A sea-gull, sailing into sunset skies;
  A child with shining eyes;
A village street; an elm-embosomed spire
  Pointing the heart up higher;
And one thin footpath, winding up a hill,
  Where memories wander still.

O sea-bird, winging quietly to the west,
  Speed on, with rose-flushed breast.
Tell them there is no strength in gold or steel
  To bind our Commonweal.
Tell them who love their maple-leaf to-day
  As England loves her may
That love and memory, when all else is gone,
  Shall triumph and live on.

327

THE ISLE OF MEMORIES

Was it so in Old England, when kings went to war?
Did the cottages grow silent, as the lads went away,
Leaving all they loved so, the wan face of the mother,
The lips of the young wives, the grey head and the golden,
While birds, in the blackthorn, made ready for the may?

It was even so, even so in Old England.
The homesteads were emptied of happiness and laughter,
The fields were forsaken.   The lanes grew lonely.
A shadow veiled the sun.   A sea-mist of sorrows
Drifted like a dream through the old oak-forest,
Flowed through our valleys, and filled them with visions,
Brooded on our mountains and crowned them with remembrance,
So that many a wanderer from the shining of the west
Finds a strange darkness in the heart of our land.
Long, long since, in the days of the cross-bow,
Unknown armies from the forge and the farm
Bought us these fields in the bleakness of death.
The may-boughs budded with the same brief glory;
And, sweetening all the air, in a shower of wet petals,
The blackbird shook them, with to-day's brave song.
His note has not changed since the days of Piers Plowman.
The star has not changed that, as curfew chimed,
In the faint green fields of the sky, like a primrose,
Woke, and looked down, upon lovers in the lanes.
Their wild thyme to-night shall be crushed into sweetness,
On the crest of the downs where, dark against the crimson,
Dark, dark as death, on the crimson of the afterglow,
Other lovers wander on the eve of farewell,
Other lovers whisper and listen to the sea.

It was even so, even so in Old England.
In all this bleak island there is hardly an acre,
Hardly a gate, or a path upon the hillside,
Hardly a woodland, that has not heard or seen them
Whispering good-bye, or waving it for ever.
This rain-drenched, storm-rocked earth we adore,
These ripening orchards, these fields of thick wheat
Rippling into grey light and shadow as the wind blows;
These dark rich ploughlands, dreaming in the dusk,
Whose breath in our nostrils is better than life;
This isle of green hedgerows and deep rambling lanes;

This cluster of old counties that have mellowed through the ages,
  Like apples in autumn on a grey apple tree;
These moorlands of Cornwall, those mountains of Cumberland,
  Ferny coombs of Devonshire and gardens of Kent;
Those russet roofs of Sussex, those farms and faint spires,
  Those fields of known flowers, whose faces, whose fragrance,
Even in this darkness, recall our lost childhood,
  Sleep like our own children, and cherish us like angels,—
All these are ours, because of the forgotten.

THE REMEMBERING GARDEN

HE brought me into a deep remembering garden;
  And I was like one that wakes from a dream of pain
To hear the cry of a thrush in the woods at evening,
  And the sound of a brook, and the whisper of Eden again.

He drew me out of the throngs of the fog-bound City;
  And, if they forget my songs, and the fond dreams die,
It will not be the only forgetting while, here in the stillness,
  The sea breathes low, and the high stars wake in the sky.
For it is not true that the wonder is lost in childhood;
  It is not true that, in manhood, the music is gone;
It is not true that the soul is mocked by its Maker,
  When the high priest sneers in its face, and the night draws on.

His brooks run down from the hills to feed my lilies.
  His clouds drift up from the sea to redden my rose.
He scatters His broken sun through the grass of the orchard
  Where the jonquils laugh with delight, and the daffodil glows.

I know how heaven was lost and won in a garden;
  I know what fruitful mist to the hill-side clung,
When God looked up at the sky, and the day was breaking,
  And, under the grey old olives, the flowers grew young.

His unseen Paradise quickens my breathing borders;
  And out of his guarded Eden each larkspur springs;
For His wild birds carry the seed over all His fences,
  And His merciful angel smiles at their careless wings.

A DEAD POET

I HAVE gone up into the hills of morning
    By the long glen I used to call my own;
Gone quietly up, among the hills of morning
    By that wild crag which was my boyhood's throne.
Far down, on earth, dark in the gulf below me,
    They have sealed the rest in cedar, lined with lead,
While scribes who never knew, and cannot know me,
    Think they dissect my soul, and call me dead.

I hear the clear hill-water softly falling
    Thro' tall wet rocks where fern and harebell sway;
And grey wood-pigeons in the fir-wood calling
        Who, who is this that knows so well the way?

And the deep firs reply—
                'Tis our lost brother!
    He has come back to our unchanging skies.
    But he is changed. Like many and many another,
        He comes from earth with horror-haunted eyes;

Mind-bruised, wing-broken, covered with derision,
    Pierced to the quick by things too dire to tell;
For he has seen on earth that monstrous vision,
    The hate of man, which is the gate of hell.
Yet would I gain my rock-bound couch of heather,
    Which sees, below the gorse, the Atlantic shine,
And hear the ferns and sea-winds talk together,
    And listen long to those old friends of mine.

And the salt wind shall whisper through the bracken,
    We knew him well in years that are long past,
Shall whisper, very gently, through the bracken,
    We always thought he would return at last.
Then shall the rolling cloud-rack fold and hide me
    Close to the hearts that knew my childhood best
For all my wanderings they will never chide me,
    Rain on the face will tell them all the rest.

THE VISITANT

BEAUTY forsakes her sky
And wakes, a changeling, in our realm of night;
    Love, in immortal ecstasy,

Dies, to be born in worlds of fading light;
  For, breathing mortal breath,
They win their heaven at last, and conquer death.

  From worlds too great to grasp,
They turn to all these dear small mortal things.
  With dying mortal hands they clasp
A mortal hand, a small warm hand that clings;
  Knowing that those who fold
Love to their hearts have more than heaven to hold.

  They dwell in man's dark mind
Lest absolute light should melt their lives like dew;
  And sight of all things leave them blind,
Even to the faces and the flowers they knew.
  They look through mortal eyes
To save their souls from those unbounded skies.

  So Merlin taught me well
Long since, in those old morning-coloured woods,
  To see the moment's miracle,
And how all beauty in one may-tree broods,
  And heaven is brought to birth
Only through lesser heavens that walk on earth.

ROSA MUNDI

Here, at the foot of the cypress, the rose of the whole world lies.
Hard rest, and an iron slumber, have darkened the radiant eyes.
Gods of lead in the garden, stand by the steps of stone;
Flute them a careless music. One rose is all our own.

What shall be said of morning, when eyes are closed for aye?
What shall be said of evening, when night is one with day?
How shall our feet turn homeward, when home and hope are fled?
Where is the throne worth winning, when heart's desire lies dead?

Out of her room they bore her—lilies from head to feet;
But left one rose behind her, upon the cold white sheet.
Turn the salt seas to favour, and prettiness, and jest.
Never shall they behold it—that rose within the breast.

We shall go out and face them—the world and its long untruth!
Never shall they behold it—that wound in the heart of youth.
Laugh, under yew and cypress. Lift up your hearts of lead!
Let all deep things be buried, when heart's desire lies dead.

THE GREY SPRING

I SAW the green Spring
  Wading the brooks
With wild jay laughter
  And hoyden looks.

I saw the grey Spring
  Weeping alone
Where woods are misty
  And buds unblown.

Red were the lips
  Whence laughter leapt;
But Oh, it was Beauty
  Herself that wept.

A TREE AGAINST THE SKY

FALL, happy leaves, that danced so high in the air,
  The One I love was hidden in your gay crowds.
Fall, you thronged joys. A Spirit far more fair
  Slept in your rustling clouds.

One lean dark Form, with arms upstretched in prayer,
  Emerges now, from dreams that drift and die.
Fall, yellowing leaves, and let the tree stand bare
  Against the wintry sky.

DISTANT VOICES

REMEMBER the house of thy father,
  When the palaces open before thee,
    And the music would make thee forget.
When the cities are glittering around thee,
  Remember the lamp in the evening,
    The loneliness and the peace.

When the deep things that cannot be spoken
  Are drowned in a riot of laughter,
    And the proud wine foams in thy cup;
In the day when thy wealth is upon thee,
  Remember thy path through the pine-wood,
    Remember the ways of thy peace.

Remember—remember—remember
When the cares of this world and its treasure
Have dulled the swift eyes of thy youth;
When beauty and longing forsake thee,
And there is no hope in the darkness,
And the soul is drowned in the flesh;

Turn, then, to the house of thy boyhood,
To the sea and the hills that would heal thee,
To the voices of those thou hast lost,
The still small voices that loved thee,
Whispering, out of the silence,
Remember the house of thy father,
Remember the paths of thy peace.

SPRING, AND THE BLIND CHILDREN

THEY left the primrose glistening in its dew.
With empty hands they drifted down the lane,
As though, for them, the Spring held nothing new;
And not one face was turned to look again.

Like tiny ghosts, along their woodland aisle,
They stole. They did not leap or dance or run.
Only, at times, without a word or smile,
Their small blind faces lifted to the sun;

Innocent faces, desolately bright,
Masks of dark thought that none could ever know;
But O, so small to hide it. In their night
What dreams of our strange world must come and go;

Groping, as we, too, grope for heavens unseen;
Guessing—at what those fabulous visions are;
Or wondering, when they learned that leaves were green,
If colours were like music, heard afar?

Were brooks like bird-song? Was the setting sun
· Like scent of roses, or like evening prayer?
Were stars like chimes in heaven, when day was done;
Was midnight like their mothers' warm soft hair?

And dawn?—a pitying face against their own,
A whispered word, an unknown angel's kiss,

That stoops to each, in its own dark, alone;
　　But leaves them lonelier for that breath of bliss?

Was it for earth's transgressions that they paid—
　　Lambs of that God whose eyes with love grow dim—
Sharing His load on whom all wrongs are laid?
　　But O, so small to bear it, even with Him!

God of blind children, through Thy dreadful light
　　They pass. We pass. Thy heavens are all so near.
We cannot grasp them in our earth-bound night.
But O, Thy grief! For Thou canst see and hear.

THE CORMORANT

EAST of the garden, a wild glen glimmers with fox-gloves,
　　And there, through the heat of the day,
In a fern-shadowed elf-ring of sand, with pine-logs round it,
　　Three bird-voiced children play;
With a palm to shelter their golden heads from evil
　　When the noon sun grows too strong;
And in Orchard's cove, unwatched, there's a cormorant diving
　　All day long.

Long years ago, from the coasts of my own far childhood
　　I watched him ride the wave,
And his way is no more changed than the wave's long whisper,
　　Though a world has gone to the grave.
He swims the unwrinkled swell of the opaline water
　　Like a small black pirate swan;
Then, quietly lifting a long sleek neck, dips over,
　　Slips under, and is gone.

And the bay is as bare as the unstained sky for a minute;
　　But, while you wonder and stare,
Though there's never a bubble to hint at the place of his rising,
　　All at once he is riding there,
With his long beak flicking a sliver of quick cold silver
　　Shivering and alive to the light,
As he rode on the dawn-red seas before man first sailed them,
　　And shall ride, after man's last night.

When the elf-ring under the palm is choked with nettles,
   And the golden heads are grey,
If they ever revisit the haunts of their own lost childhood,
   And return to Orchard's Bay,
They may watch him awhile, a small black speck; and remember
   How, once, I made them a song;
In Orchard's cove, unwatched, there's a cormorant diving
   All day long.

THE CAVE

HERE was once a cave, at the foot of the fir-clad mountains,
   Where the hawk towers over the gorse and the herring-gulls cry,
In a lonely coast where the long bright sea-wave crumbles,
      And never a foot goes by.

And there is no other sound in the sunlit stillness,
   But a slipping stone on the high steep mountain walls,
Or a trickle of sun-baked earth where the red fox passes,
      Or a dry hot fir-cone falls.

Long years ago, when I was a boy and a pirate,
   We built us a driftwood fire at the mouth of that cave,
And fished for our food, or sang round the fire, or listened,
      While time died out with the wave.

Long years ago, when I was a boy and a pirate,
   We swam in that sea, and basked in that sun, and heard
The pulse of the world in the breathing sound of the waters,
      And asked for no lovelier word.

Was it dark in the cave? Was it dark as the night that re-echoes
   The cry of our joyous crew from that timeless coast,
Calling me—back to the past, or on, to the future,
      As a man coming home, or a ghost?

In that life to come, shall we stumble out of a cave-mouth,
   As Lazarus groped through the sepulchre's open door,
Where the smooth warm stones that were wet with our naked foot-
   prints
      Gleam grey in the sun once more . . . ?

TO RONSARD

Ronsard, the night is dark. The paths you might have known
  Are choked with brambles now. The weeds run everywhere.
The little garden gods are chipped and overthrown;
  Yet, like the ghost of Spring, a fragrance haunts the air.

Perhaps, if you should grope by yonder crumbling wall,
  Beyond the dark old yew, the broken urn—who knows?—
A nook may yet remain where memory, after all,
  May dwell awhile with peace—and love's perennial rose.

I cannot see your face. But beautiful old rhyme,
  Music in lucid form that leads to lovelier light,
And one clear lyric cry, across the gulf of time,
  May still the night-jar's note, and put ill dreams to flight.

Oh, happy morning-star, lift up your heart and sing
  The beauty of the sun, so ancient and so new!
Earth, in her blind old heart, foretells your heavenly Spring;
  And men, who are nearing home, believe the tale is true.

AT ASSISI

Scandentisque Asis consurgit vertice murus.—Propertius, IV, 125.

I know a city on a crag, a mountain's castled crown,
Where, like the stairs the angels tread, the streets go up and down;
A city very small and kind, and full of strange renown.

It stands upon an eastern height, and looks towards the west.
Far off it sees Perugia, its ancient foe, at rest;
And all the birds of Italy are gathered to its breast.

So small and kind; but smaller far, in the dim gulf below,
The world of men, and all the tides that toss them to and fro,
While on its crag that city stands, crowned with the sunset glow.

Still, like a lean dark cypress there, against the clouds on high,
Brother of sun and moon and star, he towers into the sky,
As long ago, with arms upstretched, while all things else went by.

Stone of his own immortal hill has made those ramparts bright,
The warm white stone that glows at dusk with a soft unearthly light,

336

And delicate tones of heaven's own rose, when the plains are lost in
   night.

They told me of the lamp-lit tomb where dust in dust was laid;
Of painted wings from Paradise that on their walls decayed;
But not of this—this flower of light that fades, and cannot fade.

They did not tell me how it chanced that the small kind streets were
   bare
And hushed for love, as love went up, by cloister and winding stair,
Till a little lighted window shone, like an altar lit for prayer.

   .   .   .   .

Oh, bravely, bravely flash the swords beneath St. Peter's dome!
Proudly the silver trumpets ring across the world from Rome!
But this—was on a higher hill, and a little nearer home.

A little nearer home that night, when skies had ceased to glow,
And the great vale of Umbria was dark as death below,
Assisi grew into the light, as flowers and children grow.

ON THE WESTERN FRONT

(1916)

I

I FOUND a dreadful acre of the dead,
   Marked with the only sign on earth that saves.
The wings of death were hurrying overhead,
   The loose earth shook on those unquiet graves;

For the deep gun-pits, with quick stabs of flame,
   Made their own thunders of the sunlit air;
Yet, as I read the crosses, name by name,
   Rank after rank, it seemed that peace was there;

Sunlight and peace, a peace too deep for thought,
   The peace of tides that underlie our strife,
The peace with which the moving heavens are fraught,
   The peace that is our everlasting life.

The loose earth shook.   The very hills were stirred.
The silence of the dead was all I heard.

We, who lie here, have nothing more to pray.
  To all your praises we are deaf and blind.
We may not ever know if you betray
  Our hope, to make earth better for mankind.

Only our silence, in the night, shall grow
  More silent, as the stars grow in the sky;
And, while you deck our graves, you shall not know
  How many scornful legions pass you by.

For we have heard you say (when we were living)
  That some small dream of good would "cost too much."
But when the foe struck, we have watched you giving,
  And seen you move the mountains with one touch.

What can be done, we know.   But, have no fear!
If you fail now, we shall not see or hear.

THE VICTORY BALL

THE cymbals crash,
  And the dancers walk,
With long silk stockings
  And arms of chalk,
Butterfly skirts,
  And white breasts bare,
And shadows of dead men
  Watching 'em there.

Shadows of dead men
  Stand by the wall,
Watching the fun
  Of the Victory Ball.
They do not reproach,
  Because they know,
If they're forgotten,
  It's better so.

Under the dancing
  Feet are the graves.
Dazzle and motley,
  In long bright waves,

Brushed by the palm-fronds
   Grapple and whirl
Ox-eyed matron,
   And slim white girl.

Fat wet bodies
   Go waddling by,
Girdled with satin,
   Though God knows why;
Gripped by satyrs
   In white and black,
With a fat wet hand
   On the fat wet back.

See, there is one child
   Fresh from school,
Learning the ropes
   As the old hands rule.
God, how that dead boy
   Gapes and grins
As the tom-toms bang
   And the shimmy begins.

"What did you think
   We should find," said a shade,
"When the last shot echoed
   And peace was made?"
"Christ," laughed the fleshless
   Jaws of his friend,
"I thought they'd be praying
   For worlds to mend,

"Making earth better,
   Or something silly,
Like white-washing hell
   Or Picca-dam-dilly.
They've a sense of humour,
   These women of ours,
These exquisite lilies,
   These fresh young flowers!"

"Pish," said a statesman
   Standing near,
"I'm glad they can busy
   Their thoughts elsewhere!

We mustn't reproach 'em.
  They're young, you see."
"Ah," said the dead men,
  "So were we!"

Victory! Victory!
  On with the dance!
Back to the jungle
  The new beasts prance!
God, how the dead men
  Grin by the wall,
Watching the fun
  Of the Victory Ball.

THE OLD MEETING HOUSE

(NEW JERSEY. 1918)

Its quiet graves were made for peace till Gabriel blows his horn.
  Those wise old elms could hear no cry
  Of all that distant agony—
Only the red-winged blackbird, and the rustle of thick ripe corn.

The blue jay, perched upon that bronze, with bright unweeting eyes,
  Could never read the names that signed
  The noblest charter of mankind;
But all of them were names we knew beneath our English skies.

And on the low gray headstones, with their crumbling weather-stains,
  —Though cardinal birds, like drops of blood,
  Flickered across the haunted wood,—
The names you'd see were names that woke like flowers in English lanes.

John Applegate was fast asleep; and Temperance Olden, too.
  And David Worth had quite forgot
  If Hannah's lips were red or not;
And Prudence veiled her eyes at last, as Prudence ought to do.

And when, across that patch of heaven, that small blue leaf-edged space
  At times, a droning airplane went,
  No flicker of astonishment
Could lift the heavy eyelids on one gossip's upturned face.

For William Speakman could not tell—so thick the grasses grow—
  If that strange humming in the sky

Meant that the Judgment Day were nigh,
Or if 'twere but the summer bees that blundered to and fro.

And then, across the breathless wood, a Bell began to sound,
   The only Bell that wakes the dead,
   And Stockton Signer raised his head,
And called to all the deacons in the ancient burial-ground.

"The Bell, the Bell is ringing!   Give me back my rusty sword.
   Though I thought the wars were done,
   Though I thought our peace was won,
Yet I signed the Declaration, and the dead must keep their word.

"There's only one great ghost I know could make that 'larum ring.
   It's the captain that we knew
   In the ancient buff and blue,
It's our Englishman, George Washington, who fought the German king!"

So the sunset saw them mustering beneath their brooding boughs,
   Ancient shadows of our sires,
   Kindling with the ancient fires,
While the old cracked Bell to southward shook the shadowy meeting
      house.

PRINCETON

(1917)

These lines were written for inscription on the first joint memorial to the American and British soldiers who fell in the Revolutionary War. This memorial was dedicated at Princeton in 1916.

> *Here Freedom stood, by slaughtered friend and foe,*
> *And, ere the wrath paled or that sunset died,*
> *Looked through the ages: then, with eyes aglow,*
> *Laid them, to wait that future, side by side.*

"THE AVENUE OF THE ALLIES"

THIS is the song of the wind as it came
Tossing the flags of the nations to flame:
      I am the breath of God.   I am His laughter.
I am His Liberty.   That is my name.

So it descended, at night, on the city.
So it went lavishing beauty and pity,
Lighting the lordliest street of the world
With half of the banners that earth has unfurled;
Over the lamps that are brighter than stars,
Laughing aloud on its way to the wars,
Proud as America, sweeping along
Death and destruction like notes in a song,
Leaping to battle as man to his mate,
Joyous as God when he moved to create,—
          Never was voice of a nation so glorious,
Glad of its cause and afire with its fate!
Never did eagle on mightier pinion
Tower to the height of a brighter dominion,
Kindling the hope of the prophets to flame,
Calling aloud on the deep as it came,
          Cleave me a way for an army with banners.
I am His Liberty.   That is my name.

Know you the meaning of all they are doing?
Know you the light that their soul is pursuing?
Know you the might of the world they are making,
This nation of nations whose heart is awaking?
What is this mingling of peoples and races?
Look at the wonder and joy in their faces!
Look how the folds of the union are spreading!
Look, for the nations are come to their wedding.
How shall the folk of our tongue be afraid of it?
England was born of it.   England was made of it,
Made of this welding of tribes into one,
This marriage of pilgrims that followed the sun!
Briton and Roman and Saxon were drawn
By winds of this Pentecost, out of the dawn,
Westward, to make her one people of many;
But here is a union more mighty than any.
Know you the soul of this deep exultation?
Know you the word that goes forth to this nation?
          I am the breath of God.   I am His Liberty.
Let there be light over all His creation.

Over this Continent, wholly united,
They that were foemen in Europe are plighted.
Here, in a league that our blindness and pride
Doubted and flouted and mocked and denied,
Dawns the Republic, the laughing, gigantic

Europe, united, beyond the Atlantic.
That is America, speaking one tongue,
Acting her epics before they are sung,
Driving her rails from the palms to the snow,
Through States that are greater than Emperors know,
Forty-eight States that are empires in might,
But ruled by the will of one people tonight,
Nerved as one body, with net-works of steel,
Merging their strength in the one Commonweal,
Brooking no poverty, mocking at Mars,
Building their cities to talk with the stars,
Thriving, increasing by myriads again
Till even in numbers old Europe may wane. . . .
How shall a son of the England they fought
Fail to declare the full pride of his thought,
Stand with the scoffers who, year after year,
Bring the Republic their half-hidden sneer?
Now, as in beauty she stands at our side,
Who shall withhold the full gift of his pride?
Not the great England who knows that her son,
Washington, fought her, and Liberty won;
England, whose names like the stars in their station,
Stand at the foot of that world's Declaration.
Washington, Livingston, Langdon, she claims them,
It is her right to be proud when she names them,
Proud of that voice in the night as it came,
Tossing the flags of the nations to flame:
> *I am the breath of God.   I am His laughter.*
I am His Liberty.   That is my name.

Flags, in themselves, are but rags that are dyed.
Flags, in that wind, are like nations enskied.
See, how they grapple the night as it rolls
And trample it under like triumphing souls.
Over the city that never knew sleep,
Look at the riotous folds as they leap.
Thousands of tri-colors, laughing for France,
Ripple and whisper and thunder and dance;
Thousands of flags for Great Britain aflame
Answer their sisters in Liberty's name.
Belgium is burning in pride overhead.
Poland is near, and her sunrise is red.
Under and over, and fluttering between,
Italy burgeons in red, white, and green.
See, how they climb like adventurous flowers,

Over the tops of the terrible towers. . . .
There, in the darkness, the glories are mated.
There, in the darkness, a world is created.
There, in this Pentecost, streaming on high,
There, with a glory of stars in the sky.
There the broad flag of our union and liberty
Rides the proud night-wind and tyrannies die.

THE GARDEN OF PEACE

PEACE?   Is it peace at last?
In the grey-walled garden I hear,
Under the rambling golden-crusted roofs,
The beautiful lichened roofs of Horsham stone,
Only the whisper of leaves,
And a blackbird calling.
Peace, and a blackbird calling his bright-eyed mate;
Peace, and those young, those beautiful hosts of the dead,
So quietly sleeping, under the mantle of June;
Peace, and the years of agony all gone by
As if they had never been!
Is it peace at last?

The blackbird flutters away in a rain of petals.
Under the open window a land-girl passes,
Dainty as Rosalind, in her short white smock,
Corduroy breeches and leggings and soft slouch-hat.
She swings her basket, happy in her new freedom,
And passes, humming a song.

She walks through the grey-walled garden,
Watched by the formal shadows of older days,
The shadows her grandam knew, in poplin gowns
And arched sun-bonnets, like old dry crumpled rose-leaves.
They peep at her, under the dark green peacock-yew.
They smile at her, under the big black mulberry boughs.
With an exquisite self-reproach in their wise old eyes,
They whisper together, like dim grey lavender blooms,
Glad of her careless joy, *"She will not grow old,*
Never grow old, as we did."

See, she pauses,
Now, at the grey sun-dial,

344

Whose legend, lichen-encrusted in rusty gold,
Lux et Umbra vicissim,
Semper Amor,
Was read by those that rustled in hooped brocades,
Admiringly round it, once, in its clear-cut youth.

A moment, there, she pauses, youthful, slim.
She reads the hour on its old dim dreaming face,
Half mellowed by time, half eaten away by time.
She does not see the shadows around it now.
It is only the hour she sees.
The rest is a dazzle of hollyhock shadows and sun.

She goes her way.
She darkens the deep old arch in the clipped yew-hedge,
And vanishes, leaving an arch of light behind her.
Lux et Umbra vicissim,
Semper Amor!
Is it all a dream,
This unbelievable peace?
The sunlight sleeps on the boughs.
The bees are drowsy with heat.

Tap-tap, tap-tap!
Ah no, not the telegraph giving the range to the guns;
It is only a dreamer, knocking the ash from his pipe,
On the warm grey crumbling wall at the garden's end,
Where the crucified fruit-trees bask,
Those beautiful fruit-trees,
Fastened, with arms outspread.

Tap-tap, tap-tap!
Now all is quiet again.   There is only a whisper,
Calm as the whisper of grass,
On a sunlit grave.

Is it peace?   Was it only a dream
That, under this beautiful cloak of the sunlit world,
We saw a blood-red gash in the clean sweet skin,
And the flesh rolled back by the hand of the surgeon, War;
And there, within,
Alive and crawling,
The cancer;
The monstrous cancer of hate,

With octopus arms,
Gripping the blood-red walls of its tortured hell?
Is it peace at last?

Oh, which is the dream?   I hear
Now, in the grey-walled garden,
Only the whisper of leaves;
And now, on the southerly wall,
The dreamer, knocking the ash from his pipe again,
Tap-tap, tap-tap;
And the cry of a bird to his mate.

THE PACT

THEY have no pact to sign—our peaceful dead.
   Pacts are for trembling hands, and heads grown grey.
Ten million graves record what youth has said,
   And cannot now un-say.

They have no pact to sign—our quiet dead
   Whose eyes in that eternal peace are drowned.
Age doubts, and wakes, and asks if night be fled;
   But youth sleeps sound.

They have no pact to sign—our faithful dead.
   Theirs was a deeper pledge, unseen, unheard,
Sealed in the dark; not written; sealed with red;
   And they will keep their word.

They have no pact to sign—our happy dead.
   But if—O God—if *we* should sign in vain,
With dreadful eyes, out of each narrow bed,
   Our dead will rise again.

THE LOST BATTLE

IT is not over yet—the fight
   Where those immortal dreamers failed.
They stormed the citadels of night
   And the night praised them—and prevailed.
So long ago the cause was lost
   We scarce distinguish friend from foe;

But—if the dead can help it most—
    The armies of the dead will grow.

The world has all our banners now,
    And filched our watchwords for its own.
The world has crowned the "rebel's" brow
    And millions crowd his lordly throne.
The masks have altered.   Names are names;
    They praise the "truth" that is not true.
The "rebel" that the world acclaims
    Is not the rebel Shelley knew.

We may not build that Commonweal.
    We may not reach the goal we set.
But there's a flag they dare not steal.
    Forward!   It is not over yet.
We shall be dust and under dust
    Before we end that ancient wrong;
But here's a sword that cannot rust,
    And where's the death can touch a song?

So, when our bodies rot in earth
    The singing souls that once were ours,
Weaponed with light and helmed with mirth,
    Shall front the kingdoms and the powers.
The ancient lie is on its throne,
    And half the living still forget;
But, since the dead are all our own,
    Courage, it is not over yet.

THE ESCAPE OF OLD GREY SQUIRREL

OLD GREY SQUIRREL might have been
    Almost anything—
Might have been a soldier, sailor,
    Tinker, tailor,
(Never a beggar-man, though, nor thief),
Might have been, perhaps, a king,
Or an Indian chief.

He remained a City clerk
    Doubled on a great high stool,
Totting up, from dawn to dark,
    Figures, figures, figures, figures,

Red ink, black ink, double rule,
Tot-tot-totting with his pen,
Up and down and round again—
    Curious Old Grey Squirrel.

No one ever really knew
    What he did at night,
In his room so near the roof,
    Up those steep and narrow stairs
Old Grey Squirrel wasn't quite
    The same as other men.
What he said was always true;
    He was like a little child
    In a thousand things.
Something shy and delicate,
Cold and grave and undefiled,
    Seemed to keep him quite aloof.
You could never call him lonely,
    Though he lived with memory there.

When he knelt beside his bed
    He had nothing much to say
But the simplest little prayer
    Learned in childhood, long ago,
And he didn't know or care
    Whether Calvinists might call it
Praying for the dead.

Father, mother, sister, brother,—
    Memories clear as evening bells;
Yes, the very sort of thing
    All your clever little scribblers
Love to satirize and sting,
So let's talk of something else.
    He collected stamps, you know,
Commonplace Old Squirrel.

Ah, but could you see him there,
    When the day's grey work was done,
Poring over his new stamps
    With that wise old air;
Looking up the curious places
    In his tattered atlas, too—
Lands of jungle and of sun,
Ivory tusks and dusky faces,

Whence his latest treasure flew
Like a tropic moth, he thought,
    To flutter round his dying lamp. . . .

    Visions are not bought and sold;
But, when the foreign mail came in
    Bringing his employers news
Of copper, sulphide, zinc and tin
    (And the red resultant gold),
Envelopes were thrown away,
    So, of course, one clearly sees
He could pick, and he could choose,
    Having, as he used to say,
"Very great advantages."
    Rarities could not be bought.
Bus fares don't leave much for spending
    On a flight to Zipangu.

All the same, one never knew.
    All things come to those who wait—
Isles of palm in rose and blue,
India, China and Peru,
    And the Golden Gate.

So he'd turn his treasures over—
    Mauve and crimson, buff and cream—
Every stamp an elfin window
    Opening on a boy's lost dream.
"Curious, curious, that's Jamaica,
    That's Hongkong (the two-penny red),
I've no doubt they are well worth seeing,
    Well worth seeing," Old Squirrel said.

"*Curious*"—curious was his word—
    Old Grey Squirrel remembered a day
Sitting alone in a whispering fir-wood
(This was in boyhood before they caught him)
    Writing a story of far Cathay,
A tale that his friends would think absurd
But would make him famous when he was dead.
"*Curious*"—thinking of all those years,
    All those dreams that had drifted away—
Once, he had thought—but the years had taught him,
Taught him better, and bowed his head.

"*Curious*"—memory clings and lingers—
    Clings—the smell of the fir-wood—clings. . . .
Through his wrinkled ink-stained fingers,
    "*Curious, curious*," trickled the tears,
Curious Old Grey Squirrel.

No, you'd hardly call it weeping.
    Old Grey Squirrel could not weep.
Head on arm, he might have been
    Sleeping; but he did not know.
Most of us are sound asleep;
    And, that Christmas Eve, it seems,
He awoke, at last, from dreams.
    Gently as a woman's hand
Something touched him on the brow,
And he woke, in that strange land—
    Where he lives for ever now.

All things come to those who wait—
    Palms against a deeper blue,
    Far Cathay and Zipangu,
And the Golden Gate.

A NEW MADRIGAL

(It is supposed that Shadow-of-a-Leaf uses the word "clear" in a more ancient sense
of "beautiful.")

As along a dark pine-bough, in slender white mystery
    The moon lay to listen, above the thick fern,
In a deep dreaming wood that is older than history
    I heard a lad sing, and I stilled me to learn;
So rarely he lilted his long-forgot litany,—
    Fall, April; fall, April, in dew on our dearth!
Bring balm, and bring poppy, bring deep sleepy dittany
    For Marian, our clear May, so long laid in earth.

Then I drew back the branches.   I saw him that chanted it.
    I saw his fool's bauble.   I knew his old grief.
I knew that old greenwood and the shadow that haunted it,—
    My fool, my lost jester, my *Shadow-of-a-Leaf!*
And "why," I said, "why, all this while, have you left me so
    Luckless in melody, lonely in mirth?"
"Oh, why," he sang, "why has this world then bereft me so
    Soon of my Marian, so long laid in earth?

"In the years that are gone," he said, "love was more fortunate.
  Grief was our minstrel of things that endure.
Now, ashes and dust and this world grow importunate.
  Time has no sorrow that time cannot cure.
Once, we could lose, and the loss was worth cherishing.
  Now, we may win, but, O, where is the worth?
Memory and true love," he whispered, "are perishing,
  With Marian, our clear May, so long laid in earth."

"Ah, no!" I said, "no!   Since we grieve for our grief again,
  Touch the old strings!   Let us try the old stave!
And memory may wake, like my *Shadow-of-a-Leaf* again,
  Singing of hope, in the dark, by a grave."
So we sang it together—that long-forgot litany:—
  Fall, April; fall, April; bring new grief to birth.
Bring wild herb of grace, and bring deep healing dittany,
  For Marian, our clear May, so long laid in earth.

MEMORIES OF THE PACIFIC COAST

I KNOW a sunset shore
  Where warm keen incense on the sea-wind blows,
And dim blue ranches (while these March winds roar)
  Drown to the roofs in heliotrope and rose;

Deserts of lost delight,
  Cactus and palm and earth of thirsty gold,
Dark purple blooms round eaves of sun-washed white
  And that Hesperian fruit men sought of old.

The exquisite drought of love
  Throbs in that land, drought that forgoes the dew
And all its life-springs, that the boughs above
  May bear the fruits for which it thirsts anew.

And those pure mountains rise
  Behind it, shutting our sad world away,
With shadowy facets where the sunset dies,
  And cliffs like amethyst at the close of day.

An arm's length off they seem
  At dawn, among the sage-brush; but, at noon,
Their angel trails wind upward like a dream,
  And their bright crests grow distant as the moon.

351

All day, from peaks of snow,
　　The dry ravines refresh their tawny drought,
Till, on the grey-green foot-hills, far below,
　　Like clusters of white grapes the lamps come out.

Then, breaths of orange-bloom
　　Drift over hushed white ranches on the plain,
And spires of eucalyptus cast their gloom
　　On brown adobe cloisters of old Spain.

There, green-tressed pepper grows,
　　In willowy trees that drop red tassels down,
And carpet the brown road with tints of rose
　　Between the palms that aisle the moon-white town.

　．　　．　　．　　．　　．　　．　　．　　．　　．　　．

Oh, to be wandering there,
　　Under the palm-trees, on that sunset shore,
Where the waves break in song, and the bright air
　　Is crystal-clean, and peace is ours once more.

There the lost wonder dwells,
　　Beauty, reborn in whiteness from the foam;
There Youth returns with all its magic spells,
　　And the heart finds its long-forgotten home.

There, in that setting sun,
　　On soft white sand the big slow breaker falls.
There brood the huts where West and East are one,
　　And the strange air runs wild with elfin calls.

There, gazing far away,
　　Those brown-legged fisher-folk, with almond eyes,
Crouch by their nets, and through the rose-tinged spray
　　See their own Orient in those deepening skies.

Through fringes of the West,
　　They see the teeming East, beyond Japan,
Mother of races that, in age-long quest,
　　Have rounded earth, but end where they began;

End in the strange recall
　　To that far childhood, that faint flowering past,
Where some dear shade, loved, lost, the first of all,
　　Opens the door to their dim home at last.

Home,—home! Where is that land,
  Beyond the bounds of earth, the old hungering cry
Aches in the soul, drives us from all we planned,
  And sets our sail to seek another sky.

RIDDLES OF MERLIN

I

As I was walking
  Alone by the sea,
"What is that whisper?"
  Said Merlin to me.
"Only," I answered,
  "The sigh of the wave"—
"Oh, no," replied Merlin,
  " 'Tis the grass on your grave."

As I lay dreaming
  In churchyard ground
"Listen," said Merlin,
  "What is that sound?"
"The green grass is growing,"
  I answered; but he
Chuckled, *"Oh, no!*
  'Tis the sound of the sea."

As I went homeward
  At dusk by the shore,
"What is that crimson?"
  Said Merlin once more.
"Only the sun," I said.
  "Sinking to rest"—
"Sunset for East," he said,
  "Sunrise for West."

II

Tell me, Merlin,—It is I
  Who call thee, after a thousand Springs—
Tell me by what wizardry
  The white foam wakes in whiter wings
Where surf and sea-gulls toss and cry
Like sister-flakes, as they mount and fly,

Flakes that the great sea flings on high,
  To kiss each other and die.

Tell me, Merlin, tell me why
  These delicate things that feast on flowers,
Red Admiral, brown fritillary,
Sister the flowers, yet sail the sky,
Frail ships that cut their cables, yet still fly
  The colours we know them by.

Tell me, Merlin, tell me why,
The sea's chaotic colour grows
Into these rainbow fish whose Tyrian dye
In scales of gold and green reply
To blue-striped mackerel waves, to kelp-brown caves,
And deep-sea blooms of gold and green and rose;
Why colours that the sea at random throws
Were ordered into this living harmony,
This little world, no bigger than the hand,
Gliding over the raw tints whence it came,
This opal-bellied patch of sand,
That floats above the sand, or darts a flame
Through woods of crimson lake, and flowers without a name.
See all their tints around its body strewn
In planetary order.   Sun, moon, star,
Are not more constant to their tune
Than those light scales of colour are;
Where each repeats the glory of his neighbour,
In the same pattern, with the same delight,
As if, without the artist's labour,
The palette of rich Chaos and old Night
Should spawn a myriad pictures, every line
True to the lost Designer's lost design.

Tell me, Merlin, for what eye
Gathers and grows this cosmic harmony?
Can sea-gulls feed, or fishes brood
On music fit for angels' food?
Did Nescience this delight create
To lure the conger to his mate?
If this be all that Science tells
The narrowest church may peal its bells,
And Merlin work new miracles;
While every dreamer, even as I,
May wonder on, until he die.

IMMORTAL SAILS

Now, in a breath, we'll burst those gates of gold,
   And ransack heaven before our moment fails.
Now, in a breath, before we, too, grow old,
   We'll mount and sing and spread immortal sails.

It is not time that makes eternity.
   Love and an hour may quite out-span the years,
And give us more to hear and more to see
   Than life can wash away with all its tears.

Dear, when we part, at last, that sunset sky
   Shall not be touched with deeper hues than this;
But we shall ride the lightning ere we die
   And seize our brief infinitude of bliss,

With time to spare for all that heaven can tell,
While eyes meet eyes, and look their last farewell.

MOUNTAIN LAUREL

I HAVE been wandering in the lonely valleys,
   Where mountain laurel grows
And, in among the rocks, and the tall dark pine-trees
   The foam of the young bloom flows,
In a riot of dawn-coloured stars, all drenched with the dew-fall,
   And musical with the bee,
Let the fog-bound cities over their dead wreaths quarrel.
   Wild laurel for me!

Wild laurel—mountain laurel—
   Bright as the breast of a cloud at break of day,
White-flowering laurel, wild mountain laurel,
   Rose-dappled snowdrifts, warm with the honey of May!
On the happy hill-sides, in the green valleys of Connecticut,
   Where the trout-streams go carolling to the sea,
I have laughed with the lovers of song and heard them singing
   "Wild laurel for me!"

Far, far away is the throng that has never known beauty,
   Or looked upon unstained skies.
Did they think that my songs would scramble for withered bay-leaves
   In the streets where the brown fog lies?

They never have seen their wings, then, beating westward,
    To the heights where song is free,
To the hills where the laurel is drenched with the dawn's own colours,
    Wild laurel for me!

Wild laurel—mountain laurel—
    Where Robert o' Lincoln sings in the dawn and the dew,
White-flowering laurel—wild mountain laurel
    Where song springs fresh from the heart, and the heart is true!
They have gathered the sheep to their fold, but where is the eagle?
    They have bridled their steeds, but when have they tamed the sea,
They have caged the wings, but never the heart of the singer,
    "Wild laurel for me!"

If I never should find you again, O, lost companions,
    When the rose-red month begins,
With the wood-smoke curling blue by the Indian river,
    And the sound of the violins,
In dreams the breath of your green glens would still haunt me,
    Where night and her stars, drawing down on blossom and tree,
Turn earth to heaven, and whisper their love till daybreak.
    Wild laurel for me!

Wild laurel—mountain laurel—
    O, mount again, wild wings, to the stainless blue,
White-flowering laurel, wild mountain laurel,
    And all the glory of song that the young heart knew.
I have lived. I have loved. I have sung in the happy valleys,
    Where the trout-streams go carolling to the sea,
I have met the lovers of song in the sunset bringing
    "Wild laurel for me!"

THE ELFIN ARTIST

In a glade of an elfin forest
    When Sussex was Eden-new,
I came on an elvish painter
    And watched as his picture grew.
A harebell nodded beside him.
    He dipt his brush in its dew.

And it might be the wild thyme round him
    That shone in that dark strange ring;
But his brushes were bees' antennæ,

356

His knife was a wasp's blue sting;
And his gorgeous exquisite palette
  Was a butterfly's fan-shaped wing.

And he mingled its powdery colours
  And painted the lights that pass,
On a delicate cobweb canvas
  That gleamed like a magic glass,
And bloomed like a banner of elf-land,
  Between two stalks of grass;

Till it shone like an angel's feather
  With sky-born opal and rose,
And gold from the foot of the rainbow,
  And colours that no man knows;
And I laughed in the sweet May weather,
  Because of the themes he chose.

For he painted the things that matter,
  The tints that we all pass by,
Like the little blue wreaths of incense
  That the wild thyme breathes to the sky;
Or the first white bud of the hawthorn,
  And the light in a blackbird's eye;

And the shadows on soft white cloud-peaks
  That carolling skylarks throw,
Dark dots on the slumbering splendours
  That under the wild wings flow,
Wee shadows like violets trembling
  On the unseen breasts of snow,

With petals too lovely for colour
  That shake to the rapturous wings,
And grow as the bird draws near them,
  And die as he mounts and sings;—
Ah, only those exquisite brushes
  Could paint those exquisite things.

THE MATIN-SONG OF FRIAR TUCK

I

If souls could sing to heaven's high King
  As blackbirds pipe on earth,

357

How those delicious courts would ring
  With gusts of lovely mirth!
What white-robed throng could lift a song
  So mellow with righteous glee
As this brown bird that all day long
  Delights my hawthorn tree.
      Hark!   That's the thrush
       With speckled breast
      From yon white bush,—
       Chaunting his best,—
    Te Deum!   Te Deum laudamus!

II

If earthly dreams be touched with gleams
  Of Paradisal air,
Some wings, perchance, of earth may glance
  Around our slumbers there;
Some breaths of may will drift our way
  With scents of leaf and loam;
Some whistling bird at dawn be heard
  From those old woods of home.
      How souls would listen
       In those high places!
      What tears would glisten
       On glorious faces,—
    Te Deum!   Te Deum laudamus!

III

All, still as frost, the heavenly host
  Would touch no golden wire,
If but one cry of joy went by
  From this, our greenwood choir:
Then, at one flash of daffodils,
  Where those sweet cries resound,
Their heaven would seem the shadowy dream
  And earth the holy ground;
      Ay, angels then
       Would jostle and clamour
      To hear the wren
       And the yellow-hammer,—
    Te Deum!   Te Deum laudamus!

For birds by nature must enjoy
    The Lord their God for aye;
Therefore their music cannot cloy
    As lutes of angels may.
Break, wild-flowers, through the golden floor
    Where long-faced martyrs sing.
Then, let the carolling sky-lark soar
    And flood their Heaven with Spring.
        O, what a pæan
            Of joy would shake
        The empyrean.
            Awake!   Awake!—
    Te Deum!   Te Deum laudamus!

V

No king or priest shall mar my feast
    Wherever my soul may range.
I have no fear for heaven's good cheer
    Unless our Master change.
But, when death's night is dying away,
    If I might choose my bliss,
My love should say, at break of day,
    With her first waking kiss:—
        "Hark!   That's the thrush
            With speckled breast,
        From yon white bush
            Chaunting his best,—
    Te Deum!   Te Deum laudamus!

EARTH AND HER BIRDS

(SHADOW-OF-A-LEAF SINGS)

BRAVE birds that climb those blue
    Dawn-tinted towers,
With notes like showers of dew
    From elf-tossed flowers,
Shake your mad wings in mirth,
    Betray, betray
    The secret thoughts of May,
That heaven, once more, may marry our wild earth.

Dark gipsy, she would dance
  Unmated still,
Challenging, glance for glance,
  Her lord's high will,
But that her thoughts take wing
  While she lies sleeping;
  And, into glory leaping,
Like birds, at sunrise, to her bride-groom sing.

See how with cheeks aglow
  And lips apart,
While warm winds, murmuring low
  Lay bare her heart,
She dreams that she can hide
  Its rosy light
  In ferns and flowers this night,
And swim like Dian through this hawthorn-tide.

Then shame her, lavrocks, shame her,
  At break of day,
That heaven may trap and tame her
  This mad sweet May.
Let all your feathered choir
  Leave those warm nests
  Between her dawn-flushed breasts,
And soar to heaven, singing her young desire.

PETER QUINCE

PETER QUINCE was nine years old,
When he see'd what never was told.

When he crossed the fairy fern,
Peter had no more to learn.

Just as the day began to die,
He see'd 'em rustling on the sky;

Ferns, like small green finger-prints
Pressed against them rosy tints,

Mother-o'-pearl and opal tinges
Dying along their whispering fringes,

Every colour, as it died,
Beaconing, *Come, to the other side.*

Up he crept, by the shrew-mouse track,
A robin chirped, *You woant come back.*

Through the ferns he crept to look.
.   .   .   .

There he found a gurt wide book;

Much too big for a child to hold.
Its clasps were made of sunset gold.

It smelled like old ship's timbers do.
He began to read it through.

All the magic pictures burned,
Like stained windows, as he turned

Page by big black-lettered page,
Thick as cream, and ripe with age

There he read, till all grew dim.
Then green glow-worms lighted him.

There he read till he forgot
All that ever his teachers taught.
.   .   .   .

Someone, old as the moon, crept back,
Late that night by the shrew-mouse track.

Someone, taller maybe, by an inch.
Boys grow fast.   He'll do at a pinch.

Only, folks that know'd him claim
Peter's wits were never the same.

Ev'ryone said that Peter Quince
H'aint been never the same child since.

Now he'd sit, in a trance, for hours,
Talkin' softly to bees and flowers.

Now, in the ingle-nook at night,
Turn his face from the candle-light;

Till, as you thought him fast asleep,
You'd see his eyes were wide and deep;

And, in their wild magic glow,
Rainbow colours 'ud come and go.

Dame Quince never could wholly wake him,
So they say, tho' she'd call and shake him.

He sat dreaming.   He sat bowed
In a white sleep, like a cloud.

Over his dim face at whiles,
Flickered liddle elvish smiles.

.   .   .   .   .   •   •

Once, the robin at the pane,
Tried to chirp the truth again.

Peter Quince has crossed the fern.
Peter Quince will not return.

Drive the changeling from your chair!
That's not Peter dreaming there.

Peter's crossed the fern to look.
Peter's found the magic book.

Ah, Dame Quince was busy sobbin',
So she couldn't hear poor Robin.

And the changeling, in a dream,
Supped that night, on pears and cream.

Night by night, he cleared his platter;
And—from moon to moon—grew fatter;

Mostly dumb, or muttering dimly
When the smoke blew down the chimley,

Peter's turned another page,
I have almost earned my wage.

Then the good dame's eyelids shone.

.   .   .   .

This was many a year agone.
Peter Quince is reading on.

THE SUSSEX SAILOR

O, ONCE, by Cuckmere Haven,
  I heard a sailor sing
Of shores beyond the sunset,
  And lands of lasting spring,
Of blue lagoons and palm trees
  And isles where all was young;
But this was ever the burden
  Of every note he sung:—

O, have you seen my true love
  A-walking in that land?
Or have you seen her footprints
  Upon that shining sand?
Beneath the happy palm trees,
  By Eden whispers fanned . . .
O, have you seen my true love
  A-walking in that land?

And, once in San Diego,
  I heard him sing again,
Of Amberley, Rye, and Bramber,
  And Brede and Fairlight Glen:
The nestling hills of Sussex,
  The russet-roofed elfin towns,
And the skylark up in a high wind,
  Carolling over the downs.

From Warbleton to Wild Brook
  When May is white as foam,
O, have you seen my dearling
  On any hills of home?
Or have you seen her shining,
  Or only touched her hand,
O, have you seen my true love
  A-walking in that land?

363

And, once again, by Cowfold,
  I heard him singing low,
'Tis not the leagues of ocean
  That hide the hills I know.
The May that shines before me
  Has made a ghost of May.
The valleys that I would walk in
  Are twenty years away.

Ah, have you seen my true love
  A-walking in that land . . .
On hills that I remember,
  In valleys I understand,
So far beyond the sunset,
  So very close at hand,—
O, have you seen my true love
  In that immortal land?

THE LAST OF THE SNOW

I

Now, feathered with snow, the fir-tree's beautiful sprays
Pensively nod in the sun, while young April delays,—
  "Yes—yes—*we* know
  How briefly our hearts with the light of the may-tide shall glow,
Ere the darkness of winter return; and the green boughs and gold
  Shall all be choked down by the snow
    In the end, as of old.

II

"Yes, white snow, you will have your revenge for the warm dreams that
      stir
In the sap of my boughs," said the wise old heart of the fir.
  "None the less you shall go!
  For my brother, the hawthorn, has dreamed of a new kind of snow,
With honey for bees in its heart; and it's worth it, I say,
  Though you'll freeze us to death, as we know,
    At the end of our day.

III

"There's a glory in fighting for dreams that are doomed to defeat;
So perhaps it's because you'll return that the bloom smells so sweet.
  There's our victory, too,

364

Which you cannot prevent, for we're stronger in one thing than you,
Since we win the one prize that's worth winning, win heaven on earth;
  And, if truth remain true,
    Find in death our re-birth."

IV

So, feathered with snow, the beautiful boughs of the fir
Dipped to the thaw of the world as the spring touched them there;
  And the lane, like a brook,
    Sang in the sun, and the pretty girls came out to look,
Saying, "Spring is begun!   Look, look, how the snow runs away!
It is only the snow on the fir-tree that seems to delay!"

V

"That's true," said the fir, "and if only the wind of the spring
Would whisper a tale that I know, or a black-bird sing,
I think I might shake off this ghost!"—
"Oh, pouf!   If that's all,"
Chuckled the spring-wind, "Listen!   I think that's the call
Of a black-bird!   And what d'you suppose is that other faint sound—
Snow melting?—leaves budding?—or young lovers whispering all round,
In forest and meadow and city?   Oh, yes, they've begun!
Wake up!   Tell that spectre to go!"
And the fir-tree listened and shook, and the last of the snow
Slipped from its hold and plumped down on the daffodil bed;
And the green-plumed branches danced for delight in the sun;
And a black-bird alighted, at once, on the bright wet boughs,
And called to his bright-eyed mate on the roof of the shed,
"O, see what a beautiful hiding-place for our house!"
  —"That's better," the fir-tree said.

A SPRING HAT

Dear Poet of the Sabine farm,
  Whose themes, not all of blood and tears,
Beneath your happy trees could charm
  Your lovers for two thousand years,
You would not blame a modern pen
For touching love with mirth again.

For Dick and Joan went up to town,
  And Joan must choose a hat for Spring;
And, though Melpomene may frown,

There is no jollier theme to sing.
Younger and happier than they knew
Into the faëry shop they flew.

Then she began to try them on.
    The first one had a golden feather,
That like the godling's arrow shone
    When first he pierced their hearts together.
"Now, what d'you think of that," she said,
Tilting it on her dainty head.

The next one, like a violet wreath
    Nestled around her fragrant hair;
But O, her shining eyes beneath,
    The while she tipped it here and there;
And said, with eager face aglow,
"How do you like it? So? Or so?"

The next one was an elfin crown.
    She wore it as Titania might.
She gave the glass a smile, a frown,
    And murmured, "No. It isn't *quite!*
I think that other one, the blue,—
Or no, perhaps the green,—don't you?"

Maidens, the haughtiest ever seen,
    Like willing slaves around her moved.
They tried the blue. They tried the green.
    They trembled when she disapproved;
And, when she waved the pink away,
They tried the lilac and the grey.

She perched the black upon her nose.
    She hid an eye behind the blue.
She set the orange and the rose,
    With subtle artistry, askew.
She stripped the windows of their store,
Then sent her slaves to search for more.

And while they searched . . . *O, happy face,*
    Against the dark eternal night,
If I could paint you with the grace
    The Master used! . . . A lovely light
Shone in the laughter of her eyes.
They glowed with sudden sweet surprise,

She saw—the very hat for Spring!
   The first one, with the golden feather,
Dropt from a laughing angel's wing
   Through skies of Paradisal weather.
She pinned it on her dainty head.
"This is the very thing," she said.

"Now, don't you like me?"—"Yes, I do,"
   Said Dick.   The slaves were far away.
"Your eyes have never looked so blue."
   "I mean the hat," she tried to say.
He kissed her. "Wait a bit," said she.
"There's just one more I want to see."

Who knows but, when the uproar dies,
   And mightier songs are dead and gone,
Perhaps her laughing face may rise
   Out of the darkness and live on,
If one—who loves—should read and say
This also happened, in that day.

THE NEW DUCKLING

"I WANT to be new," said the duckling.
   "O, ho!" said the wise old owl,
While the guinea-hen cluttered off chuckling
   To tell all the rest of the fowl.

"I should like a more elegant figure,"
   That child of a duck went on.
"I should like to grow bigger and bigger,
   Until I could swallow a swan.

"I *won't* be the bond slave of habit,
   I *won't* have these webs on my toes.
I want to run round like a rabbit,
   A rabbit as red as a rose.

"I *don't* want to waddle like mother,
   Or quack like my silly old dad.
I want to be utterly other,
   And *frightfully* modern and mad."

"Do you know," said the turkey, "you're quacking!
　　There's a fox creeping up thro' the rye;
And, if you're not utterly lacking,
　　You'll make for that duck-pond.　Good-bye!"

But the duckling was perky as perky.
　　"Take care of your stuffing!" he called.
(This was horribly rude to a turkey!)
　　"But you aren't a real turkey," he bawled.

"You're an Early-Victorian Sparrow,
　　A ball of conventional fluff!
Do you think *I* believe in that narrow,
Banal, hypocritical stuff?

I shall break all your fetters and tethers,
　　And rock my dear Reynard to sleep.
I shall pillow his head on my feathers
　　And give him the best ones to keep.

Now the curious end of this fable,
　　So far as the rest ascertained,
Though they searched from the barn to the stable,
　　Was that *only his feathers remained.*

So he *wasn't* the bond slave of habit,
　　And he *didn't* have webs on his toes;
And *perhaps* he runs round like a rabbit,
　　A rabbit as red as a rose.

THE RIVER OF STARS

(A TALE OF NIAGARA)

The lights of a hundred cities are fed by its midnight power.
Their wheels are moved by its thunder.　But they, too, have their hour.
The tale of the Indian lovers, a cry from the years that are flown,
　　While the river of stars is rolling,
　　Rolling away to the darkness,
Abides with the power in the midnight, where love may find its own.

She watched from the Huron tents till the first star shook in the air.
The sweet pine scented her fawn-skins, and breathed from her braided
　　　　hair.

368

Her crown was of milk-white blood-root, because of the tryst she would
         keep,
      Beyond the river of beauty
         That drifted away in the darkness
Drawing the sunset thro' lilies, with eyes like stars, to the deep.

He watched, like a tall young wood-god, from the red pine that she
         named;
But not for the peril behind him, where the eyes of the Mohawks flamed.
Eagle-plumed he stood.   But his heart was hunting afar,
      Where the river of longing whispered . . .
         And one swift shaft from the darkness
Felled him, her name in his death-cry, his eyes on the sunset star.

   .   .   .   .

She stole from the river and listened.   The moon on her wet skin shone.
As a silver birch in a pine-wood, her beauty flashed and was gone.
There was no wave in the forest.   The dark arms closed her round.
      But the river of life went flowing,
         Flowing away to the darkness,
For her breast grew red with his heart's blood, in a night where the stars
         are drowned.

Teach me, O my lover, as you taught me of love in a day,
Teach me of death, and for ever, and set my feet on the way,
To the land of the happy shadows, the land where you are flown.
      —And the river of death went weeping,
         Weeping away to the darkness.—
Is the hunting good, my lover, so good that you hunt alone?

She rose to her feet like a shadow.   She sent a cry thro' the night,
Sa-sa-kuon, the death-whoop, that tells of triumph in fight.
It broke from the bell of her mouth like the cry of a wounded bird,
      But the river of agony swelled it
         And swept it along to the darkness,
And the Mohawks, couched in the darkness, leapt to their feet as they
         heard.

Close as the ring of the clouds that menace the moon with death,
At once they circled her round.   Her bright breast panted for breath.
With only her own wild glory keeping the wolves at bay,
      While the river of parting whispered,
         Whispered away to the darkness,
She looked in their eyes for a moment, and strove for a word to say.

Teach me, O my lover!—She set her foot on the dead.
She laughed on the painted faces with their rings of yellow and red,—
I thank you, wolves of the Mohawk, for a woman's hands might fail.—
    —And the river of vengeance chuckled,
        Chuckled away to the darkness,—
But ye have killed where I hunted.   I have come to the end of my trail.

I thank you, braves of the Mohawk, who laid this thief at my feet.
He tore my heart out living, and tossed it his dogs to eat.
Ye have taught him of death in a moment, as he taught me of love in a
        day.
    —And the river of passion deepened,
        Deepened and rushed to the darkness.—
And yet may a woman requite you, and set your feet on the way.

For the woman that spits in my face, and the shaven heads that gibe,
This night shall a woman show you the tents of the Huron tribe.
They are lodged in a deep valley.   With all things good it abounds.
      Where the red-eyed, green-mooned river
        Glides like a snake to the darkness,
I will show you a valley, Mohawks, like the Happy Hunting Grounds.

Follow!   They chuckled, and followed like wolves to the glittering
        stream.
Shadows obeying a shadow, they launched their canoes in a dream.
Alone, in the first, with the blood on her breast, and her milk-white
        crown,
      She stood.   She smiled at them, *Follow,*
        Then urged her canoe to the darkness,
And, silently flashing their paddles, the Mohawks followed her down.

   .   .   .   .

And now—as they slid thro' the pine-woods with their peaks of midnight
        blue,
She heard, in the broadening distance, the deep sound that she knew,
A mutter of steady thunder that grew as they glanced along;
      But ever she glanced before them
        And danced away to the darkness,
And or ever they heard it rightly, she raised her voice in a song:—

The wind from the Isles of the Blesséd, it blows across the foam.
It sings in the flowing maples of the land that was my home.
Where the moose is a morning's hunt, and the buffalo feeds from the
        hand.—

And the river of mockery broadened,
   Broadened and rolled to the darkness—
And the green maize lifts its feathers, and laughs the snow from the land.

The river broadened and quickened.   There was nought but river and
         sky.
The shores were lost in the darkness.   She laughed and lifted a cry:
Follow me!   Sa-sa-kuon!   Swifter and swifter they swirled—
      And the flood of their doom went flying,
         Flying away to the darkness,
Follow me, follow me, Mohawks, ye are shooting the edge of the world.

They struggled like snakes to return.   Like straws they were whirled on
         her track.
For the whole flood swooped to that edge where the unplumbed night
         dropt black,
The whole flood dropt to a thunder in an unplumbed hell beneath,
      And over the gulf of the thunder
         A mountain of spray from the darkness
Rose and stood in the heavens, like a shrouded image of death.

She rushed like a star before them.   The moon on her glorying shone.
Teach me, O my lover,—her cry flashed out and was gone.
A moment they battled behind her.   They lashed with their paddles
         and lunged;
      Then the Mohawks, turning their faces
         Like a blood-stained cloud to the darkness,
Over the edge of Niagara swept together and plunged.

And the lights of a hundred cities are fed by the ancient power;
But a cry returns with the midnight; for they, too, have their hour.
Teach me, O my lover, as you taught me of love in a day,
      —While the river of stars is rolling,
         Rolling away to the darkness,—
Teach me of death, and for ever, and set my feet on the way!

THE MAY-TREE

THE May-tree on the hill
   Stands in the night
So fragrant and so still,
   So dusky white,

That, stealing from the wood
    In that sweet air,
You'd think Diana stood
    Before you there.

If it be so, her bloom
    Trembles with bliss.
She waits across the gloom
    Her shepherd's kiss.

Touch her.   A bird will start
    From those pure snows,
The dark, the fluttering heart
    Endymion knows.

AFTER RAIN

LISTEN!   On sweetening air
    The blackbird growing bold
Flings out, where green boughs glisten,
    Three splashes of wild gold.

Daughter of April, hear;
    And hear, O barefoot boy!
That carol of wild sweet water
    Has washed the world with joy.

Glisten, O fragrant earth
    Assoiled by heaven anew,
And O, ye lovers, listen,
    With eyes that glisten, too.

THE WAGGON

CRIMSON and black on the sky, a waggon of clover
    Slowly goes rumbling over the white chalk road;
And I lie in the golden grass there, wondering why
        So little a thing
    As the jingle and ring of the harness,
        The hot creak of leather,
        The peace of the plodding,
    Should suddenly, stabbingly, make it
        Strange that men die.

Only, perhaps, in the same blue summer weather,
Hundreds of years ago, in this field where I lie,
Cædmon, the Saxon, was caught by the self-same thing:
The serf lying, dark with the sun, on his beautiful **wainload**,
The jingle and clink of the harness,
The hot creak of leather,
The peace of the plodding;
And wondered, O terribly wondered,
That men must die.

A FOREST SONG

Who would be a king
That can sit in the sun and sing?
Nay, I have a kingdom of mine own.
A fallen oak-tree is my throne.
Then, pluck the strings, and tell me true
If Cæsar in his glory knew
The worlds he lost in sun and dew.

Who would be a queen
That sees what my love hath seen,
The blood of little children shed
To make one royal ruby red!
Then, tell me, music, why the great
For quarrelling trumpets abdicate
This quick, this absolute estate.

Nay, who would sing in heaven,
Among the choral Seven
That hears—as Love and I have heard,
The whole sky listening to one bird?
And where's the ruby, tell me where,
Whose crimsons for one breath compare
With this wild rose that all may share?

THE BLINDED SOLDIER TO HIS LOVE

I did not know you then.
I cannot see you now;
But let my hands again
Feel your sweet hair and brow.

Your eyes are grey, I am told,
Your hair a tawny gold.

Yet, if of these I tire,
    I shall not need to stray.
Your eyes shall feed my fire
    With brown or blue for grey;
And your deep hair shall be
As mutable as the sea.

Let forms and colours flow
    Like clouds around a star.
I clasp the soul and know
    How vain those day-dreams are;
Dreams, from these eyes withdrawn
Beyond all hope of dawn.

But what is dawn to me?
    In Love's Arabian night,
What lover cares to see
    The unwelcome morning light?
With you, O sweetest friend,
My night shall never end.

RESURRECTION

WHEN all the altar lights were dead,
    And mockery choked the world's desire;
When every faith on earth had fled,
    A spirit rose on wings of fire.

He rose and sang.   I never heard
    A song of such ecstatic breath;
And, though I caught no throbbing word,
    I knew that he had conquered death.

He sang no comfortable things;
    But as a shaft had pierced him through;
And the dark stain between his wings
    Grew darker as the glory grew.

He sang the agonies of loss;
    Of dumb farewells, and love's last kiss.

He sang in heaven as on a cross,
 A spirit crucified with bliss.

Over these ruined shrines he rose,
 These crumbling graves where all men grope,
Racked by the universal throes,
 And singing the eternal hope.

THE DOUBLE FORTRESS

TIME, wouldst thou hurt us?   Never shall we grow old.
 Break as thou wilt these bodies of blind clay,
Thou canst not touch us here, in our stronghold,
 Where two, made one, laugh all thy powers away.

Though ramparts crumble and rusty gates grow thin,
 And our brave fortress dwine to a hollow shell,
Thou shalt hear heavenly laughter, far within,
 Where, young as Love, two hidden lovers dwell.

We shall go clambering up our twisted stairs
 To watch the moon through rifts in our grey towers.
Thou shalt hear whispers, kisses, and sweet prayers
 Creeping through all our creviced walls like flowers.

Wouldst wreck us, Time?   When thy dull leaguer brings
The last wall down, look heavenward.   We have wings.

THE MESSENGER

AND, in the night, the Spirit came
 And softly smiled, and said—
I am the messenger of God.
 I am the happy dead.

I cannot tell you what I see
 Or whisper what I know;
But through and through your three-walled sleep
 Our shining legions go.

From worlds outside your Time and Space
 (You cannot know how near)
You cannot see the happy face
 That bends above you, dear.

375

I cannot grieve to see your grief
　　More than a mother may
Who stoops above her child to soothe
　　Its midnight fears away.

I have been near you all the while,
　　I watched you, while you slept—
Then morning broke, then morning broke,
　　And I forgot, and wept.

THE ANVIL

STAND like a beaten anvil, when thy dream
　　Is laid upon thee, golden from the fire.
Flinch not, though heavily through that furnace-gleam
　　The black forge-hammers fall on thy desire.

Demoniac giants round thee seem to loom.
　　'Tis but the world-smiths heaving to and fro.
Stand like a beaten anvil.　Take the doom
　　Their ponderous weapons deal thee, blow on blow.

Needful to truth as dew-fall to the flower
　　Is this wild wrath and this implacable scorn.
For every pang, new beauty, and new power,
　　Burning blood-red shall on thy heart be born.

Stand like a beaten anvil.　Let earth's wrong
Beat on that iron and ring back in song.

RAIN AT SUNSET

LUCID arrows of delight, rose-feathered and moon-white,
　　Shoot from an irised bow
Round the fern-fringed wood, making little pools of light
　　Where the wild white violets grow.

Lift up your face, lift up that rain-kissed flower,
　　And show how tears can shine;
Eyes, lips, and hair that change the clinging mist of the shower,
　　By miracle, into wine.

Now, as the cloud passes, in the clear hush after the rain,
  And the green boughs drip with the sky,
Let the whole earth, while the thrush makes merry again,
  Fade into our joy and die.

THE CLEAR MAY

I saw once a clear May, was in a dark garden,
  Lilting for joy to the babe at her breast,
"Lullay, my little one; oh, lullay, my darling;
  Earth is in tumult, but heaven is at rest.

"Herod hath crushed out the grapes of the wine-press.
  Proud ride the emperors to slaughter their fill.
Lullay, my little one; the green leaves are growing;
  Earth is in torment, but the stars are so still!

"Music," said my May to me, "music surroundeth us,
  Whatsoever agonies entangle our feet!
Though the sun die, and the stars leave their courses,
  Heaven moveth round them in a music most sweet.

"Therefore I sing," she said, "I too sing *Magnificat*,
  Caught up, as one voice, in that choir of delight;
For heaven hath stooped down to be clothed with our weakness
  And looked through the eyes of a child in our night."

So darkly she sang, as that bird of old legend,
  The bird whose warm breast was pierced through by a thorn,
Lullay, my little one, oh, lullay, my darling,
  Out of earth's anguish our heaven is reborn.

SHADOW-OF-A-LEAF

Elf-blooded creature, little did he reck
  Of this blind world's delights,
Content to wreathe his legs around his neck
  For warmth on winter nights;
Content to ramble away
Through his deep woods in May;
  Content, alone with Pan, to observe his forest rites.

Or, cutting a dark cross of beauty there
    All out of a hawthorn-tree,
He'd set it up, and whistle to praise and prayer,
    Field-mouse and finch and bee;
And, as the woods grew dim
Brown squirrels knelt with him,
    Paws to blunt nose, and prayed as well as he.

For, all his wits being lost, he was more wise
    Than aught on earthly ground.
Like haunted woodland pools his great dark eyes
    Where the lost stars were drowned,
Saw things afar and near.
'Twas said that he could hear
    The music of the spheres which had no sound.

And so, through many an age and many a clime,
    He strayed on unseen wings;
For he was fey, and knew not space or time,
    Kingdoms or earthly kings.
Clear as a crystal ball
One dew-drop showed him all,—
    Earth and its tribes, and strange translunar things.

But to the world's one May, he made in chief
    His lonely woodland vow,
Praying—as none could pray but Shadow-of-a-Leaf,
    Under that fresh-cut bough
Which with two branches grew,
Dark, dark, in sun and dew,—
    "The world goes maying.   Be this my maypole now!

"Make me a garland, Lady, in thy green aisles
    For this wild rood of may,
And I will make thee another of tears and smiles
    To match thine own, this day.
For every rose thereof
A rose of my heart's love,
    A blood-red rose that shall not waste away.

"For every violet here, a gentle thought
    To worship at thine eyes;
But, most of all, for wildings few have sought,
    And careless looks despise,
For ragged-robins' birth

Here, in a ditch of earth,
    A tangle of sweet prayers to thy pure skies."

Bird, squirrel, bee, and the thing that was like no other
    Played in the woods that day,
Talked in the heart of the woods, as brother to brother,
    And prayed as children pray,—
Make me a garland, Lady, a garland, Mother,
    For this wild rood of may.

THE HILLS OF YOUTH

ONCE, on the far blue hills,
Alone with the pine and the cloud, in those high still places;
    Alone with a whisper of ferns and a chuckle of rills,
And the peat-brown pools that mirrored the angels' faces,
Pools that mirrored the wood-pigeon's grey-blue feather,
    And all my thistledown dreams as they drifted along;
Once, oh, once, on the hills, thro' the red-bloomed heather
    I followed an elfin song.

    Once, by the wellsprings of joy,
In the glens of the hart's-tongue fern, where the brooks came leaping
    Over the rocks, like a scrambling bare-foot boy
That never had heard of a world grown old with weeping;
Once, thro' the golden gorse (do the echoes linger
    In Paradise woods, where the foam of the may runs wild?)
I followed the flute of a light-foot elfin singer,
    A god with the eyes of a child.

    Once, he sang to me there,
From a crag on a thyme-clad height where the dew still glistened;
    He sang like the spirit of Spring in that dawn-flushed air,
While the angels opened their doors and the whole sky listened:
He sang like the soul of a rainbow, if heaven could hear it,
    Beating to heaven, on wings that were April's own;
A song too happy and brave for the heart to bear it,
    Had the heart of the hearer known.

    Once, ah, once, no more,
The hush and the rapture of youth in those holy places,
    The stainless height, the hearts that sing and adore
Till the sky breaks out into flower with the angels' faces!

379

Once, in the dawn, they were mine; but the noon bereft me.
  At midnight now, in an ebb of the loud world's roar,
I catch but a broken stave of the songs that left me
  On hills that are mine no more.

THE SHADOW

A SHADOW leaned over me, whispering, in the darkness,
      Thoughts without sound;
Sorrowful thoughts that filled me with helpless wonder
      And held me bound.

Sadder than memory, sharp as remorse, in the quiet
      Before I slept,
The whisper I heard of the one implacable Shadow,
      And my heart wept.

"Day by day, in your eyes, the light grows dimmer,
      With the joy you have sung.
You knew it would go; but, ah, when you knew it and sang it,
      Your heart was young;

"And a year to you, then, was an age; but now," said the Shadow,
      Malignant and cold,
"The light and the colour are fading, the ecstasy dying,
      It is time to grow old."

Oh, I could have borne the worst that he had to tell me,
      Lost youth, age, death;
But he turned to breathe on the quiet heart sleeping beside me
      The same cold breath.

And there by the throat I grappled him.   "Let me bear all of it.
      Let her dream on."
Soundlessly, shadow with shadow, we wrestled together,
      Till the grey dawn.

THE WEED-BURNER

I emptied a basket of weeds
On the gardener's crackling fire—
Nettle, and colt's foot and dock,
Till the smoke, like the white acrid clouds

That arose with the African djinn
In the wizard Arabian tale,
Making eyes tingle and smart
Went wreathing aloft to the blue;
And still the crammed basket disgorged
Burdock and nettle; and then . . .

Had you no warning, O heart?—
For, sudden and last, there out-poured
The wreckage of yesterday, too,
Rose upon perishing rose,
Yellow, and crimson, and white,
Over-blown, rotting and wet,
But sweeter than Spring in the air . . .

O heart, heart, what have you done?
Have you caught the whole world in your net?
O, colour and glory and light—
How should I know you were there?

THE GIPSY

THERE was a barefoot gipsy-girl
   Came walking from the West,
With a little naked sorrow
   Drinking beauty at her breast.
Her breast was like the young moon;
   Her eyes were dark and wild.
She was like evening when she wept,
   And morning when she smiled.

The little corners of her mouth
   Were innocent and wise;
And men would listen to her words,
   And wonder at her eyes;
And, since she walked with wounded feet,
   And utterly alone,
It seemed as if the women, too,
   Would make her grief their own.

Ah, had she been an old hag
   With shrivelled flesh and brain,
They would have drawn her to their hearts
   And eased her of her pain;

But, since her smooth-skinned loveliness
    Could only hurt their pride,
They dipped their pins in poison;
    And, by accident, she died.

FEY JOAN

SHE stood in the dark, where the crab-apples blow,
And told her own fortune for no man to know,
Crooning low to the bloom on a dew-dabbled spray
As, petal by petal, she plucked it away:
        "Wonder and wonder,
          And wonder again!
        This for the beauty,
          And this for the pain!
        This for the big star
          That shines through the tree;
        But all for the love
          That gave Robin to me."

She crooned like an elf that is drunk with the dew,
To a melody sweeter than earth ever knew;
Then she swayed like a fern at the flight of a wing,
And warbled aloud like an ouzel in Spring:
        "Wonder and wonder,
          And wonder again!
        This for the nest
          In the dark of the lane!
        This for the home
          That I never shall see;
        But all for the love
          That gave Robin to me."

She touched her red mouth to the lips of a flower,
And she breathed in her pain (it was nigh to her hour)
"Oh, one kiss for happiness, one kiss for tears,
And one for old age that must come with the years.
        Wonder and wonder,
          And wonder again!
        This for grey Scotland,
          And this for brown Spain!
        This for the tall ship
          That walked the wide sea;
        But all, all for love
          That gave Robin to me."

THE GREAT NORTH ROAD

Just as the moon was rising, I met a ghostly pedlar
  Singing for company beneath his ghostly load,—
Once, there were velvet lads with vizards on their faces,
  Riding up to rob me on the great North Road.

Now, my pack is heavy, and my pocket full of guineas
  Chimes like a wedding-peal, but little I enjoy
Roads that never echo to the chirrup of their canter,—
  The gay Golden Farmer and the Hereford Boy.

Rogues were they all, but their raid was from Elfland!
  Shod with elfin silver were the steeds they bestrode.
Merlin buckled on the spurs that wheeled thro' the wet fern
  Bright as Jack-o'-Lanthorns off the great North Road.

Tales were told in country inns when Turpin rode to Rippleside
  Puck tuned the fiddle-strings, and country maids grew coy,
Tavern doors grew magical when Colonel Jack might tap at them
  The gay Golden Farmer and the Hereford Boy.

What are you seeking then?   I asked this honest pedlar.
  —O, Mulled Sack or Natty Hawes might ease me of my load!—
Where are they flown then?—Flown where I follow;
  They are all gone for ever up the great North Road.

Rogues were they all; but the white dust assoils 'em!
  Paradise without a spice of deviltry would cloy.
Heavy is my pack till I meet with Jerry Abershaw,
  The gay Golden Farmer and the Hereford Boy.

THE WOOING OF DOROTHY PERKINS

'Twas Dorothy Perkins, so dainty and gay,
Peeped out of her window one midsummer day,
When a lad in a raggedy jerkin and hood
Crept out of the fern at the edge of the wood.

He stole up the path, and he tapped at her door,
And her heart began beating as never before,
For she knew it was either a footpad or fate
When he saw her and spoke, like a thrush to his mate:

"If you'll be my bride, dear, I'll build you a house
With windows that open on pomegranate boughs;
And you shall be crowned like a queen in a bower
All tricked out and trellised with love-knots in flower."

"Kind sir, I have heard, when a young man is wed,
He will often forget what the bachelor said;
And, as for your love-knots, I've blossoms more fair
Than any you dream of, to wind in my hair."

"O, but you shall have platters of Paradise fruits!
I'll make you soft music on ivory flutes.
White peacocks at sunset shall walk on your lawn,
And airs of Arabia wake you at dawn!"

"Kind sir, these be favors, I will not deny;
But a maid was created to sithe and to sigh;
And, for all your soft music, I'm harder to please
Than any cold mermaid that swims in the seas."

"It was all just a dream, then!   I cannot say more;
And I walked in my sleep when I knocked at your door;
For I'm just Johnny Briar that lives down the glen,
In a little thatched cottage not fit for a wren."

"Is it Adam's old stock with its roots in the clay
Which we use for our grafting, then prune it away?"
"Ay, the rest was but thorns, dear, and so we must part.
I've nothing to give you, excepting my heart."

"Kind sir, if you'll give me the things you despise,
Like the truth in your mind and the love in your eyes,
I'll come to your cottage down there in the glen,
And I'll live in your heart till you want it again."

She leaned to him smiling with eyes full of dew,
And he knew, if he dreamed, that his dream had come true;
Then he stretched up his arms, and he stood on his toes;
And—Dorothy Perkins . . . she turned to a rose!

DICK TURPIN'S RIDE

THE daylight moon looked quietly down
Through the gathering dusk on London town.

A smock-frockt yokel hobbled along
By Newgate, humming a country song.

Chewing a straw, he stood to stare
At the proclamation posted there:

Three hundred guineas on Turpin's head,
Trap him alive or shoot him dead;
And a hundred more for his mate, Tom King.

He crouched, like a tiger about to spring.

Then he looked up, and he looked down;
And, chuckling low, like a country clown,

Dick Turpin painfully hobbled away
In quest of his Inn—*The Load of Hay.*

.   .   .   .

Alone in her stall, his mare, Black Bess,
Lifted her head in mute distress;

For five strange men had entered the yard
And looked at her long, and looked at her hard.

They went out, muttering under their breath;
And then—the dusk grew still as death.

But the velvet ears of the listening mare
Lifted and twitched.   *They were there—still there;*

Hidden and waiting; for whom?   And why?
The clock struck four.   A step drew nigh.

It was King!   Tom King!   Dick Turpin's mate.
The black mare whinneyed.   Too late!   Too late!

They rose like shadows out of the ground
And grappled him there, without a sound.

"Throttle him—quietly—choke him dead!
Or we lose the hawk for a jay," they said.

They wrestled and heaved, five men to one;
And a yokel entered the yard, alone;

A smock-frockt yokel, hobbling slow;
But a fight is physic, as all men know.

His age dropped off.   He stood upright.
He leapt like a tiger into the fight.

Hand to hand, they fought in the dark;
For none could fire at a twisting mark,

Where he that shot at a foe might send
His pistol-ball through the skull of a friend.

But *"Shoot, Dick, shoot!"* gasped out Tom King.
"Shoot, or damn it, we both shall swing!

Shoot and chance it!"   Dick leapt back.
He drew.   He fired.   At the pistol's crack

The wrestlers whirled.   They scattered apart,
And the bullet drilled through Tom King's heart.

.   .   .   .

Dick Turpin dropped his smoking gun.
They had trapped him now, five men to one.

A gun in each hand of the crouching five,
They could take Dick Turpin now, alive;

Take him and bind him and tell their tale
As a pot-house boast, when they drank their ale.

He whistled, soft as a bird might call;
And a head-rope snapped in his bird's dark stall.

He whistled, soft as a nightingale.
He heard the swish of her swinging tail.

There was no way out that the five could see,
To heaven or hell, but the Tyburn tree;

No door but death; and yet, once more,
He whistled, as though at a sweetheart's door.

The five men laughed at him, trapped alive;
And—the door crashed open behind the five!

Out of the stable, a wave of thunder,
Swept Black Bess, and the five went under.

He leapt to the saddle.   A hoof-spurned stone
Flashed blue fire, and their prize was gone.

II

Away, through the ringing cobbled street, and out by the Northern Gate,
He rode that night, like a ghost in flight, from the dogs of his own fate.

By Crackskull Common, and Highgate Heath, he heard the chase be-
    hind;
But he rode to forget—forget—forget—the hounds of his own mind.

And cherry-black Bess on the Enfield Road flew light as a bird to her
    goal;
But her Rider carried a heavier load, in his own struggling soul.

He needed neither spur nor whip.   He was borne on a darker gale.
He rode like a hurricane-hunted ship, with the doom-wind in her sail.

He rode for the one impossible thing; that, in the morning light,
The towers of York might waken him—from London, and last night.

He rode to prove himself another, and leave himself behind;
And the hunted self was like a cloud; but the hunter like the wind.

Neck and neck they rode together; that, in the day's first gleam,
Each might prove that the other self was but a mocking dream.

And the little sleeping villages, and the breathless country-side,
Woke to the drum of the racing hoofs; but missed that ghostly ride.

They did not hear, they did not see, as the drumming hoofs drew nigh,
The dark magnificent thief in the night that rode so subtly by.

They woke.   They rushed to the wayside door.   They saw what the
    midnight showed,—
A mare that came like a crested wave along the Great North Road;

A flying spark in the formless dark, a flash from the hoof-spurned stone,
And the lifted face of a Man, that took the star-light, and was gone.

They heard the shout of the pounding chase, three hundred yards away.
There were fourteen men in a steam of sweat and a plaster of Midland
    clay.

The star-light struck their pistol-butts, as they passed in a clattering
  crowd,
*But the hunting wraith was away like the wind at the heels of the hunted
  cloud.*

He rode by the walls of Nottingham; and, over him as he went,
Like ghosts across the Great North Road, the boughs of Sherwood bent.

By Bawtrey all the chase but one had dropt a league behind,
Yet that one Rider hunted him, invisibly, as the wind.

And northward, like a blacker night, he saw the moors up-loom,
And Don and Derwent sang to him, like memory in the gloom,

And northward, northward as he rode, and sweeter than a prayer
The voices of those hidden streams, the Trent and Ouse and Aire;

Streams that could never slake his thirst.   He heard them as they flowed.
But one dumb Shadow hunted him along the Great North Road.

Till now, at dawn, the towers of York rose on the reddening sky,
And Bess went down between his knees, like a breaking wave, to die.

He lay beside her in the ditch.   He kissed her lovely head;
And a Shadow passed him like the wind, and left him with his dead.

He saw, but not as one that wakes, the City that he sought;
He had escaped from London town, but not from his own thought.

He strode up to the Mickle-gate with none to say him nay;
And there he met his Other Self, in the stranger light of day.

He strode up to the dreadful Thing that in the gateway stood;
And it stretched out a ghostly hand that the dawn had stained with
  blood.

It stood, as in the gates of hell, with none to hear or see.
"Welcome!" it said, *"thou'st ridden well; and outstript all but me."*

THE CONDUCTOR

Like oranges, friend?—No poem in those three words?
Wait.   You shall hear them again.

When London sweated and choked with heat and drought,
A man, like a sack of bones,
With a pinched, white, delicate face, and a soft brown beard
(Saint John of Clapham!), climbed to the top of the bus,
Painfully, hauled up the stair by the vigorous hand
Of a buxom wench in front, and sturdily pushed
By their two small boys below.
There was only one seat;
And the hot conductor bawled, *"One only outside!*
Grr! Inside only! One only outside, I said!"

The Cockney Juno looked at him, half amused,
With her bold, black, honest eyes.
                    "Right-o," she said.
They settled their sack of bones on the vacant seat.
Saint John was breathing with care, a little afraid
It might bring on that coughing.
                "That's right!" said Juno,
"I'll stand. 'E mustn't!"—
             "Nor any one else up 'ere!"
The conductor snarled like a man with a rat at his liver.
She smiled at him again with her bold black eyes,
Taking her time to obey.
             She liked fresh air.
The doctor, of course, had said it was good for her man,
And good for the children.
              With one Amazonian arm
She lifted the younger child against her breasts
That, under the cool blue leaves of the thin print gown,
Shook, with the jolting bus, like fruit on a tree.
The smooth little colt-like legs of the child in her arm
Shone in the sunlight, over the passengers' heads.

The bus pulled up with a jerk. Mother and children,
Obeying the law, went down to their inside place.
The dying man, with a flicker of male pugnacity,
Paying three sixpences out, and strong in the fact
That journeys like this were not made every day,
Looked up at the grim conductor.
                "You'll tell 'em," he said,
"As soon as a seat is vacant, to come up 'ere."

The bus rolled on. The houses thinned, and the smell
Of lilac and may, like breezes from Eden Garden,
Met the sad fugitive out of the City of Death.

This day of the spring was his.   Yet he looked troubled;
Till, after a while, two twopenny passengers rose,
Rang the bell for the bus to stop, and descended.

He cocked his head to listen, his delicate face
Tense with the over-anxiety of the weak
Who, all too often in life, had been pushed to the wall;
But now he heard them.
                            Children and mother, all smiles,
Ascended the stair.   They patted his arm as they passed.
"Now, ain't that nice?   Look, Will, it's the very front seat!"
They took their places, the elder boy at her side,
Up and down restlessly bobbing and staring around;
The child astride on her knee.
                            Saint John's wan face
Looked happy now, and quietly brightened to see her
Drinking her fill of the wholesome country air.
He watched her, glad that the joyous moment absorbed her.
Whatever might follow, he found his joy in her joy.
He watched her, alive to the sights and sounds of the fields,
Was aware of them all through *her*,—
The spires of chestnut blossom, the loaded boughs
That made the outside passengers duck their heads;
The cows in the cooling stream, under shadowy willows;
The hens by the shed, with the little arched hole in the door;
The white horse under the elm-tree, dappled with shadows;
All streaming by, like a picture, a coloured film,
A story thrown upon darkness—for him.
                            But, for her,—
The thought grew bright in his face—it was life, real life,
A real substantial earth.
                            At last, the bus
Pulled up at the end of their world, the country inn
That marked the very last inch of their sixpenny ride.

They rose.   They looked at the fields to left and right.
Juno lifted an arm, round, strong, and bare,
And pointed over a meadow.   *"We mustn't walk far,
We'll 'ave to go back by the six o'clock bus,"* she said.
*"That's where we'll 'ave our dinner, under that 'edge,
Among them ox-eye daisies.   Come along, Will."*

They gathered him up and helped him, carefully, down.
They stood on the dusty road, a little bewildered
To find they were free of the kingdom of summer at last

For one whole day.
But, as they slowly led their bundle of bones
To a stile in the flowering hedge, the conductor's voice
Rasped out on the bee-buzzing stillness, *'Arf a mo!*
He stooped for a moment, rummaging under the stairs;
Then, running across the road to Saint John of Clapham,
He awkwardly thrust an orange into his hand,
Like oranges, friend?
                    Saint John, without a word,
Took it, as children accept a gift from the sky.
Back to his bus the conductor hurried again
And tugged at his bell.   As he turned the corner he saw
Saint John at rest on the stile, in the flowering hedge;
Peeling the fruit with his teeth, spitting out pips,
And munching the pulp with the strange voracious delight
Of a man to whom death brings gifts.
                              Like oranges, friend?

SEA-THRIFT

FLOWER of the sea,
Brave thrift, you wake for me,
Fifty years back, one ageless memory,

Whose roots entwine
A childhood where you shine
Clear as to-day against the quivering brine.

Wet with salt spray
Your roseate heads to-day
Beckon me, from a world long past away.

Clear, and more clear
You grow, until I hear
The voice that named you first in childhood's ear.

Wars ebb and flow;
And still your petals glow
Crisp, roseate, clear, as fifty years ago;

Never to fall   ·
Or fade beyond recall,—
A small bright cloud—that clings—to a grey wall.

AT VENICE

HOME from their fishing, over the quiet water,
The coloured sails returned.
Before them all the domes and towers of Venice
In the deep sunset burned.

The still lagoon was full of coloured shadows.
Your face was like a flower.
The wingéd Lion darkened on the splendour,
And it was Titian's hour.

Over the shining flood the sails came softly,
Saffron and rose and white.
Brown throats among the tawny nets uplifted
A love-song to the night.

The sunset moved before them like a banner
That into darkness flows.
The sunset and the sails moved on together,
Saffron and white and rose.

THE HAPPY HUNTING GROUND

I KNOW a cottage on the coast of Maine . . .
You walk thro' a wood, by a winding lane,
Till you come to a clearing where the waves say "woosh"
And the sea-swallow nests in a wild-rose bush.
There you will find it, as the honey bees know,
With the rocks and the tide twelve yards below;
And, in among the rocks, with the dragon-fly and bee,
A foot-wide path takes the swimmer to the sea.

And the little wild strawberries redden under foot,
And the woodchuck nibbles at the rose marie root,
And the green snake basks on the path as it goes
Down thro' the rocks with the wild red rose.

Then, a shining cloud-winged spirit of the sky,
A lone three-masted ship sails by;
And, out and away, in the deep-sea blue,
The dark pines cluster on an island or two;
Salt, hard, flower-bright islands of the blest,
Where the blueberries grow and the herring-gulls nest,

And the fish-hawk over his pine-tree wheels,
And the cormorant cries to the barking seals,
While you thrust through the firs with their dew on your face,
And the long grass misty with the Queen Anne's lace;
Till the Red Man's ghost in a birch-canoe
Dips his paddle in the creeks *he* knew,
And glides thro' the old old sights and sounds
By the shores of the shadowy hunting grounds.

I know a cottage on the coast of Maine. . . .
Let a salt wave whisper, and I'm living there again.
By the tang of the rosin from a blue spruce bough,
Or the red of a maple, I am living there now,
Looking thro' a window at my heart's delight,
As the sea falls quiet and the West turns bright,—
Bare-foot children, in the sunset-glow
Running up the rocks from the little beach below,
Climbing up the crags from the shell-strewn shore
With a bucket-full of clams to the open door;
Through the scent of the briars where the sea-swallow stirs
And the squirrel chirrups in the sun-warmed firs.

I know a haven on the coast of Maine. . . .
Let a pine-wood rustle and I'm living there again,
Writing or reading by a pine-log fire,
Or looking thro' a window at my heart's desire,—
Skies of vision, and a sea at rest,
And the face of my belovèd as she turns to the West,
On a rock above the water with a creel in her hand,
And her bright eyes gazing at the sunset-land. . . .

Skies of vision, and a world of light,
And a white sail homing at the fall of night.

OLD MAN MOUNTAIN

AT SANTA BARBARA

OLD MAN MOUNTAIN had a one-mule track,
And a lump of quartz in the hump of his back;

Quartz that glinted with a hint of gold.
His bones were granite.   He was eons old.

But he slept like a child, with a squirrel on his breast,
And his eagle's feather and his chickadee's nest;

While the chipmunks nibbled at the nuts in his bed,
And the mountain-deer walked over his head.

Old Man Mountain had honey for the bear.
He had sage at his feet, and snow on his hair.

His beard was a pine-wood.   His knuckles and his knees
Were hard and gnarled as his live-oak trees.

He was kin to the Rockies,—those bleak-souled kings;
But his heart was fixed upon kindlier things;

And he liked the song that a chickadee sings.

So he looked at the ranch on the slopes below
Where the peach-bloom shone like a rosier snow

And the Angelus called like a ghost again
From an old white tower that remembered Spain.

For the purple canyons grew dark and deep;
And the sea and the palm-trees whispered sleep;

But, softly aglow, on her cypressed hill,
Santa Barbara, hushed and still,

Shone like a pearl of that rosary strung
By the brothers in grey when the West was young,

And their worn feet straightened the King's highway
From San Diego to Monterey.

Then the ghost of a bell at Capistrano
Called to a ghost in lost Solano.

The rose-light died from the soft white walls;
And, alone with his crags, where the wild hawk calls.

Old Man Mountain felt the sky growing cold;
But he knew that the tale was not yet told.

He looked at the stars, as a mountain dares;
And the clouds drew round him, while he said his prayers.

WIZARDRY

THERE'S many a proud wizard in Araby and Egypt
  Can read the silver writing of the stars as they run;
And many a dark gypsy, with a pheasant in his knapsack,
  Has gathered more by moonshine than wiser men have won;

But *I* know a Wizardry
  Can take a buried acorn
And whisper forests out of it, to tower against the sun.

There's many a magician in Bagdad and Benares
  Can read you—for a penny—what your future is to be;
And a flock of crazy prophets that by staring at a crystal
  Can fill it with more fancies than there's herring in the sea;

But *I* know a Wizardry
  Can break a freckled egg-shell
And shake a throstle out of it, in every hawthorn-tree.

There's many a crafty alchemist in Mecca and Jerusalem;
  And Michael Scott and Merlin were reckoned very wise;

But *I* know a Wizardry
  Can take a wisp of sun fire
And round it to a planet and roll it through the skies,
  With cities, and sea-ports, and little shining windows,
And hedgerows and gardens, and loving human eyes. . . .

THE ISLES OF YESTERDAY

Mariners all, declare
  Where those lost islands lie,—
The Fortunate, the Fair,
  Under what deeper sky
Robed with what shining air?

No keel of oak, they said,
  Can plough those unknown seas,
No mortal sail be spread
  For those Hesperides
Where dwell our happy dead.

Time hath no word to say
  Where that strange ocean smiles.
Far, far beyond Cathay
  We sail to seek those isles,
Those isles of yesterday.

There—memory wakes from sleep.
  Set sail where'er you will,
There youth and wonder keep
  Their music for you still. . . .
Thrust out into the Deep.

Death shall unseal your eyes.
  Fear nothing. Ye shall see
Against those purer skies
  Like clouds of ecstasy
The immortal islands rise.

In that ethereal clime
  Beyond all wrack and storm,
Pure as in Eden's prime
  Abides the immortal form
Of all that died in Time.

So, on those lovelier hills
  The wildflowers are not strange;
And the new spring-tide fills
  The fields through which ye range
With the old brave daffodils.

And violets, dim as prayer,
  Make sweet the woods ye knew;
And oh, with sun-lit hair
  And eyes of star-lit dew,
Lost love shall meet you there. . . .

Lost love shall meet you there.

BIRD IN THE BLACKTHORN

Tell me, you
  That sing in the blackthorn,
Out of what Mind
  Your melody springs.

396

Is it the World-soul
  Throbs like a fountain
Up thro' the throat
  Of an elf with wings?

Five sweet notes
  In a golden order,
Out of that deep realm
  Quivering through,
Flashed like a phrase
  Of light through darkness.
But *Who* so ordered them?
  Tell me, *Who*?

You whose throats
  In the rain-drenched orchard
Peal your joys
  In a cadenced throng;
You whose wild notes,
  Fettered by Beauty,
Move like the stars
  In a rounded song;

Yours is the breath,
  But *Whose* is the measure
Shaped in an ecstasy
  Past all art?
Yours is the spending;
  Whose is the treasure?
Yours is the blood-beat;
  Whose is the heart?

Minstrels all
  That have woven your housen
Of withies and twigs
  With a Mind in-wrought;
Ye are the shuttles;
  But out of what Darkness
Gather your thoughtless
  Patterns of thought?

Bright eyes glance
  Through your elfin doorways,
Roofed with rushes,
  And lined with moss.

Whose were the dumb, dark
    Pangs of creation?
Yours is the wild bough;
    Whose is the Cross?

Carols of light
    From a lovelier kingdom,
Gleams of a music
    On earth unheard,
Scattered like dew
    By the careless wayside,
Pour through the lifted
    Throat of a bird.

DAYBREAK

EVERY morning, a bird
    Alights on the topmost bough of the silver birch-tree
Between the house and the lake,
    And sits there alone for an hour
Looking in, looking in at my window.

It may be a blackbird or thrush,
    But the light at that hour is deceptive.
I only know it is different from all other birds.

It utters no cry, no song.
    I have never seen it alighting.
And yet, when the sky is like apple-bloom over the lake,
    And my eyes have grown used to the light,
It is always there,
    At the very same time by the sun,
A little while after daybreak.
    It always chooses the same bare bough,
And it sits there alone, for an hour,
    Looking in, looking in at my window.

Is it so that our lost ones return
    With eager inquisitive love,
Using strange eyes for an hour,
    To glance through an open window
And discover how much we have changed?

398

It is daybreak now,
   And the bird is not here;
But strange and terrible thoughts bewilder one's mind
   Before it is half-awake,
And my heart sinks,
   With fear of some evil that may have befallen my bird.

Wings rustle.
   The topmost bough of the silver birch-tree
Suddenly dips and sways,
   And all is well.
Dark on an apple-bloom sky
   A silent bird
Sits there alone, looking in,
   Looking in, looking in at my window.

MESSAGES FROM THE DEAD

MESSAGES,—from the dead?
Thou hast not heard them?   No;
Nor shalt thou ever hear
What whisperings come and go.
But, when thou hast bowed thy head
In the quietude of despair
When thou hast ceased to listen,
A meaning shall draw near
And startle thee like a light
From valleys of surprise
Opening, out of sight
Behind thee; for 'tis written
They must not meet thine eyes.
Between the effect and cause
They dare not intervene.
From the unseen to the seen
Their roads are Nature's laws;
But, through them, they can breathe
What none could speak aloud;
And quietly interwreathe

Through sea-wave and white cloud
Strange gleams of loveliness
Whose deep unearthly drift
Thou couldst not even guess;
Light that no eyes can see;
Music no ear hath heard;

Till they strike home to thee
Through star and sunset rift
Or the cry of a wandering bird;
And where the rainbow shone
Across unshadowing skies,
Clear as through tear-lashed eyes
Thy love smiles, and is gone.

Rememberest thou that hour
Under the naked boughs
When, desolate and alone,
Returning to thy house,
Thou stoodst amazed to find
Dropt on the lintel-stone
Which thou hadst left so bare
A radiant dew-drenched flower—
And thou couldst never know
Whose hand had dropt it there,
Fragrant and white as snow,
To save thy soul from hell?
Yet, in thy deepest mind,
Thou *didst* know, and know well.

Not thine to understand
How the two worlds accord,—
The will of Love, our Lord,
With this dark wheel of Time.
Yet thou didst hear them chime
Like one deep Sanctus bell
For the pure Host revealed
In the exquisite miracle
Of that white chance-dropt flower;
A flower from a known field,
And dropt by a mortal hand;
But, breathing its wild dew,
Oh, simply as tears flow,
Thou didst most surely know
The hand from which it fell
Was thy lost angel's, too.

THE RETURN OF PYTHAGORAS

Guard the immortal fire.
Honour the glorious line of the great dead.
To the new height let all thy soul aspire;
But let those memories be thy wine and bread.

Quench not in any shrine
The smouldering storax. In no human heart
    Quench what love kindled. Faintly though it shine,
Not till it wholly dies the gods depart.

    Truth has remembering eyes.
The wind-blown throng will clamour at Falsehood's gate.
    Has Falsehood triumphed? Let the world despise
Thy constant mind. Stand thou aside, and wait.

    Close not thine eyes in sleep
Till thou hast searched thy memories of the day,
    Graved in thy heart the vow thou didst not keep,
And called each wandering thought back to the way.

    Pray to the gods! Their aid,
Their aid alone can crown thy work aright;
    Teach thee that song whereof all worlds were made;
Rend the last veil, and feed thine eyes with light.

    Naught shall deceive thee, then.
All creatures of the sea and earth and air,
    The circling stars, the warring tribes of men,
Shall make one harmony, and thy soul shall hear.

    Write not thy thoughts on snow.
Cut them in rock to front the thundering sky.
    From Earth and Time, when it is time to go,
Take the dark road; bid one more world good-bye.

    Out of this earth, this dust,
Out of this flesh, this blood, this living tomb,
    Out of these cosmic throes of wrath and lust,
Breaks the lost splendour from the world's blind womb.

    Thou that wast brought so low,
And through those lower lives hast risen again,
    Kin to the beasts, with power at last to know
Thine own proud banishment and diviner pain;

    Out of this prison of clay
With lifted face, a mask of struggling fire,
    With arms of flesh and bone stretched up to pray,
Dumb, thou shalt hear that Voice of thy desire:

401

Courage, O conquering soul!
For all the boundless night that whelms thee now,
Though worlds on worlds into that darkness roll
The gods abide; and of their race art thou!

LINNÆUS

It was his garden that began it all,
A magical garden for a changeling child.

"The garden has bewitched him!
Carl! Carl! O, Carl! Now where is that elfkin hiding?"

It was the voice of Christina, wife of the Pastor,
Nils Linnæus, the Man of the Linden-tree.
Youthful and comely, she stood at her door in the twilight,
Calling her truant son.
                        Her flaxen hair
Kerchiefed with crisp white wings; her rose-coloured apron
And blue-grey gown, like a harebell, yielding a glimpse
Of the shapeliest ankle and snowiest stocking in Sweden;
She stood at her door, a picture breathed upon air.

She called yet again, and tilted her head to listen
As a faint, flushed, wild anemone turning aside
From a breeze out of elf-land, teasing her delicate petals,
The breeze of the warm, white, green-veined wings of her wooer;
And again, a little more troubled at heart, she called,
"Supper-time, Carl!"
                        But out of the fragrant pinewoods
Darkening round her, only the wood-pigeon cooed.

Down by the lake, from the alders, only the red-cap
Whistled three notes.   Then all grew quiet again.
Yet, he was there, she knew, though he did not answer.
The lad was at hand, she knew, though she could not see him.
Her elf-child, nine years old, was about and around her,
A queer little presence, invisible, everywhere, nowhere,
Hiding, intensely still. . . .
                        She listened; the leaves
All whispered, "Hush!"

402

It was just as though Carl had whispered,
"Hush!   I am watching.
"Hush!   I am thinking.
"Hush!   I am listening, too."

She tiptoed through the garden, her fair head
Turning to left and right, with birdlike glances,
Peeping round lichened boulders and clumps of fern.
She passed by the little garden his father gave him,
Elfdom within an elfdom, where he had sown
Not only flowers that rightly grow in gardens,
The delicate aristocracies of bloom,
But hedgerow waifs and ragamuffin strays
That sprawled across his borders everywhere
And troubled even the queendom of the rose
With swarming insurrections.
                              At last she saw him,
His tousled head a little golden cloud
Among the dark green reeds at the edge of the lake,
Bending over the breathless water to watch—
What?
              She tiptoed nearer, until she saw
The spell that bound him.   Floating upon the lake,
A yard away, a water-lily closed
Its petals, as an elfin cygnet smooths
Its ruffled plumes, composing them for sleep.

He watched it, rapt, intent.
                              She watched her son,
Intent and rapt, with a stirring at her heart,
And beautiful shining wonder in her eyes,
Feeling a mystery near her.
                              Shadow-of-a-Leaf
Whispered.   The garden died into the dark.
Mother and child had gone—I knew not whither
It seemed as though the dark stream of the years

Flowed round me.
              Then, as one that walks all night
Lifts up his head in the early light of dawn,
I found myself in a long deserted street
Of little wooden houses, with thatched roofs.
It was Upsala.
              Over the silent town
I heard a skylark quivering, up and up,

As though the very dew from its wild wings
Were shaken to silvery trills of elfin song.
Tirile, tirile, tirile, it arose,
Praising the Giver of one more shining day.

Then, with a clatter of doors and a yodelling call
Of young men's voices, the Svartbäcken woke;
And down the ringing street the students came
In loose blue linen suits, knapsack on back
And sturdy stick in hand, to rouse old Carl
For their long ramble through the blossoming fields.
I saw them clustering round the Master's door.
I heard their jolly song—*Papa Linnæus:*

    Linnæus, Papa Linnæus,
      He gave his pipe a rap.
    He donned his gown of crimson.
      He donned his green fur cap.
    He walked in a meadow at daybreak
      To see what he might see;
    And the linnet cried, "Linnæus!
      O hide!   Here comes Linnæus.
    Beware of old Linnæus,
      The Man of the Linden-tree."

    So beautiful, bright, and early,
      He brushed away the dews,
    He found the wicked wild-flowers
      All courting there in twos;
    And buzzing loud for pardon,
      Sir Pandarus, the bee:
    "Vincit Amor, Linnæus,
      Linnæus, Papa Linnæus!"
    O, ho, quoth old Linnæus,
      The Man of the Linden-tree.

    Quoth he, " 'Tis my conviction
      These innocents must be wed!"
    So he murmured a benediction,
      And blessed their fragrant bed;
    And the butterflies fanned their blushes
      And the red-cap whistled in glee,
    They are married by old Linnæus,
      Linnæus, Papa Linnæus!

Vivat, vivat Linnæus,
　The Man of the Linden-tree.

Vivat Linnæus!　And out the old Master came,
Jauntily as a throstle-cock in Spring,
His big bright eyes aglow; the fine curved beak,
The kindly lips, the broad well-sculptured brow,
All looked as though the wisdom that had shaped them
Desired that they should always wear a smile
To teach the world that kindness makes men happy.
He shook his head at his uproarious troop,
And chose his officers for the day's campaign:
One, for a marksman, with a fowling-piece,
To bring down bird or beast, if need arose;
One for a bugler, to recall their lines
From echoing valley and hill, when something rare
Lay in the Master's hand; one to make notes
Of new discoveries; one for discipline; all
For seeking out the truth, in youth and joy.
To-day they made for Jumkil, miles away
Along the singing river, where that prize
The *Sceptrum Carolinum* used to grow.
And, ever as they went, Linnæus touched
All that they saw with gleams of new delight.
As when the sun first rises over the sea
Myriads of ripples wear a crest of fire;
And over all the hills a myriad flowers
Lift each a cup of dew that burns like wine;
And all these gleams reflect one heavenly light;
He changed the world around him; filled the woods
With rapture; made each footpath wind away
Into new depths of elfin-land.　The ferns
Became its whispering fringe; and every stile
A faerie bridge into a lovelier world.
His magic sunlight touched the adventurous plants
That grew on the thatch of wayside cottages,
Crepis and *Bromus,* with the straggling brood
Of flowers he called *tectorum,* dancing there
Above the heads of mortals, like swart gnomes
In rusty red and gold.
　　　　　　　　"My Svartbäck Latin,"
Linnæus laughed, "may make the pedants writhe;
But I would sooner take three slaps from Priscian
Than one from Mother Nature."
o*　　　　　　　　　　405

Had made their pretty pattern of the world.
They had named and labelled all their flowers by rote,
Grouping them in a little man-made scheme
Empty of true significance as the wheel
Of stars that Egypt turned for her dead kings.
His was the very life-stream of the flowers;
And everywhere in Nature he revealed
Their subtle kinships; wedded bloom and bloom;
Traced the proud beauty flaunting in her garden,
To gipsy grandsires camping in a ditch;
Linked the forgotten wanderers to their clan;
Grouped many-coloured clans in one great tribe;
And gathered scores of scattered tribes again
Into one radiant nation.
                              He revealed
Mysterious clues to changes wild as those
That Ovid sang—the dust that rose to a stem,
The stem that changed to a leaf, the crowning leaf
That changed to a fruitful flower; and, under all,
Sustaining, moving, binding all in one,
One Power that like a Master-Dramatist,
Through every act and atom of the world
Advanced the triumph that must crown the whole.
Unseen by man that drama—here on earth
It must be—but could man survey the whole,
As even now, in flashes, he discerns
Its gleaming moments, vanishing sharp-etched scenes,
Loaded with strange significance, he would know,
Like Shadow-of-a-Leaf, that not a cloud can sail
Across a summer sky, but plays its part.
There's not a shadow drifting on the hills,
Or stain of colour where the sun goes down,
Or least bright flake upon the hawk-moth's wing
But that great drama needs them.
                              The wild thrush,
The falling petal, the bubble upon the brook,
Each has its cue, to sing, to fall, to shine,
And exquisitely responds.   The drunken bee
Blundering and stumbling through a world of flowers
Has his own tingling entrances, unknown
To man or to himself; and, though he lives
In his own bee-world, following his own law,
He is yet the unweeting shuttle in a loom

That marries rose to rose in other worlds,
And shapes the wonder of Springs he cannot see.
O, little bee-like man, thou shalt not raise
Thy hand, or close thine eyes, or sigh in sleep,
But, over all thy freedom, there abides
The law of this world-drama.
                              Under the stars,
Between sweet-breathing gardens in the dusk,
I heard the song of the students marching home.
I saw their eyês, mad nightingales of joy,
Shining with youth's eternal ecstasy.
I saw them tossing vines entwined with flowers
Over girls' necks, and drawing them all along,
Flags flying, French horns blowing, kettle-drums throbbing,
And Carl Linnæus marching at their head.
Up to the great old barn they marched for supper,
Four rounds of beef and a cask of ripened ale;
And, afterwards, each with his own flower-fettered girl,
They'd dance the rest of the summer night away.

Greybeards had frowned upon this frolic feast;
But Carl Linnæus told them "Youth's a flower,
And we're botanic students."
                              Many a time,
In green fur cap and crimson dressing-gown,
He sat and smoked his pipe and watched them there
On winter nights; and when the fiddles played
His Polish dance, Linné would shuffle it too.
But now, to-night—they had tramped too many miles.
The old man was tired. He left them at the door,
And turned to his own house, as one who leaves
Much that he loved behind him.
                              As he went
They cheered their chief—"Vivat, vivat Linnæus!"
And broke into their frolic song again.

I saw him in the shadowy house alone
Entering the room, above whose happy door
The watchword of his youth and his old age
Was written in gold—*Innocue vivito.*
Numen adest.
                              I saw him writing there
His last great joyous testament, to be read
Only by his own children, as he thought,

407

After he'd gone; an ecstasy of praise,
As though a bird were singing in his mind,
Praise, praise, to the Giver of life and love and death!

God led him with His own Almighty Hand,
And made him grow up like a goodly tree.
God filled his heart with such a loving fire
For truth, that truth returned him love for love.
God aided him, with all that his own age
Had yet brought forth, to speed him on his way.
God set him in a garden, as of old,
And gave him, for his duty and delight,
The task that he loved best in all the world.
God gave him for his help-mate, from his youth
Into old age, the wife he most desired
And blessed him with her goodness.
                                God revealed
His secrets to him; touched his eyes with light,
And let him gaze into His Council Hall.
God so determined even his defeats
That they became his greatest victories.
God made his enemies as a wind to fill
His homeward-rushing sails.   Wherever he went
The Lord was with him, and the Lord upheld him.

And yet, O yet, one glory was to come;
One strangest gate into infinitude
Was yet to be swung back and take him home.
I know not how the fields that gave us birth
Draw us with sweetness, never to be forgotten
Back through the dark.
                          I saw him groping out,
As through a mist, into a shadowy garden;
And this was not Upsala any more,
But the lost garden where his boyhood reigned.
The little dwindling path at Journey's End
Ran through the dark, into a path he knew.

Carl!   Carl!   Carl!   Now where is that elfkin hiding!
Down by the lake, from the alders, only the red-cap
Whistled three notes.   Then all grew quiet again.

Carl! O Carl! Her voice, though he could not answer,
Called him. He knew she was there, though he could not see her.
He stood and listened. The leaves were listening, too.

He tiptoed through the garden. His grey head
Turning to left and right with birdlike glances.
He passed by the little garden his father gave him.
He knew its breath in the night.
                    His heart stood still.
She was there. He saw her at last. Her back was towards him.
He saw her fair young head, through the deepening shadows,
Bending, breathlessly, forward to watch a child
At the edge of the lake, who watched a floating flower.
He watched her, rapt, intent. She watched her son,
Intent and rapt.
Tears in his heart, he waited, dark and still,
Feeling a mystery near him.

EPILOGUE

Up the Grand Canyon the full morning flowed.
I heard the voices moving through the abyss
With the deep sound of pine-woods, league on league
Of singing boughs, each separate, each a voice,
Yet all one music;
                    The Eternal Mind
Enfolds all changes, and can never change.

Man is not exiled from this Majesty,
The inscrutable Reality, which he shares
In his immortal essence. Man that doubts
All but the sensuous veils of colour and sound,
The appearances that he can measure and weigh,
Trusts, as the very fashioner of his doubt,
The imponderable thought that weighs the worlds,
The invisible thought that sees; thought that reveals
The miracle of the eternal paradox—
The pure unsearchable Being that cannot be
Yet Is, and still creates and governs all;
A Power that, being unknowable, is best known;
For this transcendent Being can reply
To every agony, "I am that which waits

Beyond the last horizon of your pain,
Beyond your wildest hope, your last despair,
Above your heaven, and deeper than your hell.
There is not room on earth for what ye seek.
Is there not room in Me?"

                        Time is a shadow
Of man's own thought.   Things past and things to come
Are closed in that full circle.   He lives and reigns;
Dies with the dying bird; and, in its death
Receives it to His heart.   No leaf can fall
Without Him; who, for ever pouring out
His passion into worlds that shall attain
Love in the highest at last, returns for ever
Along these roads of suffering and of death,
With all their lives upgathered to His heart
Into the heaven of heavens.   How else could life
Lay hold on its infinitude, or win
The strength to walk with Love in complete light?
For, as a child that learns to walk on earth,
Life learns these little rhythms of earthly law,
Listens to simple seas that ebb and flow,
And spells the large bright order of the stars
Wherein the moving Reason is revealed
To man's up-struggling mind, or breathed like song
Into the quiet heart, as love to love.
So, step by step, the spirit of man ascends
Through joy and grief; and is withdrawn by death
From the sweet dust that might content it here
Into His kingdom, the one central goal
Of the universal agony.   He lives.
He lives and reigns, throned above Space and Time;
And, in that realm, freedom and law are one;
Fore-knowledge and all-knowledge and freewill,
Make everlasting music.

                      Far away
Along the unfathomable abyss it flowed,
A harmony so consummate that it shared
The silence of the sky; a song so deep
That only the still soul could hear it now:
New every morning the creative Word
Moves upon chaos.   Yea, our God grows young.
Here, now, the eternal miracle is renewed
Now, and for ever, God makes heaven and earth.

DEDICATION
TO M. A. N.

Under the Pyrenees,
  Where the warm sea-wind drifts thro' tamarisk boughs,
There is a lonely house upon a hill-top
  That I shall never forget or see again.

I shall not see that garden, filled with roses,
  On the high sun-burnt plateau, girdled round
With that low parapet, on the lonely hill-top,
  By sunlight, or by moonlight, ever again.

In that lost garden stands a little chapel,
  And the strange ship wherein we made our voyage,
Our little mortal ship of thoughts and visions,
Hangs there, in chains, before the twilit altar.
  The doors are locked. The lamp is quenched for ever;
Though, at one corner of the house, Our Lady
  Looks out, across the valley, to the sea.

And, on the landward side, across a valley
  Purple as grapes in autumn, the dark mountains,
With peaks like broken swords, and splintered helmets,
  Remembering Roland's death, are listening still.

Look down, look down, upon the sunlit valley,
  Over the low white parapet of that garden;
And you shall see the long white road go winding
  Through the Basque vineyards. . . .
                    But you shall not see
One face, nor shall you hear one voice that whispered
  Love, as it died. . . .
                  Only one wooden Image
Knows where she knelt, among the lonely mountains
  At Roncesvalles, in one last prayer for me. . . .

   .   .   .   .

AND, when it was darkest, I came to a strong City.
  No earthly tongue can tell how I journeyed there,
Deaf to this world's compassion,
  Blind to its pity,
With a heart wrung empty, even of its last dumb prayer.

I had left the chattering throng in the night behind me,
  And stumbled into a desert that had no name.
Torn, bleeding of foot,
  Through cactus and thorn I stumbled,
And, when it was darkest, to that strong City I came.

Gate there was none, nor window. It towered above me
  Like a vast fortress into the midnight sky.
And I beat on the granite walls,
  But I found no doorway;
And the blood ran over my wrists, but I heard no reply.

Yet, I knew well—no tongue can tell how I knew it—
  Though the walls were harder than adamant, blacker than night,
Within that City
  Was glory beyond all glory
Of wisdom and power enthroned in absolute light.

Could I have entered there, all doubt were over.
  Stones would be bread at last, and water wine;
All questioning closed
      In absolute vision;
The long sad riddle solved, and the answer mine.

But oh, on those cloud-wreathed walls there stood no sentry.
Naked as cliffs they towered, abrupt as doom.
  No shining gate,
    No shadowy postern,
No least small spark of a window broke their gloom.

Hour after hopeless hour I groped around them.
  League after league, I followed that girdling wall.
Burning with thirst,
I dragged through the drifted sand-heaps
  Round its great coigns, and found them adamant all.

Once, every league, a shadowy buttress,
  Like a vast Sphinx, outstretched in the moon's pale sheen,
Loomed through the night,
With flanks worn sleek by the sand-storms,
  And calm strange face that gazed as at worlds unseen.

I groped around them; I groped around them;
  Stared up at their cold eyes and found them stone;

And crawled on, on,
Till I overtook strange foot-prints
  Going my way, and knew them for my own;

Strange foot-prints, clotted with blood, in the sand before me,
  Trailing the hopeless way I had trailed before;
For, in that night,
I had girdled the whole dark City,
  Feeling each adamant inch, and found no door.

I fell on my face in the rank salt of the desert.
  Slow, hot, like blood, out of my hopeless eyes,
The salt tears bled.
The salt of the desert drank them,
  And I cried, once, to God, as a child cries.

Then, then, I cannot tell
What strange thing happened,
  Only, as at a breath of the midnight air,
These eyes, like two staunched wounds, had ceased their bleeding
  And my despair had ended my despair.

Far over the desert, like shadows trailed by a moon-cloud,
  I saw a train of mourners, two by two,
Following an open coffin.
  They halted near me.
And I beheld, once more, the face I knew.

Blissful the up-turned face—the cold hands folded,
  Blissful the up-turned face, cold as cold stone.
Cold as a midnight flower.
  I bent above it—
Sweet, sweet cold kiss, the saddest earth had known.

Quietly they move on, in slow procession.
  They breathed no prayer.   They sang no funeral song.
Up to the adamant walls
  Of that strong City,
Slowly they moved, a strange inscrutable throng.

Behind their shining burden they stole like shadows
  Up to the shadowy City, two by two.
And like two ponderous doors of a tomb revolving

Two stones in the wall swung back,
    And they passed through.

I followed after.   I followed after.
    Theirs was the secret key, and the sure goal:
And the adamant doors
    Revolved again like midnight,
And closed, like a silent thunder, behind my soul.

Dark!   It was dark; but through that strange new darkness
    Great aisles of beauty rapturously burned;
And I stole on,
    Like a remembering pilgrim
From a long exile now at last returned.

All round me burned strange lights and banners.
    Above, great arches grasped and spanned the sky.
Then, like a bell,
    In the armoured hands of Michael,
I heard Time ring its æons out and die.

I saw that strange procession winding
    On through a veil that shielded my dazed sight
From the absolute Dark that would have drowned me
    At the first dreadful touch of absolute Light.

Yet I saw glory on glory on glory
    Burning through those ethereal folds,
Dusked by a myriad dawns, a myriad sunsets
    With smouldering mercies, merciful blood-red golds.

Before it smoked the Eternal Altar
    Branched with great trembling lights that shone
As though at last all stars, all constellations,
    Had swung to their true place before God's throne.

There, there, at last, they burned in order,
    Round that high Altar, under that rich East.
All clouds, all snows, on that pure Table
    Were spread like one white cloth for God's own feast.

And I heard *Sanctus, Sanctus, Sanctus,*
    Dominus Deus, echoing everywhere,
In tongues of earth, in tongues of ocean,
    In tongues of fire, in tongues of air.

414

Far off, I heard once more the centuries pealing
  Like one brief sacring bell, I heard Time die.
I saw Space fading, forms dissolving,
  I saw the Host uplifted high.

Spirit and Substance, Victim-Victor,
  One life in all, all lives in One,
Fast-bound to feed man's bounded vision
  Shone through that strict concentering Sun.

Anima Mundi, World-Sustainer,
  Sower to whom all seeds returned,
Through earth's dissolving mist of atoms
  The Body of God in splendour burned.

And I heard *Agnus, Agnus Dei*,
  Pleading for man with Love's own breath;
And Love drew near me,
  And Love drew near me
And I drank Life through God's own death.

NIGHT JOURNEY

Thou who never canst err, for Thyself art the Way,
Thou whose infinite kingdom is flooded with day;
Thou whose eyes behold all, for Thyself art the Light,
Look down on us gently who journey by night.

By the pity revealed in Thy loneliest hour
Forsaken, self-bound and self emptied of power,
Thou who even in death hadst all heaven in sight,
Look down on us gently who journey by night.

On the road to Emmaus they thought Thou wast dead,
Yet they saw Thee and knew in the breaking of bread.
Though the day was far spent, in Thy face there was light.
Look down on us gently who journey by night.

THE ASSUMPTION

BEFORE Earth saw Him she had felt and known
  The small soft feet that thrust like buds in Spring.
The body of Our Lord was all her own
  Once. From the cross her arms received her King.

Think you that she, who bore Him on her breast,
  Had not the Word still living in her heart?
Or that, because one voice had called her blest
  Her inmost soul had lost the better part?

Henceforth all generations . . . Ah, but that
  You think was but an ancient song she knew!
Millions this night will sing Magnificat,
  And bring at least one strange prediction true.

Think you His heaven, that deep transcendent state,
  Floats like Murillo's picture in the air?
Or that her life, so heavenly consecrate,
  Had no essential habitation there?

Think you He looked upon her dying face,
  And, throned above His burning seraphim,
Felt no especial tenderness or grace
  For her whose life-blood once had throbbed in Him?

Proof of His filial love, His body on earth
  Still lives and breathes, and tells us, night and day,
That earth and heaven were mingled in His birth
  Through her, who kneels beside us when we pray;

Kneels to the word made flesh; her living faith
  Kneels to incarnate Love, "not lent but given"
Assumed to her on earth, and after death
  Assuming her to His own heart in Heaven.

CATS AND KINGS

WITH wide unblinking stare
  The cat looked; but she did not see the king.
She only saw a two-legg'd creature there
  Who in due time might have tit-bits to fling.

The king was on his throne.
   In his left hand he grasped the golden ball.
She looked at him with eyes of bright green stone
   And thought, *what fun if he should let it fall.*

With swishing tail she lay
   And watched for happy accidents, while he,
The essential king, was brooding far away
   In his own world of hope and memory.

O, cats are subtle now,
   And kings are mice to many a modern mind;
And yet there throbbed behind that human brow
   The strangely simple thoughts that serve mankind.

The gulf might not be wide;
   But over it, at least, no cat could spring.
So once again an ancient adage lied.
   The cat looked; but she never saw the king.

SLUMBER SONG

Sandman's coming—childhood echoes
   All that age may know—
Soft and grey the streams of slumber
   Through his fingers flow.
Nearer now his quiet footsteps
   Creep and creep and creep.
Sandman's coming. Little pilgrim,
   Tuck you up and sleep.

Sandman's coming—rose and opal
   Tinge the glimmering west.
Earth is hushed. The solemn ocean
   Rocks the ship to rest.
Cry of watchman shall not wake you
   On that boundless deep.
Sandman's coming. Little sailor,
   Tuck you up and sleep.

Sandman's coming through the ages,
   Pouring darker streams,

Drowning wars and broken kingdoms
    In this drift of dreams.
Now the unremembering shepherds
    Nod beside their sheep.
Sandman's coming. Little soldier,
    Tuck you up and sleep.

Darker grows the night and darker,
    And poor Tom's a-cold.
Age that cannot solve the riddle
    Leaves the tale untold.
He who ends the tale hereafter
    Endless watch must keep.
Sandman ends the endless ages.
    Tuck you up, and sleep.

THE VISION

AND what did you find in the heart of that valley?
    A phantom, a gypsy, a wraith or a fay?
O, taunt me no more! It was but a moment
    I looked on her face ere she went on her way.

Could you dream that she dwelt where the mountains and fir wood
    Go down in the west to those evening seas?
You were only a boy then. *Ay, only a boy then.*
    My friends were the conies, the birds and the bees.

You saw her? *I stood in the stillness and listened*
    The fall of a fir cone, the cry of a bird:
And then, in a silence far deeper than music,
    Without a word spoken, I saw and I heard.

She passed, and the wild flowers that trembled before her
    Were poor little fragments of love at her feet,
But they looked at the light of her face and remembered,
    Perfected, transfigured, fulfilled and complete.

And did she not see you? *I knelt, a poor shadow,*
    And looked on the light of her face till the last,
And then, though the twilight of time was around me
    I think that she smiled on me once ere she passed.

Did you search in the grey of the dew for her foot-prints,
   Or find any proof she had truly been there?
I searched, but I knew she could never be followed
   By footsteps on earth or by wings in the air.

And what did she leave you? *A need to be shriven*
   For all that was mine and for all that was I,
A need to be lost and reborn and forgiven;
   Or just to behold her once more and to die.

SEA DISTANCES

Above the purple heather, the pasture of the bee,
A summer cloud came softly as a swan from the sea,
And bright and clear below me, a mile or so away,
A sail like the *Windflower* was beating up the bay.

Could I have come aboard her, as if there had not been
The long years of havoc, the bitter years between,
My old friend would be steering, and I should find him there,
With a line out for mackerel, and a line perhaps to spare.

A fair sky above him, the flowing wave beneath,
A head wind to master, and a pipe between his teeth,
His hand on the tiller and his finger on the line,
There'd be creels of blue and silver for that old friend of mine.

Heaps of quick and slippery silver, all bestreaked with green and blue,
And I'd take a turn at steering while he filled his pipe anew,
And he should talk of timeless things and watch the changing skies
With a jest on his lips, and the wisdom of his eyes.

O softly flowed the white clouds above that pleasant lea,
But the grey shadows followed and began to dusk the sea.
I could not see the white sail; I could not see the bay;
For my friend and the *Windflower* were forty years away.

SAINT GEORGE AND THE DRAGON

Saint George he slew the dragon,
   But he didn't shout hurray.
He dumped it in the wagon
   Just to clear the mess away.

But the waggoner he sold it
   To a showman at the fair
And when Saint George was told it,
   He was almost in despair.

For the people crowded round it
   To admire its teeth and claws,
But Saint George he was an Englishman
   And did not like applause.

"The creechah weighed a ton at most,"
   He muttered through his vizahd,
"I do not feel inclined to boast
   About that puny lizahd."

BALLADE OF THE NEW STOICISM

James Epictetus Hall possessed at most
   A yacht at Cowes, a shipyard on the Clyde,
Expense accounts, a cook for boiled or roast,
   A Rolls, and all the horse that he could ride.
   And when a distant cousin faintly tried
To touch him with a passage from St. Paul,
   He murmured, in a tone of stoic pride:
"Hope thou not much, and fear thou not at all."

In London he became the perfect host.
   He wangled that O.M. for Mr. Hyde
Who called his God a turnip lantern ghost
   But said that Sex must never be denied.
   Tahiti, he observed, should be our guide;
So Mrs. Hyde ran off with Mr. Hall
   While Nanny, from the nursery window, cried:
"Hope thou not much, and fear thou not at all."

He left his Dido on the Libyan coast
   And took his peerage at a single stride.
He bought the Morning Star and Evening Post,
   And all the Muses nestled to his side.
   Left wingers, leaping o'er the Great Divide,
Ate oysters in the new baronial hall.
   Was any still small want unsatisfied?
"Hope thou not much? Great Heaven, why hope at all?"

Envoi

Gallows bird Villon, with your thief's neck wried,
　You nailed one ballade, soiled with blood and gall,
Fast to the gibbet where a comrade died,
　In fearful hope, forgiven and shriven for all.

IN THE TAVERN

A Song for King Harry, Defender of the Faith

'Twas Harry our King to his headsman swore
　"If the Churchmen fetter my fancy,
You may take the head of Sir Thomas More
And roll it over the chancel floor!
Do they think that a King can live like a monk?
　I'm going to marry my Nancy!"

Chorus
　　Her name was Anne but, when he was drunk,
　　He frequently called her Nancy!

Sir Thomas he laughed as he leapt from bed,
　"Now is it my leg they are pullin'?
There was never a jollier game," he said,
"Than playing at bowls with my poor old head,
For I shall be merrier when I'm dead
　Than the King F.D. with his Bullen!"

Chorus
　　Merrier, merrier, far when dead
　　Than the King F.D. with his Bullen!

Quoth the headsman, "Merry though all men be,
　My jest will be better than any
When Harry, our noble King F.D.,
Sends Anne, sweet Anne, with his love to Me!
I shall hone my axe for a farthing fee,
　While wives go six for a penny!
Can a great king live like a mouldy monk?
　He's going to marry his Jenny!"

Chorus
　　Her name was Jane but, when he was drunk,
　　He frequently called her Jenny!

421

Now Anne of Cleves was a **Flemish lass**
   Whom a saddle would fit right snugly,
And she cared not much for the looking-glass,
But Harry our King was bold as brass.
"It is written," he groaned, "all flesh is grass,
   And the one thing true is the ugly.
So Jane, my Pretty, it's *tecum pax*;
   I'm going to marry my Ugly."

Chorus

    And the headsman grinned as he polished his axe.
    "He's going to marry his Ugly."

Then Harry our King, though a trifle late,
   Went back in thought to his first one.
"I think," said he, "that her name was Kate,
A fact that points like the finger of fate
To young Kate Howard as my new mate.
   I warrant she won't be the worst one.
There's even a hope it will please the Pope,
   For she bears the name of the first one."

Chorus

    But he headsman chuckled, "It won't be the last,
    And it certainly isn't the first one."

"With a little reform and an inch more rope,
   And a realm that is less dogmatic,"
Said bluff King Hal, "I should have more scope.
I might even explain to our father the Pope
That Katherine H. is beginning to mope,
So Katherine Parr is my last fond hope,
   Though I fear I am growing rheumatic.
I'm glad that we kicked old Wolsey out.
   His morals were most erratic."

Chorus

    Oh, the pick of the bunch is the last, no doubt,
    But Katherine Parr is beginning to pout,
    So we mustn't be *too* dogmatic.

BALLADE OF THE BREAKING SHELL

And must the Spring inform me I am old,
   That violets wake unseen at Orchard's Bay;

Unseen by me where croziered ferns unfold
   Rivers of primrose through the beechwood stray?
   "Tempus abire tibe!" screams the jay,
That blue winged thief, "Your songs have all been sung,"
I cannot see him but my heart is young.

And oh, my little thrush, be not too bold.
   Blue pirates have such murderous tricks to play.
You know what happens. It has all been told
   So many a thousand times before today.
   Your mate remarks she has an egg to lay!
Her nest? My dear, you'd better hold your tongue.
   A nest's a thing no warbling should betray.
I cannot see her but my heart is young.

And I've a secret too. This cracked and cold
   Shell of a skull which time will toss away
Was my poor lanthorn. Think you it can hold
   No candle to the feathers you display?
   Believe me, it may house a sprite more gay
Than any you shall meet the leaves among.
   The shell will break and mingle with the clay,
My Ariel wake, to be for ever young.

Sing on, dear thrush. Lost in the twilight grey,
   I hear a vesper bell so sweetly rung,
I lift my heart up to the night and say
   "Veni Creator, all my heart grows young."

IN THE COOL OF THE EVENING

In the cool of the evening, when the low sweet whispers waken,
   When the labourers turn them homeward, and the weary have their
      will,
When the censers of the roses o'er the forest-aisles are shaken,
   Is it but the wind that cometh o'er the far green hill?

For they say 'tis but the sunset winds that wander through the heather,
   Rustle all the meadow-grass and bend the dewy fern;
They say 'tis but the winds that bow the reeds in prayer together,
   And fill the shaken pools with fire along the shadowy burn.

In the beauty of the twilight, in the Garden that He loveth,
   They have veiled His lovely vesture with the darkness of a name!

Thro' His Garden, thro' His Garden, it is but the wind that moveth,
  No more; but O, the miracle, the miracle is the same!

In the cool of the evening, when the sky is an old story
  Slowly dying, but remembered, ay, and loved with passion still,
Hush! . . . the fringes of His garment, in the fading golden glory,
  Softly rustling as He cometh o'er the far green hill.

THE OLD FOOL IN THE WOOD

"IF I could whisper you all I know,"
  Said the Old Fool in the Wood,
"You'd never say that green leaves 'grow',
  You'd say, 'Ah, what a happy mood
The Master must be in today,
  To think such thoughts'."
That's what you'd say.

"If I could whisper you all I've heard,"
  Said the Old Fool in the fern,
"You'd never say, 'The song of a bird.'
  You'd say, 'I'll listen, and p'raps I'll learn
One word of His joy as He passed this way,
  One syllable more',"
That's what you'd say.

"If I could tell you all the rest,"
  Said the Old Fool under the skies,
"You'd hug your griefs against your breast
  And whisper with love-lit eyes,
'I am one with the sorrow that made the may,
  And the pulse of His heart',"
That's what you'd say.

THE MAN WHO DISCOVERED THE USE OF A CHAIR

THE man who discovered the use of a chair,
  Odds-bobs—
        What a wonderful man!
He used to sit down on it, tearing his hair,
  Till he thought of a highly original plan.

For years he had sat on his chair, like you,
    Quite-still!
              But his looks were grim,
For he wished to be famous (as great men do),
    And nobody ever would listen to him.

Now he went one night to a dinner of state,
    Hear! hear!
              In the proud Guildhall!
And he sat on his chair, and he ate from a plate,
    But nobody heard his opinions at all;

There were ten fat aldermen down for a speech,
    (Grouse! Grouse!
              What a dreary bird!)
With five fair minutes allotted to each,
    But never a moment for *him* to be heard.

But each being ready to talk, I suppose,
    Order! Order!
              They cried, *for the Chair!*
And, much to their wonder, our friend arose
    And fastened his eye on the eye of the Mayor.

"We have come," he said, "to the fourteenth course!
    High-time,
              For the Chair," he said.
Then, with both of his hands, and with all of his force,
    He hurled his chair at the Lord Mayor's head.

It missed that head with the width of a hair.
    Gee-whizz!
              What a horrible squeak!
But it crashed through the big bay-window there
    And smashed a bus into Wednesday week.

And the very next day, in the dignified *Times*
    (Great-Guns!
              How the headlines ran!)
In spite of the kings and the wars and the crimes,
    There was nearly a column about that man.

Envoi

Oh, if you get dizzy when authors write
    (My stars!
              And you very well may!)

That white is black and that black is white,
  You should sit, quite still, in your chair and say:

It is easy enough to be famous now
  (*Puff-puff!*
                How the trumpets blare!),
Provided, of course, that you don't care how,
  Like the man who discovered the use of a chair.

DOBBIN

THE old horse, Dobbin,
  Out at grass
Turns his tail
  To the winds that pass;

And stares at the white road
  Winding down
Through the dwindling fields
  To the distant town.

He hears, in the distance,
  A snip-snap trot,
He sees his master,
  A small dark dot,

Riding away
  On the smart new mare
That came last month
  From Pulborough Fair.

Dobbin remembers
  As horses may
How often he trotted
  That ringing way.

His coat is ragged
  And blown awry.
He droops his head
  And he knows not why.

Something has happened.
Something has gone.
The world is changing.
His work is done.

But his old heart aches
With a heavier load
As he stands and wonders
And stares at the road